HISTORY
OF AFRICA
Volume III
From 1945
to Present

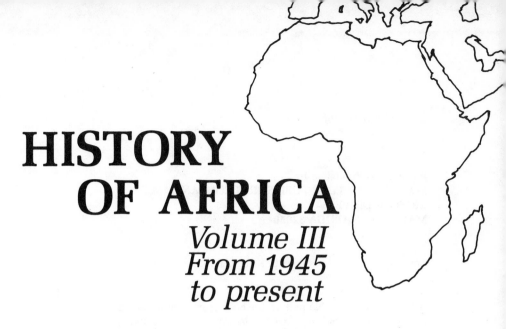

HISTORY
OF AFRICA
Volume III
From 1945
to present

HARRY A. GAILEY, JR.
San Jose State University

ROBERT E. KRIEGER PUBLISHING COMPANY
MALABAR, FLORIDA
1989

Original Edition 1989

Printed and Published by
ROBERT E. KRIEGER PUBLISHING COMPANY, INC.
KRIEGER DRIVE
MALABAR, FLORIDA 32950

Library of Congress Cataloging-in-Publication Data

Gailey, Harry A.
    History of Africa

    Vol. 1 originally published: New York: Holt, Rinehart, and Winston, 1970. It was reprinted by Krieger in 1981 as part of the 2 v. Krieger ed. of History of Africa. The 1981 issue of v. 1 is now part of this 1981–1989 3 v. work.
    Vol. 2: 2nd ed.
    Vols. 2–3 have imprint: Malabar, Fla.: R.E. Krieger.
    Includes bibliographies and indexes.
    Contents: v. 1. From earliest times to 1800 —
v. 2. From 1800 to 1945 — v. 3 From 1945 to present.
    1. Africa—History.   I. Title.
DT20.G3 1981b   960   88-9114

ISBN 0-89464-296-0 (v. 3)

10   9   8   7   6   5   4   3   2

for
MELANIE, MICHELLE, KIMBERLY, KATHERINE,
KRISTINA and CASSANDRA

Preface

Twenty years ago when planning to write a history of Africa, I conceived it at first in terms of a single volume. It soon became obvious that such a book would be overly long unless I wanted to ignore a large portion of the continent and deal with other segments in a very cursory manner. The decision was then made to issue the work in two separate but complementary volumes. This format was adequate when revisions were made for an updated edition of Volume II in 1980. It was necessary in that revision to treat the more recent developments, particularly in some of the smaller states, in a very general fashion. When the present revision was planned, it was decided that this method would no longer do justice to the many complex developments in all areas. Too much had happened since the first edition to merely add a few words to the last chapter of Volume II surveying independent Africa. Thus the decision was made to expand the work to three volumes. The first volume was kept intact since very little had been discovered about pre–1800 Africa which would alter significantly the materials in that work. Ending Volume II at the conclusion of the Second World War kept intact the coverage of that period of African history dominated by the European powers. The new final volume could then relate the nationalistic drive for an end to that European political imperialism and the subsequent difficult years of independence.

In the original prefaces to the first two volumes, I stated the reasons for attempting the difficult task of writing a survey of the history of Africa. There is no need to repeat much of what was then written except to point out the difficulty of maintaining a sense of continuity in a multivolume history. It may seem that I have ignored in Volume III very important information without which the reader could not understand subsequent events in the post–World War II period. Fully understanding that this was a problem, it was nevertheless decided not to reintroduce the reader to materials already covered in detail in the second volume. To have attempted a paraphrase of subjects already delineated in that book would only have increased the size of the text and made rational organization more difficult. The emphasis was thus placed upon a survey of how independence came to each sub-Saharan African state and how Africans have responded to the manifold problems of self-government. In this context I repeat a portion of the earlier preface pointing to the difficulties of undertaking a history of modern Africa.

The amount of information available on almost any African area is now so great that it is impossible for one person, or for that matter a team, to be equally knowledgeable in all of them. African studies is in the fortunate state where hundreds of specialists are active in research in many fields. New books and monographs are added weekly to the already impressive list of materials available to the student, teacher, and generalist. However laudatory, this presents the author of a textbook with many problems. One cannot read all the new books and articles, much less be aware of the large body of unpublished information known only to specialists which might seriously modify his interpretations. Every attempt has been made in this work to minimize outright error and to guard against over-speculation. Wherever there is inadequate information, I have tried to qualify my statements in such a way as to indicate the tentative nature of the conclusion.

It is hoped that the reorganization with the new information will allow more flexibility to instructors of university history and political science courses wile giving to the general reader a capsulated description of what has occurred in each country of this complex continent during the near half-century since World War II.

Harry A. Gailey

Los Gatos, California

Contents

Preface   *vii*

One   **Postwar political developments: French Africa**   *1*

General political changes   *1*
Devolution of power and consolidation of African rule:
the AOF   *6*
    Dahomey   *6*
    Guinea   *10*
    Ivory Coast   *12*
    Mali (Soudan)   *14*
    Mauritania   *16*
    Niger   *18*
    Senegal   *20*
    Upper Volta   *22*
Devolution of power and consolidation of African rule:
the AEF   *23*
    Central African Republic   *23*
    Chad   *26*
    The Republic of the Congo (Brazzaville)   *27*
    Gabon   *29*
Devolution of power and consolidation of African rule:
the French trust territories   *30*
    Cameroun   *30*
    Togo   *32*

Two   **Postwar political developments: British Africa**   *37*

General political changes   *37*
Devolution of power and consolidation of African rule:
British West Africa   *40*
    Gambia   *40*

Ghana   43
Nigeria   48
Sierra Leone   56
Devolution of power and consolidation of African rule:
British Central Africa   *59*
  Central African Federation   59
  Rhodesia   61
  Malawi (Nyasaland)   65
  Zambia (Northern Rhodesia)   67
Devolution of power and consolidation of African rule:
the high commission territories of Southern Africa   *69*
  Basutoland (Lesotho)   69
  Bechuanaland (Botswana)   73
  Swaziland   75
Devolution of power and consolidation of African rule:
British East Africa   *79*
  Kenya   79
  Tanzania (Tanganyika)   84
  Uganda   89
  Zanzibar   93

Three   **Postwar political developments: Belgian Africa**   *97*

Devolution of power and consolidation of African rule   *100*
  The Republic of the Congo   100
  Ruanda-Urundi   110
  Rwanda (Ruanda)   111
  Burundi (Urundi)   113

Four   **The Portuguese speaking territories**   *117*

Devolution of Power and Independence
  Angola   118
  Mozambique   127
  Guinea-Bissau and Cape Verde   133
  São Thome & Principe   137

Five   **Supranational organizations**   *139*

Conseil de l'Entente   *140*
Ghana-Guinea-Mali Union (Union of African States)   *141*
Union Africaine et Malagache (UAM) and successors   *143*
The Casablanca group   *145*
Organization of African Unity (OAU)   *146*

Six   **The special case: the Republic of South Africa,
           1910–1987**   *153*

           Political developments to 1948   *153*
           Economic developments, 1910–1948   *156*
           Developments in the non-Euopean sector through 1948   *159*
           South Africa since 1948   *164*

Seven   **Troubled independence: West Africa**   *187*

           English Speaking West Africa   *189*
             Ghana   189
             Sierra Leone   194
             Nigeria   195
             The Gambia   201
             Liberia   202
           French Speaking West Africa   *205*
             Mauritania   206
             The Saharawi Democratic Republic   207
             Senegal   208
             Mali   209
             Guinea   211
             Niger   214
             Burkina Faso (Upper Volta)   215
             Cameroon   218
             Ivory Coast   220
             Togo   222
             Benin (Dahomey)   223

Eight   **Troubled independence: Central and Southern Africa**   *225*

           Central Africa   *225*
             Gabon   225
             Central African Republic   226
             Equatorial Guinea   228
             Congo   230
             Chad   231
             Zaire   235
             Rwanda and Burundi   240
           Southern Africa   *244*
             Zambia   244
             Malawi   246
             Zimbabwe   248
             Lesotho, Botswana, and Swaziland   255

Nine   **Troubled independence: East and Northeastern Africa**   *261*

East Africa   *261*
   Tanzania   261
   Kenya   265
   Uganda   268
Northeastern Africa   *273*
   Somalia   273
   Ethiopia   277
   Djibouti   284
   Sudan   285

Ten   **Epilogue**   *293*

Selected Bibliography   *295*
Index   *305*

List of Maps

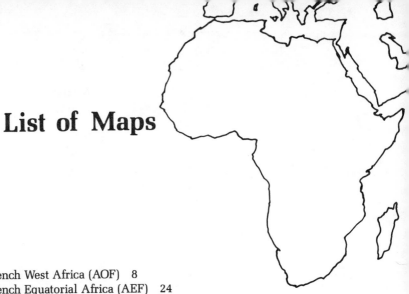

Map 1   French West Africa (AOF)   8
Map 2   French Equatorial Africa (AEF)   24
Map 3   Peoples of West Africa   41
Map 4   Central African Federation   60
Map 5   Kingdoms and Peoples of East Africa   78
Map 6   The Congo: Towns and Provinces, 1960   98
Map 7   Portuguese Central Africa   119
Map 8   The Republic of South Africa   166
Map 9   Peoples of the Congo Basin   236
Map 10   Northeastern Africa   275
Map 11   Political Divisions and Peoples of Ethiopia   279

ONE

Postwar political developments: French Africa

General political changes

The rapid German victory over France in 1940 had serious ramifications for the French territories in Africa. The establishment of the Vichy government dominated by the threat of a victorious Germany split the loyalties of Frenchmen. In the French West African Federation (AOF), Governor-General Pierre Boisson remained loyal to the Petain government until the end of 1942. Felix Eboué, the governor-general of the French Equatorial African Federation (AEF), declared his support for the Free French government of Charles de Gaulle. These divergent policies had a direct influence upon the peoples of the two federations. In West Africa, Boisson, to further his control over the federation, increased the use of the arbitrary penalty system called the indigénat whereby the administration could punish Africans without the formality of a trial. He also intensified practices which were already resented by Africans such as forced labor. The few existing politically oriented organizations were repressed; so were labor groups. Despite these more rigid controls, Governor Boisson was faced with the defection of an increasing proportion of the population as the war progressed. Some chiefs and some of the African soldiers refused to accept the Vichy regime. Many of the latter escaped to the Cameroun or to the AEF to join the Free French. The chief of the Mossi in Upper Volta was the most vocal of African rulers in his opposition to the Vichy settlement. Ultimately he committed suicide after extracting a promise from his heir not to become chief until the "true French" returned. After Boisson led the West Africans into the Gaullist camp in December 1942, many of the active tensions within the federation disappeared. However, his repressive regime was remembered by both the African intellectuals and traditional leaders. Economic dislocation caused by the war was an added stimulus to their demand for a larger voice in their own affairs.

1

French Equatorial Africa provided an example of loyalty to the Free French. Politically aware Africans realized that they could reasonably demand political rewards for that loyalty. Perhaps as important was General de Gaulle's recognition that the relationship between metropolitan France and its colonies would have to be altered significantly after the war. In January and February 1944, a group of Free French politicians and colonial officials met at Brazzaville and adopted a number of resolutions concerning the future of the French empire. They proposed that Africans be given a larger role in governmental affairs. However, they specifically ruled out self-government for the territories. Instead, they called for a strengthening of the ties binding France to its empire by giving Africans more representation on the colonial level and in the French parliament. After the war Africans should be chosen to the constituent assembly which would be responsible for drawing up the new constitution for France.

The Brazzaville Conference of 1944 set new directions for French colonial policy. However, the hopes of many African leaders for more of a share of power in their territories were blunted in the period 1945–1950 by political considerations in metropolitan France. The reorganization did not result in as much participation as many Africans wished. Nevertheless, there were sweeping changes made in the colonial system by the constitution of 1946 and the Loi Lamine Guèye named for its sponsor, the Senegalese socialist deputy. The major change was the creation of the French Union which consisted of metropolitan France, overseas departments (that is, French Guiana, Réunion, Guadeloupe, and Martinique), and the overseas territories. There was also categories for associated states such as Indochina, Tunisia, and Morocco.

The political structure of the French Union was composed of a president (the president of the Republic), the *Haut Conseil de l'Union Française,* and the *Assemblée de Union Française.* The *Haut Conseil* whose major function was to help the French government in instituting policy for the union was never established. The *Assemblée* was, however, and it was composed of 204 members. One-half of these represented metropolitan France. Two-thirds of the metropolitan members were chosen by the National Assembly while one-third were selected by the *conseil de la république.* Of the 104 overseas members, forty members came from the two African federations with the AOF selecting twenty-seven members. These representatives were chosen by the territorial assemblies. The *Assemblée de l'Union Française* appeared to embody the federal principle, but in fact it had little real power. It was to be utilized generally as an advisory body and decisions which it could make independently relating to overseas territories were not binding on the government.

The overseas territories of France also received substantial representation in the central government by the reforms of 1946. In the National Assembly there were eighty-three overseas deputies. Of these, thirty came from Algeria, ten from the overseas departments, and forty from the AOF and AEF. The territories also were represented in the *conseil de la république.* Deputies to the National Assembly from the AOF and Togoland were elected by the qualified voters in each territory from a common roll. In the AEF and the Cameroun, they were chosen by the two-college system. Representatives to the *conseils de la république* were chosen by the territorial assemblies and the deputies. Although representation in both metropolitan legislative bodies was small, it did associate the leading African intellectuals with the government of France. Thus, far from being disassociated from the central government as in British Africa, these potential leaders were directly involved at the highest level.

Of more direct importance to Africans was the reorganization of the councils which had been designed to aid the governor-general and the lieutenant-governors. In each one of the territories in the AOF, *Assemblées Territoriales* (referred to as *Conseils Généraux* until 1952) were established. In the AEF they were called Representative Assemblies. Their function was a financial one, although they were consulted by the administration on a variety of matters. Like the *conseils* which had existed before the war, they were advisory bodies. The most noticeable improvement of the territorial assemblies over the prewar *conseils* was in the method of selecting the members. They were chosen by a two-college system of direct election. In order to understand this complicated method of election it is necessary to know what changes had been made in citizenship status.

Originally there had been two broad classes of persons in the French African territories. Those who were citizens of France were *citoyens de statut civil.* They could be Africans who met the necessary qualifications as for example the qualified inhabitants of the communes of Senegal. The larger portion of this class, however, were not Africans but Frenchmen. In the previously protected areas the Africans were normally subjects or those persons who were judged by local statutes or customary law. The wording of some of the decrees creating the French Union indicated the intention of abolishing these distinctions and making all persons in the overseas territories citizens of the French Union. In general, these statements tended to confuse the issue because the large mass of Africans kept their customary laws and were not given the same rights of franchise as those holding *statut civil.* Even those persons still under customary law designated *statut personnel* were not all granted the right to vote. Only certain sections of the mass of Africans were allowed the franchise. Through the mid-1950s these categories were expanded until for certain elections in most territories the majority of the Africans did have the vote.

Election to the *Conseils Généraux* was decided on by a two-college system of franchise. The first college was composed of all voters who were entitled to the *statut civil* while the second college was made up of persons of the *statut personnel.* The reasons for this system of voting was the recognition of the differences in education of the people of French Africa. The policy of assimilation was not negated by this system. It merely admitted that the policy had resulted in the conversion of only a relatively few evolved Africans to the class of *statut civil.* Metropolitan French citizens and assimilated Africans were guaranteed the selection of more members to the assemblies than their mere numbers would warrant. The persons who voted in the second college chose more members than did the voters of the first college. The number of representatives chosen by the two electoral colleges varied from territory to territory. However, the voters of the second college chose between three-fifths and four-fifths of the members of the assemblies.

At the federal level the postwar reforms created a new advisory body, the *Grand Conseil*, which represented the entire federation and was chosen by the territorial assemblies of each federation. Each assembly chose five of its own members to the *Grand Conseil*. These bodies in an expanded fashion served the same purpose as had the prewar *Conseil de gouvernements*.

Despite the conservative reaction which occurred in France in late 1946 and lasted for almost a decade, there were three important laws enacted which affected the African federations. The first of these was the Second Loi Lamine Guèye of 1950 which assured Africans of equal conditions of work and pay with their European counterparts in the civil service. The Overseas Labor Code of 1952 guaranteed African workers minimum wages, hours of work, family allowances, and collective bargaining equal to French workers. The third piece of legislation was the Municipal Law of 1955 which provided for the creation of elected mayors and councils selected from a common roll for a number of selected municipalities in French Africa.

The ten-year period of relatively static attitudes by the French government was, nevertheless, marked by events which eventually allowed for a rapid devolution of power to Africans. Outside of the continent the conservative imperial policy of France was rudely shocked by events in Indochina. By 1954 the French had admitted their failure in Southeast Asia by agreeing to the Geneva accords. The revolt in Algeria was well under way by 1956 and the cause of the Algerian guerrilla fighters was receiving considerable support in government circles. Any relaxation of French attitudes toward Algeria also affected the attitude of colonial authorities toward the rest of Africa. It was obvious that France did not wish a reiteration of Indochina and Algeria anywhere else in Africa.

This period also witnessed the creation of the first specific African political parties. Before World War II political parties were present only in Senegal and these tended to be reflections of domestic French parties. The first important postwar party was the intraterritorial *Rassemblement Démocratique Africain* (RDA) organized by Felix Houphouët-Boigny of the Ivory Coast. At first associated with the French Communist party, it had become by 1951 a party of cooperation. The other major party was the loose association of African Socialist deputies put together by Léopold Senghor and called the *Indépendants d' Outre-Mer* (IOM). The 1956 elections to the National Assembly confirmed the RDA as the most important political organization in French Africa and Houphouët-Boigny was made a minister in the French government. This government urged on by the liberal Minister of Overseas France, Gaston Defferre, moved to reform the entire structure of control in Africa. The *Loi Cadre,* or framework law, which accomplished this reflected many of the ideas of Houphouët-Boigny who helped design it. The *Loi Cadre,* contrary to the usual French approach of legislating even the minute details of government procedure, only specified the areas where changes were to be effected. The administration would make the law effective by issuing decrees which would be approved by the territorial legislatures. These decrees framed within the context of the generalizations of the *Loi Cadre* would be the specifics of change in the colonies.

The major intent of the *Loi* and subsequent decrees was to create a decentralization of colonial government. In this aim the framers of the law were breaking with a half-century of colonial legislation that had attempted to create larger units of government directly tied to metropolitan France. The two major reasons for this reversal were the demands for more territorial autonomy from within the two large federations and the pressure created by events elsewhere in Africa. Britain was in the process of moving many of her territories toward independent status. These developments were closely followed by French statesmen and French African politicians. Another force for change was the Algerian revolt which served to divide the allegiance of African leaders and which also predisposed the French government to make sweeping reforms before the spirit of North African nationalism could spread into sub-Saharan Africa. It should be noted that Senghor and the other representatives of the IOM opposed the *Loi* because of its Balkanizing effect upon the federations.

The decrees established the territorial assemblies as the most important institution in the previous federations. The governor-generals became high commissioners, representatives of metropolitan France, and also the chief executive for the *Grand Conseil.* The *Grand Conseil's* area of concern and deliberations was restricted to matters of common concern. Its financial powers were similarly restricted. There was no central ministry provided for the collection of territories. On the territorial level, however, ministries were created called *Conseils de gouvernement* varying in size up to twelve members. These ministries were responsible to the territorial assemblies. The assemblies were given many more powers of legislation in health, education, planning, and economic development for the territory. The chief representative of the administration was the *chef de territoire,* formerly called the lieutenant-governor, who served as the head of the *Conseil de gouvernement.* All acts of the assembly had to be certified by the *chef de territoire.* The chief political figure in the territory was the vice-president of the council who exercised great powers over legislation and through the media of his political party was in a strong position to coerce the French administration.

The *Loi Cadre* was passed over the objections not only of many Frenchmen, but of a large number of important African leaders who wanted to build upon the existing federal structure to achieve a larger working political union than that of territories. Nevertheless, the *Loi* was in the mainstream of African opinion. It established workable territorial units of government at the expense of the federation. Ties of unity to France were shifted from the larger units to the territories. Thus the French Union or later de Gaulle's ideas of the Community were henceforth based on the territory. Where previously the most prestigious and important positions for Africans had been in metropolitan France or in Dakar and Brazzaville, they now became territorial cabinet positions. The expanded duties of the assemblies and the selection of the *conseil* from the members of the assemblies spurred the formation of political parties and political agitation in the smaller units.

The founding and development of new political parties in the territories which followed the reforms of 1956 will be discussed more thoroughly elsewhere. It is necessary to note here certain developments in metropolitan France that aided the cause of African nationalists. The Algerian conflict had caused France to send over one-half million men there, spend huge sums of money, and it eventually pushed France to the brink of civil war. Charles de Gaulle was called upon to give leadership to a sadly divided France. He agreed, but only on the conditions of a new constitution which would give him the necessary executive power to deal with the crisis. In the summer of 1958 his government prepared the new constitution for a Franco-African Community. As envisioned by de Gaulle, this would be a federal republic with France at the head of a number of all but autonomous states. A plebiscite was to be held in all overseas territories in September to determine the willingness of these areas to become a part of this system. In August de Gaulle traveled throughout Africa conferring with the native political leaders. He informed them that any territory could have its independence from France simply by a majority of its people voting No on the plebiscite. However, any area taking this position could expect to receive no further aid from France. In the ensuing election only Guinea chose this alternative.

By the time of the referendum in 1958, the proposed community had already become that of semi-independent territories tied to France. The defection of Guinea and the differential political movements in the territories convinced even the most adament defenders of the community such as Houphouët-Boigny that independence was the logical goal of the territories. In retrospect, the *Loi Cadre* provided the changes necessary to make the final shift to independence in 1960 smooth and easy.

With this general overview of the French method of devolving power to their African territories, one can begin to examine in more detail the development of political parties and nationalistic aspirations in each of the territories.

Devolution of power and consolidation of African rule: the AOF

DAHOMEY

Dahomey, bounded on the east by Nigeria and on the west by Togo, has an area of almost 45,000 square miles and had a population of 2,250,000. It is an agricultural state whose main products are cassava, palm kernels, and yams. As with so many of the recently independent West African states, it is too chronically short of funds to undertake any major economic and social projects. France in 1964 continued to support the government financially and took seventy percent of Dahomey's exports and provided fifty-nine percent of her imports.

A key factor in the instability of the politics of Dahomey is the north-south split caused by tribal, religious, historical, and personal factors. Post World War II political activity in Dahomey first centered on a French priest, Father Aupiais, and then on his protégé, a southerner, Serou Apithy, whose political center of power was Porto Novo. Apithy was the dominant political figure in Dahomey until 1959. At first he and his followers associated themselves with the RDA, but they broke with Houphouët-Boigny in 1948 and formed the *Parti Républicaine Dahoméenne* (PRD). Later Apithy affiliated the PRD with the aims of Léopold Senghor of Senegal. The success of Apithy's moderate pro-French policy was confirmed by the implementing elections of the *Loi Cadre* of 1957 when the PRD won thirty-five of the sixty seats in the Dahomean Assembly. In opposition to Apithy was Hubert Maga, a northerner, and Justin Ahomadegbe, another southerner and member of the Fon tribe whose power base centered on Abomey. Maga's party, the *Mouvement Démocratique Dahoméenne* (MDD), won fourteen seats and the *Union Démocratique Dahoméenne* (UDD), led by Ahomadegbe, won eleven.

All three parties in 1958 supported de Gaulle's proposal for the French Community. Apithy attempted to bring Dahomey into the Senghor-Keita designed Mali Federation. However, the political and economic pressure of the Ivory Coast's Houphouët-Boigny upon Niger, Upper Volta, and Dahomey caused Apithy to withdraw his support of Mali and his party from association with Senghor's socialists.

In the election of April 1959, the PRD won thirty-seven seats, the MDD twenty-two, and the UDD only eleven despite the fact that UDD candidates had won almost 30,000 more popular votes than did the PRD. In protest against what they considered unfair districting, UDD supporters displayed a violent reaction which culminated in serious riots throughout the country. These disturbances forced Apithy to concede nine seats to the UDD and join a coalition government with Maga as premier. He and Ahomadegbe agreed to serve as ministers under Maga's leadership. In late 1959 Apithy formed a new front in coordination with Senghor's PFA to secure the independence of Dahomey and this action broke up the coalition. Maga, with MDD and UDD support, removed Apithy from the cabinet.

Dahomey became an independent republic on August 1, 1960, with a seventy-man National Assembly and a president as chief executive. In December 1960, in the first elections after independence, Maga's MDD won a sweeping victory and Maga was elected president. By early 1962 Maga felt strong enough to reshuffle his cabinet "to streamline" the government, ostensibly in order to carry out the recently adopted four-year economic

French West Africa (AOF)

and social development plan. Correlate with the strengthening of Maga's power was a reorganization of parties to form a national front party, the *Parti Dahoméen de l'Unité* (PDU).

Although Maga's power through his control of the government and the PDU seemed at first glance unassailable, there were many disaffected areas. His real power was based in the north, particularly among the Bariba tribe. In the south, Apithy and Ahomadegbe still maintained a large following. The economic sector was basically unhealthy and was maintained primarily with French help. Unemployment, particularly among the white-collar workers, grew, and Maga was accused of squandering money on such projects as a $3,000,000 presidential palace.

This incoherent unrest was increased by a further cabinet reshuffle in September 1963, in which Maga became premier and defense minister in addition to being president. Widespread disorders followed this reorganization and in October 1963, the army, commanded by Colonel Christrophe Soglo, intervened and forced Maga's resignation. In November a provisional government was formed. The most important members were Soglo, Maga, Apithy, and Ahomadegbe. This government was an extra constitutional regime whose authority rested primarily on Soglo and his control of the small army of 800 men. In December 1963, Soglo carried the reorganization further by forcing Maga's resignation and placing him under house arrest. On January 20, 1964, Colonel Soglo resigned from politics. On the previous day Apithy had been elected president of the reconstituted government of Dahomey and Ahomadegbe was named president of the council. The government, a forty-two member assembly and ten-man cabinet, was ostensibly a national one. That this was an illusion was shown by the revolt of Bariba tribesmen against the new government in March 1964 in support of the deposed President Maga. The rebellion, after some loss of life, was suppressed by French-trained units of the army. A further source of friction within the state was the problem of the recognition of China. Apithy since 1963 had favored the recognition of mainland China and close contacts with the Ivory Coast and the *Entente* group. Apithy's viewpoint eventually prevailed and Red China was recognized. In the confusing period that followed both Chinese governments maintained embassies in Cotonou. In addition to personal rivalry between Apithy and Ahomadegbe, Dahomey was beset with almost insoluable economic problems which could have been alleviated only by massive aid. Ahomadegbe, attempting to curb spending in July 1965, cut the salaries of the civil service by twenty-five percent. The General Dahomey Workers Union thereupon called a strike. However, Ahomadegbe won his point and the strikes were ended, but these measures provided only partial relief in trying to reduce government expenditures.

The sub-rosa conflict between President Apithy and Ahomadegbe came into the open in November 1965. The two men could not agree over the appointment of the head of the Supreme Court. The coalition government broke apart over this issue and disturbances again rocked the country. General Soglo and the army intervened once more, overthrew the government in December 1965, and appointed an interim president, Tairou Concagou, and a four-man technician government. Soglo also requested that the leading politicians cooperate with one another to create a new stable government. However, in this atmosphere the three leading politicians formed new parties. These were the *Alliance Démocratique Dahoméenne* (ADD) of Ahomadegbe, the *Union National Dahoméenne* (UND) led by Maga, and the *Convention National Dahoméenne* (CND) headed by Apithy. When it became obvious within ten days that the politicians were not going to cooperate with each other to form a stable government, Soglo and the army once more took power and Soglo stated that the military regime was made necessary because of "the incapacity of the politicians to govern." Ahomadegbe and Maga fled to the Ivory Coast and Soglo after the third coup formed a military "technicians" government.

GUINEA

For almost eight years after World War II, Guinea was practically devoid of the political activity so common elsewhere in West Africa. This was largely because the most important native political leader, Yacine Diallo, a school teacher, was a moderate whose political goals were modest and evolutionary. He was supported by one of the most important Muslim leaders in West Africa, Cherif Fanti Mahdi of Kankan, and many of the influential chiefs.

Sekou Touré was one of the founders of the RDA and in 1952 he became the secretary-general of the *Parti Démocratique de Guinée* (PDG), a branch of the RDA. The rise to prominence of Touré and the success of the PDG is closely tied to the trade-union movement in Guinea. Although an extremely poor territory, Guinea did have some iron and bauxite which the French began to mine seriously in the late 1940s. This resulted in a modest-sized African industrial working class. The largest union in Guinea was the *Conféderation Générale des Travailleurs* (CGT) controlled from France and largely Communist-dominated. Touré had become a member of the trade-union movement while still a government employee, and in 1948 had risen to be the secretary-general of the CGT in Guinea and in 1950 secretary-general of the coordinating committee in West Africa. In 1953 Touré and the CGT managed a successful general strike which lasted for over two months. After the capitulation of the movement, Touré became one of the most important politicians in Guinea.

In 1954 Yacine Diallo died, thus removing from the political scene the one important Guinean moderate politician trusted by both the French and Africans. In the elections which followed for the vacant seat in the French Assembly, Barry Diawadou, the leader of the *Bloc Africain de Guinée* (BAG), defeated Touré. The election was marred by charges of election tampering by the officials. In 1955 Touré was elected mayor of Conakry and a deputy to the French Assembly. Despite these victories, the PDG in 1955 did not have a single seat in the Territorial Assembly. In this period there developed serious differences between the PDG and the other RDA branches in West Africa. Houphouët-Boigny had decided after 1950 to rid the party of its radical label and disassociate it from the Communist movement. The logic of the situation in Guinea dictated a totally different approach. Thus while the main RDA was moving to the right, the PDG appeared to become more radical.

In the elections of 1957 occasioned by the *Loi Cadre*, the PDG won fifty-six of the sixty seats in the Territorial Assembly and Touré became vice-president of the executive council. He was now in a position to begin to implement some of his programs for the economic and social development of the country through government planning and control. The major block to such reform was the traditional system of chiefs who resisted the PDG's implementation of agrarian reforms. In 1958 after continuing opposition of the chiefs, Touré's government abolished the system, replacing it with some 4,000 village councils elected by the people. The new system was designed to be more amenable to control by the central authorities than the traditional form of rule.

Touré came into more open conflict with the CGT and in order to stress the African nature of the Guinea unions, he organized the *Confédération Générale de Travail Africaine* (CGTA) in 1956. In 1957 this merged with dissident union groups to form the one union of Guinea, the *Union Général des Travailleurs d'Afrique Noire* (UGTAN). This union was separate from all metropolitan unions and control of the union was in African hands. Thus by 1958 Touré was the master of the one union in the country, the strongest party, and also controlled the territorial government. His position as an independent agent was not, however, all that secure. This was clearly shown by the referendum of 1958.

As late as his meeting with de Gaulle in August 1958, Touré had not indicated any serious desire for independence for Guinea outside the French Community. His subsequent position against the de Gaulle referendum seems to have been dictated by disappointment in the proposed future union, distrust of de Gaulle, and pressures from the more radical elements within the PDG. These still powerful radical groups could not be ignored, and Touré and the PDG campaigned against the proposed French Community. Guinea was the only area in French Africa to vote No on the referendum of September 28. The vote was a convincing 1,136,000 No to only 57,000 Yes votes. French reaction was swift and emotional. On September 29, Guinea was informed that this rejection meant its separation from French West Africa. French authorities ordered home their teachers, doctors, civil servants, and removed all equipment that could be crated and carted away. Over 4,000 skilled Frenchmen left Guinea.

On October 2, 1958, the Territorial Assembly proclaimed itself a constituent assembly, declared Guinea an independent republic, and named Touré head of state, aided by a sixteen-member cabinet. A new constitution was drawn up embodying these ideas and was adopted on November 12, 1958.

Touré gained desperately needed financial assistance from Ghana in December 1958 and later received loans and technicians from the Communist bloc. This direct aid and guarantees of more support were enough to enable Guinea to weather the first year of independence. By this time Western nations, including France, had reexamined their positions and Touré could begin cautiously to withdraw from what had seemed irrevocable commitments to the Soviet bloc. The quick action of the French after the referendum had strengthened Touré politically. In December 1958, the chief opposition party, the BAG, and the much smaller group, the *Parti Démocratique Socialiste de Guinée,* had merged with the PDG. Barry Diawadou, the leader of the BAG, became a member of the cabinet.

Touré's emancipation from the radical elements within the PDG and the Soviet bloc did not come until late 1961. In November 1961, the Teachers Union precipitated a crisis throughout the country in conjunction with officials of the Soviet Embassy. The disturbances were calmed by Touré and the moderates, and the leaders of the action were arrested and imprisoned. On December 16, 1961, the Soviet Ambassador and key aides were expelled from the country. Soviet Deputy Premier Mikoyan visited Guinea in January 1962 to reassure Touré of the continuing interest of the Soviet Union and to give assurance that its diplomats in the future would not interfere in the political affairs of Guinea. The events of 1961 set the stage for a further loosening of the close ties of Guinea and the Soviet Union. Although the bulk of technicians continued to come from the Eastern bloc, Touré appealed for more Western aid after 1962. This period also witnessed more active participation by Guinea in contacts with other African states and the Western powers.

In November 1964, Touré named resident ministers for the four major regions of Guinea, these ministers to be responsible directly to the central executive. Touré also took steps to restrict membership in the PDG only to the militantly active socialists who had proved themselves. Thus the party was directed away from a mass movement to one that could more accurately reflect the desires of the executive.

The only political opposition to the PDG and Touré was a clandestine one and the party has been vigilant in filling the prisons with those who could be suspect. In November 1965, it announced the discovery of a plot to assassinate Touré and overthrow the government. The chief plotter in the abortive coup was a distant cousin of the president, Mamadou (Petit Touré). Mamadou, who until 1964 was a part of the hierarchy, was one of the leaders of an underground political group, the *Parti de l'Unité Nationale de Guinée* (PUNG).

IVORY COAST

In 1944 Felix Houphouët-Boigny founded a farmers' union, the *Syndicat Agricole Africain* (SAA), which in 1945 grew into the more radical *Parti Démocratique de la Cote d'Ivoire* (PDCI). Partly as a reaction to the second constitution of the Fourth Republic, Houphouët-Boigny and other deputies met at Bamako in October 1946, to found a new, mass, intraterritorial party, the *Rassemblement Démocratique Africain* (RDA). Under the influence of French socialists, the Senegalese did not send representatives and thus began the polarization of nationalistic activity in French West Africa between the Ivory Coast and Senegal. Houphouët-Boigny was chosen the first president of the RDA, and the PDCI became the Ivory Coast branch of the RDA.

From the beginning the RDA associated itself with the Communists. Open clashes with the administration in French West Africa and the Ivory Coast in particular during 1949 and 1950 culminated in widespread loss of life in early 1951. The French administration clamped down on all political activity in the Ivory Coast and the RDA was radically weakened by the mass arrests. Houphouët-Boigny was saved from this because he was a member of the French Assembly. Soon afterward, the PDCI and RDA changed these tactics to cooperation with the French administration and broke their ties with the Communists. Houphouët-Boigny then urged continued cooperation with France and stated that the RDA must become a purely African party. Most of the other territorial political parties associated with the RDA agreed to this change. The weakness of the RDA was shown in the 1951 elections for the French Assembly when only Houphouët-Boigny and two other RDA members were elected. However, the decision to move to a more moderate stance was the correct one since the RDA gained the confidence of the government and the moderate French business community. This confidence was shown in January 1956, when the RDA won nine of the twenty-one contested seats in West Africa for the French Assembly. Houphouët-Boigny was elected mayor of Abidjan and was given cabinet rank by the French government. It was in this capacity that he had so much influence on the *Loi Cadre* of 1956 which gave universal suffrage based on a one-roll electoral system to French West Africa, created executive councils on the territorial level, and broadened the deliberative powers of the territorial assemblies. In the elections of 1957 for the new territorial assemblies, the RDA swept the elections in most of the areas, winning a total of 236 out of 474 contested seats in the eight assemblies. It gained majorities not only in the Ivory Coast, but also in Guinea, Upper Volta, and the Soudan. In the Ivory Coast the opposition gained only five percent of the popular vote.

The question of the future of the areas of the French Community divided the RDA. Sekou Touré and the PDG-RDA Guinea segment wanted independence quickly, and the Soudan, Upper Volta, and Dahomey were moving closer to Léopold Senghor's position. Houphouët-Boigny, despite his ideas concerning devolution of power to the territories, stood for continuing close association with France and threw his considerable influence in West Africa behind a Yes vote for the 1958 referendum. Houphouët-Boigny utilized the economic power of the Ivory Coast to dislodge the Upper Volta and Dahomey from their newfound agreement with Senegal. This move checked the construction of a potentially powerful federation and resulted instead in the creation of a much weaker Mali Federation. Soon afterward Houphouët-Boigny associated the Ivory Coast with Upper Volta, Dahomey, and Niger in the loosely organized, weak *Conseil de l'Entente*. This new creation was dominated by the wealthy Ivory Coast.

French agreement for independence for Mali within the Community led Houphouët-Boigny and the other leaders of the member states of the *Conseil* to demand independence also. This was granted, and on August 7, 1960, the Ivory Coast became independent.

The grant of independence to Mali and the *Entente* states effectively ended any chance of a larger territorial unity. This fact and the defection of Guinea minimized the effect of the RDA as an intraterritorial party. The territorial branch parties tended to become more independent of Houphouët-Boigny's control. The PDCI's domination over the Ivory Coast remained. Houphouët-Boigny was elected president in November 1960, and the PDCI-RDA won all seventy seats in the Ivory Coast National Assembly.

All of the smaller parties in the Ivory Coast were either dissolved or absorbed into the PDCI between 1952 and 1958. The *Action Démocratique et Social de la Côte d'Ivoire* was dissolved in 1958 and the small *Parti Regroupement Africaine* disappeared with the deportation of its leader, Camille Adam, in 1959. Earlier the *Parti Progressiste* and the *Bloc Démocratique Eburnéenne* had been absorbed into the PDCI. Houphouët-Boigny continued in this period to strengthen constitutionally his control of the Ivory Coast, particularly since the discovery of plots directed at his assassination in early 1963. In April 1964, another plot to kill Houphouët-Boigny was discovered. The alleged chief conspirator, Ernest Boka, a former minister, later committed suicide in prison. The controls of the PDCI, although less onerous than in most other African one-party states, are just as effective.

However, Houphouët-Boigny's strength lay not in political or police controls, but in the strength of the economy of the Ivory Coast and the success of his domestic and foreign policies. Disdaining a doctrinaire socialistic approach, Houphouët-Boigny made the Ivory Coast into one of the model states of Africa by blending state control with free enterprise. The economy of the Ivory Coast is more balanced than neighboring states. Although coffee is the major export, wood products, cocoa, and palm products also account for over one-half of the exports of the Ivory Coast. Houphouët-Boigny has been one of the most pro-Western of all African leaders, and this attitude has provided a continuing flow of development capital, largely from France.

The PDCI was unopposed in the 1965 elections for president, an enlarged eighty-five member National Assembly, and for 140 local counselors. Of the more than 1,800,000 votes cast, Houphouët-Boigny received all but 332 votes. One might question whether under a contested election the percentage of votes cast for the PDCI would have been so overwhelming, but in Africa, where political success is tied so closely with economic development and prosperity, it is doubtful whether the overall results of the elections would have been different.

MALI (SOUDAN)

The first genuine political party in the French Soudan was the *Parti Soudanais du Progrès* (PSP) formed in the early 1950s by a canton chief, Fily

Dabo Sissoko. This was a very conservative organization and the more radical, educated groups did not find a voice in politics until an ex-teacher, Momadou Konaté, organized a territorial branch of the RDA. Until 1956 Sissoko and Konaté were the dominant native political figures in the Soudan. Konaté's support was in the cities and Sissoko's came from the traditional rural areas. By 1956 the RDA in the Soudan had outgrown its earlier Communist associations and was more acceptable to the authorities and the chiefs. In that year Konaté died and the leadership of the RDA in the Soudan devolved upon a young Bambara politician, Modibo Keita, who had been a close associate of Houphouët-Boigny since 1946. After spending some time in French jails, he had become a member of Soudan's territorial assembly. In 1953 he was elected mayor of Bamako and in 1956 he was the Soudanese representative to the French Assembly.

In the elections of 1957 occasioned by the *Loi Cadre,* the RDA won sixty of the seventy seats for the Soudan Assembly. Sissoko and his deputy, the Socialist Hamadou Dicko, were both defeated. In the referendum of 1958 occasioned by de Gaulle's rise to power, Keita swung the Soudan behind de Gaulle and Houphouët-Boigny's policy of the French Community.

On December 29–30, 1958, at Bamako, Keita met with the leaders of Senegal, Dahomey, and Upper Volta to discuss federation. At a later conference in Dakar in January 1959, the delegates of the four areas agreed upon a federation plan which provided for a federal executive and legislature. This marked a definite break with Houphouët-Boigny's policy of autonomous members with the Community. Houphouët-Boigny brought pressure to bear on the leaders of Upper Volta and Dahomey, and these two states withdrew from the scheme, later forming a loose *entente* with the Ivory Coast. Keita had by this time created out of the Soudan branch of the RDA a new political party, the *Parti de la Fédération Africaine* (PFA). Keita, in conjunction with Léopold Senghor of Senegal, had presided over the Bamako and Dakar conferences. Despite the defection of Dahomey and Upper Volta, Keita and Senghor decided to go on with the plans for establishment of the Mali Federation. Although Keita would have preferred the new polity of Mali to be a unitary state, he bowed to the desire of Senegal for a federal structure. In 1959 the PSP merged with the dominant party led by Keita; and its leaders, including Sissoko, were integrated into the government. In the confirming election of March 1959, the PFA won over seventy-five percent of the popular vote and secured all the eighty seats in the Soudan Assembly. The *Parti Régroupement Soudanaise* (PRS) led by Dicko contested the election but was dissolved soon afterward and Dicko himself abandoned politics.

In April 1959, Keita was named premier of the Federation and Senghor became president of the federal assembly. In September in Paris at a meeting of the French Community's Executive Council, Keita and Mommadu Dia of Senegal presented Mali's wishes for an independent state. In December de Gaulle announced French adherence to the independence of Mali although such a move would mean the effective end of de Gaulle's newly created Community, and in June 1960, the Mali Federation became an independent state. However, stresses which had been overlooked in the emotion of creating the Federation soon divided the two parties. Differences in the economies, social needs, and methods of colonization were the root of the divisions. The immediate reason was a disagreement over apportionment of seats in the Malian federal executive, particularly the position of president. The crisis came to a head on August 19, 1960, when Keita dismissed federal Defense Minister Dia and claimed that the state was in danger. Under the guidance of Senghor the Legislative Assembly of Senegal reacted to Keita's actions on the next day by voting to take Senegal out of the Federation. Keita and other Soudanese leaders were arrested in Dakar and immediately deported. Keita's attempts to save the Federation failed and on September 22 the Soudanese legislature formally pronounced the establishment of a new Republic of Mali. Relations were broken off with Senegal, the frontier sealed, and Malian trade hastily rerouted through the Ivory Coast. The PFA was reconstituted as the *Union Soudanaise* with Keita as its leader. Keita became president of the Republic, and the *Union Soudanaise,* the only party in the state, was Keita's instrument to further his concepts of the socialistic reconstruction of the state. On January 20, 1961, Keita strengthened his control of the government by assuming the portfolios of foreign minister and defense minister. On April 29, an accord was signed with Ghana which aligned Mali with Ghana and Guinea in a union which would, in time, standardize the diplomatic, economic, and monetary policies of the three states. Keita after 1961 followed a policy of radical government control at home and nonalignment abroad. Relations with France were normalized, and with the resumption of friendly relations with Senegal in 1963, Mali once again could utilize the railroad and the port of Dakar. Despite the stringent control of the state by the *Union Soudanaise,* few incidents occurred in Mali which threatened Keita's position. One of these was when Mali merchants in July 1962 demonstrated against the introduction of the new currency regulations. Ninety-one persons were arrested and charged with attempting to overthrow the government. Among those detained were Dicko and Sissoko, and on October 1, 1962, they were sentenced to death on charges of plotting to overthrow the government. One week later their sentences were commuted to life in prison. In July 1964, the government announced that both political leaders had died in prison. Few details were given. In April 1964, the single list of candidates for the Malian National Assembly sponsored by the *Union Soudanaise* received eighty-nine percent of the total possible vote. On May 13, Modiba Keita was reelected president for a new four-year term by the National Assembly.

MAURITANIA

Mauritania is one of the most sparsely settled areas of West Africa, having a population of only slightly more than 700,000 nomadic people. Most of the Mauritanians are Moors and their typical political organization, left relatively undisturbed by the French, was that of rule by emirs. French rule in Mauritania after 1910 was an extremely stormy one. The population was highly mobile and divided by incessant petty wars involving different Berber groups. The stability of French rule was based largely upon control of the great emirs of Trarza, Brakna, and Adrar, and the possession of a first-rate military force which could implement French policy in the more difficult areas of Mauritania. Officially, before World War II the governor was assisted by a territorial council or *Conseil d'Administration*, all members of which were appointed by the governor. After the war, the French introduced a system of elections to choose members of the *Conseils*. This revised system called for a two-college method of voting. The first college was made up of all those electors in Mauritania who were residents of metropolitan France or those Mauritanians who could qualify for the classification of *statut civil*. The second roll was composed primarily of African voters who could qualify for the classification of *statut personnel*. Until 1956 there were twenty-four members in the *Conseil d'Administration*. Of these, eight were selected by the first college and sixteen were selected by the second college, despite the fact that there were only slightly over 700 non-Africans in the territory.

The first political party in the territory was created by Horma Ould Babana who was the first Mauritanian to sit in the French National Assembly. This party was primarily a government sponsored one and was called *L'Entente Mauritanienne*. Some of Babana's programs seemed to be too advanced for the traditional rulers of Mauritania, and they combined with some of the younger men to form an opposition group called the *Union Progressiste Mauritanienne*. The name of this group was later changed to the *Parti du Régroupement Mauritanien* (PRM). The leader of the PRM was Sidi el Mokhtar. In the *Conseil* election of 1952, the PRM won twenty-two of the twenty-four seats on the council. In 1956 el Mokhtar again defeated Babana for the .French Assembly and Babana fled Mauritania for the protection of the king of Morocco where he became an adherent of the king's claims to territory in Mauritania. Soon after this, Morocco launched a series of invasions of Mauritanian territory that were contained only with extreme difficulty by the French African troops and paratroopers. In the plebiscite occasioned by de Gaulle's assumption of power, Mauritania followed the pattern of most of the French West African territories and voted to remain within the French Community. Following the referendum, the territory was reorganized and given the name of the Islamic Republic of Mauritania. In this reorganization the legislative body of Mauritania was increased to forty members and the principle of responsible government was instituted. With the flight of Babana in 1956, Mauritania had become for all practical purposes a one-party state. In the confirming elections of May 1959, the PRM gained all forty seats in the Assembly. The premier of Mauritania after 1959 was Mokhtar Ould Daddah, a kinsman of el Mokhtar and the only lawyer in Mauritania. Ould Daddah was educated in France, but he also had close association with the traditional rulers of Mauritania because of his family. After the practical breakup of the French Community in 1960, Mauritania became an independent state with a Legislative Assembly and ministry

Ould Daddah became the first premier, and the PRM the chief political organization of Mauritania. A new constitution was adopted in May 1961 which established a presidential system while retaining the forty-seat National Assembly. Ould Daddah was then elected president unopposed in August 1961.

At the beginning of independence Mauritania seemed to have two basic problems. One concerned the continuing border troubles between Mauritania and Morocco, and the other was the economic nonviability of the state. After 1960 the border troubles between Morocco and Mauritania have eased in intensity. Many of the African states which had supported Morocco's claim to hegemony over Mauritania have since either adopted a neutral position or have changed sides completely. Although the problem remains, it has become less pressing than in the immediate past. Mauritania's economic position has been strengthened to the point where it is potentially one of the richest of the newly independent states of West Africa because of the discovery and exploitation of iron ore and, to a lesser extent, copper. Ould Daddah's moving of the capital from its long-time location at St. Louis in Senegal to the new city of Nouakchott reflects this growing prosperity.

There were two opposition parties to the PRM, the *Union Nationale Mauitanienne* (UNM) and the *Nahda*, a radical organization. The latter group was banned and Boyagui Ould Abride and other leaders were jailed for a brief time. Later at a series of meetings, outstanding differences between the three parties were adjusted and Ould Daddah formed a new ministry which included Boyagui and Hodrami Ould Khatny of the UNM. An attempt, late in 1964, by three former ministers to form a new political party was thwarted by Ould Daddah who declared that it was a move to destroy national unity. The major threat to continuing political control by the PRM, however, comes not from a Western-organized political party, but from the traditional schismatic elements within the Mauritanian state led by men such as the emir of Trarza and Horma Ould Babana from Morocco.

NIGER

The most outstanding feature of the Niger Republic was its poverty. In 1963 the negative difference between imports and exports was approximately $12,000,000. It is a landlocked state, depending for the export of its crops, primarily peanuts, on the foreign ports of Cotonou and Lagos. The population is ethnically divided between nomadic Tuaregs and Fula in the north and the sedentary Hausa-Songhai people in the south.

Niger gained its independence in August 1960, after voting in 1958 to stay in the French Community. Legislative power after independence was vested in a unicameral National Assembly and executive power in a president who conducts policy, initiates legislation, and has wide powers in times of emergency.

The first major political party in Niger was the *Parti Progressiste*

Nigérien (PPN), which was created in 1946 as the Niger section of the RDA. In 1950 a split occurred in the PPN when the RDA broke with the Communists. The more radical Djibo Bakary split with the party and formed his own *Union Démocratique Nigérienne* (UDN). The major leader of the PPN after the break was Bakary's cousin, Hamani Diori. In the territorial elections of 1957, the UDN in coalition with a smaller party, the *Bloc Nigérien d'Action* (BNA), won forty-one seats while the PPN won only nineteen. Bakary thus became the first premier of Niger. In 1958 he campaigned strenuously against the de Gaulle proposed French Community. The subsequent Yes vote forced his resignation, and Diori and the PPN returned to power. The strength of the new regime was seen in the elections of December 1958 when Diori's party, renamed the *Union pour la Communauté Franco Africaine* (UCFA), won fifty-four of the sixty seats in the legislature.

In October 1959, all opposition parties to the UCFA were banned. The UDN, which had changed its name to the *Sawaba* party and was still led by Bakary, was forced into exile in Mali. Another party which operated clandestinely was the Freedom party whose exiled leader, Andaly Douda, was assassinated in Bamako in May 1962. Douda's party stood for closer association with Mali.

Douda's assassination was blamed on Diori and the Niger government. This was but one of Diori's problems. Economic unbalance and growing tribal conflict made his position in the UCFA far from secure. Serious indications of this could be seen in the conflict between the army and the state in 1963. Certain high officials including the Minister for African Affairs, Zodi Ikhia, were arrested at that time. Bakary from his sanctuary in Mali continued to harass his cousin's government.

Relations with Dahomey became increasingly strained after the deposition of President Maga. Dahomeans living in Niger were expelled and Cotonou was closed to Niger trade. In September 1964, the Niger government announced that a plot, directed against Diori and organized by the *Sawaba* party, had been discovered. In October it was announced that the *Sawaba* party was responsible for a series of violent outbreaks against the government. These abortive attempts to overthrow the government were supposedly led by *Sawaba* "commandos." Diori announced the complete failure of this treasonable plot and that a number of the leaders had been publicly executed. Ghana and Dahomey, particularly, were accused of harboring *Sawaba* members and facilitating their activities against Niger.

In April 1965, while attending the Moslem celebration of Tabasky in Niamey with members of the government, Diori narrowly escaped assassination. A grenade was thrown which killed a child and wounded five other persons. The man arrested for the attempt was linked to the *Sawaba* party and it was alleged that he had been trained in Ghana. The action was denounced by all of the *Entente* members. Thus, while relations with Dahomey had improved, those with Ghana grew progressively worse during 1965.

SENEGAL

In 1945, reacting to the climate of the Brazzaville Conference, Leopold Senghor and Lamine Guèye formed the *Bloc Africain,* affiliated with the French Socialist party, SFIO. Regarding the second constitution of 1946 which established the French Union as insufficient, the African deputies to the French parliament met at Bamako to form the interterritorial RDA. Senghor and Guèye, on orders from the SFIO, did not attend this meeting, thus casting Senegal in a different political mold than the other territories which aided in the founding of the RDA. In 1948 Senghor, demanding more autonomy from the SFIO, began the *Bloc Démocratique Sénégalais* (BDS). In 1951 the BDS won both seats to the French Chamber of Deputies. In the meantime, Senghor had become the dominant force of the *Indépendents d'Outre Mer* (IOM), deputies to the French National Assembly who believed in federalism and rejected association with French political parties. This brought Senghor and the BDS in increasing conflict with the RDA in West Africa. Until 1960 the RDA concept was more popular in France and Africa than Senghor's.

In 1956 the *Bloc Progressiste Sénégalais* (BPS) was formed by blending the BDS with a number of smaller political groups. This became the Senegalese section of the *Convention Africaine* which was the successor to the IOM and was dominated by Senghor and his associates. In 1957 the *Convention Africaine* fused with the *Mouvement Socialist Africaine* (MSA) to oppose the RDA, and in the following year Senghor and Guèye merged their followings to form the *Union Progressiste Sénégalaise* (UPS) as the local agency of the interterritorial *Parti du Régroupement* Africain (PRA). Notwithstanding Senghor's stand against French control, the UPS swung behind de Gaulle's 1958 referendum. In December 1958, discussions were begun in Bamako looking toward a federation of Senegal, Soudan, Dahomey, and Upper Volta which was to be called the Mali Federation. However, pressure from the Ivory Coast caused the defection of Dahomey and Upper Volta. The two remaining partners did form the Mali Federation in March 1959. The UPS was fully in control in Senegal, and Senghor was selected president of the federal assembly of the Federation. With the breakup of the French Union, the Mali Federation became independent in June 1960. However, internal pressures, doctrinal differences, and different pressing social and economic problems brought an end to the Mali Federation in August 1960. Modibo Keita and other Soudanese leaders were deported and Senegal became a separate independent state.

The new constitution for Senegal approved on August 25 called for a president chosen by an electoral college to serve a seven-year term, a premier to act as chief executive, and an eighteen-member cabinet selected by the National Assembly. The legislative power was conferred on the eighty-member National Assembly. All members of the National Assembly were UPS men. Thus power and responsibility in Senegal were balanced between President Senghor, Premier Mamadou Dia, and the president of the assembly, Lamine Guèye. For over two years, with minor exceptions, these three men worked in close harmony to implement economic development under a four-year plan. However, the government system could be utilized by factions within the UPS if harmony among the leaders was lost.

In the period after 1960 there developed two major factions within the UPS. The younger, more radical deputies who were eager for faster economic and social change were led by Dia while the more conservative section of the assembly and the country followed Senghor. The first overt signs of the depth of the rift between Dia and Senghor occurred in the winter of 1961 when the state of emergency first decreed in August 1960 was tightened. Dia was accused of being dictatorial and, in the struggles in the party councils, Senghor proved too popular to unseat. Dia lost some supporters in high places when a cabinet reshuffle of early 1962 replaced them with Senghor adherents.

On December 15, 1962, thirty-nine deputies of the Senegal National Assembly tabled a vote of censure against Dia's government. They accused him of corruption and refusing to lift the unnecessary emergency decrees. On Dia's orders, gendarmes and part of the territorial guards on December 17 surrounded the assembly and members of the assembly were forced to leave. Senghor had meantime ordered loyal paratroops into the city and authorized Guèye to convene a parliamentary session in his home. Forty-eight members of the assembly voted for Dia's overthrow and called upon Senghor to assume dictatorial powers. The bulk of the army proved loyal to Senghor, and Dia and his chief lieutenants were arrested. The assembly immediately authorized Senghor to draw up new constitutional instruments to be submitted to the nation by referendum.

In May 1963, Dia was sentenced to life imprisonment and three of his former ministers were sentenced to twenty years each. The new constitution which was adopted by referendum on March 3 eliminated the position of premier. The functions previously exercised by Dia were taken over by the president who is elected separately from the National Assembly. No vote of censure can bring down the government, nor can the president dismiss the assembly. Thus Senghor gained full control of the executive of Senegal. Within the UPS the elements of Senghor's old party, the BDS, were more powerful than Guèye's following or that of Gabriel d'Arboussier. Senghor thus dominated the UPS. Lesser Senegalese parties such as the *Mouvement de Libération Nationale* (MLN) joined the UPS. The PRA-Senegal which broke with the UPS over the referendum in 1958 still continued its separate existence after the disturbances. Its leaders by restricting themselves to the academic world hoped to avoid conflict with Senghor and thus keep the PRA alive. However, in November 1964, the party leader, Abdoulaye Ly, was arrested and charged with incitement to revolt. The extreme Marxist party, the *Parti Africaine de l'Indepen-dence,* was outlawed. Another small party, the *Front National Sénégalais* (FNS), whose leader was Cheikh Anta Diop, the historian, was dissolved by government order in October 1964. This was probably because a number of former supporters of Dia had drifted into the FNS. Thus Senegal became for all practical purposes a one-party state firmly controlled by Senghor.

UPPER VOLTA

Upper Volta is a large, landlocked area of 105,869 square miles with a population of approximately 4,250,000. It is an agricultural state whose major exports are peanuts, maize, and livestock. It is dependent to a very large extent for extra capital from France which takes eighteen percent of the exports and provides Upper Volta with fifty-two percent of its imports.

The only political force in Upper Volta was the RDA until 1957 when the *Mouvement Démocratique Voltaique* (MDV) was formed. There were two other smaller parties which also contested the *Loi Cadre* election of 1957. These were the *Mouvement Populaire de l'Evolution Africaine* (MDEA) led by Nazi Boni and the *Parti Social d'Education des Masses Africaines* (PSEMA). In the 1957 election for the assembly the RDA won thirty-seven seats, the MDV twenty-seven, and the MDEA seven. The RDA and MDV formed a short-lived coalition under the leadership of Ouezzin Coulibaly. However, later in 1957 this coalition split and the MDV, the MDEA, and the PSEMA coalesced in opposition to the RDA, electing Nazi Boni as president of the assembly. In early 1958, Coulibaly regained control of the government by the defection of several MDV members to the RDA. Chief among these men was Maurice Yameogo. The RDA supported the de Gaulle Community and Upper Volta returned an overwhelming Yes vote in the 1958 referendum. Later in 1958, the death of Coulibaly made Yameogo the head of government of the autonomous republic.

Yameogo led the Volta RDA into a coalition with the opposition parties which allied themselves briefly with Senegal's *Parti Régroupement Africain* (PRA). This movement was the opening wedge in Yameogo's drive to unite Upper Volta with the projected Mali Federation. However, pressures from Houphouët-Boigny of the Ivory Coast rendered these attempts abortive. Later Volta's economic dependence on the Ivory Coast was underscored by its adhesion to the *Conseil de l'Entente* (Ivory Coast, Niger, Dahomey, and Upper Volta). Those who favored the Mali Federation broke with the government. Yameogo's following, now known as the *Union Démocratique Voltaique* (UDV) won sixty-four of the seventy-five seats in the subsequent elections of April 1959.

Yameogo's major political opponent, Nazi Boni, later in 1959 formed the *Parti National Voltaique* (PNV), closely associated with the chief party of Mali, the *Parti Féderaliste Africain* (PFA). This organization underscored Boni's conclusion that Volta's future rested in a close association with Mali. Both were soon banned by Yameogo and the now dominant UDV. Boni created a new party, the *Parti Républicaine de la Liberté* (PRL), which was also banned early in 1960. Boni escaped to Mali where he continued his efforts to undermine Yameogo and his one-party regime.

In July 1960, the necessary arrangements were made in Paris and, on August 5, Upper Volta became a sovereign state. The new constitution adopted by national referendum on November 27, 1960, provided for a presidential system. The first president was chosen by the seventy-five members of the National Assembly. Yameogo was selected in December 1960 to be the first president of the Republic and, in November 1965, was again elected president by gaining 2,132,418 of a possible 2,188,241 votes. Although this vote certainly indicated support, dissatisfaction could be seen in the fact that over one-third of the electorate at Ouagadougou did not vote in the elections for the National Assembly. Ostensibly this was in protest to the exclusion of certain persons from the voting list.

Yameogo's major problems in the early 1960s concerned lack of money and the need for an outlet to the sea. Forced out of the proposed Mali Federation and into the *Conseil de l'Entente,* Yameogo, nevertheless, negotiated better economic and political arrangements with Volta's other rich southern neighbor, Ghana. Poverty and its attendant pressures, coupled with government overspending, proved too complex for the UDV government of Yameogo. The president built a sumptuous country palace, and other politicians lived in lavish style while the economic ills of the country went unsolved.

To curb overspending on government services, Yameogo proposed in December 1965 a twenty percent cut in government salaries. This caused four days of demonstrations against the government in Wagadugu. The president reshuffled the cabinet, reduced its size from sixteen members to thirteen, and he assumed the position of defense minister. This precipitated the revolt of the military under the command of Lieutenant Colonel Sangoule Lamizana. The coup was bloodless, and even Yameogo publicly praised the take-over. Lamizana became president, holding in addition five ministries. None of Yameogo's ministers were retained in the new regime. However, no representative of the labor groups which had led the disturbance were included either. Lamizana established a state of emergency, proclaimed a curfew in the cities, and announced his intention of instigating an austerity program. He created a consultative committee composed of civilians to act as an intermediary group under the central government. Despite the obvious military nature of the regime, Lamizana declared that the military take-over was only temporary.

Devolution of power and consolidation of African rule: the AEF

CENTRAL AFRICAN REPUBLIC

The Central African Republic, formerly the territory of Ubangi-Shari, is a landlocked, poor area of 238,224 square miles, composed ethnically of a number of Bantu groups, with a population in 1960 of approximately 1,300,000. It is primarily an agricultural country, hampered by poor soil and lack of minerals, the exception being diamonds of which 265,000 carats were mined in 1965. The bulk of the nation's trade is with France which in 1965 supplied sixty-one percent of the imports and took fifty-seven percent of the republic's exports. In addition, France supplied the funds to meet the recurrent deficit in the government budget. The major problem facing any government of the newly independent Central African Republic was how to make the necessary social and economic improvements without the proper base.

The Central African Republic attained autonomy in the French Community in 1958 after voting ninety-eight percent Yes to the de Gaulle

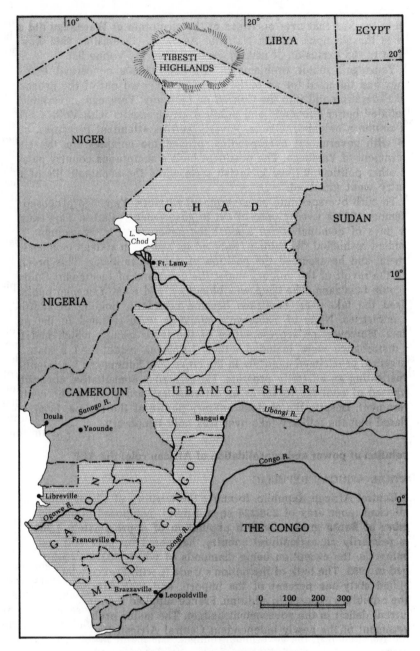

French Equatorial Africa (AEF)

referendum. The first political party in the territory was the *Mouvement pour l'Evolution Sociale de l'Afrique Noire* (MESAN). It was the creation in 1952 of Barthélemy Boganda who was a member of the French Assembly and had the support of the French party, *Mouvement Républicain Populaire*. Boganda wanted a closer federation of the four equatorial republics (Central African Republic, Congo, Gabon, and Chad) but was defeated by affluent Gabon's reluctance to join such a union. However, in 1959 the republic joined with her sister states in the Equatorial Customs Union. In 1965 the range and functions of this union were broadened by the establishment of the Central African Customs and Economic Union. A new constitution of February 1959 established a Legislative Assembly of fifty members and a president elected by the assembly as chief executive. Boganda's death in 1959 threw the politics of the country temporarily into disorder on the eve of elections for the Legislative Assembly in 1959. However, his chief lieutenant and twenty-six year old nephew, David Dacko, succeeded to power as head of the party and was elected president of the republic in April 1959. In July 1960, Dacko signed the necessary constitutional instruments with France, and on August 13 the Central African Republic was proclaimed a sovereign state.

Differences within MESAN led to the creation in 1960 of a rival party, *Mouvement pour l'Evolution Démocratique de l'Afrique Centrale* (MEDAC), led by Abel Goumba. However, in December 1960, MEDAC was ordered dissolved and Goumba and his most important followers were arrested. From that date onward the Central African Republic has been a one-party state. In early 1962, Goumba and another leading politician, Pierre Maleombko, were sentenced to jail for six months for "endangering the state," and later in the year all opposition parties were dissolved. In late 1963, an election for the assembly was held on the basis of a single list of candidates and, in January 1964, Dacko was elected to a seven-year term as president. In March 1964, he was unanimously reelected chairman of MESAN. Thus it appeared that Dacko was finally in full control of the state. However, the economic problems of the republic could not be solved without massive economic reconstruction. The funds provided by France, no matter how important, were not sufficient to undertake such designs. The mode of life of the politicians was not indicative of the poverty of the land. The form of political protest against the government in such a one-party state could only be a violent one.

On January 1, 1966, Colonel Jean Bedel Bokassa, a fourth cousin of Dacko and commander of the 800 man army, led his forces against the government. He charged Dacko and the other politicians with corruption, moral laxity, and becoming pawns of the Chinese Communists. Little resistance to the army was encountered, and as had been true in other military coups in Africa, Dacko and the other leading politicians immediately proclaimed their loyalty to the government. Bokassa dissolved the National Assembly and created a Revolutionary Council which guided by him would establish the laws for the new regime. Bokassa's first acts were an attack upon what were considered the major problems of the republic.

Polygamy was abolished and Bokassa in a number of public statements stressed the ideal of work as a major ingredient in solving the nation's economic problems. Expense allowances for government workers were canceled, taxes were cut, and a government austerity program was announced. Since the key to the republic's shaky future was continued economic cooperation with the West, Bokassa immediately took steps to assure these supporters of his hostile feelings toward the Red Chinese. Alleging the discovery of evidence linking them with paramilitary training and actvity, the new regime broke diplomatic relations with Red China.

CHAD

With an area of almost one-half million square miles, Chad is one of the larger African states. Like some of its neighbors in the former AOF, it is very poor, having a base of subsistence agriculture. Its major export item is raw cotton which provides two thirds of the export income. Chad runs a huge import-export deficit yearly and depends upon continuing French aid and investment for its economic stability.

Chad, together with Gabon, the Congo, and the Central African Republic, formed the pre-World War II administrative federation of French Equatorial Africa. It is a poor, landlocked territory with a sparse population of less than three million persons. It is divided as is Niger and Mali into two broad cultural groups—Muslims in the north and Bantu ethnic groups in the south. Despite its poverty and isolated position, Chad played an important role in the development of African nationalism in French Africa. After the French defeat in 1940, when many of the colonies remained loyal to Vichy, Chad, under the influence of its West Indian governor, Felix Eboué, declared for the Free French. It was later joined by the other component areas of Equatorial Africa. Eboué in this favorable climate was the moving force behind the Brazzaville Conference of 1944 which proposed sweeping reforms in French Africa. The failure to carry through on these promises set the stage for the development of political parties, particularly the RDA, in the ten years after the war.

The first major party, the *Parti Progressiste Tchadien* (PPT), in Chad was created by another West Indian, Gabriel Lisette, in 1947. The PPT became the local version of the intraterritorial RDA. Lisette led the PPT and the government through the reorganization caused by the *Loi Cadre* of 1956. However, mounting pressure from the Muslim north eventually forced his resignation as premier. He was succeeded by François Tombalbaye who was more acceptable to the north. Chad, in the referendum of 1958, voted overwhelmingly to remain in the French Union. Tombalbaye soon ousted Lisette as head of the party and exiled him in 1960. Some of the Muslim support defected from Tombalbaye and formed a separate party, the *Parti National Africaine* (PNA), to contest the elections of 1960. On August 11, 1960, Chad became an independent nation. The National Assembly of eighty-five members was composed of sixty-seven PPT members, ten PNA, and six independents. Tombalbaye became the president of the new republic.

In early 1961, Tombalbaye effected a compromise with his chief opposition, the PNA, and in March a fusion of the two groups, the *Union pour le Progrès du Tchad* (UPT), was announced. In January 1962, Tombalbaye declared all opposition parties a danger to the state and they were dissolved. Not surprisingly in the Chad National Assembly elections of March 1962, the PPT won all the seats and Tombalbaye was again selected head of state by the assembly. From this time Tombalbaye worked to get rid of all his potential political rivals and to further consolidate the power of the PPT. In March 1963, five leading politicians were arrested and the National Assembly was dissolved. In July two of the five were sentenced to death for subversion. Again in September 1963, Tombalbaye declared a state of emergency following clashes between demonstrators and the army. Three major politicians, including Ahmed Koulmallah, former head of the PNA, were arrested. A Chad government in exile with headquarters in Khartoum was later formed; it continued to operate until late 1965.

In April 1964, a quarrel developed between the government and some French nationals. The Chad National Assembly asked that all French troops be removed from the country. However, Tombalbaye rejected the notion that this should be carried out since Chad needed the 1,000 man French force for security as well as for the economic value of the military to the nation.

The periodic violent disturbances in outlying districts directed against Tombalbaye's government continued through 1965. The most serious was located in the Mangalme district northeast of Fort Lamy where seven government officials were killed in October. The movement at Mangalme ostensibly was backed by the Muslim rulers who wanted some of their feudal privileges returned. At the same time less serious antigovernment moves were organized in the south. In November three ministers of state and three members of parliament were arrested and accused of plotting to kill the president. Following upon these events, the National Assembly voted a change in the constitution. The section of the constitution which gave persons the right to form political parties was deleted. Thus Chad officially became a one-party state. Despite this, Tombalbaye's control of the state continued to be fraught with danger. The coups in ostensibly more stable neighboring states acted as a spur to the activities of the dissident elements within Chad.

THE REPUBLIC OF THE CONGO (BRAZZAVILLE)

Immediately after World War II, the only territorial political party in the Middle Congo was the *Mouvement Socialiste Africaine* (MSA) which was a section of the French Socialist party (SFIO). The most important African member of the MSA was Jacques Opangault. The RDA was early represented in the Congo by an efficient organization headed by Felix Tchicaya. In 1956 the *Union Démocratique de la Défense des Intérets Africains* (UDDIA) was founded by Abbé Fulbert Youlou, a Catholic priest and former mayor of Brazzaville. Although the church later defrocked the abbé, he continued to wear the habit, largely because of the effect it had on many of his supporters. Much of this support came from the Bakongo who had elevated one of their deceased leaders, Sergeant Matswa, to the position of semidiety. Some of this earlier allegiance was transferred to Youlou.

In the 1957 territorial elections, the MSA and UDDIA each won twenty-one of the forty-five seats. However, Opangault was called to form the government. Later in 1957, the UDDIA became affiliated with the RDA. Both the MSA and the UDDIA stood for autonomy within the French Community in 1958 and the electorate returned a ninety-nine percent Yes vote on the de Gaulle referendum. By the defection of one MSA supporter, Youlou was named the first premier in late 1958. Rioting between factions supporting each party occurred in January 1959. The riots took on the character of tribal warfare with the M'Bochis supporting the MSA and the Bakongo and Balalis supporting the UDDIA. French troops finally restored order, but only after one hundred persons had been killed. Opangault and other leading MSA figures were subsequently jailed. A new constitution was adopted in February which provided for a legislative assembly of sixty-one members and responsible government. The elections of June gave the UDDIA fifty-one seats and the MSA only ten. Two members of the MSA were included in the cabinet and the MSA was merged into the UDDIA before independence in 1960.

In February 1960, Youlou reshuffled his cabinet to eliminate all Europeans, and on July 12 he signed an agreement with France providing for the independence of the Republic of Congo. Under a new constitution of March, 1961, chief executive authority was conferred on a president elected by universal suffrage. The president appointed the cabinet and the vice-president, and these were not responsible to the National Assembly. Youlou was elected to a five-year term as president on March 26, 1961, and the UDDIA won over ninety-seven percent of the popular vote in the elections for the assembly. Youlou seemed to be at the height of power. He held, in addition, the positions of premier, minister of defense, and minister of the interior.

Youlou espoused a militant foreign policy, demanding freedom for Africans while at the same time developing at home a policy to restrict all opposition to the "nationalist government." The authoritarian bent of Youlou's government became more pronounced after the disturbances of September 1962, when a state of emergency was proclaimed after a disputed soccer game with the Gabon. Youlou's most vocal opponents were the various labor union leaders who were dissatisfied with the economic progress of the country and its close ties with France. Charges of corruption and mismanagement were also made against the UDDIA-dominated government. In the summer of 1963, the most important union leaders were arrested and, despite the growing signs of unrest throughout the country, Youlou persisted in his aim of establishing constitutionally an authoritarian regime. In late August, mobs in Brazzaville stormed the jails and released the unionists and forced Youlou from power. The army intervened to restore order and prevent the establishment of a left-wing unionist government. A provisional government was formed under the leadership of Alphonse Massemba Debat, an ex-minister in Youlou's government. On December 8, a new constitution was approved by a plebiscite. It provided for a one-house legislature of fifty-five members elected for five years. The head of state was to be a president chosen by an electoral college composed of the legislature and urban and provincial councils. His length of office was also five years.

Relations between Brazzaville and Leopoldville worsened in 1964 with the development of civil strife in the larger republic. Part of the rebel forces utilized the Brazzaville area as a staging ground for their invasions. Debat's government was openly hostile to the West and maintained good relations with the Chinese Communists whose regime it had recognized in February 1964. In October Leopoldville expelled all Brazzaville Congolese. In July 1964, the Congo became officially a one-party state with the establishment of the National Revolutionary Movement as the only legal party. Massemba Debat became the secretary-general of the party. On December 22, 1964, the electoral college confirmed Debat as president and made concessions to the radical left by appointing Pascal Lissouba as his prime minister.

GABON

The Gabon Republic is located on the equator with a population in 1960 of less than 500,000. It is extremely rich in hardwood timber, uranium, iron, gold, and oil. The dominant political party in the Gabon has been the *Bloc Démocratique Gabonais* (BDG) which was formed in 1953 as an outgrowth of an earlier group, the *Mouvement Mixte Gabonais*. Both of these parties were the local sections of Houphouët-Boigny's intraterritorial RDA. The leader of the BDG and first head of state was Leon M'Ba. Another important party was the *Union Sociale Gabonaise* (USG) whose leader was Jean Aubame. In the elections of 1957, occasioned by the *Loi Cadre,* Aubame's party won eighteen of the forty seats in the territorial assembly. This was the high-water mark for Aubame; afterward the BDG under M'Ba increased its influence at the expense of the opposition.

Gabon became independent on August 17, 1960. In the first elections neither party gained a majority in the forty-seat assembly. Four independent members, however, supported the BDG and M'Ba was selected premier. Because of the inability of the first government to act decisively in establishing new programs, a new constitution was drawn. The constitution of February 1961 provided for a president to serve a seven-year term and also a sixty-seven member National Assembly whose members serve a term of five years. For the elections of that same month, the two parties agreed to cooperate, and a single list of candidates was submitted to the voters. M'Ba became president and Aubame vice-president, and the ministry was almost equally divided between adherents of the two parties. M'Ba's policy was to discourage close ties with other independent African states and depended heavily economically, culturally, and defensively on France. In February 1963, Aubame's USG was given the choice of merging with the BDG or having their ministers resign from the government. The USG ministers chose to resign and oppose M'Ba's government. They criticized M'Ba for his dependence on France, his budget-cutting programs, and legislation concerning the High Court.

The president dissolved the National Assembly in January 1964, called for new elections under new regulations favorable to the BDG, and arbitrarily reduced the size of the assembly to forty-seven members. Angered by these events, on February 17, 1964, Gabon's 400 man army staged a coup which deposed M'Ba from power. Under duress he resigned and a provisional government headed by Aubame was created. However, the next day in answer to M'ba's request, French and African troops from Brazzaville and Dakar arrived, honoring the 1961 defense treaty, and M'Ba was restored to office. Elections were then held in April under the new rules and the BDG won thirty-one of the forty-seven seats in the assembly. The leaders of the coup were tried in August and received relatively mild sentences, but Aubame was sentenced to ten years for his activity. Thirteen of the opposition members later joined the BDG leaving only three members in the assembly who were not members of M'Ba's party.

Devolution of power and consolidation of African rule: the French trust territories

CAMEROUN

Politics in the Cameroun was complicated by the divisions of the territory between France and Britain as mandatory powers. In the larger French area, the first important party was the *Union des Populations du Cameroun* (UPC) created in 1947 which agitated for an end to mandate status and reunification of all parts of the Cameroun. Because of its activities, French authorities in 1955 resorted to repressive measures against the UPC and it was proscribed. The UPC leader, Reuben Um Nyobe, in the following year launched a guerrilla war to force the French departure. However, the party lost much of its drive with the death of Nyobe in 1958. Felix Moumie succeeded Nyobe as head of the party and continued to follow a terroristic policy.

Another important early party was the *Bloc Démocratique Camerounais* (BDC) led by Andre Mbida and Ahmadou Ahidjo. Benefiting from divisions in the party, Ahidjo broke away in 1956 to form his own party based primarily on northern support called the *Union Camerounaise* (UC). Ahidjo, a Fulani, had been elected to the Territorial Assembly in 1952 and became vice-premier in 1956, serving under Mbida's leadership. Mbida's political strength lay in the largely Catholic areas near Yaounde, but it proved insufficient to stem the mounting criticism over his handling of the UPC and certain of his long range goals. He resigned in January 1958, and Ahidjo and the UC formed a new government. After negotiations in Paris were completed early in 1958, full internal self-government was promised French Cameroun on January 1, 1959, and full independence a year later. Both Mbida and Ahidjo had, with French troops, continued the war against the UPC and Moumie. In 1959 Ahidjo dismissed parliament and ruled by decree. On January 1, 1960, the country became independent and Ahidjo became president with Charles Assale as premier. The power of the UPC was further weakened by the death of Moumie in November 1960.

The British-governed portion of the Camerouns was divided into two parts, both areas administered as a part of Nigeria. The Northern Camerouns until the 1961 plebiscite formed a segment of the Northern Region while the Southern Camerouns had a separate administration under the control of the governor of Nigeria acting as high commissioner for the territory. In both areas two contrary ultimate solutions for the future of the Camerouns were presented to the Africans and the United Nations. One was the unification of the British and French trust areas to form a new state. The other was permanent division with the British trusts becoming a part of the Federation of Nigeria. This latter solution was done irreparable damage by the prolonged government crisis in the Eastern Region of Nigeria in 1953. Prior to this time thirteen elected members from the Camerouns sat in the Eastern House of Assembly and cooperated with the dominant party, the National Council of Nigeria and the Camerouns. The deadlock in the Eastern regional government convinced many of the Cameroun politicians that association with Nigeria would not serve their best interests.

Two different parties were operative in the British areas in the early 1950s—the Kamerun United National Congress (KUNC) and the Cameroons National Federation (CNF). These were eventually merged to form the Kamerun National Congress (KNC) under the leadership of Dr. Emmanuel Endeley. The KNC advocated the absorption of the British Cameroun into a region of Nigeria. In 1955 as a result of the political differences in Eastern Nigeria, Dr. John Foncha resigned from the KNC and created the Kameroun National Democratic party (KNDP) which advocated the union of French and British areas.

On March 13, 1959, the United Nations General Assembly called for a plebiscite in the northern British segment to determine whether it would enter the Federation of Nigeria. The plebiscite, held under United Nations supervision in November 1959, resulted in a vote to continue the trustee status rather than join Nigeria. The United Nations in October 1959, by resolution, called for another plebiscite to be held in the Camerouns to decide its future. On October 1, 1960, the Northern Cameroun was separated from Nigeria and administration was placed under a special British administration. Meanwhile in January 1959, elections to a thirty-two member House of Assembly based on universal suffrage were held. The KNDP won fourteen of the twenty-six contested seats and Foncha became the prime minister. On July 18, 1960, Prime Minister Foncha met with Premier Ahidjo of the French Cameroun and they declared their substantial agreement on a federation of their two areas.

The plebiscites called for earlier by the United Nations were held in February 1961, with the result that the Northern Cameroun chose to join Nigeria and the southern region selected association with the French

Cameroun through a federal system of government. On June 1, 1961, the northern area became Sarduana Province of Northern Nigeria. On October 1, 1961, the southern region became the West Cameroun with its own regional assembly controlled by the KNDP. On the federal level West Cameroun sent ten representatives to the fifty-member Cameroun Federal Assembly. Ahidjo remained the president of the Federal Republic and Foncha became vice-president. Federal elections were held for the first time in April 1964. President Ahidjo's party, the UC, won all forty of the seats allotted to the east. In the west, vice-president Foncha's KNDP won all ten seats.

After unification, both Ahidjo and Foncha worked closely together attempting to weld their respective parties into one national party. In the spring of 1962, the UC and KNDP formed a "National Unity Group" to ensure unanimity in the Federal Assembly. The principle of a united party was accepted by both major groups but the mechanics were difficult to work out and a coordination committee was formed to work out the details of fusion. In East Cameroun most of the lesser political parties such as the *Mouvement d'Action Nationale* (MAN), *Rassemblement du Peuple Camerounais* (RPC), and *Démocrates Camerounais* (DC) declared for a union of all parties. In West Cameroun the Cameroon Peoples National Convention (CPNC), which was organized to fight unification, did not oppose, in principle, a one-party establishment, but again the structure of such a party presented the major obstacle to fusion. In May and September 1964, new meetings were held and a seventeen-man committee was appointed to strengthen cooperation between the parties. The ease with which federation of the two widely differing areas was carried out and the harmony displayed between the UC and the KNDP promised well for Cameroun politics. The only dark spot in this otherwise excellent example of cooperation was the civil war which Nyobe had begun in 1956. Although the French-trained troops of the Cameroun government had the upper hand since the beginning of the revolt and contained the rebels, it is estimated that some 70,000 people were killed in this little-known conflict in the five years after independence.

TOGO

During the scramble for Africa, Germany claimed direct possession of the coastal area between the Gold Coast and Dahomey. It had taken a long time to penetrate the interior, and German control there was barely effective before the start of World War I. Togoland was one of the most unfortunate victims of the boundary delimitations of the nineteenth century. There are many tribes in Togo such as the Gourmas, Lambas, and Akebas with the largest single group being the Ewe. Tribal boundaries tend to run east and west, while the state boundaries were drawn north and south by the European powers. Thus many of the tribes are also located in Ghana and Dahomey.

After World War I the small sliver of territory was divided between the two major liberating powers. Britain became responsible for the portion adjacent to the Gold Coast which was administered as a part of that territory. The French portion, with a population of slightly over one million, was administered separately from the neighboring French areas of Dahomey or Upper Volta. In 1945 these mandates were transferred to the United Nations to be administered as Trust Territories. The United Nations ordered a plebiscite to be held in the British trust to determine its future. The plebiscite held in 1956 confirmed the territory's long association with the Gold Coast. The voters in British Togoland chose by a substantial margin to have their section integrated with Ghana. Thus the originally small, poor area of Togoland was reduced even further. The future independent state of Togo, therefore, was constructed out of only the French Trust Territory.

The political reforms immediately after World War II gave Togo representatives in the French Union and also in the two representative bodies in metropolitan France. Togoland also was given a representative Assembly of thirty members, chosen by the two-college system of election. Initial nationalist leadership after the war proved to be too radical for the French administrators and some of the conservative chiefs. With some slight alterations, a more conservative group of politicians came to power under the leadership of Nicolas Grunitzky. Grunitzky's party was called the *Parti Togolais du Progrès* (PTP) composed primarily of non-Ewes and opposed to the reconstitution of a Ewe state. The party of Ewe nationalism became the *Comité de l'Unité Togolaise* (CUT). Due to divisions of West Africa from the 1880s, the Ewe peoples were assigned to the Gold Coast, the two Togos, and Dahomey. In 1951, Sylvanus Olympio became the leader of CUT. Realizing that by standing for Ewe unification his party could hope for little support from the other tribes, he changed the party's demands to a unification of the two Togos. Another early party was the *Union des Chefs et des Populations du Nord*. This party was renamed the *Union Démocratique des Populations Togolaises* (UDPT) in 1958. Its power was based on the northern section which is dominated by conservative Muslim chiefs.

By the general reforms instigated by the *Loi Cadre*, France made Togoland an autonomous republic within the French Union. This called for a ministry and a chief minister, and a legislature selected from a common roll. In the ensuing elections the PTP gained the majority and Grunitzky became the first premier. Following the reconstruction of the government, the people were called upon in October 1956 to vote in a referendum whether they wished the new republican statute or a continuation of trusteeship status. Olympio, feeling that his party could not win, called a boycott of the referendum. The United Nations refused to send observers since they maintained that the referendum did not give the voters wide enough choice. Despite these factors, seventy percent of the electorate approved the new status.

On this basis France attempted to have trusteeship status revoked in 1957. However, the United Nations called for UN supervised elections to decide the future of the area and what party really represented the people. Under threats of violence by all parties and fears of a possible *putsch* from Ghana, the elections were held on April 27, 1958. The results surprised most observers. The CUT won nineteen of the twenty-three seats in the south and even ten of twenty-three in the supposed hostile north. The popular vote was over sixty percent of the votes cast for the CUT.

Olympio as premier also surprised the French by his moderate, pragmatic approach to the many problems of Togo. He negotiated full internal autonomy for Togo beginning in January 1959. In late 1959, he received guarantees from France for the independence of Togo in April 1960. Before independence, Olympio's government successfully withstood an attempt by Ghana to integrate Togo into Ghana. Charging a breakdown of law and order in Togo, Kwame Nkrumah came forth as the protector of all Ewes. Nkrumah also charged that Togo was planning an invasion of Ghana and moved troops to the border. Olympio stated that an invasion under whatever pretext would be resisted and he would appeal to France and the United Nations for help. This open power play was thwarted and was one of Nkrumah's earliest major defeats.

The great victory of the CUT in 1958 left the opposition parties shattered. But Olympio's moderate, basically pro-French and anti-Ghana attitude created other forces of opposition within the CUT. His approach to the many problems of economically poor Togo was pragmatic. This called for economy in government, reduction of the armed forces by half, and continued close economic contacts with France in order to keep the budget balanced and continue minimum development of the country. The youth wing of the CUT, Le Mouvement de la Jeunesse Togolaise (JUVENTO), demanded more radical, socialist programs. The leader of JUVENTO, Anani Santos, a brilliant lawyer, had been quite influenced by Ghanaian socialism. In reality, JUVENTO was a separate party even before its open break with the CUT. There were rumors in January 1959 of a JUVENTO coup against the government backed by Ghana. However, despite military precautions supported by the French, nothing occurred.

A new constitution was drawn up and approved by the electorate in April 1961. This new instrument of government provided for a presidential system with a unicameral legislature. The Chamber of Deputies was composed of fifty-one members elected by universal suffrage. In the elections of 1961, Olympio was elected president. Grunitzky formed an alliance with JUVENTO to contest the election. The election lists of the alliance were disallowed and the CUT won all the seats in the legislature. Grunitzky left Togo soon after the elections, and JUVENTO was later outlawed. Previously, in the elections of 1958, the UDPT and the PTP had ceased to be effective political parties. Therefore, after 1961, Togo had only one political party, the CUT, and Olympio seemed firmly in control of the government.

Olympio's conservative approach to the needs of Togo led directly to the overthrow of his government and his assassination in January 1963. Togo is a poor country, and Olympio resisted all demands to increase the budget by adding new government posts. Unemployment, always a problem, increased. By far the most important question concerned the size of the Togolese army. The ex-soldiers demanded an increase in its size and this demand was continually refused. These ex-soldiers served as the nucleus of the revolt. Despite Olympio's record as an administrator, capable of balancing the budget and maintaining excellent relations with Europe, the military forces numbering in the hundreds took over the government on January 13, 1963, and killed President Olympio.

A revolutionary committee of eight officers was formed. Grunitzky, who was in exile in Dahomey, was informed of the coup and arrived in Lome three days after the overthrow of Olympio's government. Until his arrival there was considerable confusion in Togo. However, the committee appointed Grunitzky provisional president and some order was reestablished. New elections were promised within six weeks. Grunitzky calmed the dangerous situation by promising reforms and increasing the size of the army to employ the ex-servicemen who had been so instrumental in the coup.

One of the complicating features of these crucial days was Ghana's possible involvement. Relations between Ghana and Olympio's government had been poor since before the independence of Togo. From December 1959 through May 1960, there was a possibility of armed conflict. In December 1961, eighteen men were arrested by Togolese police and charged with plotting to overthrow the government. They were allegedly supported by Ghana. JUVENTO was actively pro-Ghana, and many of the leaders of the opposition to Olympio had gone to Ghana. Ghana was the first state to offer de jure recognition to the new regime. However, Grunitzky and Antoine Meatchi, the foremost politician from the north, made it clear that they intended to maintain the integrity of Togo.

In conjunction with other members of the provisional government, Grunitzky called for national unity. The constitution was revised to provide for a National Assembly of fifty-six members. Each of the four parties in Togo was to have equal representation in the legislature. These parties were the CUT, the UDPT, JUVENTO, and the Mouvement des Populations Togolaises (MPT). This represented a revival of political activity, although the competition was restricted. Each party would nominate proposed members. From this list the voters would choose the legislators. The presidential system was also to be retained. Before the elections of May 5, 1963, there was considerable conflict and confusion among the leaders. Grunitzky was challenged briefly for the leadership of his now revived party, the UDPT, by Meatchi who wanted to be the presidential nominee. Also, from Guinea, M. Mally, the interior minister under Olympio, broadcast charges against the provisional government. Despite threats of a coup against the provisional government, the elections were held. Grunitzky was elected president, the constitution was adopted, and the single list submitted was approved by the electorate. Mally was later arrested and sentenced to twenty years imprisonment for his actions in the days prior to the election.

Subsequently, the Togo government was recognized by most of the African states, and their representatives were present as observers at the Addis Ababa conference. In August 1963, Togo was formally admitted to the *Union Africain et Malagache* (UAM). Even Ghana opened an embassy in Lome and entered into economic discussions with Grunitzky's government. Although Grunitzky's government could not solve many of the problems which led to the overthrow of Olympio, it did restore law and order, and gave Togo a stability which many observers believed impossible in the spring of 1963. Indicative of this stability was the joint meeting of representatives of the four parties making up the coalition government in December 1965. The congress of the four—JUVENTO, UDPT, MPT, and CUT—called for studies which would perhaps lead to their merging into a single political party.

TWO

Postwar political developments: British Africa

General political changes

The British government indicated an alteration of attitudes toward its dependent empire during World War II by a number of separate actions. The Colonial Development and Welfare Acts showed that the prewar penurious attitudes were at an end. The Colonial Office early in the war sent a directive to the governors of all its territories to design coordinate postwar development plans for all colony and protectorate areas. This was the first time that the Colonial Office was presented with complex, integrated analyses of the situation in each territory and with projections for the future. Despite the economic stringencies of postwar Britain, funds were provided for many of these projected improvements. At the same time the Labor government committed itself to opening more mid-range positions and equalizing pay scales and conditions of work in the civil service for Africans. This Africanization, although it did not proceed as rapidly as many believed necessary, did provide within a decade a much larger cadre of trained personnel at all levels in all British African territories.

Before the end of the war most governors had indicated that the governmental instruments for their areas were inadequate. With the concurrence of the Colonial Office new constitutions were granted to all of Britain's dependent empire in the five years following the war. Before granting these constitutions Britain consulted African nationalists only in a minimal fashion. Thus such reforms as the Richards Constitution in Nigeria were from the outset unpopular because they granted the elite too little power. Nevertheless, these new government instruments brought many more Africans on the upper levels into the legislative and executive councils. On the local level reforms in municipal government gave Africans a larger share in determining local policy. The Colonial Office also tried to improve the all but moribund concept of vital, developing systems of indirect rule for the protectorates. The new emphasis was upon native authorities rather than a chief and his traditional council. An effort was made, wherever possible, to admit the elective principle in the selection of the native authorities. Thus the major question after 1950 was no longer whether Africans should be given more responsibility but concerned the timing for increased authority to the Africans.

Reforms of the central government structure presented the British government with an unforeseen problem. Heretofore the dichotomy between the government of the colony areas and the protectorates had produced few problems. It was apparent that the grant of increased influence to Africans in the central government was incompatible with the older concepts of indirect rule. The now politically influential, educated Africans made it clear that the old and, in many ways, inefficient local government system would have to be modified. Semi-independent states could not function with two such incompatible philosophies of government. Every advance of the British territories toward independence witnessed the commensurate shrinkage in power of the protectorate chiefs. British concerns for the future of the protectorate Africans and their traditional rulers dictated a slower policy of political advance than was desired by the African political parties.

Thus the rate of advance became the key problem in the 1950s. Political agitation such as that first undertaken in the Gold Coast was designed to show the British a united native front and force the Colonial Office to grant concessions earlier than the British authorities wished. But in West Africa, Kwame Nkrumah, Benjamin N'namdi Azikiwe, Obafemi Awolowo, Milton Margai, and other African politicians did not have to convince the British that eventually the African should control the destinies of their territories. Initially British authorities as well as most African nationalists had envisioned a long period of continued, responsible British control which would devolve power to the Africans when they were able to meet the responsibilities of that power. British experience in India and observation of the Dutch in Indonesia and the French in Indochina and Algeria, however, had shown the futility of attempting to maintain control against the wishes of the people. Thus the major contribution of activist parties such as Nkrumah's CPP was to convince British authorities to speed up the granting of authority to Africans. The transition from British to African control was a relatively smooth one even though it was accomplished far faster than many responsible officials believed was safe. The presence in West Africa of only a small number of European residents also facilitated the transfer of power to the Africans. It was more difficult elsewhere.

Once the change was decided upon, the method by which Britain accomplished the shift of power was relatively simple. There was never any attempt to bring all the British territories to the same level of development at the same time or to associate them directly with the mother country. The crown colony system of government was merely expanded and elaborated upon. The change from total dependency to independence was accomplished by a series of modifications. The first was to associate

Africans with the government by nominating more of them to the legislative and executive councils. The next step was to provide for the elections of some Africans to the Legislative Council. The third was to increase the number of Africans, usually elected, to the Legislative Council until they controlled an unofficial majority. Normally at this time ministries were formed having basically advisory functions to the civil service departments. The African quasi-ministers were part of the Executive Council. The next to last step was to increase the size of the legislature and hold elections throughout the territory for its members. A ministry could then be formed responsible to the legislative body. This ministry took the place of the Executive Council and the ministers exercised real executive power over the departments under their control. Normally at this point a chief minister with the responsibility of coordinating policy and legislation was also chosen. It was at this time that the African territory gained full internal self-government. The governor, still appointed by the Colonial Office, exercised some powers of review and veto over domestic matters, but these were seldom exercised. Only in the areas of foreign trade, defense, and foreign affairs did the British government still retain its preeminent position. The final step was complete independence of the territory and voluntary association in the Commonwealth.

This is a generalized pattern of evolution of the British African states toward independence. In non-multiracial areas this evolution proceeded in an orderly fashion with a minimum of friction. This was not the case where the British government attempted a compromise between the demands of Africans and Europeans. There were only two areas of Britain's African empire where there was a significant resident, white population—Kenya and the Rhodesias.

In 1944 Kenya's population was slightly over four million. Of these only 32,000 were Europeans. Yet they possessed an inordinate amount of political and economic power and influence. Although it is a mistake to believe that the Nairobi government was a rubber stamp for these colonists, one cannot deny that basically it reflected the desires of the Europeans. Thus the postwar government reforms came late to Kenya and they were much less sweeping than in West African areas. By 1948 there were only four nominated Africans on the Legislative Council. The proposed reforms of 1952 contemplated the introduction of a system of indirect election for six Africans on this council while the Europeans had fourteen seats. Long-standing grievances over land, growing urban unemployment, high prices, and the conviction that Britain was not going to grant them the same measure of freedom which it was giving West Africans drove some of the Kikuyu into revolt. Mau Mau was bloody and costly. Although few other tribes in Kenya joined the revolt, it took the British four years to pacify the country, and the era left scars which will take long to heal. However, after 1957, the British government realized that it had to choose between the African majority and the white minority. After deciding for the former, political evolution in Kenya followed the general pattern of development of other British colonies.

The problems in Central Africa were similar to those of Kenya, but due to the creation in 1952 of the Central African Federation they were more difficult to resolve. The Central African Federation of Nyasaland, Northern and Southern Rhodesia was created over the objections of almost all the African political leaders of these territories. The major force which created and held this union together was the white population of Southern Rhodesia and their leader, Sir Roy Welensky. Although the outlook of the whites in Southern Rhodesia and the 38,000 Europeans in Northern Rhodesia was generally not as extreme as the Afrikaners in South Africa, they had no intention of allowing Africans the measure of political authority which their numbers would have indicated. The problem facing political leaders such as Kenneth Kaunda and Hastings Banda was, therefore, more complicated than elsewhere in Africa. The federation had to be broken before independence for its northern territories became a reality. It was not until 1963, after considerable violence in all these areas combined with pressures from the now independent African states, that the Colonial Office decided finally to jettison Welensky and the federation and allow the independence of Malawi and Zambia. The problem of a largely disenfranchised African majority and a controlling white minority, nevertheless, remained in Southern Rhodesia.

Aside from the multiracial areas, Britain's record of colonial guidance in the years following World War II was excellent. Its central government system, pragmatic from the earliest days, was simply expanded to meet the new demands. In the protectorates the traditional systems were changed to function primarily as agencies of local government while the responsibility for the protectorate as a unit was merely shifted from a loose system of direct rule to a more complex method controlled by the newly expanded organs of the central government. A brief examination of each British territory will show how the grant of authority to Africans was accomplished in each area.

Devolution of power and consolidation of African rule: British West Africa

GAMBIA

For such a small area (approximately 4,000 square miles, population 250,000) which was touched late by nationalistic feelings, the Gambia has had a large number of political parties. Until the decade of the 1950s the typical British dual rule of crown colony government for the colony and guided, traditional rule for the protectorate seemed sufficient. Britain granted more liberal constitutions to the Gambia in 1946, 1950, and 1954 with little organized pressure from the Gambians themselves. Not until after 1959 did the leading politicians of the Gambia begin to demand eventual independence for the small, economically poor area. They had previously proposed direct federation with Britain or a federal union with Sierra Leone as their goals. With the creation of the West Indies Federation and independence for other tiny areas such as Malta, the idea of a direct federation with Britain was no longer feasible. Sierra Leone on the

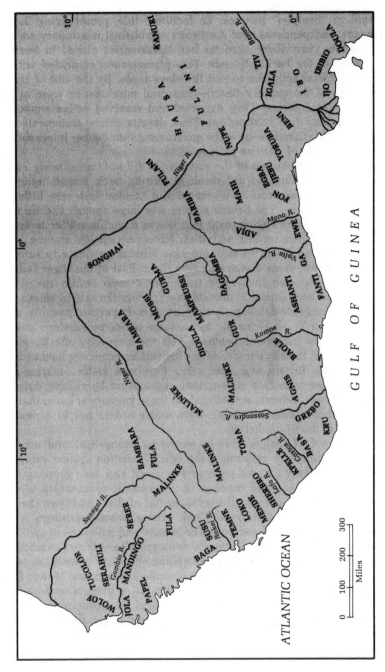

Peoples of West Africa

41

eve of independence was not in the mood for adding more responsibilities. The only alternatives left for Gambians became continued dependent status, amalgamation with Senegal, or independence. Growing dissatisfaction with the British administration ruled out the first. Thus the only goals left were independence or absorption by Senegal.

The first political parties in the Gambia were of necessity colony-based and were formed to contest the 1951 election. The first of these was the Democratic party (DP) which served as a vehicle for the election of its leader, the Reverend J. C. Faye, to the Legislative Assembly. The second party also created in 1951 was the Muslim Congress which was formed out of a number of smaller Muslim cultural and political groups. Its leader, I. M. Garba-Jahumpa, wanted to mobilize the Muslim majority of the Gambia not only for the Legislative Council elections but possibly to control the future political development of the Gambia. Formed soon after P. S. N'Jie was defeated for the Legislative Council in 1951, the United party (UP) was also personality oriented. It gained great support from the colony by N'Jie's opposition to the British administration and the fact that he held no government office.

The first constitution to genuinely reflect Gambian articulate opinion was that of 1960. It provided for a greatly increased Legislative Council and appointed ministers. It was the first to apply the elective principle to to the numerically superior protectorate. As such, it was the first definite breach in the authority of the chiefs in the protectorate. A number of changes occurred in political alignments before the election. David Jawara formed the first protectorate-oriented party, the Peoples Progressive party (PPP). Failing support for their programs caused the Muslim Congress and Democratic Party to merge into the Democratic Congress Alliance (DCA) just weeks before the elections. The elections resulted in a standoff between the PPP and the UP. The UP won six seats, five of which were in the colony. The PPP won eight protectorate seats. Neither of the leaders of the DCA was elected, although the party captured three seats. The balance of power was held by eight indirectly elected chiefs. In early 1961, the governor appointed the first chief minister. The role of the chiefs was decisive in this selection and P. S. N'Jie, leader of the UP, was appointed.

None of the political parties were satisfied with the constitution, and constitutional discussions with the Colonial Office were held in mid-1961. A new constitution was put into effect in 1962 and elections were held for a greatly expanded House of Representatives. The colony was to have only eight elected members while the protectorate directly elected twenty-five. The chiefs had only four indirectly elected representatives. In the elections of 1962 th PPP gained eighteen seats, the UP thirteen, and the DCA only one. A responsible ministry was formed by the PPP and David (later Sir Duada) Jawara became premier. Despite considerable confusion and debate over the election registers, this government was confirmed and the PPP has never since been out of power. In the fall of 1963 the Gambia was granted full internal self-government.

One of the major questions that Jawara's government had to deal with was independence or amalgamation. The PPP government instituted a number of discussions with Senegal and asked for a United Nations team to investigate possible courses of action. The United Nations report published in mid-1964 recommended federation with Senegal as the ultimate political solution. However, opposition in the Gambia and a cooling off of Senegal's receptiveness postponed any action in this direction. Therefore, in July 1964, discussions with British officials established the date for independence as February 19, 1965. The form of government for the new independent state was a constitutional monarchy with a governor-general representing the crown and responsible government with a prime minister and ministry based on the Westminster model. No new elections were held for the newly independent state. Thus Jawara carried over into independence the majority he controlled in the House of Representatives.

In 1965 Garba-Jahumpa and his followers withdrew from the DCA which had by then been all but swallowed up by the PPP. They formed their own small but vocal group called the Gambian Congress. The UP continued to be the major opposition but until late in the year, except for the all but defunct election issue, there were few points which they could contest with the PPP. Jawara then proposed a major alteration in the system of government. He wanted a presidential system with the president chosen not by direct election, but by a majority vote of the thirty-six member House of Representatives. Jawara proposed a referendum on this question to be held in November. The UP and the other small groups opposed the measure while the PPP fought for it. Thus it was strictly a political contest. The referendum to amend the constitution required a two-thirds majority and Jawara was certain that he, with better facilities at his disposal and a stronger campaign, would secure the requisite vote. However, the plebiscite showed the PPP failing to secure their goal by 758 votes. Thus Gambia remained a reflection of Westminster. However, this issue along with unification with Senegal was far from settled and Jawara indicated that he would go to the polls again on the issue to bring the Gambia more in conformity with the presidential systems of other African states.

GHANA

Ghana was the first African territory to exchange colonial status for independence. As such it served as a model of political agitation for nationalists elsewhere in Africa. In transforming the Gold Coast colony and protectorate into a nation state, Britain, in cooperation with the political leaders of the Gold Coast, worked out the forms which would later be applied to other British African territories. After independence Ghana, because of its premier position, helped determine, by its policies, the domestic and foreign policies of other newly independent states.

In 1946 the Gold Coast was granted a new instrument of government, the Burns Constitution, which gave the territory the first Legislative Council in Africa with a majority of African members. However, the constitution did not go far enough to satisfy many African leaders. Dissatisfaction with their status led to the formation of the first powerful political voice for Gold Coast Africans, the United Gold Coast Convention (UGCC). The party was created in the fall of 1947 by Dr. Joseph Danquah and other middle-class urban Africans.

In November 1947, a new factor was introduced into Gold Coast politics when Kwame Nkrumah returned from Britain to assume the post of general secretary of the party. Nkrumah, then thirty-eight years old and a member of the Nzima tribe, had been educated at the Achimota secondary school, and in 1935, upon the advice of the Nigerian nationalist, Dr. Azikiwe, left the Gold Coast for the United States. He attended and later taught at Lincoln University in Pennsylvania and did graduate work at the University of Pennsylvania. He was introduced to the writings of Du Bois, Garvey, Ghandi, Marx, and many other Socialist and Communist authors. In addition he had carefully observed the organization and tactics of American political parties. In 1945 he left the United States for Britain where he met George Padmore and other British African nationalists. Nkrumah played a prominent role in organizing the fifth Pan African Congress at Manchester. Thus when he arrived in Accra he was far more politically knowledgeable and radical than the founders of the UGCC.

Nkrumah immediately began to create a mass political party with a European style of organization. This called for Nkrumah and other younger members of the party to address African audiences in all parts of the Gold Coast to prepare them for direct action against the British authorities. In the spring of 1948 economic problems led to demonstrations by ex-servicemen and a general African boycott of European and Syrian traders. Nkrumah welcomed this type of confrontation because it could be utilized to the advantage of the UGCC. British authorities attributed much of the disorder to the inflammatory activities of the UGCC, and the six leaders of the party were arrested. This was the beginning of the split between Nkrumah and his more conservative colleagues. On their release he was removed from the position of general secretary and, although continuing to work for the UGCC, he founded the Committee on Youth Organization (CYO). In June 1949, the CYO converted itself into a new party, the Convention Peoples party (CPP) with Nkrumah as its head.

A commission of inquiry into the disorders of 1948 recommended an increase in membership of the Legislative Council and greater African responsibility in the executive. In 1949 an all African committee was appointed under the chairmanship of Judge Coussey to examine the entire constitutional position of the Gold Coast. The commission report formed the basis for the new constitution issued in 1951. In the months that followed the issuance of the Coussey report, the CPP made clear its opposition to the moderate changes proposed by the commission and conducted positive action against its implementation. In January 1950, after numerous mass disturbances occasioned by CPP demonstrations, the CPP leaders, including Nkrumah, were arrested.

The 1951 constitution provided for a Legislative Assembly partially elected by direct suffrage. Of the eighty-four members, thirty-eight were popularly elected. In the Executive Council six of the eleven members were to be in charge of government departments. The work of the African members of the Executive Council was to be coordinated by a leader of government business. Despite its previous opposition to the constitution, the CPP contested the election held in February 1951 and won thirty-four of the elected seats. Dr. Danquah's UGCC won only three seats. Nkrumah was released from prison to become leader of government, and this office was upgraded to prime minister in 1952. Under pressure from the CPP and its mass organization, Britain announced in 1953 further government concessions. A new constitution promulgated in April 1954 provided for a responsible cabinet and a 104 member, all elective Legislative Assembly. In 1954 the Northern Peoples party (NPP) which, as the name implies, drew much of its strength from the poorer northern regions was created. In the general elections of June 1954, the CPP won seventy-one of the seats while the NPP could gain but twelve, becoming the official opposition. The Gold Coast in 1954 thus had reached the stage before complete independence. The major question which concerned Nkrumah's government and the Colonial Office was what should be the new form of the independent state.

The NPP was afraid that the coastal politicians would dominate the new government and force upon the north measures unpalatable to the traditional society there. Of more actual concern to the CPP government was the National Liberation Movement (NLM) formed by Dr. K. A. Busia in September 1954. This party spoke for the separatist feelings of the Ashanti. Instead of a unitary state, they wanted a federal system. The asantahene and the fifty chiefs of the Asanteman Council signed a petition to Britain demanding this type of government. Nkrumah opposed the federal scheme and the Colonial Office also registered its disapproval.

Disturbances in Ashantiland postponed the smooth movement of the Gold Coast toward independence. In 1955 a commission headed by Sir Frederick Bourne was invited by the Gold Coast government to review the extant government and make suggestions for the future of the Gold Coast. The NLM refused to meet with Bourne and continued to demand a federal system even after Bourne had made his report. The report of 1955 recommended a unitary state with substantial devolution of power from the central government to provincial assemblies in order better to protect the minorities in the state. Nkrumah's government was in substantial agreement with these proposals. However, the CPP leadership never forgot the disturbances and the refusal of the NLM to advise the government. The attitudes of the northerners had postponed the grant of independence. Finally on May 11, 1956, Britain announced its intention of granting independence after the conclusion of the new elections. In May a plebiscite in British Togoland resulted in a favorable vote for integration of that territory with the Gold Coast.

In the elections of 1956, the CPP won seventy-two of the 104 seats including eight of twenty-one in Ashanti and eleven of twenty-six in the northern territories. The NPP gained twelve seats and the NLM twelve. Nkrumah announced in the fall of 1956 his government's intention to call the new state Ghana and set the date for independence as March 6, 1957. After independence, six opposition groups in October 1957 came together to form the United party (UP) under the leadership of Dr. Busia.

Immediately after independent Nkrumah moved to secure control over decision making for the central government in all areas of Ghana. This resulted in a series of confrontations with traditional authorities. The CPP made it clear that it considered opposition a luxury which the new state could not afford. In February 1958, following disturbances in Ashantiland, the government deposed two paramount chiefs. In March six persons including two members of parliament from Togoland were sentenced to prison for creating disturbances. Nine members of the UP in Ashantiland were deported in April. The CPP-dominated assembly passed the Preventive Detention Bill in July which gave the government the right to imprison suspects without trial for up to five years. In September the government took over direct control of the Kumasi region due to alleged misappropriation of funds for the use of the NLM. In November forty-three members of the UP were arrested on charges of plotting against the government, and the government withdrew passports from all opposition members. This reaction of the CPP majority against opponents continued throughout 1959, forty-five persons being imprisoned under the Preventive Detention Act by the end of November. Dr. Busia, the leader of the opposition, was disqualified from the assembly and fled the country. By the end of 1959 Ghana had practically become a one-party state.

In April 1960, by a combined plebiscite and presidential election, Ghana became a republic and Nkrumah, its first president, was given more executive power. The CPP controlled eighty-six seats in the 104 seat unicameral National Assembly. In addition there were ten differentially elected women members. Nkrumah further extended his control by taking over full executive direction of the CPP on May 1, 1961, and instituting a series of austerity measures on the party and throughout the country. In September 1961, a dock and railroad workers' strike, which was briefly dangerous, was settled. The next month Nkrumah reorganized his cabinet and the government arrested forty-nine persons allegedly connected with the strike. On October 30, the National Assembly passed a bill establishing special courts empowered to try political cases with the right to impose the death penalty. By 1962 the CPP controlled one hundred seats in the assembly and the UP only nine.

In 1962 there was an easing of restrictions in Ghana. Several hundred persons held under the detention act were released. This policy was sharply reversed by the first major attempt on Nkrumah's life on August 1, 1962. The grenade blast wounded Nkrumah, killed four persons, and injured fifty-six. Other terroristic attacks in October claimed more lives. Hundreds were arrested including Ako Adjei, the foreign minister, Tawia Adamafio, minister of information, and H. Cofie-Crabbe, executive secretary of the CPP. In October Nkrumah rejected the offer of the assembly for a lifetime tenure as president but reiterated his previous statements that Ghana, in order to survive, would continue to be a one-party state. In April 1963, five of the chief conspirators of the fall of 1962 were sentenced to death, and in August 1963, the trial of the ex-ministers and other alleged conspirators began. In December 1963, the three judges, including Chief Justice Sir Arku Kosah, acquitted Adjei, Adamafio, and Cofie-Crabbe. In the ensuing constitutional crisis, the chief justice was dismissed from office by Nkrumah and the accused were not released.

The New Year's broadcast of 1964 by Nkrumah suggested certain further changes in the constitution which were adopted by a plebiscite and the legislature between January 31 and February 21. These made Ghana officially a one-party state. The president received the power to remove any judge from office, not just the chief justice as had been the case. Subsequently Nkrumah removed three supreme court justices and one lesser judge. Even the national flag was changed to reflect the red, white, and green colors of the CPP. Seven of the eight UP members in the assembly changed to the CPP. The eighth was arrested under the terms of the Preventive Detention Act.

On January 2, 1964, the fifth attempt since 1956 was made on Nkrumah's life. A police constable fired, missed the president, but killed the chief security officer. Partially because of the danger and partially due to Nkrumah's growing feeling of omnipotence, he withdrew himself more and more from the public. The state-controlled press extolled his virtues as the savior of the African people and castigated all who opposed him as agents of neo-imperialism. His active saber-rattling had frightened Ghana's neighbors and the majority of African leaders rejected both Nkrumah and his policies. There was a worsening of Ghana's relations with the United States in 1964 and an improvement of those with Red China. The visit of Chou En-lai in January was followed by a Chinese loan of eight million Ghanian pounds. Despite the attempt on his life, Nkrumah's hold on Ghana seemed secure in 1964. The CPP appeared to be a docile, willing agent for the leader. The young pioneers and students at the Ideological Institute at Winneba were systematically indoctrinated in a manner reminiscent of Fascist Europe. The Volta Dam, one of the great projects sponsored by Nkrumah, was over eighty percent complete, and the cocoa crop brought an excellent price. The government in 1964 announced its seven year plan which envisioned a capital expenditure of 1,017 million Ghanian pounds. More than half of this was to come from the private rather than the government sector. In February 1965, Adamafio, Adjei, and Cofie-Crabbe were found guilty by a jury of twelve drawn from the Ideological Institute. The government also announced the death in a detention camp of Dr. Danquah, founder of the UGCC.

In late 1964 the first indications of a financial crisis in Ghana became apparent. There was a significant fall in the world market price of cocoa, and this, combined with the near exhaustion of the surplus fund, dictated a policy of retrenchment. However, the government continued its policies of establishing ventures of questionable merit heavily subsidized by the state. Many of these were poorly managed and lost great sums. Others such as Ghana Airways attempted too much and were a constant drain on government money. Foreign governments were reluctant to advance funds to Nkrumah to check the growing economic crisis. An investigation agency of the International Monetary Fund in 1965 was extremely critical of the state corporations and short-range inflationary loans and refused to advance funds until Ghana altered its financial priorities. Reluctantly the government agreed to put into effect some of the recommendations of the commission.

Nkrumah's grandiose plans for leadership of larger African political groupings had received repeated setbacks after 1960. The final blow to his prestige as a spokesman for Africa occurred in October 1965. Accra was the host city for the third conference of the Organization of African Unity. The Ghana government spent over fifty million dollars preparing new facilities for the meeting. However, only nineteen heads of state attended the conference and the delegates were divided on almost every issue. The ex-French states of Africa were not represented. This Accra meeting was a stunning expensive defeat for Nkrumah and his dreams of leadership of a united Africa.

Nkrumah left Accra in late February 1966, on a state visit to Peking, seemingly unaware of the growing dissatisfaction with his regime. In his absence the Second Brigade of the Ghana army stationed at Kumasi marched on Accra on February 24. Soon the leaders of the revolt, Colonels Kotoka and Ocran, and Major Afrifa, had gained the support of the rest of the army. Overpowering the presidential guard, they assumed control of the state. The junior officers called upon Joseph Ankrah, who had retired in 1965, to become commander in chief of the army and head of a seven man National Liberation Council. A state of emergency was proclaimed, political prisoners were released, the CPP was banned, and the Ideological Institute was closed. The revolution was greeted by large, joyous crowds throughout Ghana.

The new regime announced that the military phase would be temporary until a new constitution could be developed which would provide for a separate executive, legislative, and judicial branch. Political freedom was guaranteed and assurances were given that Ghana would no longer be used as a base for subversion against its neighbors. The new regime labeled Nkrumah a tyrant and began at once to deport Soviet and Chinese technicians. Nkrumah flew from Peking to Guinea and immediately announced his intention to return to Ghana, and Sekou Touré named him honorary president of Guinea. His hopes of ever regaining power were dealt a severe blow with the recognition by the Soviet Union of the new military government.

NIGERIA

Despite encouragement from outside sources and some participation in Pan African conferences, there was very little nationalistic activity in

Nigeria before the early 1940s, and then until the close of World War II it tended to be Lagos based. The first real Nigerian party was the Nigerian National Democratic party (NNDP) created by Herbert Macaulay, the doyen of Nigerian politics, and it was a good example of the Lagos bias. In 1934 the Lagos Youth Movement was formed to agitate for better Nigerian education. In 1936 the name was changed to the Nigerian Youth Movement (NYM) and it became the focal point for the political education of young Nigeria. Based partially upon the popularity of Benjamin Nnamdi Azikiwe's newspapers, the NYM was the major protest party in Lagos by 1938 and had organized branches in many of the major cities. In 1941, however, the NYM was all but destroyed by the defection of Azikiwe and his followers. Only in Ibadan did the NYM remain potentially powerful.

In 1942 Azikiwe formed the Nigerian Reconstruction group, and in August 1944, at a conference in Lagos, the Nigerian National Council was created. The name was changed later to the National Council of Nigeria and the Cameroons (NCNC). It absorbed many separate tribal and cultural organizations and Macaulay's NNDP. The party stood for more African participation at all levels and a definite timetable for an independent federal Nigeria.

In 1945 the Richards Constitution was put into effect by Britain. Although it was an advance over the previous government instruments, it was not designed in consultation with the Nigerians. The NCNC opposed it. Labor disputes rocked the government and the prestige of Azikiwe and the NCNC soared with their protest delegation to London in 1947. The dissatisfaction in Nigeria abated somewhat with the discussions which led to the MacPherson Constitution. In the meantime Obafemi Awolowo and others had formed in London the *Egba Omo Oduduwa* which became the Yoruba cultural base for a new political party. This party, the Action Group, was created to contest the elections of 1951 called for by the MacPherson Constitution. The Action Group based its power on the wealth of the Western Region. In the north the Northern Peoples Congress (NPC) was formed in 1949, first as a cultural union. However, when more radical elements led by Mallam Aminu Kano formed the Northern Elements Progressive Union (NEPU), the NPC converted itself into a political party. Its leader was Ahmadu Bello, Sardauna of Sokoto, who was aided by a young progressive Muslim, Abubakar Tafewa Balewa. Thus by the time of the elections of 1951, Nigeria had its three major parties, each strongly based on an ethnic group with their strength concentrated in different regions.

The 1951 constitution provided for a semifederal system with divisions of power between the central government and the governments of the three regions. The Northern and Western Regions had a two-house system with a House of Chiefs and a predominantly elected House of Representatives. The Eastern Region had only a House of Assembly. Each region had its own Executive Council which was responsible to the lower house for its continuance in power. On the federal level there was a House of

Representatives of 148 members, 136 of whom were elected. There was a Federal Council of Ministers of eighteen members, twelve of whom were nonofficials. Although the governor and his lieutenants in the regions retained wide executive powers, the MacPherson Constitution was a major step forward toward self-government in that Nigerians were given freedom, within certain limits, to enact and carry out government policy for themselves.

Dr. Azikiwe attempted to make the NCNC a national party, but the Action Group which had won the elections in the West prevented his election to the federal House of Representatives in 1951 and Azikiwe was relegated only to leader of the opposition in the West. In 1952 Azikiwe began a purge of those who disagreed with him in the NCNC. This resulted in the formation of the National Independence party (NIP), and when the Eastern Region House of Assembly was dissolved in 1953, Azikiwe returned to the East as undisputed leader of the NCNC. The NIP won only nine out of the ninety-seven seats in the subsequent elections.

Questions not adequately explained by the MacPherson Constitution concerning the regional and central government soon brought demands for a new government instrument to clarify these disputed points. The Action Group in the West and the NCNC in the East both demanded that 1956 should be the date fixed for Nigerian independence. This demand led to conflicts with the North whose representatives wanted a slower development and more guarantees for their institutions. Four members of the Council of Ministers resigned in March 1953 on this issue. Serious riots broke out in Kano in May between Action Group and NPC followers. Also, in May the Eastern assembly defied the government and was dismissed by the lieutenant-governor. With this type of disorder as a background, the Colonial Office convened constitutional discussions in London and Lagos beginning in July 1953, and the new constitution went into effect on October 1, 1954. It called for a strengthening of the federal system, an expanded House of Representatives with 184 elected members, and better definitions of the role of the central and regional governments. The Council of Ministers at the center was reduced in size to thirteen members. The major political leaders chose to remain on the regional level, Awolowo becoming premier in the West, Azikiwe in the East, and Ahmadu Bello in the North. The power ratio in the federal House of Representatives was NPC seventy-nine, NCNC fifty-six, Action Group and their allies twenty-seven, Kamerun National Congress six, and sixteen independents.

In May 1957, a conference held in London resulted in the grant of self-government within the federal structure for the Eastern and Western Regions. Agreement was also reached on further constitutional changes. The most important of these was the appointment of an all-Nigerian Council of Ministers and a federal prime minister. The constitution provided for a greatly expanded House of Representatives and a Senate. Regional governments would also be maintained, each with a premier and elected lower house. The federal government, by consensus, after 1957 was a national government of all three parties. Abubakar Tafewa Balewa of the NPC was chosen to head this coalition as chief minister.

In October 1954, when Awolowo became premier of the West, he tried to extend the Action Group's influence beyond that region by using modern electioneering methods. However, he failed to muster support in the North, and in 1957 when Balewa was selected chief minister, the only way that the southern area could have kept the North from power was by a coalition of the NCNC and Action Group. Dr. Azikiwe had survived another threat to his power in the East, especially from Dr. Mbadiwe, the second vice-president of the NCNC (the name was changed in 1961 to the National Council of Nigerian Citizens), and was in no mood to come to terms with his old adversary, Awolowo. Instead, after the federal elections of 1959, he negotiated an alliance with the NPC which broke up the national government that had existed since 1957. The Action Group was then left in opposition at the federal level. In the House of Representatives after the 1959 elections, the NPC held 142 seats, the NCNC eighty-nine, and the Action Group seventy-three. Each region was still controlled by a specific party with the greatest power in the hands of the sarduana in the North. Because the central government was by then the most important political arena, Azikiwe delegated his authority as premier in the East to his lieutenant, Dr. Okpara. Chief Awolowo trusted the regional government of the West to the leadership of Chief S. L. Akintola. This was the political arrangement in Nigeria when independence finally was granted in October 1960.

Between May and June 1962, a major crisis developed in the Western Region. Differences between Chief Awolowo and Chief Akintola led to the majority of the Action Group requesting Akintola's resignation as Western premier. Akintola refused to comply and the governor of the region dismissed him from office. Disturbances in Ibadan and in the regional legislature were of such seriousness that the federal prime minister, Balewa, declared a state of emergency and suspended parliamentary government in the Western Region. On July 7, 1962, the Supreme Court ruled that Akintola's dismissal was invalid, and on September 17, the federal government arrested Chief Awolowo and fifteen associates, charging them with planning to overthrow the government. The trials of the accused were prolonged through September 1963 when the court found Awolowo and his lieutenants in the alleged plot guilty. Chief Awolowo was sentenced to fifteen years in prison. The Action Group as a power in the West and at the federal level was shattered by these events. Direct federal administration in the Western Region was continued through April 1963.

The Western House of Representatives met in April 1963, for the first time since the emergency. The session was boycotted by thirty-eight members of the Action Group led by their new leader, Alhaji Adegbenro. Chief Akintola remained as the premier. His support came from a new party, the United Peoples party (UPP), composed of former Action Group members who had chosen to support Akintola in the internecine conflict. The UPP after mid-1963 was in coalition with the NCNC on the regional level and, therefore, Akintola's position as premier was far from secure. No elections were held immediately after the emergency and many Yorùbas remained loyal to the Action Group and their "lost leader." Their latent strength was shown in the 1963 Lagos municipal elections when the Action Group won all the seats.

A major policy decision was made in 1962 to create a new region, the Mid-West, out of parts of the Eastern and Western regions. Litigation introduced by the Western Region postponed effecting this division until 1963. However, a plebiscite held in 1963 in the areas concerned resulted in a favorable vote for the new region. An interim administrator, Chief Dennis Osadebay, was appointed under federal control until elections could be held for the Mid-Western House of Representatives. All the major parties in Nigeria contested these elections which were held in February 1964. A Mid-West Democratic Front (MDF) was formed which allied itself for this election with the NPC and also the Mid-West branch of the UPP despite the fact that the NPC and the NCNC were allied on the federal level. The NCNC led by Chief Osadebay thus was challenged by a coalition of all parties except the Action Group. The Action Group had an informal understanding with the NCNC for the elections. The result of the elections showed the NCNC winning forty-nine seats and the MDF only ten.

Prior to these elections Nigeria had taken another step away from older British forms of government by becoming a republic. With the exception of the change of name and creating the post of president, little was altered in the structure of government. Dr. Azikiwe became the first president in October 1963 with the same internal powers formerly exercised by the governor-general. The regional governors and other legislative and executive institutions were retained unchanged.

Early in 1964 there were signs that the coalition between the NPC and the NCNC at the federal level was wearing thin. Examples of friction between the parties were the NCNC-UPP coalition in the West and the recent elections in the Mid-West which saw the NCNC and the NPC contesting against one another. In March 1964, it was announced that a merger between the UPP and a large segment of the NCNC in the West had been effected. The new party led by Chief Akintola was called the Nigerian National Democratic party (NNDP). The census taken in preparation for new general elections placed the southern regions at an even further population disadvantage to the North and was sharply criticized by the NCNC. The census showed the North to have a population of 29,750,000 as compared to the 12,333,000 of the East, 10,250,000 of the West, and 2,500,000 of the Mid-West. As of January 1964, however, Balewa was secure with a majority in the House of Representatives even without the NCNC. Although it is difficult to determine exact alignments in the house, a conservative estimate of parliamentary strength at that time was NPC 179, NCNC 82, UPP 19, and Action Group 18.

In 1964 there was considerable unrest in all of the regions of Nigeria, even in the supposedly secure North. The Tiv country in the extreme southeast of the Northern Region was the scene of widespread violence beginning in February 1964. Over one hundred persons were killed and more than one thousand were arrested for various crimes including murder. Local politicians were restricted and the Northern government appointed a commission to inquire into the disturbances.

Part of the reason for the unrest was the historic differences between the Tiv and the Fulani-Hausa ruling group in the North. The Tiv, a Bantu people, comprise the largest homogeneous minority in the North. They had formed the chief opposition to the NPC in the southern area of the Northern Region. In the 1959 elections the United Middle Belt Congress (UMBC) was formed to agitate for a separate region. UBMC candidates won the Tiv seats handily, but this did not diminish the control of the NPC over the native authority. The defeat of a proposed Middle Belt region further intensified the hostility between the Tiv and the NPC.

The violence in 1964 began over the location of a market and spread rapidly until it involved thousands of people. The NPC finally dissolved the native authority in question and appointed a commission of inquiry. The basic question was far from settled by the end of 1965 and illustrated very well an area of great instability within what was normally considered the most stable political region of Nigeria.

By the fall of 1964 it was apparent that new elections, the first since independence, would soon be held. This accelerated the breakdown of the NPC-NCC coalition and resulted in the formation of new political alliances. Potentially the strongest of these groupings was the Nigerian National Alliance (NNA) which was composed of the NPC, the NNDP of Chief Akintola, the MDF, a small schismatic party, the Niger Delta Congress, an anarchistic new organization, the Dynamic party, and the Lagos State United Front. The chief figure in the NNA was the sardauna of Sokoto, Ahmadu Bello, whose NPC was the dominant party at the center. His confidence in victory was based largely upon the new population figures.

The NNA called forth an opposition alliance of parties, the United Progressive Grand Alliance (UPGA). The main strength of this union was the NCNC which provided the government of both the Eastern and Mid-Western regions. Also prominent in the alliance was the Action Group under the leadership of Adegbenro in the absence of Awolowo. The other two parties joined to the UPGA were the NEPU and the UMBC. The NEPU was the main opposition to the NPC in the North while the UMBC was solidly based in the Tiv areas.

In addition to these two great alliances there were a number of small, localized independent groups. The most important of these was the Socialist Workers and Farmers party (SWAFP) whose leader, Dr. Tunji Otegbeye, was a former leader of the Nigerian Youth Movement. However, the SWAFP contested only about one-fifth of the seats and its chances of success even in those constituencies were minimal.

The alliance systems assured that the coming election would be the first to be nationally contested. This did not mean that the NPC or NCNC was in danger in its region, but there was theoretically a better chance for the opposing parties to make inroads in areas previously closed to them. Thus, even before the date was set, the alliances were already contesting the election. Some of the speechs, including those of President Azikiwe, publicly reminded the people that they were Nigerians and not members of a party, province, or tribe.

The preelection controversies continued through the period of balloting in January 1965. Dr. Okpara, leader of the UPGA, already disturbed over the census figures, declared that the election was being manipulated in many districts. This was believed to be particularly true in the Northern Region where forty UPGA candidates had been jailed and over twenty other candidates had not been allowed to register despite the fact that the Northern Region, already controlled by the NPC, was allotted 167 of the 312 seats in the National House of Representatives. In the minds of Eastern politicians such activities only confirmed their suspicions of the sardauna and the NPC. When the NNA announced that sixty-four of their candidates from the North would be returned unopposed, Dr. Okpara replied that the UPGA would boycott the elections until the question of irregularities had been thoroughly investigated. The boycott was fairly effective in the Eastern and Western regions. However, this decision brought Nigeria to the brink of civil war and dissolution of the federation. Okpara stated that if the political situation continued to deteriorate, the UPGA coalition would consider proposals to break up the federation. Rioting was endemic throughout the southern part of Nigeria, particularly in the Western Region. There was a protest strike by civil service workers in Lagos supporting the UPGA position.

Only last-minute appeals by President Azikiwe and Prime Minister Balewa saved the situation. Balewa agreed to accept UPGA members into his ministry which in effect would create, at the federal level, not a partisan, but a coalition government. While still protesting the validity of the election returns, the UPGA leadership eventually accepted the offer. Thus by a very hasty compromise more bloodshed was avoided and the federation was saved.

The next important test for the stability and unity of Nigeria was the Western regional elections held in October 1965. Due to the suspension of the civil government in the West in 1962 and early 1963, the region had not had an election since independence. Many of the troubles which had plagued the federal elections in January 1965 had their source in the conflict between the Action Group and Chief Akintola's NNDP. There was more than political rivalry involved in the West. Genuine hatreds had been generated by the arrest and subsequent imprisonment of Chief Awolowo. Chief Adegbenro of the Action Group had accused Premier Akintola of a whole range of unfair practices even before the dates for the regional elections had been set. In the early stages of the balloting Chief Adegbenro accused the NNDP of a number of flagrant violations of election rules. The Federal Electoral Commission, however, certified the results of the election which gave the NNDP of Akintola seventy-one of the ninety-four seats in the Western House of Assembly. Such an overwhelming victory was a surprise to many observers who believed that the contest would be close.

Adegbenro, obviously disappointed and distressed, protested vainly to the governor of the Western Region, Chief Fadahunsi. The governor, however, refused to see him and called upon Akintola to form a new government. At this juncture Adegbenro and the Action Group announced their computations of the election results. These estimates, if approximately true, would have reversed the official figures and given the UPGA a majority of over fifty seats. During the exchange of views by the political leaders, the violence which had been endemic during the elections spread. These disturbances were particularly bad in Ondo Province where many public buildings were burned. Ijebu Province and Lagos were also scenes of antigovernment UPGA violent protests. Most observers agree that the majority of the participants of these activities were UPGA supporters. In Ibadan a dusk to dawn curfew was imposed and four of the major newspapers in the region were banned.

The UPGA did not file election petitions challenging any of the contested seats. The leadership obviously believed that federal authorities would intervene in the deeply divided riot-torn region. However, Prime Minister Balewa was not eager to repeat the state of emergency proclamations of 1962 and refrained from utilizing the central government as an agent for either of the contending parties. Therefore, whatever the validity of the UPGA charges, the failure to challenge any of the contested seats officially left Akintola and the NNDP in control of a deeply divided Western Region.

At the same time events in the Mid-Western Region also created tension and a sense of disunity. There, a federal board of inquiry was investigating the activities of the Owegbe cult, a semireligious society composed of Benis. This had been organized to give voice to the desires of the Benis and to protect them from imagined Ibo oppression. The cult had as members some of the most influential men in the region such as the oba of Benin and Chief Omo-Osagie. The Federal board was concerned with the activities of the cult in intimidating candidates for office and the electorate.

Over a year of tension in Nigeria was climaxed by the overthrow of the government by the army. On Friday evening, January 14, 1966, the main elements of the 10,000 man army led by junior officers moved simultaneously against the federal and regional governments. In the North, units commanded by Major Nzeogwu attacked the palace of Premier Bello, head of the NPC. After its capture the sarduana was summarily executed. Other forces in Ibadan concentrated on the major leaders of the NNDP. Chief Akintola was taken from his home and shot. Meanwhile, the commander of the presidential guard in Lagos arrested Prime Minister Balewa and Finance Minister Okotie-Eboh. Three days later their bodies were found outside Lagos. It was later revealed that the army's plan was nonpartisan and Dr. Okpara and Osadebay, premiers of the East and Mid-West, had been scheduled for execution, but the plans went awry. President Azikiwe escaped possible assassination because he was in England. Over seventy-five other influential persons were killed during the coup.

By January 18, the revolt was stabilized by the assumption of leadership of the country by the army commander, Major General John Aguiyi-Ironsi. The constitution was suspended, the offices of president and prime minister eliminated, and military governors appointed for each of the four regions. Ironsi promised a concerted attack upon corruption, inefficiency, and partisanship. To show that he was serious, many superfluous civil service positions were abolished and travel abroad was severely restricted. The leading politicians in all the regions accepted the military coup and promised their support of the new regime. Even the North where the sarduana's power had been paramount showed no real signs of resistance to the new regime.

SIERRA LEONE

Politics in Sierra Leone through 1957 were dominated by the tension between the colony and protectorate. The colony had been administered by the British from the early eighteenth century with the active support of the Creole population. The Creoles of Sierra Leone, descendants of freed slaves, were the first Africans to develop a large Western-oriented middle class. Throughout recent history many of the doctors, lawyers, ministers, and teachers in West Africa came from, or were trained in, Sierra Leone. The protectorate with a much larger population was by comparison backward, relatively poor, and ruled by the British through traditional chiefs. The Creole attitude toward protectorate natives, developed at an earlier period, seriously prejudiced the development of national political parties.

In accordance with their policy elsewhere in West Africa, Britain put forward proposals in 1947 for an expansion of African representation in the Legislative Council. These proposals called for the protectorate to have a larger representation than the colony. Creole opposition led by Dr. H. Bankole-Bright, head of the colony-based National Council of Sierra Leone, blocked the implementation of the proposals until 1951. Then the British government instituted a Legislative Council of twenty-one elected members as contrasted to seven officials and two nominated members. Members from the protectorate were chosen by an indirect method.

The year 1951 thus signaled a radical change in the government and in the political parties of Sierra Leone. Until then all parties had been small, Creole, and colony-oriented. The formation of the Sierra Leone Peoples party (SLPP) coincided with the shift of political power to the protectorate. The SLPP was an outgrowth of the Sierra Leone Organization Society which had been created earlier to further agricultural development in the protectorate. Under the leadership of Dr. Milton Margai and his brother Albert, this became, with the backing of the chiefs, the major political instrument of the protectorate. Milton Margai blended this organization with the small colony-based Freetown Peoples party to create the SLPP. The new party became the majority group within the new Legislative Council under the leadership of Milton Margai. With the active support of the governor in the period after 1951, the six African members of the Executive Council assumed the status and responsibility of ministers.

The improvements in the government of Sierra Leone, impressive as they were, did not directly affect the majority of the population. No more than 6,000 persons had had an opportunity to vote for candidates. Responsible British and Sierra Leone officials soon began work to advance the territory toward the goal of independence. The Keith-Lucas Commission in 1954 suggested a wide franchise based, however, upon property qualifications and exercised in single member constituencies. The commission recommended that independence be granted in 1961.

In July 1956, the Colonial Office submitted to the Legislative Council a plan to reorganize the legislature. This new legislature, called the House of Representatives, was to contain fourteen elected members from the colony, twenty-five from the protectorate, and twelve chiefs who were to be selected by the district councils. The reorganization of the executive was to be left to the decision of the new house. The plan was adopted by the Legislative Council, although all the colony parties opposed the disparity between the number of colony and protectorate representatives. This plan was assented to by Britain in November and elections were set for May 1957.

The election of 1957 was heavily contested in the colony. The National Council, the Labor party, the Sierra Leone Independence Movement (SLIM), and the United Peoples party (UPP) opposed the SLPP. The results were almost a foregone conclusion since all of the other parties were primarily colony-based and the SLPP was so strongly entrenched in the protectorate that it ran its business with only twelve branch offices. The SLPP won twenty-six of the thirty-nine directly elected seats in the new house. The SLPP even won all six Freetown seats and three of the six in the immediate colony area. The National Council, the official opposition in the old Legislative Council, won no seats and soon disappeared as an active party. The UPP won five seats and became the opposition. With most of the twelve paramount chiefs supporting SLPP policy, Milton Margai's position seemed unassailable.

Immediately after the elections of May 1957, however, in the reconfirmation of the party leadership, Milton Margai was challenged by his brother Albert. Milton was conservative and his political power was strongly dependent on support from the protectorate chiefs. Albert appealed to the younger, more progressive members of the party. In closed balloting for the leadership, Albert was chosen by one vote over his brother. Later arrangements were made, Albert stepped aside, and Dr. Milton Margai continued as head of the SLPP and prime minister of Sierra Leone.

In September 1958, the split within the SLPP leadership so noticeable the previous year was confirmed by Albert Margai's resignation as national chairman of the SLPP. Together with other more radical leaders such as Siaka Stevens, former minister of lands and labor, he formed a new party, the Peoples National party (PNP). This group criticized the SLPP for its slowness to react to the many pressing needs of Sierra Leone. Because of its size, it became the government opposition party. In December 1959, the party alignment in the house was SLPP thirty, PNP-SLIM coalition seven, UPP four, and independents three.

Discussions concerning further constitutional advances were begun as early as December 1957. Serious final talks began at Lancaster House on April 20, 1960 and continued until May 4. Sir Milton Margai led a coalition group, the United Front, to the conference. The United Front was composed of all parties of Sierra Leone. Such an arrangement, it was believed, would show that all factions were united on the question of independence. The conference set the date for independence as April 1961 and decided there was no need for a general election before independence. It was on this latter issue that Siaka Stevens, a PNP delegate, demurred and refused to sign the agreement. In June 1960, Stevens was expelled from the PNP and subsequently formed his own party, the All Peoples Congress (APC).

Independence came to Sierra Leone on April 27, 1961, in the midst of what has been described as the most peaceful state of emergency in Africa. On April 18, Siaka Stevens and fifteen members of the APC were arrested and charged with planning violent acts to disrupt the independence ceremonies. Thirteen of those charged were released in May. Stevens was tried for his activities and sentenced to six months in prison. Later this conviction was reversed and Stevens' party became the chief opposition to the SLPP.

The other parties, never large and with little countrywide following, underwent a series of crises after 1957. The UPP split into two factions. The dissident group called themselves the Independent Peoples party. They were drawn into Margai's United Front of early 1960 and their members subsequently either joined the SLPP or coalesced once again with the UPP in late 1960. Having lost decisively in the elections of 1962, the UPP merged with Stevens' APC in July 1962. The SLIM, which had strength only in the Kono district, also merged with the APC. After independence the PNP was reabsorbed into the SLPP. In the first election after independence held in May 1962, there were only two really effective parties, the SLPP and the APC.

The SLPP itself was but an amalgam of local groups held together by a loose organization and the political sagacity of Sir Milton Margai. This coalition was effective because of the trust placed in Margai by the protectorate authorities and his pragmatic conservatism. The APC, although disagreeing only on a few general policies of the government, appealed to the younger, more progressive elements in Sierra Leone. In the elections of May 1962, the SLPP won twenty-eight seats in the house, the APC twenty, and independents fourteen. However, twelve of the independents associated themselves with the SLPP and it could count on the support of most of the twelve indirectly elected chiefs. Thus on major issues the real voting strength in the house after May 1962 was approximately fifty-two to twenty-two in favor of the SLPP. The closeness of the vote between the SLPP and the APC and the loose party structure of the SLPP indicated that without Milton Margai, the SLPP could well lose any future general elections.

In May 1964, Sir Milton Margai died and was succeeded by his brother Albert as head of the party and premier. The change of leadership was accomplished smoothly. Sir Milton, in a quiet, efficient manner, left a multiparty legacy to his nation. In 1965 only Sierra Leone, Gambia, and Nigeria of all independent West African states maintained a system whereby opposition groups had a legal and effective outlet. However, the new prime minister made a concerted attack upon the multiparty concept. By the end of 1965 shifts of alliances gave the SLPP forty-eight seats to only fourteen for the APC in the seventy-four member house. In December 1965, a private member introduced a motion in the house which called upon the government to consider seriously the introduction of a one-party system. This private motion was approved by the house. It appeared that Sierra Leone was going to follow the example of most other African states in rejecting a multiparty approach to government.

Devolution of power and consolidation of African rule: British Central Africa

CENTRAL AFRICAN FEDERATION

Politics in the Central African Federation in the 1950s were the most complex in Africa. This was not because the problems themselves were more complex, but because in addition to the need to solve the questions posed by a multiracial society there was added the largely unwanted mechanism of a federal government structure. The federation, composed of Southern and Northern Rhodesia and Nyasaland, was not based upon historical precedents, tribal affinity, or political similarity. It was created by the British Colonial Office in response to the pressure of the whites, primarily of Southern Rhodesia, to draw together these territories in a closer economic union and thus covertly postpone the date when Africans would receive full political equality with the whites. When the federation was created in 1953, only the electorate of Southern Rhodesia, a self-governing colony, primarily white, expressed the desire for federation. The decision for the northern territories was made by the British government.

The federal structure reserved specific powers to the central authority whose executive was a ministry and a prime minister, first Lord Malvern and after 1956, Sir Roy Welensky, responsible to a central legislature. However, governmental responsibility in certain areas was shared with the separate states. The white minority of Southern Rhodesia represented by the United Federal party (UFP) and Sir Roy Welensky tended to dominate the association. In 1957, despite the growing nation-

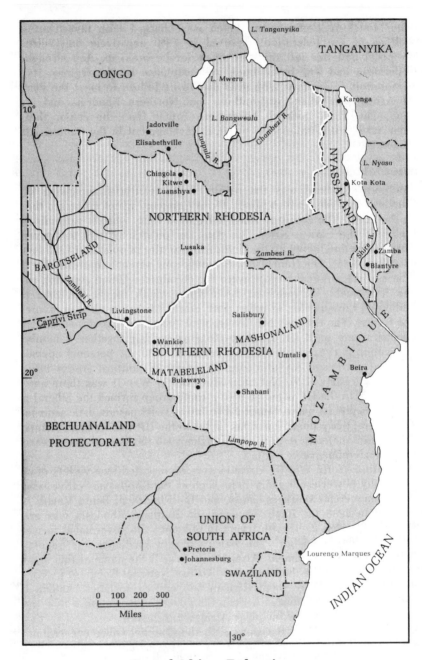

Central African Federation

alist sentiments in all the territories, Welensky began his campaign to have the federation become an independent entity within the Commonwealth. The Monckton Commission, which was charged with investigating the politics of the federation, reported in 1960 negatively on Welensky's proposal and this left the way open for its breakup. Any strength the federation had was based upon its acceptance by the regions. Its final dissolution, in January 1964, was due to its failure to meet the demands of African politicians in Southern and Northern Rhodesia and Nyasaland. Therefore, it is to the regions rather than the center that one must turn to understand the political development in the Central African Federation.

RHODESIA

Southern Rhodesia was the result of the territorial expansion of the Rhodes' controlled British South Africa Company which colonized the area in the 1890s. The company ruled there until 1923, when it surrendered its rights to the crown. After this date the politics of this self-governing colony was dominated by the small white-settler population (3,500 in 1924; 60,000 in 1955). The franchise was ninety-nine percent controlled by them. The earliest political parties were the Rhodesian Union Association and the Responsible Government Association which fought the 1922 referendum on the question of union with South Africa which was favored by the former. The Responsible Government Association governed the colony for ten years until Dr. Godfrey Huggins welded together a number of opposition parties and won the election of 1933. By personal appeal and political patronage, he later formed almost all political groups into one, the United Party (UP). Not until after World War II was there any real opposition to the UP when in 1946 a small group formed the Liberal party which, despite its name, favored a policy of strict paternalistic segregation. The Liberal party posed a serious threat to the UP and Huggins maintained only a slim majority in parliament. After 1948 the Liberal party ceased to have much influence.

Before World War II, Africans were represented by a variety of small, politically powerless organizations such as the Rhodesian Native Association, Commercial Workers Union, and the Rhodesian Bantu Voters Association. In 1938 the Bantu Congress of Southern Rhodesia was created which contented itself with trying to influence the government in matters of education and labor. The party did not challenge the segregation policies of the government. After World War II the name of this organization was changed to the Rhodesian African National Congress (ANC). The ANC absorbed many small African cooperative societies. Among these was the Rhodesia Railways African Employees' Association which brought Joshua Nkomo into the incipient African movement.

A long series of discussions with the Colonial Office concerning possible unification began in 1949 and culminated in 1953 with the creation of the federation. This was done against the fears and protests of African leaders in all areas. Nevertheless, the Colonial Office believed that the compromise by which Britain retained definite powers of intervention in

Northern Rhodesia and Nyasaland would protect African interests. The ensuing federation resulted in a reorganization of the UP. One segment was called the United Federal party (UFP) to contest federal elections, and the other was the United Rhodesians, primarily for Southern Rhodesia. Sir Godfrey Huggins of the UFP was elected federal prime minister and Garfield Todd became prime minister of Southern Rhodesia. The most important African parties carried the names of their respective African national congresses. The key leaders were Nkomo of Southern Rhodesia, Chuime of Nyasaland, and Nkumbula of Northern Rhodesia.

There was no effective opposition to the United parties until 1956 when the Dominion party led by Winston Field was formed. He advocated permanent white supremacy and the expulsion from the federation of all nonviable, non-European territories. In 1957 there was a major crisis in the United Rhodesian party. Garfield Todd had recommended gradual integration and voter privileges for the Africans. Partially for this and partially because of personal conflicts with his ministers, he was expelled from office and the party. In the ensuing election, Sir Edgar Whitehead, Todd's chosen successor as leader of the United Rhodesian party, was barely able to win over Field's Dominion party. On the federal level, however, the UFP held firm control. In 1955, Huggins had retired, becoming Lord Malvern, and his place as federal prime minister was taken by Sir Roy Welensky.

Economic agitation by Africans which had begun as early as 1945 continued to mount and the ANC in Southern Rhodesia benefited from this and the growing African dissatisfaction in the northern territories. Its leader, Joshua Nkomo, had been one of the major opposition leaders to federation in the London discussions in 1952, but four years after federation the ANC was almost moribund. Nkomo's proposals for a united ANC of all the territories had been rejected. However, in 1957, the movement began to revive and Nkomo was elected president-general. In February 1959, due to continued disturbances, a state of emergency was declared in Southern Rhodesia; the congress leaders were arrested and the organization was banned. Nkomo escaped arrest because he was in London and therefore became influential in organizing a new party, the National Democratic party (NDP) in early 1960. Elected president-general in October 1960, he returned to Southern Rhodesia. In late 1959, the British appointed a twenty-five member commission headed by Viscount Monckton to investigate the potential for future development of the federation. It recom-- mended that the federation be retained but that each area be given the right to secede after five years. It also suggested a liberalization of the franchise laws and more African representation in the legislature. After the Monckton Report, the Colonial Office began a series of discussions on the substance of the report and revision of the Southern Rhodesian constitution. Nkomo, a moderate within his party, at first was inclined to accept the compromises agreed upon in the discussions. However, pressure within his party forced him to repudiate the agreement in February 1961. In July the NDP called a general strike during the time of the referendum on the proposed new constitution and organized a referendum of its

own. This strike was a failure and the NDP referendum had little effect
on the attitudes of the Colonial Office. A group dissatisfied with Nkomo's
leadership broke away from the NDP to organize their own more radical
party, the Zimbabwe National party (ZNP). In December 1961, when
Nkomo was in Tanganyika, the Southern Rhodesian government permanently banned the NDP. Nkomo replied by organizing yet a new party, the
Zimbabwe African Peoples' Union (ZAPU). With the increasing intransigence on the part of the Southern Rhodesian government, nationalist
leadership became more radical.

The new constitution which went into effect in December 1961 called
for a legislative assembly of sixty-five elected on a two-roll system. Fifty
members were to be selected from the predominantly white upper roll
while fifteen were to come from the predominantly black lower roll. Although the Dominion party and the NDP denounced the constitution for
widely differing reasons, it had been accepted by over seventy-five percent
of the qualified voters.

Much of 1962 was taken up by discussions on new constitution instruments since the constitution of December 1961 was so unpopular. No real
agreement could be reached between Africans and whites. Further adding
to the confusion was the coalition of the right-wing parties into the
Rhodesian Front party (RF) led by Field. There was an increase in violent
activities throughout Rhodesia which led to a tightening of restrictive
native laws and these, in turn, produced more violence. It was announced
in November that elections under the new constitution would be held in
December 1963. Nkomo was arrested and ZAPU was banned which meant
that no African party would be officially represented in the new elections.
The UFP and Whitehead attempted to get as many Africans as possible
enrolled in the lower rolls. However, African leaders effectively prevented this.

In the elections the UFP was placed between the two extremes of
white ultraconservatives and African nationalists. The election results
clearly showed the fate of a middle-ground party in Southern Rhodesia.
The RF won thirty-five seats to twenty-nine for the UFP, with one independent being returned. The decision of the ZAPU leaders that Africans
should boycott the elections thus resulted in the election of a more conservative government—a government dedicated to independence for Southern Rhodesia on white-settler terms. The harsh laws of the Whitehead
and Field governments and the banning of ZAPU had temporarily dis-
organized African opposition. Nkomo and his lieutenants upon their
release from detention formed yet another African political group called
the Peoples Caretaker Councils.

Winston Field carried the demands of the RF for independence to
London in February 1964. He and other white leaders believed that their
case had been strengthened by the recent breakup of the federation and
the promised independence of the other two territories. However, the
British government was adamant in demanding a readjustment in the
electoral system to give more voice to the African majority. Thus Field

came back empty-handed to face a revolt within his party. Field was ousted and Ian Douglas Smith who had served as Field's finance minister became prime minister. Smith represented the most adamant section of the RF. His first official act was to arrest Nkomo and three officers of the Peoples Caretaker Councils. This action resulted in riots in Salisbury and the arrest of 250 Africans.

The breakup of the federation and the promises of speedy independence made by the Colonial Office to Nyasaland and Northern Rhodesia had created demands by the Europeans in Southern Rhodesia for independence within the Commonwealth. Winston Field's failure to secure some type of commitment from Britain had led to his downfall. Smith and the RF refused to consider any major reforms of the electoral laws of Rhodesia which alone would have appeased the sentiments of Great Britain. Instead, he explored the possibility of a unilateral declaration of independence. Although repeatedly stating that his government would pursue negotiations with the Colonial Office, he also said he believed these would be fruitless. His political position in Rhodesia was not strong enough to allow him to do more than make tentative moves toward pressuring Britain. The RF had only a slim five-vote majority in parliament in the summer of 1964. One of the first pronouncements of Harold Wilson's newly elected Labor government in Britain was to reiterate his hostility toward Smith's views of the native question and underline the ill effects that any precipitate independent action would have on Rhodesia's future.

In June 1964, the Rhodesian National party (RNP), formerly the UFP, held a congress and declared against unilateral declaration of independence unless Britain interfered with the internal affairs of Rhodesia. Also in June, Dr. Maurice Hirsch launched a new organization, the Reform party, whose program was much the same as that of the RNP. The major differences were in the personalities of Hirsch and Sir Edgar Whitehead. The Reform party wanted to do away with racial discrimination on the upper roll and entrench the fifteen "B" roll seats in the constitution while making adjustments for wider African representation. Such changes were necessary before Britain would contemplate granting Rhodesia independence. Fragmentation of parties among the Africans continued to hamper any coordinated African protests. The government also made difficult any meaningful opposition. The leader of the Zimbabwe African National Union (ZANU), Ndabaningi Sithole, was in and out of jail during this period. Joshua Nkomo was placed in restricted custody at Gonakudzingwa in southeast Rhodesia.

Although Smith had voiced his skepticism many times concerning an amicable agreement with Britain, the discussions between the governments continued. In March 1965, the Commonwealth secretary, Arthur Bottomley, visited Rhodesia, met various leaders, and reported back to Prime Minister Wilson. The granting of independence to Zambia the previous fall and the seeming intransigence of both the Hume and Wilson governments had created more support for Smith in Southern Rhodesia by midsummer than he had enjoyed before. In October Smith visited

London for a series of discussions with Prime Minister Wilson. Smith announced his willingness to add a senate of African chiefs to the legislature and give the right to vote to perhaps one million Africans. However, he refused to increase African representation in the house immediately over the existing fifteen out of a total of sixty-five. These promises were not sufficient for Britain, and Smith returned to Rhodesia better armed for a unilateral declaration.

The United Nations' General Assembly condemned the concept of a unilateral declaration and the white supremacy concepts of Smith's government by a vote of 107 to two. Three former prime ministers of Rhodesia spoke out to urge caution. In retaliation, former prime minister Garfield Todd, without trial, was ordered by the government confined to his farm for a year. The Rhodesian Chamber of Commerce and Tobacco Trade Association warned that the economic repercussions of any move not sanctioned by Britain could bring on a catastrophe for Rhodesia.

Smith's ministry had already met and ostensibly decided for a unilateral declaration of independence. However, Smith did not announce this immediately, but opened contacts once again with Prime Minister Wilson. He demanded independence on the same terms as before with the exception of offering a "solemn treaty" to guarantee what his government had promised. Prime Minister Wilson decided to fly to Salisbury to continue the discussions. On October 30, 1965, an agreement was reached which called for the establishment of a royal commission to investigate further. However, on November 11, Premier Smith, reacting to pressures within his party, declared the independence of Southern Rhodesia. The governor, Sir Humphrey Gibbs, dismissed Smith, but the premier ignored this and stripped the governor of any real administrative powers.

Britain refused to be stampeded into rash military action by other African states and decided instead to try to bring the Smith regime down by imposing a boycott on all goods to and from Rhodesia. By mid-December this was some ninety-five percent effective. The embargo on oil supplies had the most immediate dramatic effect on Rhodesia. No other state recognized the Smith regime. South Africa and Portugal, although sympathetic to the government, did not find it to their advanage to support directly the de facto government. The Organization of African Unity passed resolutions against the breakaway regime and condemned Britain for not taking more direct forceful action. However, even the African states bordering on Rhodesia showed little inclination for positive direct action.

MALAWI (NYASALAND)

Politics in Nyasaland was simpler than in either Southern or Northern Rhodesia because of comparative lack of resources and small European population. African politics in Nyasaland until 1958 was conducted by the Nyasaland African National Congress (ANC) whose major role had been in opposing federation. Beginning in 1957, however, a new factor galvanized the Africans in Nyasaland into a more active force. This was Dr. Hastings

Banda, a highly respected, reputable physician who had been practicing medicine in England.

The announcement of the plan for the federation aroused Banda's interest in Nyasaland politics. From his office in London and later Ghana, he gave guidance to the leaders of the Nyasaland African Congress. Finally persuaded to return to Nyasaland after an absence of many years, he was elected president-general of the party in August 1958. Banda was welcomed as a deliverer everywhere in Nyasaland, and he urged noncooperation on all levels with the federation until a new constitution could be granted. However, after a number of incidents, the government (in March 1959) declared a state of emergency in Nyasaland. Banda and his chief lieutenants were arrested. While Banda was in prison in Southern Rhodesia, The Malawi Congress party was founded to take the place of the old ANC and Banda resumed leadership of the Nyasaland nationalist movement upon his release in April 1960. In June 1960, the emergency in Nyasaland was ended and in the following month constitutional discussions were begun in London. The Congress party accepted the constitution instruments which provided twenty-eight elected seats out of a total of thirty-three in the Legislative Council. Voting was to be from two election rolls with eight seats chosen from the upper roll. Almost one year later on August 16, 1961, the elections were held and the Congress party won twenty-three of the twenty-eight elected seats. Banda and four of his congress associates joined the Executive Council in September 1961 and formed the first black government within the federation. Banda as leader of the Congress party and minister of local government continued throughout 1962 to oppose the federation even to the refusal in July of a federally planned hydroelectric project. Nyasaland was granted self-rule on November 23, 1962, representing the first great break in the federation. After lengthy high-level discussions, Banda's demands for secession from the federation were granted. A new constitution was promulgated on February 1, 1963, and Dr. Banda became prime minister. A committee to work out the manifold details of secession was formed. The many functions previously performed by the federal government were phased out by January 1, 1964.

The final step in Banda's nation-making was accomplished on July 6, 1964, when Nyasaland became the thirty-fifth independent African nation under the new name of Malawi. The major political force in Malawi was the Malawi Congress party which appeared to be totally dominated by Banda. However, in the summer of 1964, a rift occurred between Banda and some of his most important ministers. The six disaffected members contended that the prime minister was assuming too much personal power. The ministers were dismissed and the leader, ex-Education Minister Henry Chipembere, was restricted to a four-mile radius around his home in Malindi. Soon there was rioting between the pro- and anti-Banda factions in the capital. Banda survived this threat to his leadership and the leaders of the opposition were either arrested or forced into exile. The united front which had sustained Malawi in its drive for independence, however, was broken and Banda would never again have such whole-hearted support of all the people of Malawi. His party, nevertheless, in 1965 controlled fifty seats in the fifty-three member National Assembly, the other three being reserved for Europeans elected on a separate election roll.

ZAMBIA (NORTHERN RHODESIA)

When federation was imposed despite Northern Rhodesian-ANC opposition, the organization turned to boycotts and demonstrations. This led to more conflicts with the European-dominated government and prison for many of the leaders. In February 1958, the ANC proposed that twenty-one of the forty-two seats in the Northern Rhodesian Legislative Council be reserved for Africans elected by direct franchise. Instead, the Colonial Office sanctioned an extremely complex system of franchise. Harry Nkumbula's leadership of the ANC, which had been under fire for some time, was openly challenged because of his seeming noncommittal behavior. The result of this quarrel was the creation of Zambia African National Congress (ZANC) led by Kenneth Kaunda and containing a majority of the influential members of the ANC in the north. While ANC supported the elections of 1959, the ZANC actively opposed them. In March 1959, ZANC was banned and its leaders arrested. Kaunda was not released until January 1960, when he became the leader of a new party, the United National Independence party (UNIP) which announced its aim to force independence by the close of the year. After violence flared in the copper belt, the UNIP was banned from that area. Kaunda held talks with the Colonial Office in May 1960, but it was not until October 1960 that it was announced that new constitutional discussions would take place at the same time as the Federal Review Conference. These discussions began in December, and in February 1961, the tentative complex territorial constitution was announced. Under this constitution there was created a three-part electoral system. Fifteen members of the Legislative Council would be elected from an upper roll, fifteen from a lower roll, and fifteen from the composite of both. It was obvious to the federal prime minister, Sir Roy Welensky, that Africans would gain a majority in the Legislative Council unless the constitution was changed. He demanded further discussions with the Colonial Office which resulted in the revision of the proposed instrument to give a separate electoral roll for Indians, and a percentage factor was introduced which limited the effect of the African votes. Following this announcement violence again erupted in Northern Rhodesia and the UNIP was banned in the northern areas. Faced with such African protest, the Colonial Office agreed in September 1961 to reconsider the entire question. In February 1962, the Welensky revision was again revised partially to compromise with the UNIP demands. This Colonial Office compromise satisfied none of the parties concerned, and Kaunda announced that in any elections, the unwieldy constitution would produce a deadlock. The UNIP rejected the new constitution promulgated in March 1962 but later indicated that it would contest the election as a preliminary to dissolving the federation and independence for Northern Rhodesia. The United Federal party led by Mr. J. Roberts, a supporter of federation and the white party policies, strongly contested the election. Another white-dominated party, the Liberal party, had as its major premise close cooperation with the Africans.

In the elections held in October 1962, the United Federal party won a total of fifteen seats (thirteen upper roll, two national), the UNIP won fourteen (one upper roll, twelve lower roll, one special Asian), and the ANC won five (three lower roll, two national). Ten seats were left vacant on the national combined roll because none of the candidates received the ten percent minimum votes necessary. Of the 104,000 votes, the UNIP gained 64,000. The Liberal party was utterly defeated.

The complicated system of voting, as Kaunda had predicted, produced a complete stalemate, and a caretaker government of officials was appointed by the governor pending by-elections in December. The ANC and UNIP formed a coalition government in December, controlling twenty-one seats, and Kaunda became minister of local government and Nkumbula was named minister of African education. In February 1963, the first major decision of the new Legislative Council was to call for a new constitution and an end to federation. Committees were appointed by the governor to make recommendations on both points and, by June 1963, substantial agreement had been reached by the UNIP and ANC. After a number of higher level conferences, the British decided that with Nyasaland opting out of the federation and violence continuing in Northern Rhodesia, the only solution was to grant what the nationalists wanted—an end to federation.

The federation officially ended in January 1964 and the new constitution for Northern Rhodesia went into effect that same month. It provided for self-government with a ministry responsible to a seventy-five member Legislative Assembly. Elections were held on January 20, with the UNIP winning fifty-five of seventy-five seats, and Kenneth Kaunda became prime minister. Harry Nkumbula's African National Congress won only ten seats. According to the constitution, ten of the seats were to be reserved for the 77,000 Europeans until 1969.

In May Kaunda led a delegation to a further series of conferences in London. During this sixteen-day discussion period, Britain granted Kaunda's request to dispense with the usual period of symbolic rule under a governor-general and agreed upon the immediate establishment of a presidential system. The new state renamed Zambia thus became a republic on October 24, 1964. Kaunda was chosen by the assembly as the first president elected for a five-year term. For all subsequent terms the president would be elected by direct suffrage.

Rich in copper, Zambia's major economic problem is related to its landlocked position and the fact that the railway lines connecting it with the outside world passed through the disturbed Congo and its potentially hostile neighbor, Southern Rhodesia. Kaunda's own moderate position was thus reinforced by the economic situation. He, like Hastings Banda in Malawi, could not immediately afford to take a militantly hostile line toward South Africa, Southern Rhodesia, or Portugal. This type of neutralism was brought to an end by the unilateral declaration of independence by Premier Ian Smith of Southern Rhodesia.

The reactions against Smith's regime by Britain and other African states placed Kaunda in an extremely vulnerable position. The Kariba Dam which supplies power to Zambia as well as Southern Rhodesia was, in the first days after Southern Rhodesia's action, the focal point of most concern. The turbines and generators in this joint venture were on the Rhodesian side of the border. Kaunda's position was, therefore, ambivalent. He wanted Britain to deal with Smith's government, but did not feel that he could sanction the kind of actions which might have detrimental results for Zambia. Prime Minister Wilson's embargo on Southern Rhodesia was followed by a Southern Rhodesia embargo on oil transports to Zambia. Thus in November and December 1965, the British action had as much negative effect upon Zambia as on Rhodesia. To a very large extent the stability of Kaunda's government depended not only upon forces within Zambia but upon the development of events in Southern Rhodesia.

Devolution of power and consolidation of African rule: the high commission territories of Southern Africa

BASUTOLAND (LESOTHO)

The major determinant in the history of this 12,000 square mile territory is its geographic location. It is a predominantly highland area completely surrounded by the Republic of South Africa. In the nineteenth century the Basuto people were in constant conflict first with the Boer trekkers and later with their republics, particularly the Orange Free State. The Basuto, largely because of the easily defensible terrain, were never conquered by the Boers. However, the great Basuto chief, Msheshwe, realized that ultimately they would be conquered if they continued to stand alone. Repeatedly he appealed for protection to British authorities at Capetown. Finally in 1868 the British annexed Basutoland and attached it administratively to Cape Colony. In 1884 the Cape was relieved of the cost of administration and the government of Basutoland was assumed directly by the British crown.

The type of administration in Basutoland in the twentieth century prior to its independence was the dual rule of the British and Basuto. The traditional Basuto rulers have exercised more power in local affairs than was true in other areas under indirect rule. Basuto local government was also more unified since the paramount chief had substantive powers over his chiefs and subchiefs. Although no paramount chief has been as able and had as much influence as Msheshwe, they always were important enough to be consulted by the British before any major policy changes were instituted.

Basutoland was a High Commission Territory, and as such, it was administered since the 1920s under the Commonwealth Relations Office and not the Colonial Office. The chief administrator was a resident commissioner who was assisted by a secretariat and district commissioners. Since 1903 he was advised by the Basutoland Council. After 1910 this council was composed of thirty-six members elected by the district councils, fifty-two members appointed by the paramount chief, five members nominated by the government, and six representing special interests. The council not only acted to give the resident commissioner a wide sampling of Basuto opinion, but also from this body the three chief advisers to the paramount chief were selected.

The most crucial continuing problem of Basutoland concerned its future relations with South Africa. By the Act of Union, South Africa was assured that in due time all the High Commission Territories, after consultation between Britain and the Union, would be returned to South Africa. Britain's reluctance to do more than discuss this matter was based on the known opposition of the Basuto to any such union. Nevertheless, any liberalization in the government of Basutoland in recent years meant further estrangement from South Africa. South Africa completely surrounds Basutoland and a large sector of the Basuto economy depends upon the continued employment of Basutos in South African industry.

Due to the nature of dual rule, political parties in Basutoland were slow to develop. The oldest such organization, the Progressive Association, was founded in 1907 and could not be considered a political party in the usual sense. It stood for more Basuto participation in the central government, but represented a conservative, go-slow, cooperative policy. Any influence which it might have had was more than matched by the Sons of Msheshwe. Composed of the descendants of the great chief, this organization exercised considerable influence over local government and British opinion, particularly concerning association with South Africa.

In 1954 Britain, responding to pressures within Basutoland and carrying out the liberal colonial policy so noticeable elsewhere in British Africa, appointed a commission to study political reforms. The report of the Moore Commission did not recommend major changes in the system. Many of the younger educated Basutos had formed a political party, the Basutoland Congress party (BCP) before the commission had been appointed. The mild report said nothing about the BCP's foremost demand for an elected legislative council. The BCP, while not completely against traditional rule, wanted an end to British control and the grant of more power to elected representatives who in turn would limit the power of the chiefs. In 1958 the British again attempted to find a consensus on constitutional reform. BCP representatives in London made it clear that they expected the normal progression toward independence. Soon afterward Britain announced basic agreement with the BCP ideas of an elected legislature.

This announcement and the subsequent constitution changed the status of Basutoland and South Africa. After the constitution of 1959, any move to incorporate the enclave into the Union would need not just the consultation of the British government with South African officials, but also the consent of the Basutos.

The constitution of 1959 provided for a legislative council, the Basuto National Council, of eighty members. One half of the members were elected by the nine district councils. All 162 members of the district councils were directly elected from a common roll. Therefore, the indirect method of selecting a member of the Basuto National Council, although a compromise, was representative. The council had the right to legislate in all matters except external affairs, defense, police, loans, and public service. In these it acted only as a consultative body. In the elections under the new instrument held in January 1960, the BCP won seventy-three of the 162 seats on the district councils and twenty-nine of the forty elected seats to the National Council.

As was true in many other areas at the same stage of development, Basutoland has had a number of political parties. The only other party besides the BCP with a large following was the Basuto National party (BNP) led by Chief Lebua Jonathan. Another group founded in 1962 was the Marematlou Basuto Freedom party (MFP) whose leader was S. S. Matete. He was replaced in mid-1964 by Dr. Seth Makotoko. There have been other small parties with little popular support that disappeared after a few months. The Communist party was small but extremely active in Basutoland. Although all three major parties denounced Communism as alien to Africa, the BCP was in the past receptive to receiving aid from the Eastern bloc, particularly in the form of education grants. All parties demanded more power for the Basuto, exercised through a fully elected legislature and a ministry. All were opposed to union with South Africa. The differences came in their concepts of the rate and degree of Basuto advance and the position of the traditional native authorities in the future government.

The BCP was a more radical group than its opponents. It was affiliated with the Pan African Freedom Movement (PAFMECA) whose chief goal was independence of all territories from colonial rule as soon as possible. The BCP also was more hostile to granting the paramount chief, Moshaeshoe II, any real substantive powers in an independent Basutoland.

In October 1961, the BCP leader, Mokhehle, called for constitutional revision which would provide for responsible government. When this was not forthcoming, there was, in early 1962, considerable violence in Basutoland. Later twenty-three persons were sentenced in Maseru to terms up to ten years for their part in the disturbances. In May 1962, Mokhehle demanded of the United Nations Committee on Colonialism that they investigate Basutoland, and he again asked for quick independence.

A constitutional commission was appointed by Britain in early 1962. One of its greatest problems was what position the paramount chief should have if more responsible government was granted. Throughout the course of its investigations there grew among the Basutos the feeling that Britain was no longer giving them adequate protection. This was in reference to South Africa which had tightened its border controls considerably. In August 1963, in an unprecedented action, the Basuto National Council rejected the speech from the throne because of this feeling.

In October 1963, the constitutional commission published its recommendations for the future structure of the government after independence. The tentative date was suggested for 1965. The government, as conceived, was to be a constitutional monarchy with the paramount chief acting as head of state. The report called for a two-house system, the upper house mainly composed of chiefs with the lower house fully elected. The ministry, headed by a premier, was to be responsible to the lower house.

In May 1964, the British Commonwealth secretary, Duncan Sandys, announced his government's adherence to the draft constitutional instruments. Further, if the people of Basutoland desired independence, it would follow one year after the legal acceptance of the constitution. Chief Moshaeshoe immediately announced his support of the British proposal. The leaders of the major political parties also agreed to abide by the recommendations. All major political figures in Basutoland made public statements of assurance of future friendly relations with the Republic of South Africa and renounced any scheme of using their territory as a base for subversion within the republic.

On April 29, 1965, general elections were held and the new constitution came into being. Chief Moshaeshoe became the Queen's representative, and the British resident became the British government representative holding important reserve powers. The executive power was to be in the hands of a prime minister and his ministry, dependent upon the confidence of the lower house. The legislature was bicameral. The upper house, or Senate, was composed of twenty-two principal chiefs and ward chiefs, and eleven nominees of the paramount chief. The lower house, or National Assembly, was composed of sixty members elected by the Basuto people.

In the interim period, before the elections, great changes had occurred in the political parties. The BCP which had dominated the political scene for almost ten years encountered internal problems. The creation of the MFP was one result of these stresses. Further quarrels led to the diversion of much of the Soviet funds away from the BCP to the MFP. The MFP then became a force which detracted from potential BCP support. Mr. Mokhehle, the leader of the BCP, was such a dominant personality in the party that a number of younger Basuto were discouraged from supporting it. After Dr. Makotoko became leader, the MFP began to shift its policies from radicalism to a more moderate stance. This process continued so rapidly that by the end of 1964 the party was recognized as the political organ of the great chiefs. It was rumored that the paramount chief actually supported the MFP.

The BNP, led by Chief Jonathan and Mr. C. D. Malopo, represented the middle and lesser chieftains. It was avowedly pro-West and harshly critical of the Moscow and Peking connections of the other two parties. It was also much more realistic in its attitudes toward future relations with South Africa and was supported, although not openly, by the various Christian organizations in Basutoland.

Campaigning for the elections began early with each party well organized and having a considerable amount of modern equipment. Armed clashes between the BCP and MFP, in October 1964, resulted in the deaths of at least four people, and this undoubtedly caused many Basutos to support the BNP. Preelection indications were that either the BCP or BNP could win, but by a narrow margin. The results of the election, where ninety percent of the electorate participated, confirmed this prediction. The BNP emerged victorious with thirty-one seats and a popular vote of over 105,000. The BCP with a vote of more than 103,000 won twenty-five seats. The MFP gained four seats but had a popular vote of over 42,000. Post-election difficulties were avoided by the appointment of Mr. Malopo of the BNP and Dr. Makotoko, leader of the MFP, as senators. Each of these men had been defeated in the general election. Chief Jonathan, who was also defeated, later stood a by-election.

Chief Jonathan decided not to attempt a coalition but to form an exclusive BNP ministry which had but a narrow two-vote majority in the National Assembly. The middle-ground government thus formed was able to avoid an open clash between traditionalists and radicals until independence in the spring of 1966. At that time the name of the state was changed to Lesotho.

BECHUANALAND (BOTSWANA)

Bechuanaland was the largest (275,000 square miles) and most sparsely settled of the High Commission Territories. Unlike the other territories, it is not populated by only a single tribe but has eight different tribes living in separate reserves. The largest and most influential group is the Bamangwato. The Bantu population numbered slightly over 300,000 persons. In addition, there are approximately 3,000 Europeans and half as many Asians in the territory. Much of Bechuanaland is desert where only the Bushmen and Makalahari peoples can exist. Although there is some good agricultural land available, Bechuanaland is the poorest of the territories. This is reflected particularly in its systems of health, public works, and education. In Basutoland a large portion of the population is literate and, therefore, more in contact with political movements outside the territory. In Bechuanaland, however, the numbers of the educated elite are smaller and the unmodified tribal system more in evidence. Bechuanaland presented more problems than the other areas in its movement toward independence. It had a resident European population with its own confirmed rights and prerogatives, eight different tribal systems, and was poorer in resources than the smaller territories.

The British became interested in Bechuanaland in the late nineteenth century in competition with the Transvaal and to ward off German encroachment. The southern portion, since transferred to South Africa, was declared a protectorate in 1885. The territory was important for Cecil Rhodes' plans for expansion northward. After much discussion, the British government assumed, in 1896, direct control over the protectorate of Bechuanaland. This action was largely due to the protests of the chiefs over threatened incorporation into the territories ruled by Rhodes' British South Africa Company. The most powerful of the traditional rulers was

Khama III of the Bamangwato who until his death in 1923 maintained that he owed direct allegiance only to the British crown.

The system of rule in Bechuanaland after 1896 was a dual system. Because of the many tribes, no single chief was as important as in Swaziland and Basutoland. The presence of Europeans also caused a modification in the type of rule. The resident commissioner was the chief executive, operating on instructions given from the high commissioner's office in Pretoria. The resident commissioner was aided by a secretariat and district commissioners who were responsible for implementing indirect rule. In 1920 a European advisory council was created to represent European interests in the government. In that same year an African advisory council was established. It was composed of thirty-five chiefs, subchiefs, or persons appointed by chiefs. Its functions were similar to its European counterpart. In 1951 a joint advisory council was instituted, composed of eight members, each from the European and African councils.

The logical progression from this type of rule to a more liberal form was postponed by the long conflict between the Bamangwato and the British over the chieftainship of the tribe. The Bamangwato chief, Sekgoma, ruled for only two years and in 1925 left his heir the infant, Seretse Khama. His uncle, Tshekedi Khama, acted as regent and became known as one of the most enlightened rulers in southern Africa. In 1948 Seretse married an English woman and this created a crisis among the Bamangwato. However, their loyalty to Seretse eventually prevailed and the elders agreed to accept him as chief. However, the British in 1950, fearing further disturbances, deposed Seretse for a five-year period, and also exiled Tshekedi. This left the Bamangwato without a chief executive, and thus no important business could be transacted. After 1953 the British government attempted in vain to get the Bamangwato to accept a new chief. Eventually, with pressures from Africans and the British Labor party, the government was forced to allow both Seretse and Tshekedi to return to Bechuanaland. However, it was decided not to attempt to reconstruct the office of paramount chief of the Bamangwato but rather to introduce a conciliar system.

Only after the Khama crisis had been settled could Britain begin a reconstruction of the government. This was accomplished by the constitution of December 30, 1960, which established a multiracial Legislative Council. The council was composed of ten government officials, ten elected European members, one elected Asian member, and ten Africans selected by a newly formed African council. The representation to this Legislative Council was unbalanced in favor of the Europeans. Representational ratios were: for the Europeans one to 300 persons, Asians one to 1,500, and Africans one to 30,000. No direct elections were provided for the Africans either at this level or for the thirty-two seats on the African council. They were all selected by traditional authorities.

It is in this context that political parties came into being. These new parties either represented traditionalism and tribalism or reacted against these old methods. The largest party, the Bechuanaland Democratic party

(BDP), was based on the Bamangwato whose leader was Seretse Khama. The Bechuanaland Liberal party (BLP) was mainly representative of the Bangwaketze tribe. Each of these favored a slower program of political development which took account of the traditional order of society. The two most radical parties were the Federal party and the Bechuanaland Peoples party (BPP). The former was affiliated with PAFMECA while the latter was even more radical. The BPP completely rejected the Legislative Council because it was nonrepresentative. Their delegates testified in June 1962 before the United Nations Committee on Colonialism and demanded immediate independence for Bechuanaland.

It became obvious to the British that the old Legislative Council had to be drastically revised to admit the elective principle. In consultation with the politicians, a new constitution which provided for internal self-government was created and accepted by the British government in June 1964. Under the new instruments a two-house legislature was established. The lower house, the Legislative Assembly, of thirty-two members was to be elected by broad suffrage. The upper house, the Senate, was a house of chiefs which was given delaying powers similar to that planned for Basutoland. The functional executive was to be a prime minister and ministry responsible to the Legislative Assembly. A national census was completed in 1964, and a commission demarcated the thirty-two electoral constituencies.

The general election was held on March 1, 1965, and the BDP of Seretse won twenty-eight of the seats in the Legislative Assembly and thus he became the first prime minister of Bechuanaland. Almost immediately he publicly reiterated his position toward the Republic of South Africa. Although disagreeing with the Republic's native policy, he stated that he saw no reason why good economic relations could not be continued between the areas. This was most important when Bechuanaland became an independent state in September 1966 taking the name Botswana. It continued to be tied to the Republic by a customs union, used South African currency, and over 30,000 Tswana earned their living in South Africa. Prime Minister Verwoerd replied to Prime Minister Khama's statements in equally moderate terms.

SWAZILAND

Swaziland was the third of the British territories in southern Africa administered by the high commissioner under the Commonwealth Relations Office. Slightly less than 6,700 square miles in area, it had a population of approximately 280,000. There is only one Bantu group, the Swazi, resident in the territory. Although still a relatively poor area, it has greater economic potential than either Basutoland or Bechuanaland. Asbestos, sugar, cotton, timber, and rice have been the major export products, but iron deposits have been uncovered and an expensive hydroelectric project has been started. Despite these advantages, the problems of converting the political system to a more liberal form were more complex than in the other

High Commission Territories. Although there were only 8,000 Europeans resident in Swaziland, they owned almost half the land. They have established economic and political rights. There are also 2,000 Colored residents, most of whom are middle class. Thus any constitutional change had to be such that it would satisfy all these groups.

Throughout the 1950s, the dual government of Swaziland was administered by the Native Administration Proclamation of 1950. The chief administrative officer was the resident commissioner, aided by a secretariat and district commissioners. He was also assisted by a European advisory council of ten members. The native reserve of 3,516 square miles was administered by the paramount chief, Subhousa II, who was assisted by two councils. The first, the *Liqoqo*, was originally a family body and remained largely aristocratic. The second, the *Libandhla*, was a more popular council, although the elective principle in the Western sense was not practiced in selecting its members.

Political parties in Swaziland were late in developing, but as constitutional concessions were made to Basutoland and then to Bechuanaland, there was a sudden spurt of political activity. The first powerful Swaziland party was the Swaziland Progressive party (SPP) led at first by Mr. J. J. Nqutu and, after June 1962, by Dr. A. P. Zwane. It was affiliated with PAFMECA, and from the beginnings of constitutional discussions assumed the most radical position in Swaziland. The other early major Swazi party was the Swazi Democratic party (SDP) whose leader was Dr. Allen Nxumalo. Although in basic agreement with the ends announced by the SPP, it was more amenable to compromise with the traditional authorities and the British. Chief Subhousa II commanded the allegiance of more Swazis than any other figure. His position as traditional head of the Swazis was reinforced by his own knowledge of Western forms and, particularly, by his personality. At first the traditional views of the paramount chief were not represented by a political party. However, to contest the 1964 elections, the Imbokodvo party reflecting Subhousa's ideas was formed.

Another quite small Swazi party which emerged in the early 1960s was the Mbandzeni National Convention. The European community at first formed no political party, but was represented in the early political deliberations through the European advisory council. By the time of the first elections for the Legislative Council, they, too, had a party, the right-wing United Swaziland Association. The Colored of Swaziland formed a Eurafrican Welfare Association to present their views. These were basically conservative and constituted an appeal to unity and the idea of Swazi nationhood.

A constitutional committee was appointed by the British in late 1961 to study and make recommendations for a new constitution. From the first the SPP demanded elections to the Legislative Council on the basis of one man, one vote. They also asked for a bill of rights and the guarantee of Chief Subhousa's position as head of state. This position was to be largely ceremonial with the real power in the hands of a chief minister. These recommendations, if adopted, would have removed power not only from the paramount chief, but also from the European residents. Subhousa wanted his present power and prerogatives guaranteed. The Europeans wanted a certain number of seats guaranteed them to prevent being swamped by the numerically superior Swazi. All factions agreed that they wanted a better constitution than that presented to Bechuanaland.

In March 1962, the constitutional committee made its recommendations. They called for a continuation of the dual system. The governor was to be appointed by the British government and responsible to the secretary of state. The position of the paramount chief was to be recognized and protected. His authority in the native areas was to continue relatively unchanged. Executive and legislative councils were to be created and they were to be advisory to both the governor and the paramount chief. Elections of whites to the Legislative Council were to be direct for one-half of the seats. One-half of the seats were to be reserved for Swazis chosen in the traditional way.

Both the SPP and the SDP rejected the proposals as being racialistic and discriminatory. Later in 1962, a great *indaba* or formal meeting of the Swazi was called by Chief Subhousa, the first in seventy-five years. However, the delegates were so divided in their thinking that they were dismissed before reaching any specific conclusions. In 1963 the British government issued a White Paper in which it stated its compromise solution to the selection and composition of the Legislative Council. In January 1964, the British granted a constitution based on its White Paper which created a twenty-four member council. This was to be composed of eight Swazis elected in the traditional manner, eight of any race elected from a common, nonracial roll, and eight whites of which four would be elected by Europeans and four from the common roll. Except for the eight Swazis selected in the traditional manner, the basis of franchise was one man—one vote. For the contested seats on the common roll, voters in a given district had to vote for one European and two Swazi candidates.

This compromise constitution was opposed by all the political parties and even the Europeans protested that Britain was imposing a constitution on Swaziland. The constitution did not solve the political impasse but simply postponed its solution. Despite the protests, the constitution went into effect and elections were held for the Legislative Council in June 1964. The election results were a considerable surprise to most observers because the traditionalists swept all the elected seats. The king was practically guaranteed eight supporters in the Legislative Council by the traditional method of selection. Few persons believed that the Imbokodvo would win all eight of the Swazi seats on the multiracial roll. However, they did, and furthermore the right-wing United Swaziland Association won all the seats reserved for whites. The radical African parties were completely shut out. Thus in the indefinite future, the more modern-oriented African parties on the basis of these elections seemed to have no effective place in Swaziland.

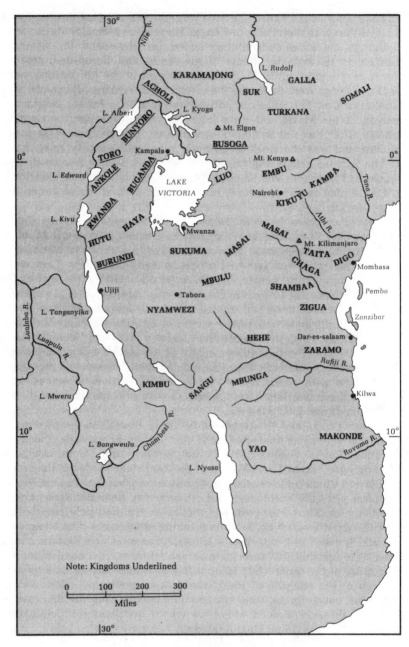

Kingdoms and Peoples of East Africa

Devolution of power and consolidation of African rule: British East Africa

KENYA

Political activity in Kenya prior to World War II was concentrated almost entirely in the small but dominant white community. From 1907 when the first Legislative Council with two unofficial white members was created until Mau Mau, European colonists managed to obtain from the government most of what they wanted. In the five years after World War I there was considerable disturbance in Kenya related to the future political role of the colony. Many European settlers wanted the home government to grant responsible government to the area which would give the settlers complete control of local decisions. Despite generally pro-European attitudes, no British government was prepared to turn the destinies of millions of Africans over to the rule of a few thousand settlers. Nevertheless, the constitution was changed to give the settlers more voice in the decisions of the legislative and executive councils. Two settlers were appointed as unofficial members of the Executive Council in 1918. The following year the elective principle was admitted in selecting eleven European members for the expanded Legislative Council. The revision contemplated having nominated Indian and Arab members and also one European nominated to represent African interests. The Indians, deeply resentful of their treatment by Europeans, refused to cooperate and for seven years there were no Indian members in the council.

The Indians comprised a significant third population in Kenya even in the 1920s. Brought at first to East Africa to work on the railroad, those who remained occupied a socioeconomic position between the dominant Europeans and the Bantu people. They were restricted from owning land and were forced to live segregated from the whites. In the early 1920s, supported by the government of India, they precipitated a crisis in Kenya. Indians wanted to own land in the highlands and secure abolition of all official discrimination. They wished to be able to compete, on the basis of merit, for positions in the police and civil service. In 1923 after the British government had gone on record as supporting Kenya for the Africans, the Devonshire White Paper supplied a formula for ending the Indian impasse. It provided for the election from a communal roll of five Indian representatives to the Legislative Council. It did nothing to remove the other restrictions which the Indians had complained about. After the Indian community eventually accepted these conditions there were no further important alterations in the Legislative Council until after World War II.

African attitudes in the interwar period were generally constrained within the context of indirect rule. Outwardly docile, the Africans were deeply dissatisfied, although they had no effective organization to present their demands. Their major concern was over the alienation of their land. Though never enunciated as official policy, the practice of government at all levels confirmed Europeans in control of the "white highlands." Despite the British White Paper in 1923 which stated "native paramountcy," there was little done during the next two decades to implement that policy. The most pressing problem for the Africans, particularly the Kikuyu, was land. The early European settlers such as Lord Delamere had purchased large amounts of land from the Kikuyu. Later the Kikuyu denied that they had sold the land. They had only given use rights since no Kikuyu, acting on his own, could dispose of communal land. In 1904 the government drew the boundaries of native reserves. All land not specifically designated as reserves was decreed to be crown land which could be disposed of by the government in any way it wished.

There was no flood of European emigrants to Kenya, but rather a steady stream with the majority coming after the Boer War and World War I. By 1950 the European population of Kenya was less than 35,000 persons yet they controlled over 12,000 square miles of land. At the same time the native reserved areas comprised 52,000 square miles for a rapidly growing population which had reached the four million level. In 1932 a royal commission, the Carter Land Commission, was appointed to investigate the whole range of problems connected with land. The commission, although adding a portion of land to the Native Reserves, did little from the African viewpoint to solve their problems because it accepted the basic European contentions.

African politics before 1945 was concerned primarily with the two factors of land and the clash of multinational interests. Little had been done in the interwar years to adjust the attitudes of the different African tribal units. Most of the African pressure upon the colonial administration had been brought by groups interested in a specific problem rather than in long-range solutions through the media of political parties. Of all African groups in Kenya, the most responsive to European attitudes and methods were the Kikuyu. It is not surprising, then, that the bulk of African political activity should have been initiated by them.

The first Kikuyu political organization was the Kikuyu Association formed by chiefs and trusted by the government. Thus its major function was to mediate between government decrees and the people. In 1921 Harry Thuku, a young telephone operator, formed the Young Kikuyu Association composed mainly of some of the younger, more educated Kikuyu. Although hampered by organizational problems, the association was the first attempt to present Kikuyu grievances through a modern, nontraditional organization. As a result of its activities, moderate though they were, Thuku was arrested in March 1922 and exiled by the government. Members of the Young Kikuyu Association formed the nucleus of a new organization, the Kikuyu Central Association (KCA). Although there were a number of smaller political groups such as the Progressive Kikuyu party, the KCA remained the most articulate spokesman for the Kikuyu. They lost no opportunity to present their complaints to either the Nairobi or London governments. However, they were never able to expand their influence beyond the Kikuyu, and the government, despite evidences of popular support, continued to treat the KCA as unrepresentative. It was in this period that the very influential Kikuyu Independent Schools Association was formed to combine, in their schools, Western concepts of education with the traditional values of the Kikuyu. Weaker, small political groups such as the offshoots of the Kavirondo Association were also operating in the 1930s among non-Kikuyu Bantu and the Luo.

During World War II the British administration in Nairobi considered the KCA a danger and it was proscribed. After the war a new organization, the Kenya African Union (KAU), was formed and Jomo Kenyatta became its president in June 1947. The KAU's influence was greatest among the Kikuyu, but it was not designed to be just a Kikuyu group. Oginga Odinga was particularly successful in his attempts to organize the Luo in Nyanza in the late 1940s. By 1950 the KAU's membership was over 100,000.

Concessions to the African majority in Kenya were slower and more grudgingly granted than to most other British African territories. Finally in 1952 Britain introduced a constitution which would have given Africans six representatives on the Legislative Council. Educated Africans protested that this reform was hardly sufficient since the Europeans had fourteen representatives on the council. Failure of the British to act definitively on such complaints led to Mau Mau.

Mau Mau was a terrorist organization designed to drive the Europeans from Kenya. It was almost entirely a Kikuyu-based movement and it utilized Western organizational practices and warped traditional Kikuyu oathing ceremonies in order to bind its adherents to the group. The first disturbances began in 1951 with attacks upon European cattle and then moved to sporadic raids against white farms. The government in October 1952 declared a state of emergency, flew in British troops, and organized European and Kikuyu militia units. Detention camps were established for all those Kikuyu suspected of belonging to Mau Mau and elaborate de-oathing ceremonies were performed to enable members to feel themselves free from their obligations to the movement. Under continuous pressure, the terrorists were forced further into the Aberdare Mountains. In September 1955, the government announced that the major threat had come to an end. By then the rebellion had cost the government over £30 million and had resulted in the loss of thousands of lives, most of them Kikuyu. The Mau Mau uprising led to the arrest of Jomo Kenyatta in November 1952, and for a brief time the KAU continued legal operation under the presidency of Walter Odede, a Luo, until the government banned all political activity. Kenyatta was tried, convicted of complicity in Mau Mau, and sentenced to seven years imprisonment. There was no legal political activity during most of the period of the state of emergency which was not lifted until early 1960.

During the disturbances in 1954 the colonial secretary, Oliver Lyttelton, announced his intention to issue a new constitution which would leave the composition of the Legislative Council unchanged but would make the African positions elective. This promise was confirmed in 1956 and elections took place in March 1957. In 1956 the Nairobi District African National Congress was formed to contest the election. By then the British government had decided to abandon its previous support of the white minority and speed up the devolution of power to Africans. A new constitution became effective in 1958 which provided for enlarged African representation on the Legislative Council and which also created a Council of State with the function of ensuring nondiscrimination in legislation.

The most important political organization at this time was the Peoples Convention party founded by Tom Mboya, general secretary of the Kenya Federation of Labor. In April 1959, Jomo Kenyatta was freed by the government but kept restricted to the northern territories. As the pace of governmental advance quickened, his release became a major issue. In August 1959, the Kenya National party was created and this soon gave way to the two parties that have since dominated Kenya politics, the Kenya African National Union (KANU) and the Kenya African Democratic Union (KADU). KANU elected Kenyatta president, but the government would not register the party under his leadership. The party was finally recognized when James Gichuru stood in for Kenyatta. Although claiming to speak for Kenya, KANU's power was based upon the urban Bantu, the Kikuyu, and Luo. KADU, led by Roland Ngala, represented the smaller tribes.

The white settlers were almost unanimous in opposing the extension of more authority and responsibility to the Africans. Their failure to achieve this goal was registered in the constitutional conference of 1960. The constitution which emerged from these discussions provided for a greatly expanded Legislative Council with thirty-three members being elected from a common roll. There were also twenty-two seats reserved for differing ethnic groups. The Executive Council was reconstructed as a Council of Ministers with twice as many unofficial as official members. One group of moderate white settlers did follow Michael Blundell's New Kenya Group of 1958–1959 with its concept of cooperation with Africans. But the mechanics of political development, the smallness of the white community, and the deep divisions within it dictated that such a compromise movement would have little success.

The general election of 1961 gave Africans a majority in the Legislative Council. KANU won eighteen seats to eleven for KADU and polled three times as many votes. KANU, however, made the recognition of Kenyatta's leadership a condition of forming the government. KADU eventually agreed to cooperate with the government and became the official government. Kenyatta was moved from the north in March and finally released unconditionally in August in time to prevent an open split in KANU between Mboya and Odinga. Kenyatta again became president of KANU in November 1961, and the rules regarding persons convicted of major crimes were changed to allow him to be elected to the Legislative Council.

A further London conference convened in February 1962, to discuss the future of Kenya. KADU, afraid of the domination of the smaller tribes by the Kikuyu, demanded a federal constitution while KANU stood for a unitary system. The stresses between the parties were important and potentially dangerous. But the conference ended with the Colonial Office deciding to compromise between the groups by providing for a strong central government and six regional governments with considerable local power. There was much disagreement to come over the degree of regionalism, but each party agreed to accept seven ministries in a new coalition government. The whole of 1962 was taken up in KANU by factions and quarrels which threatened to tear the party apart.

This factionalism within KANU led to an abortive attempt by the Kenya Federation of Labor to set up a new Labor party. Although the party was never formed, the Kikuyu-Luo split and the Mboya-Odinga quarrel were highly important. KADU's policies of tribalism undoubtedly led to the creation of the Kenya Land Freedom Army and outbreaks of violence. Charges by KANU that the Colonial Office was procrastinating caused the removal of Governor Renison in November 1962. One of the reasons for delay in granting self-government was the demarcation of the regional boundaries which was finally completed in the fall of 1962, and the boundary commission's report was published in December. Earlier in the year dissidents from the two major parties under the leadership of Paul Ngei formed the African Peoples party (APP) which seemed, at the beginning of 1963, to hold the balance between the large parties. After much delay, the new elections for a really responsible Kenya government were set for May. In the elections, KANU elected sixty-nine members of the House of Representatives compared to KADU's eight. In the Senate, the KANU-Northern Province United Association (NPUA) coalition elected twenty out of thirty-eight, and in the regions KANU won 158 seats to KADU's fifty-one. The new ministry was formed by Kenyatta with Odinga becoming justice minister, Gichuru, finance minister, and Mboya, minister of constitutional affairs.

The period of internal self-government from June 1 through December 11, 1963 was a time of heated debates in the House of Representatives between the APP-KADU coalition and the government over the power to be assigned to the regional assemblies. Ngala and his followers feared a strong centralized regime controlled by Kenyatta. The power of the government opposition in time waned as various opposition members of parliament joined the government party. The first major defection was Ngei and the APP and then finally a number of very important leaders of KADU.

Nevertheless, at the Lancaster House Conference held September 25 to October 19 to decide the final form of the Kenya government after independence, the question of regionalism versus a strong central authority was the main point of debate. At one time Roland Ngala threatened to end the discussions and establish in those regions loyal to KADU a new Republic of Kenya. KANU countered this bombastic threat by promising to break up the conference, return to Nairobi, and declare independence on October 20 without further reference to the British. This threat quickly led to substantial agreement between Britain and the KANU representatives. After the furor, the KADU leaders accepted defeat and urged support for Kenyatta's government. Kenyatta and KANU controlled the newly expanded 130 member House of Representatives. KADU elected only thirty-one persons to the house. Independence finally came to long-divided Kenya on December 11, 1963.

Defections from KADU to KANU continued after independence; KADU was officially disbanded in 1964, and Roland Ngala, its leader, was made a minister in the Kenyatta government. A new constitution was adopted in 1964 which removed the governor-general and established a republican form of government with a president as chief executive. It also created a two-house system—a forty-one member Senate and a House of Representatives of 129 members. On December 12, 1964, the new government with Jomo Kenyatta as president went into effect.

Although after 1965 there was only one party in Kenya, it was far from being homogeneous. The vice-president, Oginga Odinga, a leader of the Luo, was far more radical than the other political leaders. He wished closer contacts with the Communist bloc and was openly critical of the pro-Western attitudes of Kenyatta and Mboya. On a number of occasions in 1965 Kenyatta made clear his opposition to Odinga's ideas, and by extension to Odinga as a possible successor. Perhaps the clearest indication of Kenyatta's intention to stay clear of the Communist bloc and avoid taking sides in the cold war was the seizure, in May 1965, of a convoy of Chinese arms sent from Tanzania to Uganda over Kenya's roads. Although Kenya continued after independence to belong, with its neighbors, to the joint rail, air, road, and postal systems, Kenyatta considered this action a flagrant violation of Kenya's neutralist position. The trucks and drivers were released only after Tanzanian and Uganda officials were fully appraised of Kenyatta's determination to stay clear of Communist influence.

The same practical firmness could be noted earlier in his quick reaction to the mutiny on January 24 of a battalion of the Kenya Rifles. The uprising was a result of dissatisfaction with pay and the continued presence of European officers. The disturbance was of the same order as those which struck Tanzania and Uganda at the same time. Acting quickly, Kenyatta asked for British aid, and thus the mutiny never got beyond the embryo stage. Later sixteen of the mutineers were sentenced to prison and twenty-nine others were discharged from the service. The decisive action by Kenyatta possibly warded off a crisis of the same order as that which shook the foundations of Nyerere's power in Tanzania. Despite Kenya's poor economic position and the many long-range problems facing the state, it soon became one of the most stable of the new African states due to the moderate leadership of Kenyatta, Mboya, and Gichuru.

TANZANIA (TANGANYIKA)

After World War I Britain was confirmed by the League of Nations in its occupation of the bulk of what had been German East Africa. The two territories of Ruanda and Urundi had been detached and given to Belgium as mandates of the League. Theoretically Britain ruled Tanganyika under the direction and guidance of the League as a class "C" mandate. In actuality the League interfered very little in the administration of Tanganyika. The major advantage to the Africans of the League's presence was its reminder to the Colonial Office and British administrators that Tanganyika was held for Africans until they were sufficiently advanced to govern themselves.

In 1920 the government of Tanganyika consisted of the governor, Sir Horace Byatt, a nominated Executive Council, and a skeleton staff of European district officers. Traditional rule throughout the area was in shambles largely because the German system had minimized the importance of chiefs and headmen. Byatt's primary concerns were to bring order to all areas of Tanganyika and to restore trade. His success can be measured by the exports which in 1925 were twice the 1914 levels. It was left to his successor, Sir Donald Cameron, to attempt a reconstruction of local government under traditional leaders. Cameron, with long experience in Nigeria, believed the best format for advancing African people was through the medium of their own institutions. In Tanganyika this necessitated long, complex surveys to discover the varying systems of rule and the actual leaders of the people. Whenever these were known, Cameron constructed his form of indirect rule complete with native courts and in some cases native treasuries. By the time he left Tanganyika in 1930 this system was working in all areas except where the slave trade or the Maji-Maji rebellion had destroyed the older system. Cameron's structure of local government remained relatively unchanged for almost thirty years.

Cameron was responsible for the introduction of the first legislative council in 1926. He opposed the desires of the European community for some type of amalgamation with Kenya and the imposition of the same type of settler-dominated government as in Kenya. Demands from Europeans in Tanganyika and Kenya and the economic stringencies of the postwar years led to a number of commissions appointed by the British government to investigate the federation of some of the British East Africa and Central African territories. The first of these reports, that of the Ormsby-Gore Commission in 1924, had already pointed out that the difficulties of uniting Uganda, Kenya, and Tanganyika outweighed the economic advantages. However, after 1925 the colonial secretary, Leopold Amery, still pursued the idea of federation even against the obvious opposition of the mandates commission. Joined by Lord Delamere, who had called an unofficial conference in 1926 to discuss the union of Nyasaland, Rhodesia, and Tanganyika, Sir Edward Grigg, governor of Kenya, produced in 1927 a plan to federate Uganda, Kenya, and Tanganyika. Cameron believed that African interests, particularly in Tanganyika, would be subordinated to the wishes of the Europeans in Kenya and threatened to resign on this question. Grigg's plan for federation was not adopted, but Amery appointed yet another commission, the Hilton-Young Commission, to make recommendations on union and a number of other related problems. Finally in 1930 the new Labor government laid to rest the possibility of an immediate political amalgamation of the three areas. Despite this, government officials, Indians, and Europeans continued to be perturbed in the 1930s over the future of the territory. In the early part of the decade there was genuine fear that the League was going to end its mandate and hand Tanganyika over to a resurgent Germany. Not until 1938 did it become apparent, even to the German settlers, that Lord Milner had been correct eighteen years before when he had stated that Tanganyika had become "permanently incorporated in the British Empire."

Few alterations were made in the mode of British control in Tanganyika even after World War II. The British Labor government placed the area under United Nations control which continued the earlier pattern of administration that had as its goal the preparation of Africans for independence. Despite this objective, little had been done to help the education system provide more educated leaders; and the country stilll operated on the basis of indirect rule. One reason why Britain did not offer revised constitutional instruments to Tanganyika after the war was because African political leaders were more concerned with local than national politics. The Legislative Council remained totally nominated until 1955, with seven European, four African, and three Asian members. This imbalance reflected harshly upon the theory of British administration since there were fewer than 20,000 Europeans and only 60,000 Asians in a total population of approximately 8,000,000. In 1949 a committee on constitutional development was created which reported in 1951 that the Legislative Council should be enlarged and its influence extended. No changes were made, however, until after the investigations of W. J. M. MacKenzie, a Professor of Government from Manchester University, in 1955. Then the council was enlarged to thirty unofficial members with a rough parity between the races. All members of the council were still nominated by the governor. To offset the lack of elections, the British instituted a system whereby some of the African members became assistant ministers with restricted executive authority.

In June 1956, a bill was passed by the Legislative Council which called for a revised constitution which would allow the elective principle. The instrument which was designed to meet this demand permitted elections to an expanded council. The franchise was granted on a qualitative basis and all voters were placed on a common roll. However, the election system was very complex. Each voter in the districts had three votes and were required to vote for three candidates—one African, one Asian, and one European. The elections held in 1958 were saved from a possible impasse by the rise in importance of a new political party, the Tanganyika African National Union (TANU).

The modern political history of Tanganyika is closely tied to the career of one man, Julius Nyerere, who after returning to Tanganyika from Britain in 1952 became a power in the old Tanganyika African Association which had been created in 1929. In 1954, believing that this association was too restricted, he formed TANU. Within months the organization had branches throughout the country. In 1955 Nyerere took the nationalists' complaints concerning Britain's slowness to reform Tanganyika's political institutions to the United Nations. In the beginning

TANU was primarily a vehicle for African nationalism. However, after its initial successes it became more moderate and Nyerere was able to convince Asians and Europeans that if they cooperated with TANU their interests would be safeguarded. Nyerere's approach did much to undermine the potential of the United Tanganyika party which had been created in 1955 on the platform of multiracism. In December 1957, Nyerere again highlighted TANU's demands for faster developments by resigning from the Legislative Council. TANU cooperated in the implementation of the constitution of 1958 although the party disagreed with the division of African, European, and Asian candidates, and TANU won an overwhelming majority of the elected seats. The members of the new Legislative Council of 1958 formed themselves into the Tanganyika Elected Members Organization (TEMO) to expedite the political liberation of Tanganyika. Backed with solid African support, TANU immediately demanded that Britain grant more responsibility to Africans. Nyerere's pressure and cooperation produced the new constitution of 1960. This constitution provided, for the first time, a majority of elected members to the Legislative Council and also responsible ministerial government. Fifty electoral districts were created which chose seventy-one members. Reservations were made so that eleven of the members elected had to be Asians and ten Europeans. In the elections of August, TANU-supported candidates won seventy seats and Nyerere was asked to form a government. In the spring of 1961 a constitutional conference held at Dar-es-Salaam gave Tanganyika full self-government on May 1 and full independence at the end of December 1961. The Legislative Council was renamed the National Assembly and Nyerere became prime minister of an independent Tanganyika.

In early 1962, tensions within TANU convinced Nyerere that he should not try to hold both the position of prime minister and head of TANU until the country was more stable. There were indications that the tightly knit party which he had created was in danger of breaking apart. Therefore he resigned as prime minister to concentrate on the task of reconstructing the party throughout Tanganyika. His mild-mannered, trustworthy deputy, Rashidi Kawawa, became prime minister. In the interim, constitutional changes were proposed on June 28 to the National Assembly which would enable Tanganyika to become a republic. In early November the first presidential election was held and Nyerere returned as the head of government, and on December 9, 1962, Tanganyika became a republic within the Commonwealth. The constitution provided for a vice-president, an appointive fourteen-member cabinet, and gave the president a veto over legislation.

The first serious threat to the moderate evolutionary government of Nyerere occurred in January 1964 with the mutiny of a large segment of the 1,600 man Tanganyika Rifles. They were discontented with low pay and being still under command of British officers. Nyerere had refused to bow to growing demands to dismiss a number of British senior officers and replace them with Africans. This uprising was probably triggered by the successful military coup in 1963 which ousted the sultan of Zanzibar.

Nyerere, fearing a takeover similar to that which had occurred in Togo and Zanzibar, went into hiding, leaving the minister of external affairs, Oscar Kambona, to deal with the mutiny. Nyerere finally issued a call for British troops, and with their aid the mutiny was quelled. After the revolt Nyerere dismissed large numbers of soldiers and police, but his image had been altered by the revolt. The army was eventually disbanded to be replaced by a militia force, the Tanzanian Peoples Defense Force, which was armed primarily with weapons provided by the Chinese. The revolt of 1964 illustrated how explosive the forces were beneath the surface of even the best-managed, moderate African government.

Nyerere recovered some of his lost prestige by engineering the federation of Zanzibar and Tanganyika. In March 1964, Oscar Kambona flew to Zanzibar to discuss mutual problems with Abeid Karume, head of the new revolutionary regime. Implicit in the discussions was the possibility that Tanganyika would remove its policemen which had enabled Karume to restore order. This would have left Karume with only a mixed irregular force to maintain peace in Zanzibar. Later Karume visited Tanganyika at a time when Abdul Muhammad (Babu) was on a tour of the Far East. This series of discussions led to the announcement of the union of Tanganyika and Zanzibar. The agreements of the two leaders were later ratified by the legislatures of both areas in April 1964. By the agreement, Nyerere became president and Karume first vice-president of the Federation of Tanzania.

The articles of union called for a modification of the constitution of Tanganyika to provide for a separate executive and legislature for Zanzibar. The union was only temporary until a combined commission on the constitution made its report and a constituent assembly was called to redraft the constitution. These actions were to be completed within a year from the initial act of union. Until that time the laws in both areas remained in effect, although the president had the power to repeal any laws of Zanzibar which infringed on the power of the federal government. Areas specifically reserved to the federal government were the constitution, defense, external affairs, trade and customs, police, and emergency powers. Each area of the union maintained its own legislature to deal with specifically local issues.

Actual integration of services were predictably slow. Foreign aid throughout 1964 still came directly to Zanzibar without going through the mechanism of the central authority. As late as September 1964, there were still customs examinations between Tanganyika and Zanzibar. Nevertheless, the federation appeared on the higher levels to be a triumph for Nyerere and moderation, even though Muhammad and Hanga still remained in the government.

In late January 1965, the government of Tanzania charged two United States officials with plotting against Vice-President Karume and requested their removal. The United States retaliated by asking that Nyerere recall one of his attaches from Washington and he, in return, reacted by recalling the Tanzanian ambassador from the United States. This worsening of relations with Nyerere, who was once considered to be one of the most moderate African politicians, was paralleled by friendlier relations between Tanzania and Communist China. Tanzania received $45,000,000 in pledges from China, and in June, Chou En-lai visited Dar-es-Salaam and made a major address from there. The new-found friendliness between China and East African states embroiled Nyerere with his northern neighbor Kenya. Chinese arms designated for use in Uganda were sent from Tanzania by truck across Kenya. This was done without prior consultation with Jomo Kenyatta. The guns were seized and were not released until both Uganda and Tanzania apologized for attempting to compromise Kenya's position by such activities.

In October 1965, elections were held for the expanded 107 seat legislature. President Nyerere also was seeking reelection but ran unopposed. A new feature of elections in a one-party state was introduced. With the exception of six seats reserved for top party officials, all seats were contested. TANU nominated two men for every seat, gave each candidate equal support, and then let the incumbents and their challengers vie for voter's approval. The results were surprising. Only sixteen members of the old assembly were able to retain their seats. Nine ranking party officials, including the finance minister, Paul Bomani, were defeated.

The government of Tanzania in 1965 remained an enigma to Western observers. Nyerere, despite his overtures toward China and the worsening of relations with the United States, seemed essentially a moderate. If the president's statements were taken at face value, all he wished to do was to keep Tanzania as far from cold-war commitments as possible and retain freedom of action for his government. The great unanswered question concerning the future of the federation was how successful he would be in dealing with supporters, particularly on Zanzibar, who were unlikely to be happy under a moderate government.

UGANDA

There have been major alterations in the boundaries of Uganda since Sir Harry Johnston left. These adjustments which ceded great portions of the protectorate to neighboring Kenya and the Sudan had reduced the territory to approximately half its former size by 1926. The area which remained was a compact, well-populated, rich agricultural territory. The divisions of the protectorate based upon the agreements designed by Johnston and his predecessors did not substantially affect the unity of Uganda until the 1950s. In brief, the agreements signed with the rulers of the important kingdoms of Buganda and Bunyoro gave these areas a special relationship to the central British administration. For a half century they made British rule easier in Uganda. The existence of strong kings and their councils, while making consultation imperative, did ensure the adherence of an entire nation to policies agreed upon by the rulers and the British authorities. European colonization in the interwar period was not encouraged, thus avoiding many of the problems of adjacent Kenya.

The two factors of strong African rulers and few Europeans meant that the British governor could exercise more direct authority without the usual restrictions of a meaningful executive or legislative council. It was not until 1921 that these agencies were established with a legislative council composed of only six members, four of whom were officials. No Africans were represented. Not until 1945 were three Africans chosen as a part of the seven-member unofficial group in a fourteen-member Legislative Council. Further adjustments to the Legislative Council were made in 1947, 1948, and 1950 which resulted in increasing African unofficial representation to the level of the combined number of European and Asian members. By the early 1950s it had become apparent that any major constitutional advance by the entire protectorate in the same direction as that taken in other British territories could only come by restricting the significant power of the traditional authorities. There had been some democratization of the Buganda Lukiko (Assembly of Notables) following the disturbances of 1949, but it was still a major force for conservative Buganda nationalism. In 1953 further attempts at reform by the central government precipitated a major crisis with the kabaka.

In June 1953, in an after dinner speech, the colonial secretary, Oliver Lyttelton, suggested the possibility of the development of a meaningful East African Federation. The Baganda, their special status already threatened by Uganda constitutional reforms, reacted to this further intimidation by demanding that their country be placed under Foreign Office control and a plan be devised to grant Buganda its independence separate from Uganda. The governor, Sir Andrew Cohen, one of the architects of the new British African policy, hastily assured the Baganda that Britain had no intention of forcing a federation upon them. The Lukiko would not be mollified by such assurances and pressed its demands. The kabaka, caught between the contending parties, negotiated with the governor a plan for the future development of Buganda within the large polity. However, under pressure from his most powerful subjects, he repudiated this agreement and supported the Lukiko's demands. By not representing the British government's opinion to the Lukiko, he was in violation of the 1900 agreement. Sir Andrew reluctantly ordered the kabaka, Mutesa II, deported to Britain. Not until 1955, when he was allowed to return to Uganda, did he play a significant role in Uganda politics.

In 1954 Sir Keith Hancock of the Institute of Commonwealth Studies and a committee of the Lukiko negotiated a compromise settlement. In November 1954, on the basis of this agreement and after consultation with other segments of Uganda opinion, the government issued a new constitution. The Legislative Council was increased in size to sixty members with the thirty unofficial members being Africans. There would be ministerial government introduced with five ministers, three of whom would be African. At the same time the 1900 agreement with Buganda was modified to establish the kabaka as a constitutional monarch acting on the advice of his ministers. The Lukiko also accepted the concept that Buganda representatives should sit on the Legislative Council. These representatives were to be chosen by indirect election. Britain reiterated its pledge not to force a federation and the Baganda gave up their demand for independence. Britain also promised that there would be no change made in the form of government agreed upon until 1961. On acceptance of the agreement, Kabaka Mutesa II returned to Uganda in October 1955.

A decision in 1957 to have the speaker of the Legislative Assembly preside over its meetings was taken by the Baganda to be a breach of the 1954 agreement and they refused to send their representatives to the central government. By 1958 most African members to the council were being selected by direct elections. Buganda, however, continued its opposition, refusing to allow its five representatives to take part in the Legislative Council. Early in the year Buganda again requested that the Buganda Agreement be terminated and British protection ended. This was refused, but a new constitutional committee was established to plan for the future of Uganda. In May 1959, the government was faced with a boycott of all non-Africans by a new organization, the Uganda National Movement. The organizaton was banned, its leaders sent into exile, and a new constitution was drawn up for a greatly expanded Legislative Council of eighty-two members; and elections were held on a basis of direct suffrage in March 1961.

The general elections of March 1961, which were designed to give Uganda a large measure of self-government, were boycotted by the kabaka and his followers. The Democratic party (DP) which had been created in 1956 won the twenty seats for Buganda with a total of less than 12,000 votes. This gave them forty-four out of the eighty-two seats in the Legislative Council while the rival Uganda-wide party, the Uganda Peoples Congress (UPC) led by Milton Obote, could gain but thirty-five. Therefore, the DP, although the minority party throughout Uganda, formed the first real African government for Uganda under their leader, Benedicto Kiwanuka. In the months that followed, Britain negotiated an agreement with Buganda whereby the kabaka was recognized as the hereditary ruler. Buganda was to be federally associated with the rest of Uganda. Buganda was given twenty-one representatives in the eighty-two seat National Assembly. The Buganda Lukiko, however, was to be directly elected. The agreement was accepted on October 31, 1961, and the elections for the Lukiko were held on February 22, 1962. The Kabaka Yekka party, which had been created in November 1961 as the political extension of the kabaka's traditional power base, won sixty-five of the sixty-eight seats to the Lukiko. The UPC by agreement did not challenge this regional election. In the national election of April 25, 1962, the DP in an atmosphere of growing bitterness was soundly defeated. The UPC won forty-three seats while the DP could claim only twenty-four members in the assembly. The twenty-four selected members from Buganda gave the Kabaka Yekka the balance of power. Kiwanuka, the former head of government, was not even elected to parliament.

The months immediately following the elections of 1962 were devoted largely to discussions concerning total independence for Uganda. Major problems also arose from the demands of Ankole, Bunyoro, Toro, and

Busoga for equal status with Buganda in any federal structure. Formal discussions which opened on June 27, 1962, were troubled further by border disputes between Bunyoro and Buganda. The conference evaded many of the implications of federalism, but it did establish a system encompassing four kingdoms, Busoga, and eleven administrative districts, and October 9, 1962 was established as Independence Day. The president of the republic was to be the kabaka of Buganda, while the vice-president was to be the king of Bunyoro, Sir William Nadiope.

Conflict at the central level quickly arose because of the kabaka's idea of his position in Uganda and his power position in parliament. However, the UPC in the elections in Ankole and Toro gained control of the regional governments. Obote made good use of his position as the head of the only strong party that stood for a Uganda-wide policy against the Buganda-oriented policy of the kabaka. By June 1963, defections from the DP and the Kabaka Yekka made him master of parliament with fifty-five members out of a total of ninety-one. If the UPC could manage a two-thirds majority, then the constitution could be changed to prevent a recurrence of the weak coalition that existed before June 1963.

In January 1964, the army mutiny in Tanzania triggered a smaller outbreak in Uganda. The first battalion of the Uganda Rifles captured the minister of the interior on January 23 and held him hostage, demanding pay raises. Reluctantly Obote called for British aid and the mutiny was suppressed. The Uganda government bowed to the demands of the army and by midsummer most of the European officers had been replaced by Ugandans.

Tribal affairs throughout 1964 continued to disturb the political equilibrium of the state. In Toro, the Bwamba and Bakonjo who insisted on a separate district were attacked by Toro tribesmen. This forced a state of emergency to be proclaimed for the whole area. In August the government announced a referendum to determine the future of the two "lost counties" of western Uganda. Kabaka Yekka members walked out of the National Assembly and their coalition with Obote's UPC was dissolved on the issue. In November the voting took place and the people in the counties elected to return to the kingdom of Bunyoro.

Relations between the kabaka's party and the UPC were repaired in 1965 and Obote continued as prime minister. The major shocks to Obote in 1965 were the seizure of an arms shipment by Kenya and, toward the end of the year, charges of misappropriation of funds captured from Congolese rebels in 1964. Obote settled the former problem by a personal visit to Kenyatta where he apologized to the president of Kenya for the shipment through Kenya and promised that there would not be a recurrence of such activity. The second problem by the end of 1965 threatened to overthrow Obote since many of his own party were joining in criticism of their leader. The Kabaka Yekka and the small DP both demanded investigations of the supposed misappropriation of approximately one-third of a million dollars.

Thus the government of Uganda in practice was as unstable in December 1965 as it had been in theory since the adoption of the complex federal system. Tribalism had been enshrined into the constitution. With the kings of Buganda, Bunyoro, and Toro claiming exclusive privileges in certain areas, it is doubtful whether any politician would have been able to achieve more unity than Obote. Any increase in stability depended upon the outcome of the power struggle between Obote and the kabaka.

ZANZIBAR (SEE ALSO TANZANIA)

The islands of Zanzibar and Pemba, ruled by the sultan under British control until January 1964, had a population of one-third of a million persons, mostly African, although the traditional rulers were the minority Arabs who dominated politics. Much of the wealth of the state was controlled by Indians. Zanzibar was ruled in a dual manner in the first half of the twentieth century. Ostensibly the sultan ruled the country. However, the British protectorate officials effectively curtailed any significant independent action by the sultan. In 1914 control of the protectorate passed from the Foreign Office to the Colonial Office and in the next ten years the sultan's political agents were gradually replaced by British district officers.

In 1924 the theoretical limits of British authority in the protectorate were defined and two years later the sultan established the first executive and legislative councils. All members of the councils were appointed by the sultan. There were seventeen members of the Legislative Council of which eight were unofficials. The ethnic composition of this council—three Arabs, two Africans, two Asians, and one European—indicated the complex ethnic mix of the island. The next major political change occurring in Zanzibar was the 1944 reorganization of the Zanzibar Township Council. All members of the enlarged township council were nominated by the British resident. Membership on this council also reflected the complex mixture in Zanzibar. However, the Africans who have a majority of the population on the island did not receive a commensurate number of seats on any of the councils.

In the reorganization of government following World War II a significant difference of opinion developed between the Arab ruling class and the African majority over the ends to be achieved. The Arabs wanted a quick movement toward self-government while the Africans were more cautious, suspicious of their role in an Arab-dominated government. The British, therefore, proceeded very cautiously in their reforms. In 1956 they enlarged the executive and legislative councils. The Executive Council remained totally nominated, but in the twenty-six member Legislative Council, six of the twelve unofficial members were elected from a common roll.

Political parties in Zanzibar date from 1955 and were responses to mainland nationalistic moves and British reaction to them. The first party was the Zanzibar National party (ZNP) led by Sheikh Ali Muhsen and Abdul Muhammad (Babu). Although Arab-led, it attempted to appeal to all classes and was not originally a narrow Arab party. It stood for rapid constitutional advance toward self-government. In 1955 ZNP called for adult suffrage, a common roll, and all members of the Legislative Council to be elected. In 1957 as a result of the court's investigating commission, the new constitution was implemented and elections were held for six of the Legislative Council seats. The Afro-Shirazi party (ASP) was created to contest this election. The ASP, like the ZNP, was also a conglomerate party which attempted to win both Arab and African support although its leader, Abeid Aman Karume, appealed more to the uneducated, economically depressed Africans. At that time the major difference in the approach of the parties was the speed of approach to self-government since the ASP wanted a slower rate. The ASP won three seats to the Legislative Council in the elections. Two independents later allied themselves with the ASP. The popular voting showed approximately one-third of the voters opting for each party.

Attempts in 1958 to heal the growing breach between the parties were made by the Pan African Freedom Movement of East and Central Africa (PAFMECA). The moving force in this attempt was Julius Nyerere of Tanganyika. This conciliation failed because of the economic and social differences of the populations to which each party made its appeal. From this period onward Zanzibar became a focal point for outside influence from East Africa, the United Arab Republic, and the Chinese Republic. In December 1959, a split occurred in the ASP when Muhammad Shamte formed the Zanzibar Peoples' Party of Pemba (ZPPP). This party also was mostly African in membership and appealed to the African electorate.

Devolution of power by Britain to mainland African territories denied Britain the option of withholding further constitutional advance for Zanzibar, although after 1956 it was apparent that the African majority would no longer be satisfied with a subservient role under Arab leaders. British officials, in conjunction with African nationalists, formulated a new constitution which provided for a larger Legislative Council, a form of ministerial government, and granted the franchise to most Zanzibari. This constitution, issued in 1960, made it possible for the relatively new African-oriented parties to successfully challenge the Arabs for leadership. The Arab position was further weakened in 1960 by the death of Sultan Seyyid Sir Khalifa bin Harub who had ruled Zanzibar since 1911. The new sultan, Seyyid Abdullah, in turn died two years later. His successor, the young Seyyid Jamshid, was made sultan just before Zanzibar became a self-governing state and inherited all the problems of the Arab-African rivalry.

The new constitution, which went into effect in January 1961, provided for elections of twenty-two of the thirty Legislative Council seats. The election of January was very close. The ASP won ten seats, the ZNP nine, and the ZPPP three. Two of the ZPPP men supported ZNP and one the ASP, creating an eleven to eleven deadlock in the Legislative Council which necessitated new elections. In the second election, held in June, twenty-three seats were voted on. The ZNP and ZPPP agreed on constituencies to contest and the results were ASP ten, ZNP ten, and ZPPP three. The coalition ZNP-ZPPP formed a government and the ZPPP leader, Sheikh Shamite Homadi, became chief minister. The June elections were marked by extreme violence on election day with over sixty killed and nearly 1,000 wounded. This was the first major outbreak of racial violence between

African and Arab although the conditions which produced the riots had existed for a long time. A state of emergency was declared which lasted over a year and many important persons were arrested and jailed for their role in the disturbances. Abdul Muhammad, former secretary-general of the ZNP, was sentenced to fifteen months for sedition and eleven other persons of the ZNP were detained. The ZNP, despite being the government party, was very anti-British and was accused by many of being pro-Communist (Chinese). Certainly two of the major trade unions allied with the ZNP had been strongly influenced by the Chinese. In June 1963, Abdul Muhammad broke with the ZNP and became the dominant figure in the Red Chinese-oriented Umma party which was later banned.

Further constitutional advance toward self-government was delayed by the disturbances and the state of emergency. A constitutional conference in London, in March 1962, broke up because of nonagreement between the parties. Finally new constitutional instruments were devised and elections based upon universal adult suffrage were held in July 1963. The ZNP-ZPPP coalition won eighteen of the seats for the Legislative Council while the ASP gained only thirteen. The new government immediately asked Britain for independence. After a conference in September, the date for the independence of Zanzibar was set as December 10. Also on that date the sultan's authority over the coastal areas of Kenya would cease and these territories would come under the authority of the Kenya government.

On January 12, 1964, the Zanzibar army led by self-styled "Field Marshall" John Okello overthrew the one-month independent government of Zanzibar. After one week of rioting, more than 500 Zanzibaris, mostly Arabs, were dead and the Afro-Shirazi and Umma party leaders, Karume and Abdul Muhammad, gained control of the government. Okello was gradually eased out of power and in March, after a visit to the mainland, he was refused readmittance to Zanzibar. The ZNP leaders and the sultan were forced into exile.

Order in Zanzibar was restored largely because of the presence of 300 Tanganyika police loaned by President Nyerere to the new revolutionary government. Although Karume enunciated a moderate course for the government, he was not strong enough to keep his chief lieutenants, Abdul Muhammad and Kassim Hanga, from stating the hope of establishing a Communist regime for Zanzibar. Abdul Muhammad, the foreign minister, was pro-Communist, and Hanga, the vice-president, although less obvious, seemed to be committed to the same policies. Aside from the historic and economic connections with the coast, this drift to the left convinced President Nyerere of Tanganyika that something had to be done to negate potential extremism. In April 1964, Nyerere found President Karume amenable to a closer union. The discussions between Karume and Tanganyika officials resulted in a federation of the two states called the Union of Tanganyika and Zanzibar (Tanzania). In the new union, Julius Nyerere became president and Karume first vice-president. Details of these discussions and the subsequent federation are discussed more fully in the section dealing with Tanzania.

THREE

Postwar political developments: Belgian Africa

Belgian authorities, notwithstanding the political ferment else-where in Africa in the early 1950s, assumed that they would have time to carry out the Congo's development on an evolutionary basis. Thus, while Britain and France in colonial territories less economically viable than the Congo were granting the Africans political power, the Belgian authorities continued their white-dominated autocratic system. The first concessions to the Africans' demands for democracy came in the reforms of municipal government in 1957. Previously local government in the cities had been of a two-part type. One form was that of the native city (extra coutumiers) of the areas surrounding the large cities. The other was the government of the cities them-selves. In the native cities chiefs had been appointed by the central authorities to govern under Belgian direction. They were aided by appointive councils which the Belgians had planned to utilize at some future time as a base for extension of democracy. The cities proper had been administered directly by the Belgian authorities. In 1957 the *statut des Villes* abol-ished these distinctions in Léopoldville, Elizabethville, and Jadotville. The native cities were abolished in these areas. The cities were divided into communes each with its own elected council and mayor. These mayors were appointed from the candidates chosen by the electorate. In Léopoldville less than 50,000 persons out of a population of approximately 350.000 could qualify for the franchise. Election was from a com-mon roll.

The Belgians granted these minor reforms with consider-able reluctance after studying the long-range implications of such a move for almost ten years. The functional powers of the mayors and councils were quite limited. Further, a chief mayor was appointed by the central authorities to coordinate munici-pal government. Minor as these reforms were by comparison with those occurring in French and British Africa, they sig-naled a change in the direction of Belgian policy. The elections

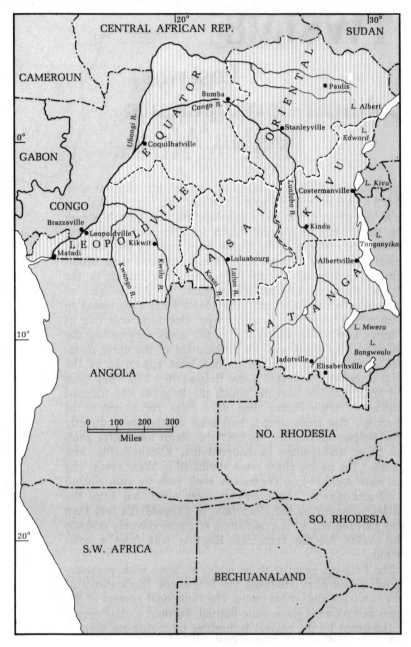

The Congo: Towns and Provinces, 1960

resulted in developing the first political parties which were not only based upon tribal affiliation but on their popularity in the urban centers.

In 1958 the government of Belgium underwent a series of changes which brought more liberal men to office. M. Leo Petillion, former governor-general of the Congo, became minister of colonies. He had long favored political changes in the Congo. Before any specific reforms were announced, Petillion was replaced by the even more liberal van Hemelrijck. In November 1958, the prime minister of Belgium, Mr. Eyskens, stated that a detailed declaration of Belgian reforms would be announced in January 1959. Before the reforms were announced, African political leaders such as Joseph Kasavubu of ABAKO made it clear that they wished no slow evolutionary change but quick independence. In early January, there were riots in Léopoldville which lasted several days and resulted in the deaths of over thirty Africans. Almost fifty Europeans were injured. These riots were triggered in part by the economic recession which had struck the Congo in early 1957. Many urban, partially detribalized Africans were without jobs and were receptive to the new propaganda calls by political leaders who blamed the Europeans and the government for these conditions. Although only a small portion of the population of Léopoldville took part in the riots, the effect upon the Belgian government was electric.

Both the king and the colonial ministers made immediate statements in which Congolese independence was promised. Although the Belgian government had decided before the riots to grant a large measure of self-government to the Congo, it appeared to the Africans that the riots had effected the change. The Belgian announcements of early 1959 resulted in the creation of new political parties and a growing political ferment throughout the Congo. Even though many Belgian officials believed that moderate reforms would suffice, African political leaders wanted a speedy advance to independence. The Belgian government adopted this point of view by late 1959 and the Congo state became independent in June 1960.

In the short period of three years after 1957, the Belgian Congo moved from a government almost totally controlled by the Belgians to complete independence. A nation as large as Europe, populated by diverse tribes actively hostile toward one another, the Congo had not been allowed to develop the proper institutional base for independence. There were few Congolese trained in the political skills of ruling such a heterogeneous state. Belgian policy before 1957 was not necessarily wrong if the Congo had been isolated from the rest of Africa, but it was not. The political advances of territories less economically developed than the Congo could not be hidden from the Congolese political leaders. The change from paternalism to fraternalism could not be achieved in a short period of time. Political education and maturity could not be legislated. When the Belgian semiautocratic regime removed itself from the Congo, the only force that had unified the Congo basin for seventy years was removed. The new Congo Republic had neither the prestige nor the experience to take the place of the old Belgian administration. Unlike British and French territories, the Belgians had not left behind an educated or trained political elite who could peacefully assume the roles of leadership. Thus the Congo, with one of the most advanced social, health, and economic systems, drifted into anarchy.

Devolution of power and consolidation of African rule

THE REPUBLIC OF THE CONGO

Events in the politically quiescent Congo moved with such rapidity and such confusion after 1959 that it is nearly impossible to synthesize them. Belgian policy after 1909 had been based primarily upon the economic interdependence of the Congo and Belgium. The central government, represented in the Congo by the governor-general and the administrative staff, sought to improve living and working conditions for the urban African and protect the rural African from undue exploitation either by Europeans or other hostile tribes. The political system was autocratic and paternalistic and at its best was geared to bringing the African into the government by a slow evolutionary process. As late as the mid-1950s, Belgian authorities had only begun to formulate plans for sharing political power with the urbanized African on the lowest levels of government.

Notwithstanding the economic development of the Congo, the pursuance of a policy of slow evolution kept the Congo politically infantile. The government discouraged higher education for Africans, did not employ them in positions of responsibility in government, and had not by the mid-1950s established a workable framework whereby peaceful transition of power from Europeans to Africans could be effected. The paternalistic Belgian regime had done little to break down tribal differences and hostilities. The reality of the Congo on the eve of independence was not an embryo nation-state but a collection of hostile tribal entities held together by an efficient Belgian administration.

Within a distressingly short period of time Belgian policy was completely reversed. The right of self-determination and the representative principle were admitted and the Congo embarked upon independence without any of the necessary preludes to self-government. All of the political parties of the Congo were formed during this period to take advantage of the weakening position of the Belgian government. These parties tended to represent tribal and regional loyalties and usually were dominated by one man.

The first major political party in the Congo, the *Association des Bakongo pour le maintien l'Unité et l'Expansion et la Défense de Langue Kikongo* (ABAKO), was originally a cultural association of the Bakongo people. Founded in 1950, it had become by 1956 a party in all but name. Joseph Kasavubu became president of the ABAKO, dedicated not to Congo independence but the unification of all the Bakongo people in the Congo, Angola, and Rhodesia.

The other major parties came into being after the Belgian government had granted a measure of political reform. In December 1957, democratic elections were held for the first time for the major urban councils. The ABAKO based its power not only on the Bakongo but also on its strength in Léopoldville. Emboldened by the changed attitudes, a number of the *evolués* addressed demands for more political power leading to independence. These demands were backed by political agitation in the cities and the countryside. The threat of violence spread throughout the Congo in 1958. Patrice Lumumba, president of the African Staff Association in Stanleyville, requested eventual independence from the Belgian government in August. Similar demands and agitation came from every one of the provinces of the Congo. The visit of Charles de Gaulle to Brazzaville in August and the announcement of the large measure of self-government which was to be granted to the French Congo speeded up political agitation in the Belgian Congo and the formation of new political groups.

In October 1958, the *Mouvement National Congolais* (MNC) was created by Patrice Lumumba and had its centrum of power in Stanleyville. The MNC soon became the only party to stand for a unitary Congolese state. Its objectives were to promote unity throughout the Congo, combat tribalism, and prepare the masses for eventual control. Branches of the MNC were soon established throughout the Congo.

By 1959 the major African personalities in the Congo began to emerge. Kasavubu and the ABAKO openly advocated separatism or as an alternative a loose federation. Lumumba and the MNC opposed any breakup of the Congo and called instead for the speedy end of Belgian control and the establishment of a strong central government. In January 1959, Lumumba, recently returned from the Accra Conference, addressed a number of large meetings in Léopoldville. Disturbances in the cities grew more commonplace. A march of the unemployed in Léopoldville brought about only one of many clashes with the Belgian government. Kasavubu was briefly arrested and the ABAKO banned. These and other punitive measures were not successful. The Belgian government then decided to compromise and promised immediate and long-term reforms with the possibility of territorial communal elections for December 1959. Instead of carrying through on these elections, the government announced that a round table discussion between the various political factions and the government would be convened in Brussels in January 1960. To present a united front, the major Congolese parties in December 1959 formed the short-lived ABAKO-Cartel. The most important parties in this grouping were the ABAKO, the MNC, a MNC breakaway group in the Kasai headed by Albert Kalonji, and the *Parti Solidaire Africaine* (PSA) of Antoine Gizenga.

Although the round table conference was stormy, it was the basis on which the Belgian government built the *loi fondamentale* which established the structure for the future independent Congo state. The *loi fondamentale* established a bicameral central legislature. The 137 member Chamber of Deputies was to be elected by universal male suffrage. An eighty-four member upper house, or Senate, was to be selected by the provincial assemblies. There was to be a president as titular head of state, but the real conduct of central policy was left to a premier and a cabinet responsible to the legislature. Although the *loi* endorsed the principle of the supremacy of the central government, it nevertheless provided for six provincial legislatures and provincial ministries. The six provinces were Léopoldville, Kasai, Katanga, Kivu, Oriental, and Equator. The system was quite complex and the balance between central and provincial government would have been hard to maintain even with a more sophisticated polity. The conference set June 30, 1960 as the date for Congolese independence.

In the Katanga the *Confédération des Associations du Katanga* (CONAKAT) had been formed in July 1959, headed by Moise Tshombe. This was a political party which based its popularity and later its power upon the Lunda people. A rival organization, the BALUBAKAT, headed by Jason Sandwe, had been formed which reflected the desires of the Baluba tribe. The major party in Equator Province was the *Parti de l'Unité Nationale* (PUNA) led by Jean Bolikango. Thus by the time of the elections of May 1960, there had been created in the space of three years a great number of political parties which, with the exception of the MNC, reflected only tribal and regional loyalties.

The elections held in May 1960 were for both the central and provincial legislatures. The MNC won forty-one of the 137 seats in the Chamber of Deputies and was the only party to show strength throughout the Congo. Gizenga's PSA won thirteen seats, the ABAKO twelve, and CONAKAT eight. The MNC was also the strongest party in the Senate, holding twenty-two of the eighty-four seats. However, ABAKO dominated the provincial elections in Léopoldville Province winning thirty-three of the ninety seats in the legislature. Together with ABAKO's allies, they controlled the province. In the Katanga, CONAKAT, despite Tshombe's later claims, did not have universal support. His party held twenty-five of the sixty seats in the provincial legislature and only with the aid of smaller groupings was he able to overcome the BALUBAKAT.

The Belgian government did nothing for its image by first ignoring Lumumba's support and asking Kasavubu to form a government. He could not get the requisite parliamentary support and Lumumba was reluctantly called upon to form the government on June 24. On the same day Kasavubu was elected president of the Republic. King Baudouin I of Belgium, at ceremonies conducted in Léopoldville, proclaimed Congolese independence six days later. The newly formed entente between ABAKO and the MNC was short-lived because of the mutiny of the Congolese *Force Publique* against their Belgian officers in June 1960. A series of clashes between these rebellious forces and Belgian civilians brought Belgian troops to the Congo to protect their nationals, and the wholesale evacuation of Belgians from the Congo was begun. This exodus left the government, educational, medical, and social departments without the necessary trained personnel to carry out the ordinary services. The state of confusion bordering on chaos which followed forced Lumumba to call upon United Nations assistance to maintain control over the Republic.

On July 15, the first United Nations caretaker troops landed. By December 1 there were over 19,000 United Nations soldiers in the country.

In the months that followed the rebellion of the Force Publique, government in the Congo became fragmented with many provincial political leaders acting independently of the central authority. In July 1960, Tshombe declared the Katanga independent, and in August he was elected head of state by the Katanga legislature. Kasavubu gradually moved back to his federalist position and in September attempted to dismiss Lumumba from office and replace him with Joseph Ileo of the MNC-Kalonji. Lumumba in turn tried to oust Kasavubu from the presidency. The Senate overthrew both dismissals. On September 15, Colonel Joseph Mobutu of the Congolese army seized power in Léopoldville, suspended both Lumumba and Kasavubu, and dismissed parliament. This confused situation in Léopoldville caused Antoine Gizenga of the PSA, who had previously reached an understanding with Lumumba, to flee to Stanleyville. There he formed a provisional government which gradually extended its control over the provinces of Oriental, Kivu, and Northern Kasai. Albert Kalonji, a Baluba chief and opponent of Lumumba, had previously formed a new state in southern Kasai.

In late September, Mobutu had reached an agreement with Kasavubu and appointed a nonpolitical caretaker government ostensibly led by Ileo. Lumumba was a virtual prisoner within his quarters, protected only by United Nations guards. Lumumba, the legal functional head of the state whose armed forces had not been successful against the breakaway regime and who felt impotent in Léopoldville, accused the United Nations of refusing to support him and acting as agents of his enemies. Ordered to act only defensively and to be neutral toward the factions, the United Nations forces, because of their inaction, did enable Kasavubu and Mobutu to effectively destroy the constitution. Lumumba, afraid for his safety, attempted to join Gizenga in Stanleyville and was arrested by Mobutu's troops on December 2. On January 18, 1961, Lumumba was transferred as a prisoner to Elizabethville in the Katanga. There under circumstances not yet totally known, he was murdered on February 13. It is known, however, that although a Belgian mercenary was the executioner, Tshombe and Kasavubu were deeply implicated in his death. Despite the United Nations' presumed neutrality, they had, in contravention of the loi fondamentale, recognized Kasavubu as head of the Congolese state in November 1960.

The United Nations, following a theoretically defensive course of action, called off a threatened invasion of the Katanga in August 1960. The central government under Kasavubu arrived at a surface rapprochement with Kalonji in the Kasai in February 1961. In March a meeting of all Congolese parties was convened in Tananarive, Madagascar. There a basic agreement was reached for a federal-type state. At a further conference in April at Coquilhatville, Tshombe, however, disagreed on the integration plans and left the meeting. He was arrested by the central authorities who immediately announced he would be tried for his crimes. He was, however, released after signing an eleven-point agreement which would have provided for a national Congolese parliament and a federal system. This agreement was repudiated in July 1961 by the Katanga legislature.

Discussions between the central government, the United Nations, and Gizenga's breakaway regime in Stanleyville went on through the summer of 1961. In August Gizenga dissolved his regime and the Congo National Convention was reconvened. A government of national unity was created and Cyrille Adoula was named as the compromise premier in the same month. Adoula had at first been associated with the MNC and later with the Kalonji group, as well as being one of the chief organizers of the *Union Féderation Générale des Travailleurs du Kongo* (FGTK). In the election of May 1960, he had affiliated himself with the PUNA of Equator Province. Antoine Gizenga was associated with Adoula in the government reorganization of late 1961 as first deputy premier. However, Gizenga refused to leave Stanleyville. He had formed a new party there called the *Parti National du Patrice Lumumba*. Two other deputy premiers in the central government were Jean Balikongo of PUNA and Jason Sandwe of the BALUBAKAT. Adoula reduced the size of the unwieldy forty-three member cabinet by nearly half. The new central government survived a shaky beginning which included a near parliamentary defeat in November 1961.

Nevertheless, the Adoula government backed by the United Nations began to take more effective measures to reunify the Congo. The major focus of their efforts was the Katanga. On September 13, 1961, United Nations' military forces attempted to seize Katanga. Tshombe's mercenary forces held them back and a cease fire was arranged on September 20. Again in early November the Congolese forces under Mobutu failed in their military attempt on Katanga. On November 24, the United Nations General Assembly passed a new resolution authorizing the use of force to unify the Congo, and the United Nations launched a general attack on the Katanga on December 5. With Elizabethville surrounded, Tshombe agreed to a conference with Adoula. At Kitona on December 19, Tshombe accepted an eight-point program which would end the Katanga secession and bring the province once again under central authority. Despite these assurances, it was not until February 16, 1962 that the Katanga Assembly accepted the Kitona agreement.

At the same time political and military pressure was exerted on the schismatic regime of the South Kasai. On January 3, 1962, Albert Kalonji was arrested and imprisoned. Antoine Gizenga was also ordered to leave Stanleyville and come to Léopoldville to face charges. Brief fighting occurred between central forces and Gizenga's followers, and Gizenga surrendered. A vote of censure in the Chamber of Deputies was passed, and on January 16, 1962, he was dismissed as deputy premier and arrested. The Katanga, however, was not yet pacified. Details of reunification of the Katanga had not been covered at Kitona, and Adoula and Tshombe met from March 18 to April 17, and May 22 to June 26, to discuss these problems. They represented two extreme positions, particularly with regard to the financial obligations of Katanga to the central government.

When no agreement was reached by August, Adoula attempted to cut off Katanga from the outside world. A compromise financial scheme submitted by the United Nations in August 1962 for sharing revenues was accepted by the central government but not by Tshombe. The total achievement of this one year of discussion was almost nil and military action against Katanga was resumed in December 1962. By December 31, Congo and United Nations forces held all the important centers of Katanga. Tshombe at first fled to Rhodesia but returned to proclaim, on January 15, 1963, the end of Katanga's secession. Soon afterward Tshombe fled the Congo.

By August 16, 1962, President Kasavubu had promulgated laws which created sixteen new provinces out of the six old provinces. Although these measures reduced immediate friction between rival tribes, they were a further concession to federalism and tribalism. On October 16, Adoula introduced a new constitution which gave the provincial governments great autonomy in local affairs while still reserving the most important functions for the central authority.

After January 1963, peace, imposed by the United Nations forces and the Congolese army, had returned to the Congo. All the major factional leaders had either been imprisoned, were dead, in exile, or working for the government. Lumumba was dead, Tshombe and Kalonji in exile, Gizenga in prison, while Kasavubu, Adoula, and Sandwe were in power. The political parties with their schismatic differences were still the major channels of political power. The unity of the Congo was a forced one created by the central government through its control of the *Army Congolaise National* (ANC) and its ability to call upon the United Nations forces in case of trouble.

During 1963 Adoula's government concerned itself with the economic as well as the political situation. The government was impoverished. The rich mines of the Katanga and Kasai had produced little revenue for the central government. The two years of civil war had disrupted trade, destroyed railroads and bridges. The Congo was solvent only because of United Nations' funds. Although not able to completely restore financial stability, the Congo under Adoula was by 1964 moving toward a restoration of order. The United Nations and the United States spent large sums to improve the quality of arms and training for the ANC. The political nature of the Congo, however, remained chaotic, and this threatened any gains made by the new government. In addition to the major parties such as CONAKAT, BALUBAKAT, ABAKO, MNC, and PSA, there were dozens of small splinter groups representing totally local and parochial viewpoints. Later in 1963, a number of exiles in Brazzaville formed the *Comité du Libération National* (CLN) pledged to the overthrow of the Adoula government. Later elements of the CLN were also based in Usumbura. Chief among the leaders of the CLN were Andre Lubaya, Christopher Gbenye, and Emile Soumialot.

Leaders of the major parties within the government attempted to counteract the splinter tendency by trying to organize larger nationwide political parties. A meeting of some fifty political groups in August 1963 resulted in the formation of a new party, the *Rassemblement Démocratique Congolaise* (RADECO). In early 1964, Premier Adoula became the president of RADECO. Another attempt at a national grouping was the formation of the *Comité Démocratique Africaine* in June 1964. This was another alliance of local groups including Kasavubu's ABAKO and the PSA-Kamitatu, a splinter of Gizenga's PSA. A most important grouping was the ABC alliance in the Katanga. This was composed of the former enemy parties of the BALUBAKAT and CONAKAT with the Tshakwe Association of Congo and the Rhodesias (AKTAT).

To work out a more satisfactory and stable government system, President Kasavubu in late 1963 appointed a 120 member constitutional commission. This group headed by Joseph Ileo had made little progress by the spring of 1964. The government, as well as all factions, were aware that June 30, 1964 would be one of the most crucial dates in Congolese history because the United Nations had previously announced the withdrawal of all their troops by that date. The new constitution had to be finished by then and the ANC prepared to take over the full responsibility for policing the state.

The first of a new series of disturbances began in Kwilu Province in December 1963. The leader of the uprising was Pierre Mulele, former minister of the interior in the Lumumba government. He had spent years in Communist areas absorbing details of guerrilla warfare. Returning to the Congo, he organized his guerrilla bands, called the *Jeunesse,* on the model of those in Southeast Asia. In Kwilu he found the native population hostile to the central government and willing to support his irregulars. Although the government announced, in late January 1964, that the area was pacified, this was far from the case. The *Jeunesse* controlled most of Kwilu. The guerrillas believed they were immune from the bullets of the ANC. The ANC seemed to believe it also. By March 1964, central Kivu was also affected. It is doubtful that Mulele was directly responsible for this outbreak, but certainly his success in Kwilu served as a good example. The fighting in Kivu was led partially by the CLN based in Burundi. Another faction in the disturbances in Kivu were the Bafulero pygmies led by Moussa Maranduru. Although better equipped, the ANC proved no match for the insurgents. Many regular soldiers feared the magic of their opponents. Time after time patrols of the ANC, numerically superior, threw away their weapons and fled. Even the appearance and personal bravery of General Mobutu served only as a palliative. To add to the confusion, a three-day riot ripped Albertville in northern Katanga. The ANC was spread so thin that, even if its troops had been more disciplined, the situation would have been critical. By June the United Nations had only 2,000 troops remaining in the Congo and these left on the appointed date.

Adoula's government was being torn to pieces. He no longer could command the allegiance of any but a few high government officials. There was no parliament since President Kasavubu had suspended it in March, probably because it was impossible to gain a quorum of the necessary forty out of a total of 137 elected members. Rumors were that approximately forty members of parliament were in the interior and fifteen had joined the CLN. Late in June 1964, Tshombe and Kalonji were allowed to return to the Congo. Premier Adoula submitted his resignation on June 30 but was persuaded by Kasavubu to remain the head of a caretaker regime. Kasavubu then asked Tshombe to sound out political leaders to see if he could gain their support to form a new government. In early July, Tshombe, who only eighteen months previously had been the chief secessionist, became the premier of the Congo. He freed Antoine Gizenga from his two and one-half year imprisonment on the island of Balambemba and included in his ministry many of his old enemies. In this government of "public salvation," President Kasavubu retained the ministry of defense; Tshombe was premier, minister of trade, and minister of foreign affairs; Albert Kalonji was minister of agriculture; Andre Lubaya was minister of health; and Tshombe's old confederate, Godefroid Munongo, became minister of the interior.

Tshombe claimed that within three months he would put down the uprisings and secure a stable Congo. However, he was hardly in office when a new threat to the state appeared. A "Popular Army of Liberation" guided by one of the CLN leaders, Emile Soumialot, aimed at capturing Stanleyville. Although the second largest city in the Congo was protected by almost 1,000 ANC, the ill-equipped rebel force inspired such fear that most of the ANC fled and Stanleyville fell to Soumialot's forces. Soumialot was soon replaced as head of the Stanleyville regime by Christopher Gbenye who established a rival government which he called the Peoples Republic of the Congo.

Tshombe's position was extremely critical. Rebels controlled Albertville and Bukavu in the east and most of the territory from Kongolo northward along the Congo River to Stanleyville. The ANC, although well-equipped, would fight only in rare instances. Tshombe turned to two sources for aid. His appeal for more material from the United States was soon met by a quantity of aircraft and technical advisers. His attempt to secure aid from the OAU, however, showed that other African states were more consumed with hate for Tshombe and his past actions than with the future of the Congo. In September 1964, he addressed the foreign ministers' meeting of the OAU at Addis Ababa detailing the Congo's position and asking for aid. He wanted African states to provide troops to police-pacified areas so that the bulk of the ANC could be thrown against the rebels. This help would thus enable him to dispense with mercenary soldiers. The foreign ministers rejected his request for troops. In October Tshombe flew to Cairo to lay his case before the heads of state of the OAU. He was not given a hearing but was held prisoner in a Cairo hotel before being deported. Thus Tshombe was thrown back on his own resources, knowing that he would receive no help from other African states. The only concrete action taken by the OAU was to establish a committee headed by Jomo Kenyatta to work for a mediation of differences in the Congo.

Tshombe's decision to use white mercenaries as a spearhead for his armies had been one of the reasons for his reception in Cairo. However, the 400 mercenaries from Europe, Rhodesia, and South Africa were the main reason why the Congo did not collapse. Used as shock troops, they drove the rebels out of town after town. The ANC following behind began to regain some confidence. By November, Bakavu and Albertville had been recaptured. Meanwhile, Gbenye at Stanleyville had seized all Europeans in the area and held them as a pledge for the safety of his regime and the withdrawal of the mercenaries. Daily the position of the Europeans became more desperate. From a moderately harsh position toward them, Gbenye drifted to one which threatened their lives as his military situation worsened. This situation brought forth further European intervention in the form of Belgian paratroopers flown in by planes supplied by the United States. This drop was coordinated with a flying column of mercenaries and ANC from Kindu. Stanleyville was taken, but only after approximately one hundred European hostages were killed by Gbenye's militant followers who had been given the name "simbas." The majority of the 1,000 Europeans in the district were safely evacuated. Gbenye, Olenga, Soumialot, and the other rebel leaders fled to the Sudan. However, when the Belgian troops were withdrawn, rebel soldiers returned and the northern area was far from secure for Tshombe. Confusion was compounded in Stanleyville by the outbreak of a typhoid epidemic in December. The Belgian intervention was condemned by most African states and a full-scale discussion of the Congo was conducted in the United Nations. It is obvious that the Stanleyville affair did not enhance Tshombe's position in Africa.

Tshombe protested to the Security Council of the United Nations the actions of certain African states giving aid to the rebels. Specifically, Burundi and the Sudan were named as areas being used as both a staging ground and training area for the rebel forces. Tshombe gave evidence that Algerian officers were training guerrillas and that Egypt, Ghana, and Algeria had all sent arms to the rebels through the Sudan. The Security Council was content to call for a general cease fire.

By mid-December mercenary and ANC units had rescued over 600 Europeans caught in the midst of the fighting. During early January 1965, over 200 hostages were killed by the hard-pressed "simbas" in the northeastern regions. Over one hundred hostages were still held in June in the Buta region north of Stanleyville after the majority were rescued by Congolese and mercenary forces. The revived ANC and the mercenaries continued their operations in disaffected areas throughout 1965. A major operation was that against Fizi in the mountains near Lake Tanganyika in September and October. The rebels were never able to seriously challenge Tshombe's government after January 1965. Support from the Sudan, Burundi, and other states sympathetic to the rebels slackened. The leaders of the revolt were killed or forced into exile. Gbenye and others were eventually expelled from their sanctuary in Egypt. At the end of 1965, the Congo had been pacified. By June 1965, most of the states of the OAU had reconsidered their previous positions and had accepted Tshombe's regime as the legal government of the Congo.

While world attention was rightly focused upon the efforts of the central government to restore stability, there had been a considerable constitutional change. In July 1964, a new, more simplified, constitution was adopted by referendum. All males over eighteen years of age were made eligible to vote for the members of the National Assembly and members of one of the twenty-one provincial legislatures. The lower house was to have 166 seats with one deputy elected to represent approximately 100,000 persons. Each provincial legislature chose six persons for the upper house or federal Senate. The executive continued to be responsible, depending upon the support of the house. In October 1964, the minister of the interior, M. Munungo, announced that general elections under the new instruments would be held in early 1965. Therefore it became doubly imperative that order be restored to the Congo before these elections.

The elections were held from the middle of March through April 30, 1965. The size of the Congo, the multiplicity of parties, and the number of candidates involved made the elections seem chaotic. There was voting for the National Assembly and for provincial representatives as well. There were sixty separate lists of candidates for office and over 230 parties represented. So complicated did the process become that in places the election had to be postponed to a date later than scheduled. As an example, the elections in Léopoldville originally scheduled to begin on March 25 were postponed until April 25.

The major political groupings involved in the elections were the ABAKO of Kasavubu and the Convention Nationale Congolaise (CONACO) led by Tshombe. CONACO was a coalition between the Katanga-based CONAKAT and some fifty smaller political parties. The MNC-Lumumba, once so powerful, was not an important factor in the election. It was allied with other Lumumbist-oriented parties such as the Parti Lumumbiste Unité (PALU) created by Gizenga in August 1964. Other important smaller parties were the PSA-Kamitatu which had some strength in Kwilu, the Union Démocratique du Congo also in Kwilu, and the BALUBAKAT and FRONKAT, anti-Tshombe parties in northern Katanga.

Tshombe's CONACO emerged from the election as the most important political force in the National Assembly. However, due to the many parties involved, it did not have a majority. President Kasavubu, obviously concerned with Tshombe's success and popularity, decided to act to minimize Tshombe's influence in the months before the presidential elections. Between May and October there developed a definite power struggle between the two men. In October Kasavubu dismissed Tshombe and his ministry, declaring that the tasks assigned in 1964 had been completed and, therefore, Tshombe was no longer needed. Kasavubu called upon Evareste Kimba, one-time foreign minister of the secessionist Katanga, to form a government. Tshombe, looking toward the presidential elections in February 1966, chose to become leader of the parliamentary opposition.

In October and November 1965, there were obvious signs of an active anti-Tshombe campaign. Kasavubu restored relations with Congo-Brazzaville, made definite contacts with Ghana, and promised to get rid of the mercenary forces. The chief of police forces, Nendaka, had begun to supervise pro-Tshombe newspapers. The growing rancor between Kasavubu and Tshombe decided General Mobutu in late November to act to end the power struggle which threatened a further civil war.

General Mobutu and the army forced Kasavubu's resignation as president and guaranteed him instead a permanent seat in the Senate. The Kimba ministry resigned to be replaced by a "government of National Union" with one minister for each of the twenty-one provinces. To head this ministry, Mobutu called upon the most able of the army combat officers, Colonel Leonard Mulamba, who had been serving as the military governor of northeastern Congo. Kasavubu, Tshombe, Kimba, and their adherents, at least outwardly, welcomed the military regime.

RUANDA–URUNDI

These two small mountainous territories were originally a part of German East Africa. After World War I, they were detached from Tanganyika and became separate League of Nations mandates administered by Belgium as a portion of the Congo. The size of each territory was slightly over 10,000 square miles and they had a combined population of almost 6,000,000. The population concentration in these territories was one of the highest in Africa. Although the land available for cultivation was better than in surrounding territories, the pressure of population combined with the ultraconservative political system made the territories poor. The Bahutu, a Bantu agricultural people, comprised over eighty percent of the population of each area. The politically dominant people, however, were the tall, aristocratic, Nilotic Watutsi. The Watutsi owned the cattle, the most obvious source of wealth. In addition, they were the traditional rulers of Ruanda and Urundi. The Watutsi had kept as their servants and workers the Batwa pygmies who comprised about one percent of the population.

The Belgians, as had the Germans before them, did little to upset the aristocratic, feudal system dominated by the Watutsi. The supreme rulers in each territory were the bami (singular mwami) who were advised by appointive aristocratic councils. Below the bami were the chiefs and subchiefs, each with their own appointive advisory councils. Belgian administration was superimposed over this system and until 1956 did not attempt to modify the almost total control of the Watutsi aristocracy over the territories. The chief Belgian administrative authority was the vicegovernor general of Ruanda-Urundi who was assisted by a totally appointed general council and secretariat. In the countryside, Belgian authority was represented by district officers who made certain that Belgian regulations were carried out. However, they normally left local administration in the hands of the Watutsi overlords. There was only one part of Ruanda-Urundi that was a *centre extra-coutumier*. This was the capital, Usumbura, which had a population of approximately 40,000.

Beginning in 1949, the Belgians utilized Ruanda-Urundi for elections which could serve as tests for possible application to the rest of the Congo. The elections held in 1949, 1951, and 1953 were actually only tests of the preferences of the population for the advisers to the Belgian local officials. The power of appointment was still retained by the Belgians. In 1956 Belgium devised an extremely complex system of direct and indirect elections for all the councils of the territories from the clan councils up through the African councils which advised the bami. The members of the African councils chose the native representatives who sat with the Belgian officials on the general council of the territories. All of these councils remained advisory with no legislative power of their own. However, the general council was empowered to examine the budget and make recommendations.

All of the changes in administrative procedure made by Belgium through 1959 were in keeping with their concept of gradualism. They had been careful not to disturb the traditional pattern of rule and their support of the Watutsi rulers. However, events in the Congo impelled them to apply new approaches in Ruanda-Urundi. They had been too inflexible in recognizing public opinion in the Congo. Thus in Ruanda-Urundi they attempted a new approach by recognizing the aspirations of the Bahutu masses. This was as much a reversal of previous policy as was their actions in the Congo. In Ruanda, particularly, this quick change of attitude did not foster continued Belgian power but rather contributed to a violent upheaval which destroyed not only Watutsi influence but also Belgian control.

RWANDA (RUANDA)

Before 1959 the Watutsi had favored a quick advance toward independence because they were positive that their domination would continue as before. In this period the Bahutu looked upon the Belgian rule as a protection which mitigated the harshness of their Watutsi overlords. In June 1959, mwami Charles Rudahigwa died suddenly. The chief council of Rwanda, fearing that the nationalism rampant in the Congo would spread into Rwanda and take advantage of the vacuum of power, quickly appointed the dead mwami's half-brother, Kigeri, as the new mwami. This action increased the now politically awakened Bahutu's fears, and some Bahutu began to plunder the villages of the Watutsi. Over one hundred persons were killed in late October and the Belgians sent in Congolese army units and paratroops to restore order. Instead of supporting the new mwami and the Watutsi, the Belgian government, reflecting their general Congolese policy, shifted to support the Bahutu and their new political party, the *Association pour la promotion des Masses* (APROSOMA). On November 10 the Brussels government announced plans to create constitutional monarchies in the two trust territories and end their dependence upon the government of the Congo. Popular elections were promised for an enlarged legislature within six months. A United Nations mission recommended in early 1960 a round table conference of all factions which would lead to elections and a speedy independence. The round table conference was never called and the Belgian authorities continued with their own plans. The election for a provisional legislature was held in July 1960.

APROSOMA and the newly formed *Parti d'Emancipation des Hutus* (PARMEHUTU) gained eighty-four percent of the votes, and the old order in Rwanda was broken. Violence between the two peoples was endemic throughout 1960.

In January 1961, Belgium, without prior consultation with the United Nations, concurred with the Rwanda parties in declaring the state independent. The provisional legislature, elected in July 1960, declared itself a parliament. Mwami Kigeri V was formally deposed and the state declared a republic. The first appointed president was Dominque Mbonyemuta, the leader of PARMEHUTU. Gregoire Kayibanda was declared premier. With Belgian aid, the machinery of government was reorganized. All of these actions were taken without consulting the Watutsi. The United Nations was presented with a dilemma. It was on record favoring independence, but the methods of achieving it was not in accord with their concepts. A United Nations investigating commission reported in March 1961 that Belgium was attempting to establish a pro-Belgian government in open defiance of the United Nations. In April the United Nations General Assembly called for new elections under United Nations control for broadly based caretaker governments in both Rwanda and Burundi. They also demanded a referendum to decide whether the mwami of Rwanda should retain his office.

The United Nations-supervised elections were held in September 1961, after a summer of constant violence. Over 300 deaths were reported in July and August. Many Watutsi fled to Burundi or took refuge at the Christian mission stations. Under such conditions it was not surprising that the referendum showed the people definitely opposed to the return of the mwami. The proposed constitution called for a forty-four member legislative committee elected by direct suffrage and for a presidential-type executive. The PARMEHUTU won thirty-five of the seats and Kayibanda became president. During all these political changes Belgium still held executive responsibility under the United Nations. Not until July 1962 did Rwanda become totally independent of outside control.

The quick reversal of power from the Watutsi to the Bahutu had caused considerable violence. Many Watutsi expected after independence to be slaughtered by the now dominant Bahutu. The excesses of July and August and the expectation of more violence caused almost 100,000 Watutsi to flee the country. It is alleged that from their places of refuge in Tanzania, Burundi, and Uganda, these displaced Watutsi continually raided Bahutu farms and villages in Rwanda. In the week before Christmas 1963, thousands of Watutsi crossed the frontier, and some of these armed bands advanced to within a few miles of the Rwanda capital of Kigale. They were repulsed by the regular Rwanda army, and then the Bahutu began a process of slaughtering the Watutsi. The Rwanda government was not directly implicated in the massacres that followed, but the statements by government officials indicated sympathy with the Bahutu terror. No accurate figures exist for the numbers of Watutsi killed during this period, but estimates vary between 10,000 and 15,000 with some 6,000 in the

Kigene district alone. The disorders culminating in these massacres spelled an end to any hope of reconciling the Bahutu and Watutsi to a coalition government similar to that of Burundi.

In June 1964, the army was forced to meet another threat to the sovereignty of the small state. The disorders then current in the eastern Congo almost spilled over into Rwanda. Elements of the rebel forces, intent on capturing Bukavu in the eastern Congo, attempted an invasion through Rwanda. They were met by the army at the Ruzzi River, defeated, and forced to turn back. Although there were sporadic raids in 1965, the year was relatively peaceful since the Congolese government threatened to expel the Watutsi refugees if they did not cease agitating against Rwanda. Disorders in neighboring Burundi occupied the attention of the dominant Watutsi group there. However, the situation was complicated by large numbers of Bahutu refugees who fled Burundi for the safety of the Bantu government of President Kayibanda.

The endemic violence between the Bahutu and Watutsi in Rwanda was made worse by the potentiality of armed conflict with neighboring unstable Burundi. After October 1965, when a revolt of Bahutus within the Burundi army was crushed, the pro-Watutsi group within the government was even more active in supporting plans for an overthrow of the Bahutu government of Rwanda.

BURUNDI (URUNDI)

Although conditions in Burundi since 1959 were similar to those in Rwanda, there were slight differences and these differences were responsible for the separate political development of Burundi. The Bahutu made up approximately eighty-seven percent of the population and were ruled by a Watutsi mwami. However, the traditional rule of the mwami of Burundi was never as centralized as in Rwanda. There was better rapport between the Bahutu and Watutsi. Most important, there was no event similar to the death of the mwami of Rwanda that could be immediately seized upon by the Belgians to change radically the traditional system. Lacking such an opportunity, early political development in Burundi followed a more standard, orderly course. Under the tutelage of the United Nations and Belgium, the once autocratic regime was transformed into a constitutional monarchy. The constitution created in the summer of 1961 established a National Assembly of sixty-four members, a crown council to advise the mwami, and a premier exercising executive authority dependent upon the support of the legislature. One of the key factors in the early relative stability of Burundi was the mwami, Mwambutsa IV, who, even under the revised constitution, still retained a strong residue of power.

The major political party in Burundi was the *Parti de l'Unité et du Progrès National du Burundi* (UPRONA). It was conservative and had the support of both Bahutu and Watutsi chiefs. In the elections of September 18, 1961, arranged by the United Nations and Belgium, UPRONA won fifty-eight of the sixty-four seats. There was also a smaller political party, the *Parti Démocratique Chrétienne* (PDC), but it never became a major factor in the government. The first premier chosen was Louis Rwangasore, son of the mwami. Despite the orderly development of self-rule, violence did not pass Burundi completely by since Rwangasore was assassinated on October 13, 1961. He was succeeded by his brother-in-law, André Muhirwa. The United Nations General Assembly voted ninety-three to zero on June 27 to approve independence for the two trust territories and Burundi became an independent state on July 1, 1962. Muhirwa remained premier until June 1963, when he was forced to resign by a vote of censure by the Assembly which charged him with attempting to assume dictatorial powers by ordering the arrest of the president of the Assembly. His successor, Pierre N'Gendandumwe, was a Bahutu.

The major question which agitated the government in early 1964 was that of the revolt in the Congo and the attitude which the government should assume toward the Red Chinese who had opened an embassy at the capital Bujumbura (Usumbura) in January. This question more than any other issue caused the resignation of pro-Western N'Gendandumwe in March. He was replaced as prime minister by Albin Nyamoya who adopted a most compliant attitude toward the activities of the Chinese. During 1964 Bujumbura was the main focal point for aid to the rebel forces operating in the eastern Congo. Chinese money had made a deep impact on members of the Burundi government and the National Assembly. The mwami finally became so concerned that Nyamoya was dismissed and N'Gendandumwe was returned as prime minister on January 8, 1965. On January 15, 1965, Prime Minister N'Gendandumwe was assassinated on the steps of the hospital in Bujumbura. The assassin was a Watutsi, and it appeared that his action was motivated more by tribal hatred than concern with cold-war issues. Former Prime Minister Nyamoya, a Watutsi, and twenty-three other Watutsi tribesmen were arrested as accomplices. Joseph Bamina, a moderate in domestic affairs and neutralist in regard to foreign policy, became premier. In early February, the mwami, now thoroughly alarmed by possible Chinese subversion, ordered their embassy closed. The Burundi army supervised the departure of the Chinese ambassador and his staff.

Mwami Mwambutsa dissolved the National Assembly in March and elections were held on May 10. These further discredited the pro-Communist faction since all the leading Watutsi figures associated with Nyamoya were defeated. The king retained the powers of the premier through the summer due largely to tensions between the Watutsi and Bahutu which had increased after N'Gendandumwe's assassination. Finally in September, Leopold Biha, a Watutsi who was considered a moderate by outside observers, became premier. Nothing substantial had been done since independence to weld the two racial groups in Burundi closer together. On the contrary, events in Rwanda, as well as Burundi, had only alienated them more from each other. Over 80,000 Watutsi refugees from Rwanda added to the government's difficulties. Many Bahutu in Burundi demanded the ouster of Mwambutsa and the establishment of a republic which would be controlled by the Bahutus. This desire and resentment against the government led, in October 1965, to a revolt of some of the police units backed by Bahutu radicals. Biha was surprised in his home and shot. The mwami hid in the palace and thus escaped the rebels until loyal troops quickly put down the rebellion. Martial law was proclaimed and thirty-four of the rebellious gendarmes were publicly executed. Large numbers of Bahutu politicians and intellectuals were arrested.

The UPRONA government formed by Biha was dissolved by the mwami, and he granted powers of government to Michel Micombero, the defense minister. Then the mwami left the country for a rest in Switzerland. On November 18, Mwambutsa reconstituted the Biha government. However, Biha, in a Belgian hospital recuperating from the attempt on his life, was in no position to effect the changes decreed by the mwami. In March 1966, Prince Charles Ndizeye arrived in Burundi to act for his father, the mwami, and bring some order to the strife wracked state. However, in July he deposed his father and became Mwami Ntare V. In turn, while on a state visit to the Congo, he was deposed by Micombero who declared the monarchy at an end. Instead, there was created a republic controlled by a thirteen-member National Revolutionary Committee. Thus after four years of independence, Burundi's politics were as stormy as ever, the cleavage between Bahutu and Watutsi remained, and the new factor of pro-Western and pro-Communist factions further divided the people.

FOUR

The Portuguese speaking territories

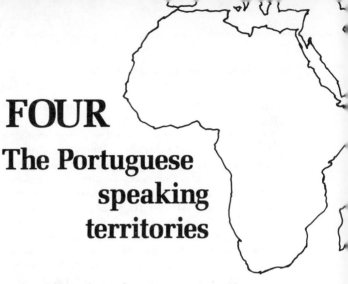

The political system as constituted in the 1920's continued in force after World War II. The assumptions upon which Prime Minister Salazar had constructed his system remained unchallenged until the uprising in Angola in 1961. Centralized control over the lives of Africans was actually increased when in 1952 the African territories were designated overseas provinces of Portugal instead of colonial possessions. Thus, while other colonial powers were modifying their rule in response to African pressures, the Portuguese made no concessions. Dual citizenship was maintained. The first class, the *populacao civilizada* (civilized), comprised all Portuguese residents, the mixed population, and the few *assimilados*. Persons in this category participated fully in the limited political life of the territories. The bulk of the population was designated *populacao não-civilizada* (uncivilized), and was controlled directly by the full machinery of the appointive European system. Portuguese neo-mercantilism and the *assimilado* system effectively prevented the development of any legal political activity for the indigenous people, the *indegenas*.

The key to Portugal's attitude toward its overseas provinces lay in its poverty. In 1959 Portugal's trade deficit with the rest of the world was over $140,000,000. In order to keep this unhealthy situation from becoming worse Portugal needed desperately the cotton, tea, tobacco, petroleum, and other supplies provided by its provinces. Angola, Mozambique, and Guinea were also constrained to import the bulk of their goods from Portugal. It should not be assumed, however, that Portugal neglected its territories economically. In order to increase their economic potential Portugal had invested millions in port facilities, railroads, roads, and irrigation systems. An integral part of its schemes for economic development had been the resettlement of Portuguese families in new agricultural communities in Angola and Mozambique. One of the largest of these *colonatos* was located north of the Limpopo River and cost

117

Portugal over $35,000,000 in the decade after 1954. In 1959 Portugal instituted a six-year development plan which projected the expenditure of $300,000,000 for new agricultural and industrial enterprises. Despite all its efforts to support white colonization, there were less than one-third million Europeans resident in Angola and Mozambique.

In March 1961, Portugal's empire was shaken to its base by a revolt in northern Angola. Salazar was forced to concentrate over 50,000 troops in Angola before African resistance was broken. In mid-1962 a further nationalist uprising began in Guinea and guerrillas trained in Tanzania started to operate in northern Mozambique. The United Nations, Britain, and the United States brought additional pressure to bear upon Portugal to alter its African political system. While implicitly denying the right of any outside agency to interfere in Portugal's domestic affairs, Salazar's government acted as early as June 1961 to moderate some of the worst features of its system. Municipal councils which had previously been appointive were in the future to be elected. Three new seats were assigned to Mozambique, three to Angola, and one to Guinea in the Portuguese National Assembly. The government announced in August 1961 a plan to abolish dual citizenship replacing it with a single set of property and educational standards for the franchise.

As the war continued in all of its African territories, the Portuguese government found it more difficult to justify its actions in purely economic terms. The largest portion of the budget of the country went to support its military operations and the casualties mounted. The death in 1968 of long time dictator Antonio Salazar weakened the central government. His successor, Marcello Caetano, was never able to control the divisive political elements in Portugal as efficiently as had Salazar. The insurgents in Mozambique and Angola made some advances in the early 1970s, but the Portuguese forces maintained control of all the cities and most of the countryside in those regions. However, the 40,000 man force was not able to contain the revolt in Portuguese Guinea. Thus this tiny, poverty striken region became the focal point of debate over the correctness of th government's policy. In April 1974, General Antonio de Spinola, former commander of the troops in Portuguese Guinea, overthrew the Caetano government and announced his intention of altering Portugal's relationship with its African territories. The government then moved rapidly to end its military involvement in all its African territories and within a few months it became obvious that all three territories would be granted independence. Events after 1961 connected with the African revolt against Portugal became so complex that only by viewing each province separately can one obtain an understanding of this period.

Angola
The government regime of Dr. Salazar both in Portugal and in the colonies precluded the normal organization and lawful practice of political parties in Angola. The territory was governed by an appointive governor-general and elected legislative council. However, the council was dominated by the white settlers and, moreover, had little real power. African political activity in

Portuguese Central Africa

Angola has, therefore, been of the clandestine, terrorist type which sought the overthrow of the centralized white regime. The political organizations operative in Angola were never recognized by Portugal and their headquarters were located in friendly African states. The political party which has demonstrated, in the past, that it had a larger amount of African support than the others was the *Uniao das Populacaes de Angola* (UPA). The UPA was founded in 1954 and was led by the Congolese-educated Holden Roberto. Roberto was widely known in African Nationalist circles, having attended all the major conferences after that in Accra in 1958. He had a close relationship with Kwame Nkrumah, and the office of the UPA was located in Léopoldville. The UPA takes credit for the March 15, 1961 uprisings which focused world attention on Angola. Certainly the strength of the UPA was in the agricultural north, particularly among the Bakongo.

Another nationalist party was the *Movimento Popular de Libertacao de Angola* (MPLA) founded in 1957 by Ilidio Alves Machado. Arrested for subversion in 1959, Machado was imprisoned in Luanda during the uprising. One of the other early leaders, Dr. Agostino Neto, also was arrested in June 1960. The movement's next leader in the absence of Neto was Mario Pinto de Andrade whose headquarters was in Guinea. At the All African Peoples Conference at Tunis in January 1960, the MPLA joined three other small nationalist organizations to form the *Frente Revolucionaria Africana para Independencia Nacional* (FRAIN) to gain independence for all Portuguese colonies. This led to a permanent coordinating organization, the *Conferencia de Organizacoes Nacionalistas das Colonias Portuguesas* (CONCP). Most of the MPLA were mulatto and the strength of its movement in Angola was in the vicinity of Luanda.

In March 1959, the government arrested several hundred people including leaders of the clandestine political parties. There were three trials subsequently where fifty-seven persons were charged with "attempts against the external security of the State." Portugal began to reinforce its garrison in Angola. The exiled MPLA in conjunction with the UPA formed a united movement, the *Frente Libertacao Nacional de Angola* (FLNA), in May 1960 and appealed to the government for a peaceful solution to the Angolan problem. The Portuguese answered by more arrests of suspects in Luanda, Lobito, Dalatando, and Malange. In July 1960, troops began intermittent raids on African quarters in Luanda. In November twenty-eight nationalists from Cabinda were executed in Luanda. Leaders of the Liberation Front in London implied in December that only direct action was left to the Africans if they wished to end Portuguese colonialism.

The first direct action was timed to coincide with the return of Henrique Galvão to Luanda. On January 23, 1961, he and seventy followers had seized Portugal's second largest ship, the *Santa Maria*, to dramatize opposition to Salazar's regime. Captured by the Brazilian navy, the *Santa Maria* was scheduled to dock in Luanda on February 4. African nationalists attacked the prisons and a military barracks. The main battle raged for three days before the revolt was quelled with a loss of African life estimated at over 2,000. Throughout February fighting between Portuguese army units and Africans was endemic in northern Angola and there was a major African uprising on March 14.

Despite its militant attitude which predated the February uprising, Portugal had not believed the Africans capable of concerted action. Therefore the entire military garrison of Angola in early March numbered less than 3,000 men. On the evening of March 14, an estimated 60,000 Africans attacked the Portuguese settlers in the provinces of Congo, Malange, and Luanda. Over 300 European men, women and children were killed in the initial onslaught. There were numerous cases of rape, torture, and mutilation. In the next three weeks approximately 1,000 more Europeans and 6,000 Africans were killed. Dr. Salazar took over the ministry of defense in Portugal and reinforcements were rushed to Angola. Armed civilians in Angola joined the military in counterattacking. Jet planes using bombs, machine guns, and napalm struck at villages and targets of opportunity throughout the disaffected area. The ferocity of the initial African attack was thus matched by the Portuguese counterattack.

Before the end of the initial crisis in October 1961, Portugal had over 15,000 troops operating in the three provinces. Eventually more than 50,000 soldiers were garrisoned in Angola. There is no way of knowing how many Africans died in northern Angola. Estimates have been made of upward of 60,000 dead. It is known that over 100,000 fled northward to join their Bakongo kinsmen in the trouble-wracked Republic of the Congo. Portugal had by the end of the year controlled the uprising at a cost of millions of dollars of its scant reserve fund. Fighting was endemic on a smaller scale in northern Angola through 1965.

Portugal, after the rebellion, responded by liberalizing its rule to a limited extent. The *assimilado* system was abolished and civil rights extended to all residents of Angola. A single set of requirements for the franchise was established. Forced labor for the production of cash export crops was stopped and the government disassociated itself from active participation in recruitment of African labor. The Legislative Council was made elective and three new seats in the Portuguese National Assembly were reserved for Angola. It should be remembered that the grant of franchise and civil rights, while an advance, is not comparable to these practices in British or French areas. The Portuguese government remained firmly in the hands of Premier Salazar and his associates and even Europeans in Portugal had few political rights.

Another result of the uprising was the speeding up of European colonization of Angola. The government announced its long-range goal of attempting to convince many of the 50,000 soldiers in Angola to settle there permanently. The Portuguese relaxed their immigration requirements and began to fund at an even higher level their land settlement schemes. The success of Portugal's colonization efforts can be seen in the following approximate figures for European population: 1940—40,000; 1950—79,000; 1955—140,000; 1960—200,000; 1964—240,000.

In reaction to the disturbances, the United Nations voted on April 20, 1961 to send a five-man fact-finding commission to Angola. The Security Council in

June, by a vote of nine to zero, called upon Portugal to cease its repressive measures against the Africans. Portugal bitterly criticized the actions of the United Nations and its fellow NATO ally, the United States, for their positions on this matter. Salazar maintained that these were internal disturbances beyond the scope of United Nations activity and refused to allow the General Assembly's committee to land. Further resolutions of the Security Council in 1962 and 1963 were likewise ignored by Portugal. The pressure of African states, even those which broke relations with Portugal, had even less effect upon Salazar's policies.

The failure of African nationalists to achieve any substantial part of their goals by 1965 was due as much to divided leadership as to Portuguese troops. After the uprising of 1961, there was a fragmentation of the MPLA and a corresponding loss of prestige of the *Frente Revolucionaria* and the CONCP. The largely mulatto leadership of the MPLA had never been popular with the African masses. There was briefly a shift in Portuguese settler thinking toward a Brazilian solution where the settlers in Angola, not the politicans in Lisbon, would determine policy. This more moderate attitude of the settlers was partially designed to undermine the MPLA. The lack of a single revolutionary organization which could coordinate guerrilla activity in Angola restricted the effectiveness of the revolution. In 1963 the OAU created a coordinating committee to investigate the relative merits of FLNA and MPLA. The investigations indicated that the MPLA had no political structure in Angola. Further, the committee discovered that MPLA militants in Angola numbererd only about 200. The goodwill commission previously had imagined that its risk would be to reconcile two revolutionary groups of almost equal power. However, it found that the FLNA was the only really effective political and military force in Angola. Holden Roberto's group at that time still controlled, by the admission of the Portuguese, over six percent of Angola. The OAU commission recommended that all future aid be channeled to the FLNA through its Léopoldville headquarters and suggested that all of the smaller revolutionary groups join the more effective and militant UPA and FLNA. Subsequently, the OAU recognized Roberto's government in exile, located in Léopoldville, as the official government of Angola.

The concentration by the Portuguese of a large, well-trained, modern army in Angola had by 1965 all but negated the guerrilla forces throughout the territory. Only a few bands were active in the Bakongo country. Further to the south those in the Kimbundu areas either had been liquidated or had vanished. Portugal was thus able to transfer a large portion of her military forces from Angola to the troubled areas of Mozambique and Guinea.

These reversals were paralleled by a loss in prestige for Roberto and the government in exile. Jonas Savimbi, his ex-foreign minister, broke with Roberto over policy. Savimbi maintained that the guerrilla losses stemmed largely from Roberto's failure to give the proper leadership. He also claimed that Roberto's Bakongo separatist sentiments had kept the FLNA from becoming an all-Angolan movement. Other defectors from Roberto's party in 1965 formed the *Congress Popular de Angola* (CPA).

While Roberto's group, perhaps as a reflection of its losses, became more

Bakongo-oriented, the MPLA based in Léopoldville recovered some of the prestige which was lost in 1963. Under the leadership of Neto and Andrade, guerrilla bands loyal to the MPLA carried out terrorist activities in Cabinda. At the close of 1965, Roberto still had the support of the OAU, but there was considerable feeling that his group had failed and that the MPLA had a better chance of eventually succeeding in Angola. The intense political rivalry between the liberation groups damaged their ability to pursue the war with more vigor. MPLA guerrillas first from their bases in Zambia and later the far eastern sections of the territory proved to be the most effective in the years immediately prior to independence. Although MPLA guerrillas raided as far west as the Cubango River, they could not take the major towns or contain Portuguese airborne troops. In the extreme south, Savimbi's forces, crippled by lack of supplies, carried out only sporadic raids and acted as a potential threat to the great Cunene River hydroelectric project. Holden Roberto was content to hold most of the FLNA in Zaire although the Bakongo regions of Angola were known to be favorable to his movement.

In December 1970, Premier Caetano announced plans to give the African territories more autonomy. In May of the following year, the National Assembly gave effect to Caetano's statement by passing legislation which altered the names of the territories to states. While the Lisbon government retained control of foreign affairs and defense, it was willing to allow a large measure of control of planning, development, and finance to state and provincial assemblies. This reorganization was denounced by all the leaders of the revolutionary movements and the fighting continued. The revolt in Angola gained further status in 1970 when the Vatican received Agostino Neto, the MPLA leader. In the following year, the United Nations voted to accept deputies of the revolutionary movements as observers and began to investigate charges that Portuguese forces had committed genocide. The Spinola coup and subsequent disorders in Portugal assured the independence of Guinea-Bissau in September 1974. After this was done it was only a matter of time before Angola became independent.

Angola's problems were compounded by the three competitive nationalist groups, each of which moved swiftly to bolster its military and political position once it was apparent that the Portuguese would withdraw. Fighting broke out between the FNLA and MPLA factions in Luanda in January 1975 and escalated sharply in the months prior to independence in November. Neto's troops held control of Luanda and oil rich Cabinda as well as those Kimbundu areas north of the Benguela-Zambia railway. Roberto's FNLA backed by Zaire invaded the Bakongo regions while Savimbi's UNITA dominated the Ovimbundu territories in the south. Although attempting to moderate the differences, the Portuguese did not wish to prolong their stay and kept their own military in a purely defensive posture until independence.

The Angolan civil war of 1975-76 soon became a focal point of big power politics. In a strange juxtaposition, the United States and China supported Roberto while Russia and Cuba immediately began to send aid to the MPLA. Jonas Savimbi received at first secret and then open support from South Africa which sent a part of its army into southern Angola to protect the Cunene River installations. It was soon apparent that the MPLA was far better organized than its opponents and that its foreign allies were prepared to invest heavily in the civil war. Roberto's troops quickly showed their lack of committment; even the Bakongo turned against the invading FNLA forces. United States aid to the anti-MPLA factions which had been given in a clandestine fashion was stopped in February 1976 when Congress learned of the deepening committment. By contrast the Soviet Union sent millions of dollars worth of supplies and sophisticated weapons and Cuba in 1975 began to send troops. By early 1976, over 10,000 Cuban regulars had reinforced the MPLA forces and this enabled Neto to launch a general offensive. By mid-year most of the country was under MLPA control.

Rich in minerals and with a great potential for agricultural development, Angola was left in shambles. Fewer than 15,000 of the half million Portuguese chose to remain after the civil war. Most of the doctors, professional men, and technicians so vital to any developing state left the country. In part this loss was compensated for by the Cuban troops whose number had escalated to over 30,000 by 1980. These helped immensely at first in providing the necessary medical and technical assistance needed, particularly in the areas near Luanda. The Soviet bloc countries continued to provide the MPLA government with massive economic and military aid which by 1987 accounted for two thirds of Angola's $3.2 billion foreign debt. Soon after independence Neto began to make overtures to the non-Communist West for the economic aid which was desperately needed to develop the natural potential of Angola. His decision caused considerable dissention in the seventy-four-member Central Committee of the party because many of the more doctrinaire Marxists viewed it as a move back to neo-colonialism. The outcome of such factional debates was not settled when Neto, who had been ill for some time, died in Moscow in September 1979. The party immediately chose the minister for planning, Eduardo dos Santos, as the new president. He quickly showed a desire to continue rapprochement with the West but was inhibited by the twin problems of UNITA and Namibia.

Jonas Savimbi in the half-decade after independence was able to extend UNITA's control over much of Ovimbundu territory, some of the most fertile agricultural land in Angola. The nucleus of his army had been created during the war of liberation. Although the exact size of this force was unknown it was believed to be in excess of 20,000 men. In that vast territory Savimbi, in addition established a governmental system and maintained markets, schools, and health facilities. From his capital at Jamba he planned raids into MPLA controlled areas. Although there were some major offensive actions initiated by UNITA such as the 1984 attempt to take the town of Sumbe, Savimbi was generally content with a defensive position ultimately dominating one-third of Angola. The Benguela railway, once the major route for Zairian and Zambian minerals, remained closed despite attempts by Angolan and Cuban troops in the late 1970s to reopen it. UNITA was also very active in hit and run raids on strategic targets in towns and cities such as the destruction of transmission towers and lines to Luanda and the bombing of the main rail yard at Benguela. In July 1984 UNITA agents operating in Cabinda blew up an oil pipeline operated then by Gulf Oil, shutting it down for a few days. UNITA also began planting claymore mines in the areas of Huambo and Bie Provinces not under their control. The object of this indiscriminate violence was to drive farmers from the land. There is no way of even estimating the number of innocent farmers who were killed or lost limbs because of these antipersonnel mines, but Savimbi's strategy worked. The cities of Angola became crowded and by 1987 only three percent of Angola's arable land was under cultivation. The annual production of grain was only 300,000 tons, only one-half the country's needs.

It was difficult to know what were Savimbi's ultimate plans. His excellent public relations program in Europe and particularly the United States stressed his anti-communist position. However, he also made clear to reporters who were flown in to Jamba from time to time that he recognized that he could not overthrow the MPLA government by military force. Instead he aimed at ultimate reconciliation and participation in a national government. This goal, if the actual one, would be difficult to achieve. In order for UNITA to participate in such a government the MPLA would have to change the entire structure of rule and give up much of their Marxist programs. It would also mean that the 30,000 Cuban troops and Soviet and East German advisors would be removed, an unlikely event as long as they were needed to protect Luanda and bolster the Angolan army. Dos Santos and his advisors saw clearly that UNITA as a political and military force had to be destroyed before the country could begin to prosper. Taking advantage of superiority in numbers, the government army yearly has tried a major invasion of UNITA held territory. The most serious of these invasions was just before the rains in 1985 and again in 1987. Both times the MPLA forces were decisively defeated, partially with South African assistance. In 1985 the Angolan army reportedly lost ninety armored vehicles and Soviet made T-62 tanks to South African tactical air strikes.

The most fateful decision of the MPLA government was to give sanctuary to the SWAPO guerrillas who used Angolan territory as a base from which to attack into Namibia. This gave the South African government the necessary excuse to attack across the border in order to destroy SWAPO bases. The bulk of military hardware needed by UNITA has either been provided by South Africa or has reached Savimbi through Namibia. Thus the anomoly of the white, conservative government of South Africa aiding a revolutionary movement led by a former Marxist is logical only from a purely pragmatic viewpoint. South Africa's policy of destabilization meant that the MPLA could not be allowed to crush UNITA. When it appeared that the regular Angolan forces might triumph, South Africa used its armed forces directly in the struggle. This occurred in 1976 when South African units penetrated hundreds of miles into Angola and this protected Savimbi's left flank. The actions of Angola in granting sanctuary to SWAPO also allowed South Africa to argue against any significant grant of independent authority to blacks in Namibia. The Botha government consistently linked abiding by the United Nations Resolution 435 to the ending of Angola's sanctuary policy for SWAPO and the removal of all Cuban troops from Angola.

President dos Santos, understanding clearly the need to neutralize the South African presence in southern Angola, entered into negotiations with Pretoria. This culminated in the Lusaka agreement of February 1984. Dos Santos promised to force the closure of SWAPO bases and in return South Africa would immediately remove all of its forces from Angola. Although a joint monitoring team was created, this agreement never had a chance of success. Even had the MPLA not been so committed to the cause of SWAPO, it is doubtful that given the size of the country and the demands elsewhere upon its military that the bases could have been shut down. Recognizing this South Africa kept troops in the disputed area over a year after they were to be pulled back. Finally in April 1985 the last South African units were removed. This was done largely at the behest of the United States which was attempting to negotiate the withdrawal of the Cubans.

The position of the United States with regard to Angola and peace in southern Africa was very difficult for most observers to understand. However crucial a role the United States was to have, it appeared not to have a logical cohesive policy. On the one hand President Reagan had stated his opposition to apartheid and his support for an independent Namibia. His opposition to the Botha regime became even more pronounced when Congress forced stringent sanctions upon the president. Despite this seemingly clear position the United States had opposed the Marxist government of Angola since its support for the FNLA in the mid-1970s and refused to have direct relations with it. To many conservatives Jonas Savimbi was a patriot fighting for a democratic government against an oppressive regime which was propped up by the Soviet Union and Cuba. Despite overtures from dos Santos the United States refused to alter its position and in 1981 Congress began to discuss the repeal of the Clark amendment, passed five years earlier, which had prohibited aid to UNITA. The repeal was finally voted and in October 1986 Congress approved covert aid to Savimbi. It was disclosed that over $15 million, mostly in hardware, had already been provided. Included in this aid were advanced Stinger antiaircraft weapons and antitank guns. President Reagan welcomed Savimbi to Washington, a recognition that mirrored that given him by South Africa in 1984 when he was a guest at the inauguration of President Botha.

It had not escaped the notice of most congressmen that such a policy of support for UNITA was at odds with the actions of American multinational oil companies in Cabinda. The operations of Chevron and Texaco there provided the government of dos Santos with over one-half of its foreign exchange earnings and this, more than anything, kept Angola's economy from collapsing. Thus in late 1986 a sense of the Congress resolution was passed deploring the continuation of American participation in petroleum production there. Later an amendment to a Department of Defense authorization bill outlawed buying any oil from Angola. During the crucial five years when the United States government opinion was swinging to direct support of UNITA, dos Santos was trying to normalize relations with the Reagan administration. He would not be successful despite the illogic of the hostile American position toward South Africa which at the same time gave military support to UNITA while American oil firms continued to pump money into the MPLA government's coffers. The reason for dos Santos's failure was not just his close ties with the Soviet Union but the continued presence of over 30,000 Cuban troops in Angola. The United States demanded their immediate withdrawal and South Africa linked this to any solution of the Namibian question. Angolan Foreign Minister Alexandre Rodriques during his meeting with Assistant Secretary of State Charles Crocker in Cape Verde in 1985 proposed a phased withdrawal of the Cubans whose maintenance was costing Angola $250 million each year. If South Africa would comply with United Nations resolution 435 and limit the size of its force in Namibia to 1,500 men, then 20,000 of the Cubans would be sent home over a three year period. Ten thousand Cubans would remain to protect Luanda and the oil sites in Cabinda. As long as Angola was threatened by a considerable South African force and was struggling against UNITA, the MPLA government could not afford the luxury of a quick removal of all the Cubans. The Rodriques proposal was not accepted by the United States and South Africa. The result was a continuation of the civil war, a continual drain on the weakened Angolan economy which had already spent $15 billion on the war, and a deepening commitment by the United States to the cause of UNITA.

The MPLA government, partially by design and partially by accident, had been caught up in the cold war since Angola's independence. It appeared obvious in 1987 that any solution to Angola's worsening economic situation lay in ending the devastating civil war. However, this would mean coming to terms with Savimbi and making a place for him and for his followers in a government of national reconciliation. This solution even if practicable was not acceptable to the Marxist hard-liners in dos Santos's government or to his Soviet advisors. Equally, any such peaceful solution would be anathema to South Africa which depended on UNITA to continue its destabilization program. Botha did not have to seek any solution to the Namibian problem as long as the conditions in Angola were chaotic. In the meantime Angola went deeper into debt to its communist allies, a large part of its great mineral resources could not be utilized, its communications infrastructure was a shambles, and potentially worst of all, despite its rich agricultural land, it could not feed itself. As with Ethiopia, the Western Sahara, Mozambique, and the Sudan, the civil war had become a way of life for so many and promised to continue with few prospects for a solution.

Mozambique

Mozambique was the most populous Portuguese territory in Africa with a population in 1964 of approximately six million of which over 65,000 were Europeans. It has a coastline over 1,500 miles long. In the north it borders Tanzania, in the west Rhodesia and Malawi, and in the south the Republic of South Africa. Most of the European population was located in the south and along the coast.

Portugal's hold over interior areas was extremely tenuous even after the agreements which settled the scramble. Before that the *prazeros*, mulatto descendants of early Portuguese settlers, controlled the Zambesi Valley. Laws unto themselves, they ignored, except when convenient, rules made in Lisbon or Mozambique. With their private armies they fought among each other, against the Africans, and against innumerable Portuguese expeditions. By use of chartered companies, such as the Mozambique Company, and more troops, the Portuguese succeeded in defeating most of the African rulers of the interior and the *prazeros*. By 1914 the Portuguese held nominal control of the interior.

Early in the twentieth century the Portuguese established the practice of sending contract laborers to São Thomé and Réunion. In 1911 the Portuguese government signed an agreement with the Union of South Africa to provide up to 80,000 workers every year for the mines. The use of the hippopotamus hide whip, beating the palms of the hands, and other methods were utilized to enforce Portuguese decrees for forced and contract labor. These methods were outlawed by 1915 but were still being practiced at a much later date.

In 1915 the Lisbon government announced the *assimilado* system which theoretically gave the African the right to rise to the status of Portuguese citizens. The home government under the control of Premier Salazar after 1931 was even less amenable to change than had been the monarchy. Thus Portuguese neo-mercantilism and the *assimilado* system have prevented the development in Mozambique of any legal political activity for the *indegenas* who made up most of the population. Thus all African political groups have been clandestine organizations such as those in Angola and Portuguese Guinea. The Salazar government made clear by its statements and actions even before the uprisings in Angola that there would be no major change in the relationship of the African territories to Portugal.

In 1952 Mozambique was declared an overseas province and an integral part of Portugal. It continued to be directed largely from Lisbon through the offices of the governor-general and his appointive staff. An advisory council and a twenty-four man Legislative Council composed of European appointees gave advice to the executive, but they had little substantive powers. The political reality of life for the *indegenas* was direct control of their affairs by European officers down to the district level. The failure of the *assimilado* system in Mozambique is seen in their numbers. Only 4,500 Africans out of a population of almost six million had become *assimilados*.

Portugal's strict paternalist relations with the African population became critical in the late 1950s when African territories of other European states were being advanced quickly toward independence. One of the main thrusts of the Pan African movement was to oust all colonial powers from the continent and replace them with African rule. It was impossible for Portugal to seal its frontiers against these new ideas. The March 1961 rebellion in Angola was the best evidence of the extent of this Portuguese problem. Following the outbreak of violence in Angola, a number of African political organizations were founded which had as their objective self-determination and independence for Mozambique. In October 1960, Adelino Gwambe and a few followers formed the *Uniao Democratica Nacional de Mocambique* (UDENAMO) with its headquarters in Tanzania. Another political faction, the *Frente de Libertacao de Mocambique* (FRELIMO), was created by Dr. Eduardo Mondlane. Its headquarters was also in Tanzania. In addition there were a large number of local groups operating generally in northern Mozambique which were not directly affiliated with either liberation party. FRELIMO claimed by 1965 to have 9,000 members inside Mozambique and they had approximately 500 men in training in Tanzania. FRELIMO was affiliated with other freedom groups operating in Portuguese territories which were opposed to Holden Roberto's party in Angola. This loose association was called the Conference of Nationalist Organization of Portuguese Colonies (CONCP). The OAU made clear its sympathies with the African revolutionaries.

Portugal replied to this increasing guerrilla activity by enlarging substantially the garrisons in Mozambique and building new forts throughout the border
areas. President Tomas on a state visit in 1965 reviewed over 5,000 troops in
Lourenço Marques and reiterated Portugal's intention to maintain itself in East
Africa. Portugal continued to send white settlers into reclaimed agricultural areas
throughout Mozambique. The largest of these was the Limpopo *colonato* composed of thirteen villages northwest of Lourenço Marques. After 1954 over 2,000
families had been settled there. A 2,100 foot dam was built on the Limpopo River
and thirteen irrigation canals carried water to the 30,000 acres of the *colonato*.
The project by 1965 had cost Portugal almost $40,000,000. Lourenço Marques
and Beira reflected the prosperity not only of Mozambique, but also of Rhodesia
and the Republic of South Africa. The bulk of Rhodesian goods passed through
Mozambique as well as much of the equipment for the mines of the Transvaal.

Portugal's resolve to hold Mozambique was aided by dissension among the
various African nationalist groups. UDENAMO and FRELIMO leaders have
often been jealous of one another and, therefore, there was never a unified
command of the guerrilla activities in Mozambique. Nor does it appear that the
organization of the peoples of northern Mozambique has been very effective.
These factors were most important for the Portuguese before they could shift
large numbers of troops from Angola. The task of holding Mozambique against
an effective coordinated African revolt was tremendous. The size of the territory
alone made policing difficult: Mozambique is larger than the state of Texas.
Other strategic difficulties related to the long coastline of Mozambique and the
Malawi salient thrust into the heart of the northern area. There are over 700 miles
of mountainous bush area along the border with Malawi.

Recognizing the vulnerability of Mozambique, Portugal strengthened its
garrisons, particularly in the northern sector. According to reports, there were
between 20,000 and 25,000 troops in this area in 1965. In addition, Portugal had
constructed five new airfields in the north and there was a considerable number
of all types of planes at these stations. A new military road between Palma and
Mueda was also constructed. Guerrilla activity was especially strong in the areas
immediately adjacent to the Tanzanian and part of the Malawi borders. However, by the end of 1964, Portuguese troop activity and massive arrests had
considerably lessened the dangers to Portuguese control. In the summer and fall
of 1964, nearly 7,000 refugees crossed the Ruvuma River from Mozambique into
Tanzania. The long-expected contest of strength between the rebels and the
Portuguese began in early 1965 in Mozambique. Dr. Mondlane at the OAU
meeting at Accra in 1965 admitted that the activities of FRELIMO within
Mozambique were accelerated during the year. Despite his optimistic statements, the year ended with FRELIMO forces restricted to smaller areas and,
because of the divisions within, the freedom movements were forced to assume
the defensive. Dr. Mondlane managed to heal the breech in the revolutionary
movement by the end of 1968. However, before any positive results could be
shown from this united front, FRELIMO was once again divided because in
February Dr. Mondlane was assassinated in Tanzania. The ensuing struggle for
power did not end for almost a year until Samora Machel was chosen president
and Marcelino dos Santos vice-president of FRELIMO. Both leaders were

confirmed Marxists and their avowed aim after victory was to establish a socialist republic.

Prime Minister Caetano pledged in 1970 to pursue the war against the insurgents until they were no longer a threat. He increased the armed forces to a total of over 40,000 by mid-1971 and appointed a new more aggressive commander who immediately launched offensives in the Tete district and along the border with Tanzania. Portugal continued its attempts to develop further the mineral and agricultural potential of Mozambique. In 1970 work began on the huge $400 million Cabora Bassa dam which was designed to provide controlled irrigation to a large part of Tete district as well as all the electricity that Mozambique would need in the forseeable future. In May 1971, the Portuguese National Assembly decreed a change in the status of all its African territories. Mozambique became a state within the Portuguese empire and was granted considerable local autonomy. FRELIMO rejected completely this unilateral decision. However, despite escalating guerrilla strikes against roads and railroads in the Tete area in 1972, the Portuguese in Mozambique showed no signs of being defeated.

World opinion had been operating against the Portuguese activities since the beginnings of the revolt. In 1973 charges were made by Catholic missionaries against Portuguese brutality. Specifically they claimed that over 400 men, women, and children were massacred in December 1972 in a village near the Rhodesian border. This brought a new round of charges by both Western and African powers in the United Nations. More ominous to Caetano was the anti-government attitudes expressed by various political groups in Portugal. Growing numbers were tired of the economic drain and the casualties suffered in defense of the empire. General Spinola's seizure of power in April 1974 based upon his promise to end the war in Guinea-Bissau undercut all of Portugal's previous military victories in Mozambique. Throughout the summer of 1974 there were frequent meetings between Portuguese and FRELIMO representatives. Agreement was finally reached on a time table for Portuguese withdrawal. On September 20, an interim government composed of six FRELIMO and three Portuguese ministers was installed at Lourenço Marques. The Portuguese withdrew completely from Mozambique in June 1975 and Machel became president of a Marxist-socialist state. The National Assembly of 210 members was appointed from the ranks of FRELIMO. The party leaders promised elections within a year after convening of a third party congress. Although this convened in 1977, the election had not yet been held by 1979.

At the time of independence the economy of Mozambique was surprisingly healthy even after years of civil strife. The FRELIMO leaders committed to a Marxist-socialistic program immediately after independence began to dismantle the free enterprise system which was so closely associated with Portuguese overrule. All land was nationalized and the large productive tea, sugar, cashew, coffee, and cotton plantations became state owned collective farms. In addition all banking and major industries were nationalized. Long before this process was completed most of the one-quarter million Portuguese residents had left the country, taking with them the bulk of their capital and most important their irreplaceable skills. The 10,000 Portuguese who chose to remain could add very little to the pool of talent available to the government which found itself chronically short of trained personnel at a time when it was instituting a major turnaround in the economic system. Even under the best of circumstances there would have been difficulties in the economic sphere with the new system in the hands of untrained and in many cases corrupt managers. By the time President Machel began to have second thoughts about his economic program the worst drought in a century struck southern Africa. Hundreds of thousands of persons were immediately affected. Only foodstuffs provided by foreign agencies kept the bulk of these from starving. To compound Mozambique's problems the world recession lowered prices for all its agricultural exports. In 1984 export earnings had fallen to only $385 million while imports cost over $735 million. Three years later export earnings amounted to less than $100 million. Faced with such a variety of economic problems, President Machel decided in 1982 to reverse the hard line socialist policies and to appeal to the West not only for aid for those stricken by the drought but for possible investment. The reversal of policy carried out over the next five years meant that the largest of the state farms, particularly those tea, tobacco, and cashew plantations, were reorganized and many turned over to private control. For most of the subsistance farmers the government instead of centralized planning began to stress local initiatives. Corrupt civil servants and police officials were brought to trial and a genuine effort was made in the state run programs to put men of talent into management positions. Many of these changes were cancelled out by the escalation of civil war. However, Machel did reopen economic dialogue with Europe and the United States. In 1984 the United States lifted its seven year ban on direct economic aid which had by 1986 grown to $40 million. Machel also in 1984 joined the World Bank and the IMF and tried to comply with IMF guidelines to combat inflation and overspending. That same year the Paris Club rescheduled payments on $860 million of Mozambique's estimated $3.2 billion debt.

Mozambique's major problem has been the civil war which began in 1976. Machel immediately after independence granted sanctuary to Robert Mugabe and his forces then seeking to overthrow the Ian Smith regime in Rhodesia. Although these bases played a key role in ending white rule in Rhodesia, the ultimate cost to Mozambique was very high. Dissident elements in Mozambique received the active support of the Rhodesian government. With aid from Rhodesia the Mozambique National Resistance Movement (RENAMO) became, at first, a nuisance and then later a definite threat to the government. When Mugabe came to power in Rhodesia the economic and military burden necessary to keep RENAMO active then passed to South Africa. Botha's government saw this as an important way of destabilizing a potentially hostile government with which it shared a long frontier. Although the aims of RENAMO were never concisely spelled out, the leaders of the movement could take advantage of the economic malaise of the early 1980s. The poorly equipped and trained Mozambique army found itself facing the same problems which had bedevilled the Portuguese— how to contain small irregular forces operating in friendly or neutral territory in a state as large as Mozambique.

There appeared to be one way of negating RENAMO—cut off its supplies of war material. Machel as a part of his reversal of policy agreed to direct negotia-tions with the South African government. He had allowed the ANC to establish a major headquarters in Maputo from which it could direct attacks on South Africa. In 1981 and again in 1983 South African strike forces had landed in Maputo to destroy that headquarters. Both sides had something to gain from the negotiations. An agreement was finally reached and the articles duly signed on March 16, 1984 at Nkomati, a small settlement 300 miles northeast of Pretoria. By this pact South Africa promised to cease its aid to RENAMO and in return Mozambique would not support the ANC. Machel immediately expelled 800 ANC members from the country, allowing only a skeleton staff of ten persons to remain at Maputo. Later in May a further agreement between the two states was signed whereby South Africa contracted to purchase the bulk of the electricity from the Cabora Bassa dam. These actions in conjunction with the ongoing program of hiring thousands of Mozambique workers to labor in South African mines indicated a normalization of relations between the two countries.

Although South Africa denied the charges, it appeared to many observers that aid to the RENAMO forces continued after the Nkomati agreement. As the guerrillas became more successful tension between Mozambique and South Africa mounted. Then in October 1986 President Machel's plane crashed on its approach to Maputo airport killing all on board. There were immediate charges that South African agents were responsible and the rumors persisted even after a high level multinational investigating committee found that the crash was due to pilot error. Machel's death catapulted his vice president and long time associate, Joaquim Chissano, into the presidency. The major problems confronting his reorganized government were the same as those which had faced Machel. Time only had made them worse. The economy by any measure was bankrupt and there appeared little hope of reversing the situation as long as the civil war continued. Some estimates placed RENAMO in control of sixty percent of the countryside. RENAMO forces showed little compunction about using terror as a weapon. In July 1987 a RENAMO unit attacked the village of Homoine northeast of Maputo killing 386 men, women, and children. In October they attacked busses and slaughtered the civilian occupants. However much these actions gained worldwide denunciation, they indicated that the Mozambique army of almost 27,000 men could not guarantee the safety of persons in the vast interior. The vital but vulnerable railways and pipelines between Zimbabwe and the ports of Beira and Ncala were struck a number of times by the guerrillas. These links were so vital to the economies of Mozambique's neighbors that they have contributed troops to help guard them. Over 15,000 men, one-third of Zimbabwe's army, were deployed to see that its agricultural and mineral exports reached Beira safely.

Mozambique's creditors were sympathetic to the plight of the erstwhile Marxist regime. The Paris Club of creditors in June 1987 agreed to the rescheduling of Mozambique's $3.2 billion debt over the next twenty years and the United States and European countries continued a high level of aid. Although the drought had ended, the ongoing civil war prevented normal agricultural production even of locally consumed foodstuff. The nation's exports in 1987 amounted to only $87 million, a fraction of what it had been when Machel ordered the turnaround in his socialistic program. Foreign aid groups estimated in mid–1987 that over one-third of Mozambique's population of 14 million persons were at risk and would need emergency food. Mozambique's infant mortality was the highest in the world. Twelve years after independence Mozambique, instead of the model socialist state projected by the planners, was being torn apart by civil strife and had become one of the continent's charity cases.

Guinea-Bissau

Portuguese Guinea, with a population of slightly over one-half million, was the smallest of the Portuguese possessions in Africa. In its 14,000 square miles are numerous tribes, many with warlike histories, and some such as the Puels were only recently subdued by the Portuguese army. It is a poor area producing chiefly agricultural products such as rice, peanuts, palm oil, and timber. Until recently it was considered one of the small, sleepy backwaters of Africa. Since mid–1962, however, the nationalist revolt against Portuguese authoritarianism has wracked the Guinea interior.

Before 1962 Portuguese Guinea was ruled by an appointed governor-general who implemented the decisions made in Lisbon by the council of ministers and the overseas ministers. The *assimilado* policy was followed as were all the other facts of Portuguese rule in Africa. The distinction can be made, however, that the harsh rule so typical in southern Mozambique and Angola was not in as much evidence in Guinea. Another noticeable difference was the smaller number of Europeans resident in the territory. The educational system can be evaluated by the fact that in 1962 there was only one secondary school in the territory with an enrollment of less than 300 students. There was no framework through which Africans could hope to gain any voice in the government. Thus the African political organizations of Portuguese Guinea were organized outside of the territory as clandestine revolutionary organizations.

A number of different nationalist groups claimed to represent the aspirations of the Africans of Portuguese Guinea. The first and most powerful of these organizations was the *Parti Africana Independencia para Guinea e Cabo Verd* (PAIGC). The nucleus of this group was composed of colonial students who in the mid-1950s began to plan for independence for Portuguese Guinea. The organization of PAIGC was correlate with those organizations formed for the liberation of Angola. The leader of PAIGC was Amilcar Cabral, a native of the Cape Verde Islands. He was quite well-educated since there was no native statute in Cape Verde to restrict African education.

Two smaller nationalist movements were the *Frente Libertacao para Independencia Nacional de Guinea* (FLING) and *Uniao Nacional de Guinea Portuguesas* (UNGP). The former had its headquarters in Dakar and was led by Francisco Mendy and Enrique Labery. The UNGP was an even smaller group whose leader was a mulatto, Benjamin Pinto Bull. Bull's brother was appointed administrative secretary-general of the colony in 1963. The UNGP was a party which tried to compromise between the extreme positions of the inflexible Portuguese and the more radical nationalists. It had practically no popular support.

The first signs of revolt in Guinea occurred in 1959 when a strike for higher wages began in the small capital city of Bissau. The police reacted violently and a number of African workers were killed. An intangible but certainly a key factor in the organization of the nationalist movement in Portuguese Guinea was the granting of independence to neighboring Senegal and Guinea. In the early 1960s, it was apparent that even tiny Gambia was being groomed for independence. To nationalist leaders the only way which seemed open to them to achieve the same ends for Portuguese Guinea was a resort to arms. The uprising in Portuguese Guinea was almost entirely the work of the PAIGC. This organization's headquarters was located in the Republic of Guinea. From there the guerrilla leaders infiltrated southern Portuguese Guinea in an area where there is an extensive network of waterways and which is densely forested. The revolt, which began in June 1962, was based upon the grievances and aspirations of native farmers. Aid was initially supplied primarily by Guinea. The nationalist revolutionaries in the south also received some aid from Algeria, Ghana, and Morocco. At a later date the revolt spread to the northern area which borders on Senegal. Raiders moving across the Senegalese border and utilizing native support did considerable damage. In both the north and the south the terrain was such that the Portuguese forces were at a disadvantage. The guerrilla nationalists knew the areas perfectly and could operate with freedom, totally supported by the African population.

Portugal followed the same procedures in dealing with the crisis in Guinea as was used in Angola and Mozambique. The small garrison of sleepy Guinea soon belonged to the past. With some 10,000 troops operating in the territory by 1965, the Salazar government showed its intention of holding the territory by force. The PAIGC claimed to have over 4,000 guerrillas operating throughout Guinea. They had shifted their activities to the northwestern part of the country, and by the end of 1965 the rebels had pinned down most of the Portuguese troops in Bissau and the other urban centers. The measure of the success of Cabral's guerrillas can be seen in the admission of the Portuguese defense minister in 1963 that the rebels controlled fifteen percent of the territory. The guerrillas continually enlarged the areas which they directly controlled until by the end of the decade almost all the country districts were dominated by the PAIGC. The Portuguese armed forces, at their peak numbering over 40,000 men, were confined to the towns or fortified strong points. Supported by modern aircraft, they would sortie from these bases on sweeps into adjacent territory. These strikes were not aimed at controlling territory and served mainly to convert recalcitrant Africans to the rebels' cause.

One of the reasons for the strength of the PAIGC was the care with which the leaders established firm civil government in the areas brought under their control. They created schools, offered assistance to traditional rulers, and shared the army's medical facilities with the people. Amilcar Cabral and his associates in less than a decade constructed a viable mass movement based upon the reality of African village life blended together with a flexible ideology drawn largely from Indo-Chinese and Cuban models. The Portuguese found that they could only destroy the people and their villages; they could not shake their adherence to the PAIGC. General Spinola, the long-time commander in Guinea, recognized this fact even before his return to Portugal. His book, *Portugal and the Future*, published in 1973 called for a new policy toward the African areas. Spinola thus joined his voice to the growing number of critics of the expensive, coercive, and seemingly fruitless military policies of the government. When the Caetano regime was overthrown in April 1974, General Spinola came to power and immediately began to wind down the war in Guinea-Bissau. His first proposals which would have enabled Guinea to remain a part of the Portuguese empire were rejected by the PAIGC. After further discussions during the summer, Portugal capitulated and on September 10, 1974, Guinea-Bissau became an independent nation.

The detailed organization of civil government during the revolt made the transition to independence relatively easy. Amilcar Cabral had been assassinated in January 1973, the result of a plot set in motion by Portuguese authorities. There had been no struggle for power between his lieutenants. His brother, Luis de Almeida Cabral, succeeded to the leadership of the PAIGC and assumed the position of president of the new republic. After some debate, Portugal reluctantly agreed to grant independence to the Cape Verde Islands in June 1975. Although Guinea-Bissau and the Cape Verde Islands were two legally separate entities, they were linked by revolutionary ties and adherence to the doctrines of the same party. Aristides Pereira, the Secretary-General of the PAIGC, became president of the Cape Verde Islands. The major problem of both socialist states was the same as that of most African politics. They were extremely poor agricultural states with little to offer in return for outside investment. Perhaps the greatest challenge to the PAIGC was how to achieve the goals established by party theoreticians within the context of such scarcity.

Guinea-Bissau and Cape Verde

There is no better example in Africa of the gulf between theory and reality than Guinea-Bissau. During the revolution against Portuguese rule much of the world's attention was focused upon Amilcar Cabral and his guerrilla forces and the egalitarian organization he created to carry on the conflict. Many naively believed that after independence the new state would be able to continue the progress witnessed in the bush enclaves. However, reality intruded on these sanguine hopes. The first blow was the assassination of Amilcar in 1973; the leadership of the PAIGC passed to the less competent hands of his brother, Luis. It is doubtful, however, whether Amilcar even with his charisma could have prevented what occurred in the decade after independence. Guinea-Bissau is small, criss-crossed by rivers and creeks, and the Portuguese had left behind no solid economic infrastructure. The relative inaccessibility of parts of the country which had played such a role in the success of the revolution now inhibited development. There were only 700 miles of paved road, half a dozen bridges, no adequate port facilities, and not even a rudimentary industrial base. There were few minerals which could be extracted without undue costs. Thus the bauxite and phosphate resources were left relatively untapped. Petroleum exploration even in the mid–1980s had proved negative. Thus when the twin disasters of drought and inflation caused by OPEC's action struck, Guinea-Bissau was less prepared than most West African states. Luis Cabral and his associates' commitment to a rigid socialistic organization of the economy only exacerbated the economic problems. Two state owned enterprises were given the sole monopoly of the import and export trade; private enterprise was restricted to small retail shops and even these had to compete with state owned ones.

By 1980 the government's inability to cope with the economic problems led to pervasive food shortages, particularly in Bissau where fifteen percent of the population lives. Basic goods were in short supply and there was smuggling across the border from Senegal and Guinea. These were the conditions which enabled Major João Vieira to overthrow Luis Cabral on November 14, 1980, and to impose a more authoritarian regime in place of the village based democratic system envisioned during the revolution. This coup led to the rupture in the union with Cape Verde which established its independence from Guinea-Bissau the following year. Since 1980 Vieira's government has struggled against a worsening economy and the suggested approaches to solving those dilemnas has led to political infighting between the country's leaders.

In May 1984 the newly created 150 person National Assembly approved a new constitution in which executive authority was vested in a fifteen member Council of State which replaced the Revolutionary Council that had existed since 1980. Not surprisingly, Vieira was elected chairman of the council for a five year term. Vieira's orchestration of these reforms further consolidated his power base which had been briefly threatened by his prime minister, Victor Saúde Maria, before he was dismissed from office in March 1984. Maria caused a brief diplomatic flurry when he was given asylum in the Portuguese embassy. However, both states needed to continue good relations and soon the incident was forgotten. A further threat to Vieira developed when Marias's replacement First Vice-President, Brigadier Paulo Correia, came to disagree openly with Vieira over economic policy. In November 1985 soon after the celebration of Vieira's revolution he and fifty others were arrested. One of those, a hero of the struggle against Portugal, Jão da Silva, the Secretary for Cultural Affairs, was shot while in prison.

This fourth challenge to Vieira's control of the state underscores how tenuous is his position as long as the ongoing economic problems remain as serious as they are. All of the problems which led to the 1980 coup were still present a half decade later. Basic goods were still in short supply, there was a continuing black market and smuggling across the borders, and corruption in the civil service increased. There were water shortages and power failures in Bissau adding to the discomfort and disenchantment of the population. No new sources of income had been added although the government was hopeful of investigations for offshore oil. The foreign debt mounted yearly reaching a level which exceeds the annual Gross National Product. Service on the debt by 1986 exceeded $10 million a year. Attempting to slow down the economic decline is dangerous for the Vieira regime since rigorous conservative actions as recommended by the IMF generally affect the working population which is already suffering from the economic malaise. Vieira's announced four year development plan inaugurated in 1983 depended largely upon foreign assistance, particularly from Portugal, and has not been the success the government hoped. Despite continuing the rhetoric of a socialist managed state, the government began in 1987 to open more contacts with states other than the Lusiad and Soviet connections. The two state run monopolies over trade were to be dismantled and private traders allowed to compete for a share of the trade. Whether this and restructuring the foreign debt and World Bank loans will be sufficient to give the citizens of Guinea-Bissau a decent standard of living is doubtful. Without that no government can be secure.

The revolution against Portuguese rule was directed largely by men who had been born and educated in the Cape Verde islands. After gaining independence the two areas were connected primarily by such leadership, a singularity in political and economic philosophy, and the rule by a single political party, the PAIGG. The unlikely union of mainland Guinea-Bissau and the collection of islands located 400 miles west of the mainland came to an end after Vieira's takeover in 1980. The following year the controlling executive of the PAIGG in Cape Verde declared the union to be ended. Aristides Maria Pereira, one of the leaders in the fight for independence, continued as head of state. Although the mainland areas have economic woes, they are nothing compared to Cape Verde. There are practically no exports and drought struck the islands with unexpected ferocity. Large numbers died and a significant portion of the population simply left the islands. Agricultural production in 1987 had not yet reached normal proportions and malnutrition remained a major problem. Most of the food consumed by the estimated 300,000 persons was provided by international agencies. That this situation was likely to continue for years can be seen in the annual trade imbalance. In 1984, for example, the islands exported only $2 million in goods and imported $68 million. Pereira's hold on the state apparently does not and cannot depend on successful economic policies but rather on the domination by a single political party which he controls.

São Thome and Principe

One of the most improbable of modern states, these two small islands comprising only 372 square miles and having a population of slightly over 100,000 persons became independent in July 1975 as a result of the collapse of Portugal's African empire. Before this the economy of the islands had been dominated by a few thousand white settlers most of whom fled before the new African government could take over. They took with them not only their wealth but their skills, leaving the new nation sadly lacking in political and economic expertise. The new African government was a republic dominated from the very first by the *Mouvement para de Libertacao de São Tome e Principe* (MLSTP), the party which had been formed earlier in Gabon to further the revolution against Portuguese rule. Soon after independence, Manuel Pinto da Costa won a power struggle within the party and became president. Da Costa was a Marxist and immediately put into effect a number of socialist schemes most of which simply made the state's economic situation worse. Further, the close relationship he fostered with the Soviet Union effectively cut off all but a trickle of aid from Western nations. President Bongo of Gabon claimed once that São Thome was the "mouth of a Soviet gun pointed at Gabon." Although da Costa denied it, rumors persisted that the Russians were developing radar sites on the islands.

The small armed force of São Thome was until 1985 bolstered by over 2,000 troops from Angola.

President da Costa and his associates in the early 1980s began a rethinking of their relationship with Western states. This was brought on by the failure of socialism and Russian aid to significantly alter the state's poverty. There are only a few tropical exports. Income from cocoa, its major foreign exchange earner, had been halved in the decade after independence. The amount of land was limited and thus São Thome had to import ninety percent of its food. Consequently, the state was continually in debt. In 1984 its exports amounted to only $9 million while it imported over $20 million. Da Costa sent home most of the troops from Angola in 1984 and reduced the role of his Soviet advisors. At the same time he began dismantling many of his socialist projects and began to improve relations first with Portugal and then later with other nonsocialist states in the hope of luring much needed aid and investment.

FIVE
Supranational organizations

Nowhere is theory and reality of action more at variance than in the different supranational organizations which have recently been constructed in Africa. An observer must carefully weigh statements concerning unity and cooperation made by heads of state or those which are released from conferences of African leaders. These pronouncements normally represented aspirations and took little account of the difficulties of achieving these ends. The most obvious example of this dichotomy is Pan Africanism. Almost every leader in Africa committed himself to the furtherance of the principle of greater unity. However, the realization of even the first steps toward the goal proved to be more difficult than at first envisioned. A further complication arises in attempting to assign reasons for failures. For example, how far are the failures of the *Conseil de l'Entente* or the Union of African States to achieve closer unity among the states directly attributable to the actual difficulties of union and how much simply to the reluctance of political leaders to surrender their own power to a larger association?

On the level of the practical, all of the political associations before the creation of the Organization of African Unity were failures. This sweeping statement is not meant to negate the intangible contributions made by statesmen of Africa meeting together and discussing common problems. However, on the wider plane of establishing viable administrative mechanisms to put into practice the theories of the various organizations, no other verdict can be given. The economic committees established by the various organizations did not really establish policies which limit or direct economic planning and development in the member states. Some of the organizations had a defense council designed to coordinate planning for the group. Strategic and logistical problems prevented any real implementation of a joint military policy. Even the much heralded announcement by the OAU of a boycott of South African goods was largely window dressing since some African states such as Malawi depend too much on South African manufactured products.

It would be presumptuous to dismiss the various movements for larger groupings as a waste of time. Slowly many of the petty differences which have separated the various blocs in Africa have been bridged and, for all its immediate impotence, the nucleus of an organization of African states was created. It would have been unreasonable to expect that African states in little more than five years would have been able to achieve a fully functioning political and economic unity. That they progressed so far, even in theory, augurs well for future development. The real power of any supranational organization in Africa rests not with that organization but with the separate national entities that comprise it. Thus even the OAU, for all of the fanfare surrounding its creation, will succeed or fail on the willingness of the separate states to surrender to it a portion of their sovereignty.

There is no way to present the extremely complex events concerned with supranational organizations in any concise integrated fashion. One must look, therefore, at each individual organization and chart its creation, development, and in some cases demise in relative isolation from the maze of sweeping changes occurring throughout Africa which affected that organization.

Conseil de l'Entente

The Conseil de l'Entente was a reaction to the original plans to establish the Mali Federation which was to include Senegal, Soudan, Upper Volta, and Dahomey. The governments of France and the Ivory Coast brought economic pressure to bear upon Upper Volta and Dahomey. France intimated that it might reconsider building new facilities at the harbor of Cotonou. The rich Ivory Coast hinted at economic sanctions, particularly against Upper Volta, if the Mali constitution was adopted. Not surprisingly, the two weaker states revised their previous commitment and chose to continue their economic association with the Ivory Coast. Upper Volta was the first to defect from the proposed federation. Then Dahomey, which depended greatly on its position as the outlet for trade for land-locked Upper Volta and Niger, soon removed itself from its commitment to Mali.

In April 1959, an agreement was reached between the Ivory Coast and Upper Volta which served as the basis of the Conseil de l'Entente or, as it is sometimes called, the Benin Union. This agreement guaranteed that the harbor of Abidjan would be utilized in common and the main railway from Abidjan north would be jointly used. Further, a customs union was created to regulate customs and taxes, a common system of road transport was established, and in time it was planned that there was to be common postal service. In addition, the Entente was to regulate affairs common to the states. A Fonds de Solidarité was established to aid in development of the two territories.

By the end of May 1959, Dahomey and Niger had joined the Conseil and further discussions had evolved basic agreements on civil service, labor, justice, and finance. These agreements were further elaborated upon after long negotiations by resolutions signed, in April 1961, by the premiers of the four states. Continuing disturbances in Dahomey created in 1964 strains on its friendship with other Entente states. By the end of the year Dahomey had been phased out of the activities of the union. Therefore the decisions by the heads of state in December 1964 to establish "dual nationality" applied only to the Ivory Coast, Niger, and Upper Volta. Houphouët-Boigny, Diori, and Yameogo stated that this was the first step in a long-range program to effect a "fusion" of the three areas. In 1965 Houphouët-Boigny utilized the Entente to oppose Ghana and the OAU summit meeting called in October. Each of the members with four other ex-French areas refused to attend the conference and thus focused attention upon the dual role which Ghana was attempting to play.

The development of the Entente to the point where it could act as a working model for other African states was hampered by two interrelated factors. One was the disparity in wealth between the rich Ivory Coast and its poorer northern neighbors. To make the association meaningful, the Ivory Coast would have to bear the major cost of financing the further development of these areas. Not only Premier Houphouët-Boigny, but also powerful factions within the Ivory Coast, did not wish to see their wealth expended for the benefit of other areas. Certainly one of the factors which made the Ivory Coast leaders adverse to keeping, in effect, modified federal mechanisms of the AOF was the feeling that the Ivory Coast had been drained in the past to support the poorer members of the French African empire.

The second reason for the nullification of the Conseil as an effective federation was the attitude of Premier Houphouët-Boigny. For a variety of reasons he opposed political federalism as a solution to African problems. He viewed the Pan African movement as being effective in removing economic barriers and building understanding between African national leaders. He had always opposed political amalgamation as an effective solution to African ills. The Ivory Coast would gain little advantage by merging politically with even its immediate neighbors. Economic liabilities to the Ivory Coast would join the political by creating a larger, less homogeneous, less stable state. The Conseil, by achieving the modest ends Houphouët-Boigny set for it, created more harmonious conditions between the states and their ten million people. Within this existing framework the Ivory Coast could lead by influence without further political commitments. Correlate with the Ivory Coast's reluctance to strengthen federal ties was the development of larger, equally loose associations such as the Afro-Malagasy Union and the Organization of African States. These attempts to meet common problems is a way which agrees with Houphouët-Boigny's philosophy and renders relatively unimportant regional agreements such as that of the Conseil which sought to do the same.

Ghana-Guinea-Mali Union (Union of African States)

The Ghana-Guinea Union, which was born in 1959 and expanded to include Mali in July 1961, was in practice no union. It came into existence in the aftermath of Guinea's No vote to the de Gaulle referendum of 1958. The immediate, almost total withdrawal of French technicians and aid left Guinea in a desperate situation. Under Nkrumah, Ghana was attempting to extend its influence and philosophies throughout West Africa. The situation was tailored for some type of rapprochement. Ghana offered a loan of £10,000,000 which along with credits and aid from elsewhere enabled Guinea to survive the first troubled months of its independence. In May 1959, discussions between Kwame Nkrumah and Sekou Touré resulted in the union. In November 1960, soon after the breakup of the Mali Federation, Nkrumah announced, following discussions with Modibo Keita of Mali, that Ghana would grant Mali a long-term loan. He also stated that Ghana and Mali would establish a political association. The expanded union was formally created in July 1961, after a declaration of joint purpose had been issued in December 1960. Again the catalyst had been Ghanaian money and Nkrumah's desire to create an effective political entity which would forward his ideals of African unity.

The declarations of 1959 and 1960 had been framed in general terms. The major purpose was to "establish a union of our three states." Details of this amalgamation were not mentioned; instead the 1960 statement established two special committees to study "practical methods for achieving objectives." Various proposals which would have created a standard currency were never implemented. Neither was the plan to have a resident minister from each country serve in the ministry of the other states put into effect. Practically speaking, the union had little effect upon the internal policies of any of the states. This inaction represented a setback for Nkrumah who attempted through 1961 to follow a Pan African policy that would lead to an actual federation of states. Thus the Union of African States (UAS) was little more effective than the Conseil de l'Entente created by Houphouët-Boigny who had never favored political integration.

Yet the UAS was not a complete failure. The presidents of the three states consulted together a number of times on matters of common interest. The UAS created a spirit of cooperation between the countries which was most notable in the united front presented on nonalignment. In general, Nkrumah, Keita, and Touré were in agreement on foreign affairs. There were noticeable exceptions to this such as the Congo where Nkrumah's policies clashed with those of the more militant Touré. Given the differences in language, culture, and general economic and social problems, it was unrealistic to believe that a real political union could be quickly achieved.

Whatever intangible value the association might have had was lessened considerably by the rapprochement between Mali and Senegal and the creation of the OAU. The final blow to the union as a potentially effective organization was the revolt in Ghana which deposed Nkrumah. The new military government of Ghana began immediately to follow policies which mitigated against the continuance of the union. Perhaps the last feeble act of the organization was the token appointment of Nkrumah as an honorary president of Guinea in early 1966.

Union Africaine et Malagache (UAM) and successors

Most durable of all the supranational organizations were the associations of independent states which had been former French colonies. This is not surprising since there had existed before independence a large degree of geographic contiguity and economic interdependence. With rare exceptions the leaders of these states tended toward moderate policies, both in foreign and domestic affairs, and they remained on good terms with France. French investment and loans for many of the poorer areas allowed them to continue to maintain services that otherwise would have been impossible. The name of the organization representing the ex-French states has changed four times since 1960 and the functions have changed accordingly. However, the degree of cooperation represented has remained fairly constant.

In October 1960, twelve African states acting on the request of the Ivory Coast met in Abidjan. The primary reason for the meeting was to explore ways by which these states, all of which had previously been a part of the French colonial empire, could act as mediators in the Algerian crisis. This initial meeting was followed by another at Brazzaville in December 1960, where it was decided to establish a more permanent organization. The Brazzaville declaration called for a quick solution to the Algerian problem while it reiterated the continuing friendship of the states with France. The declaration made clear the states' sympathy with the FLN and its objective of an independent Algeria. It also stated the support of the signatories for Mauritanian independence and their backing of the United Nations in its attempts to solve the Congo problem.

The declaration provided for a meeting of a representative commission to study the problem of establishing closer economic ties between the states involved. In January 1961, the commission met in Dakar and formed the *Organization Africaine et Malagache Coopération Économique* (OAMCE). It was primarily an economic organization which was designed to coordinate economic policies relating to industry, agriculture, and interstate trade. This establishment led to the creation of Air Afrique, an airline composed of the total aviation resources of the member states and a joint defense command. In March 1961, the charter of the *Union Africaine et Malagache* (UAM) was signed by the heads of state. The association provided for close cooperation between the governments involved and twice-yearly meetings between the heads of state. A permanent secretariat was established at Cotonou to be run by a secretary-general.

Partially as a reaction to the Casablanca Conference, invitations were sent out to all African states in May 1961 to convene for a general conference at Monrovia, Liberia. Of the twenty states attending, twelve were from the UAM. The Monrovia Conference declared for a unity of aspiration attempting to work toward African solidarity based on the realities of the African situation. Thus other African polities represented at Monrovia accepted the principle behind the UAM of not trying to create immediate political unification.

With the addition of Rwanda and later Togo in July 1963, the UAM consisted of fourteen states. Due to the unity of language and culture as well as the nonpolitical approach toward greater unity, the UAM became the best organized of all African supranational groups. It was far more successful and pragmatic than the Casablanca group and, due to its loose political nature, it could associate freely with regional organizations such as the *Conseil de l'Entente* and take part in wider discussions such as the Monrovia meeting.

By early 1963, many of the differences which separated the so-called Casablanca group from the Monrovia bloc were healed. The relations between Nigeria and Guinea had improved, Senegal and Mali had settled their differences, and the hostility between Ghana and Togo was no longer a bar. In May 1963, all independent African states met at Addis Ababa. This conference resulted in a rapprochement between the two previously hostile blocs and led to a series of important declarations. The Addis Ababa meeting established the framework of the Organization of African Unity (OAU). Many of the duties envisioned by this new organization duplicated those already functioning in the UAM.

It thus became apparent, although the UAM was not to be phased out immediately, that there would have to be major changes if the fourteen member states were serious about the development of OAU. Many of the most important political and permanent officials of the UAM in the summer of 1963 seemed to favor a shift away from the UAM. Two such officials were President Yameogo of Upper Volta and President Senghor of Senegal. In March 1964, at the end of the meeting of the heads of state of the UAM in Dakar, it was announced that the UAM was to be transformed. The new organization was to be called the *Union Africaine et Malagache Coopération Économique* (UAMCE). This was but a return to the limited aims of the original states when in 1960 they had created the OAMCE. President Tsiranana of the Malagasy Republic stated that this move would "facilitate stronger links with Mali and Guinea" and would be a "far reaching step toward African unity." There were no further meetings of the heads of state of the UAMCE in 1964. The session planned for December was postponed until the spring of 1965. However, 1964 was the year of increasing cooperation between French African leaders, even those who had previously belonged to the more radical group. The Mali-Senegal rapport was made effective and relations between Senegal and the Ivory Coast improved.

In early 1965, the name of the organization was again changed, although ostensibly its functions remained basically the same. The new title was the *Organization Common Africaine et Malagache* (OCAM). The OCAM, although conceived to be primarily an economic organization, retained considerable residual political power. This was shown by the position taken by a majority of the OCAM states toward the OAU summit meeting at Accra in October 1965. Houphouët-Boigny of the Ivory Coast began his campaign in the spring to boycott the meeting unless Ghana was willing to change its aggressive attitude toward its neighbors. At an extraordinary meeting of the heads of state of the OCAM in May, Houphouët-Boigny's views prevailed and eight members of the organization did refuse to attend the OAU conference. However, this issue and that of the relationship of Congo-Léopoldville to the OCAM sharply divided the members. At the May 1965 meeting, only eight presidents were in attendance. Two other states sent observers. The president of the OCAM, Moktar Ould Daddah of Mauritania, was one of the statesmen who did not appear. He, particularly, opposed any rapproachement with the Kasavubu-Tshombe regime in the Congo and was also hostile to Houphouët-Boigny's attitudes toward the OAU. The triumph of Houphouët-Boigny in the OCAM did aid in keeping the Accra meeting from becoming a triumph for Nkrumah. However, it resulted in the resignation later of Mauritania from the OCAM.

The developments in 1965 showed how potentially powerful the OCAM was as the largest, best-organized economic and political bloc in Africa. At that time Houphouët-Boigny and the Entente group effectively controlled the OCAM, largely because the other leaders of French Africa tended to think and act in the same moderate way as the leader of the Ivory Coast.

The Casablanca group

The Brazzaville Conference in December 1960 acted as a catalyst for those African powers which followed a more activist line toward the West and its supposed neocolonialism. The Congo situation served to isolate these states from the majority of the African states in the United Nations. Supporting the Lumumbist position in the Congo was only one of the reasons why these nations drew together after Brazzaville. Morocco, which had an outstanding quarrel with Mauritania, fearing the results of the Brazzaville group's sponsorship of Mauritania, issued invitations to a select number of states whose foreign policies paralleled its own. This call resulted in the convening of the Casablanca Conference in January 1961. Seven African states attended the conference. These were Morocco, Guinea, Ghana, Mali, the United Arab Republic, Libya, and the Algerian provisional government. In addition, Ceylon was represented at the conference.

The Casablanca meeting necessitated a number of compromises on the part of the attending powers. Morocco was primarily concerned with non-recognition of Mauritania. Three of the other states, Ghana, Algeria, and Libya, for the sake of greater unity, abandoned their previous positions and supported Morocco's claims on Mauritania. The Congo crisis was another heated issue. Most of the states were in favor of withdrawing all their troops from the United Nations' command. Further, they were in favor of open aid to the Stanleyville government of Antoine Gizenga. Only Nkrumah opposed these proposals. In the end a communique was issued which stated in general terms the position of the powers. However, the last paragraph of the communique which reserved the right for each state to take appropriate action if the United Nations did not heed their advice showed that Nkrumah had won his point. Having won on that issue, Ghana relented and supported the United Arab Republic-sponsored resolution again Israel. This was the first time that a group of African states had taken a firm position of record on the Israeli-Arab conflict.

Following the January 1961 meeting, a further conference of the foreign ministers of the Casablanca states met in Cairo in May. There the basic agreements reached at Casablanca were incorporated into a charter. This created the executive machinery of the new union. It established four committees—political, economic, defense, and cultural. The political committee was made up of the heads of state, the economic was composed of the finance ministers of each state, and the defense committee was made up of the chiefs of staff of the armies of the member states. A permanent secretariat was established, located at Bamako, Mali.

Despite the specific statements and commitments to action made by the Casablanca and Cairo conferences, the association proved less durable and homogeneous in its organization than the Brazzaville group. The first major defection from the ostensibly solid front of January 1961 was the refusal of Libya to sign the protocol in May. Four of the original seven African states in the group were northern states with their focus of interest in the Islamic world of the Middle East and only secondarily in sub-Saharan Africa. Although there was a broad area of agreement on nonalignment and the dangers of the new imperialism between the states, there was from the beginning a tacit conflict between the United Arab Republic and Ghana. The three powers most involved in the Casablanca experiment were the nations of the Union of African States—Ghana, Guinea, and Mali. The Casablanca group did not take part in the Monrovia Conference or the follow-up Lagos meeting and seemed to be going contrary to the expressed wishes of the majority of African nations. In retrospect, these differences were more apparent than real. The primary aim of President Nkrumah for some type of immediate real political union had proved illusory; even the Casablanca protocol did not provide for this. Thus after 1961, the major differences between the Casablanca group and the Brazzaville group concerned means, not ends. National and individual rivalries tended to obscure this fact.

Improved relations between Nigeria and Guinea, Mali and Senegal, Ghana and Togo, and even Morocco and Mauritania made possible the rapprochement between the two groups which took place in May 1963 at the Addis Ababa Conference. The Addis Ababa summit meeting which established the OAU ended the Casablanca and Monrovia blocs although the UAM was not disbanded as a political organization until March 1964.

Organization of African Unity (OAU)

The new African states in the period 1960–1963 attempted a compromise between nationalism and Pan Africanism. If their independence was to be permanent and meaningful it was necessary for political leaders in all states to create a sense of nationalism in their people. The synthetic boundaries drawn by European powers in the scramble for Africa had to be accepted as the limits of the new nation states. Tribal and traditional loyalties had to be minimized and the state substituted as the entity which claimed the first loyalty of the citizens. In order to achieve this end, strong central governments were established, usually of the one-party type. Economic and social progress was demanded by the people. To satisfy the real needs of the people as well as their aspirations, the politicians had to foster a sense of particularism. Opposing such nationalism were the claims made by all African leaders that they desired a united Africa. They saw Africa as a whole with all states having common internal problems, all with a heritage of colonialism, and all wishing to avoid the pitfalls of the cold war. Despite the many statements by African leaders favoring Pan Africanism, the solutions to their national problems took precedence over general African or even regional solutions. This led many observers to conclude that Africans, despite their pronouncements, were not overly concerned with African unity.

Reinforcing the apparent disunity of Africa was the rivalry between differing cultural blocs and political personalities. Differential occupation by the French, British, and Belgians for over sixty years had imposed two languages and three sets of institutions on Africa which acted as a major block to any plans for immediate political union. In the period after 1957 there emerged a number of African leaders who were jealous of their new-found prerogatives, each seeking regional or African unity on his terms. Such varied personalities as Nkrumah of Ghana, Senghor of Senegal, Touré of Guinea, Houphouët-Boigny of the Ivory Coast, Balewa of Nigeria, and Nasser of Egypt had their own solutions to African unity. Inevitably the plans formulated by such African leaders clashed. These differences were institutionalized in the formation of a number of hostile organizations such as the Ghana-Guinea-Mali Union, the *Conseil de l'Entente,* and most important, the Casablanca and the Brazzaville blocs. Although generalizations must be made with caution, one can say that the differences between these blocs concerned means and not ends. The Brazzaville (later Monrovia) bloc wanted to build toward possible political unity by rationalizing those divisive elements which could effectively be dealt with immediately. The Brazzaville group attempted economic solutions and, building on a base of common institutions, sought to create a spirit of unity. The Casablanca powers did not have these common institutions and tended to be more radical in their pronouncements of non-alignment and anti-imperialism. The Casablanca group in the statements of their leaders favored steps toward immediate political unity. From 1961 onward, however, both groups began to realize that the ends of African unity were ultimately the same. This awareness led to a conference of delegates from all the independent African nations, with the exception of Togo, at Addis Ababa in May 1963. This meeting resulted in the abolition of the Casablanca and Monrovia blocs and the creation of the Organization of African Unity (OAU).

The speeches of the heads of state at Addis Ababa reflected a new-found maturity. Different though they were, most of the speeches pressed for a charter to define the areas of agreement, an organization to work for the realization of African unity, and a body which would organize efforts to drive the last vestiges of imperialism from Africa. Although there was a recognition of areas of conflict between African states, such as Somalia's claims to Ethiopian and Kenya territory, the stress was upon unity. This spirit of cooperation resulted in the charter which established the OAU.

The charter, later ratified by all independent African states, provided for an assembly of the heads of state, a council of ministers, a general secretariat, and a commission of mediation, conciliation, and arbitration. The assembly of the heads of state or their representatives was to meet at least once a year. The council of ministers was composed of the foreign ministers of the individual states or their representatives. This council was charged with preparing the agenda for the assembly conferences, investigating matters referred to it, implementing decisions of the assembly, and coordinating policies leading to inter-African cooperation. The council of ministers was to meet at least twice a year. The secretariat was under the direction of a secretary-general and was charged with carrying out the administration of the organization. Members of the secretariat were not controlled by one state and received orders only from the organization. All member states were pledged to avoid violence in settling any dispute with another member state. It was the duty of the commission on mediation, conciliation, and arbitration to solve questions involving conflicts between states.

The budget for the organization was prepared by the secretariat and approved by the council of ministers. Contributions from member states were based upon the rate of assessment made by the United Nations. No state was to be charged with over twenty percent of the total yearly budget. In addition to the major subdivisions of the organization, specialized commissions were to be established under the direction of the assembly. These regular commissions covered the areas of defense, health, economics, nutrition, and science and research.

Aside from the establishment of the framework of a general African organization, the most important pronouncement of the Addis Ababa Conference of 1963 concerned South Africa, Rhodesia, and Portugal. The conference urged decolonization of the remaining parts of Africa still controlled by European powers. It urged the United Kingdom to prevent the "white settler" minority from consolidating its power in Southern Rhodesia and promised aid to the nationalist leaders there in securing African political rights. Apartheid in South Africa was condemned and the states pledged themselves to oppose this system through direct aid to nationalists, through mobilization of world opinion in the United Nations, and through a boycott of trade with South Africa. These same forms of opposition were to be applied to Portuguese imperialism in Guinea, Angola, and Mozambique. The heads of state recommended the breaking of diplomatic relations between African states and Portugal and South

Africa. However, a number of states such as Malawi and Zambia later showed a decided coolness toward any such action because of the adverse economic effect it would have on them.

The organization established a coordinating committee with head-quarters at Dar-es-Salaam to help national liberation movements. A liberation fund was established to aid the freedom fighters and all states promised to help train volunteers for the national liberation movements. The year following showed how difficult it was to translate these ideals into concerted action.

The second summit meeting of the OAU took place in Cairo in mid-July 1964. After a week of deliberation which had been preceded by conferences of the foreign ministers, the heads of state made a few important announcements. The permanent site of OAU headquarters was established at Addis Ababa. M. Diallo Telli of Guinea was appointed to a four-year term as secretary-general. His position was not defined in terms other than the administrative ones already outlined in the charter. Reluctance to give him more political responsibility to act in urgent cases stemmed from fear of concentrating theoretical power in the hands of the representative of a supranational organization.

There were few concrete successes to report to the heads of state. The dispute between Algeria and Morocco was settled. Little was said of the Kenya-Ethiopia-Somalia dispute except to promise that it would be the subject of special study. Later Somalia announced that it would not be bound by any decisions made by the OAU in respect to her borders. Two functional committees were established, one of which was to coordinate activities of the African states in applying sanctions against South Africa.

Illustrating the wide divergence of opinion among OAU members were the four days of speeches by the heads of state. President Nkrumah of Ghana was particularly critical of the work of the liberation committee in putting into effect any real help for those Africans struggling for freedom. President Nyerere of Tanzania was equally critical of Ghana's attitude of preaching unity but refusing to help the liberation committee.

Perhaps the major failure of the Cairo meeting was their reluctance to deal with the Congo crisis. Moise Tshombe had been appointed premier of the Congo three days before the heads of state were due to arrive in Cairo. The foreign ministers cabled President Kasavubu requesting that Tshombe not come to Cairo. Thus the premier of the most troubled area in Africa was not present. This was more than symbolic; it was an actual rejection of the Congo and undercut the OAU's later position against foreign intervention. If Tshombe was not even to be invited to present the problems of his state, then the OAU was not really the organization it claimed to be.

In September the OAU appointed a ten-member commission headed by President Kenyatta of Kenya to attempt a reconciliation of the warring factions in the Congo. After interviewing rebel leaders, some of the commission members called upon Tshombe to stop receiving outside aid. A delegation flew to the United States to protest to President Johnson any further aid to the Congo. President Kasavubu protested this action by commission members, claiming he was not consulted and the delegation was, therefore, not received by President Johnson. The Kenyatta commission was kept in force after the foreign ministers' meeting in March 1965, although it had accomplished little and its report had been rejected by Tshombe. The commission did more harm to the image of the OAU than would have been the case if they had not acted at all. Not only did they focus world attention on the weakness of the OAU to act decisively, but the commission acted as a focal point for the expression of wide differences of opinion within the OAU itself.

However, in certain areas the OAU was successful. One of its commissions had played a most important role in the resettlement of over 100,000 Watutsi who had fled Rwanda. The Algeria-Morocco border dispute was temporarily settled. The organization acted as a base for a number of bilateral and multilateral groupings concerned with such matters as riverine agreements. The liberation committee still functioned although beset with a host of problems brought on by the fragmentation of resistance movements. Perhaps the one action of the OAU in early 1965 which could have the most far-reaching effects was the establishment of the African Development Bank. By the spring of 1965, $32,000,000 of the initial capitalization of $250,000,000 had been subscribed from African sources.

Despite all of these positive actions, the OAU was deeply divided. At the conference of foreign ministers in Nairobi in March and in the months immediately following, most member states were polarized into a pro- or anti-Ghana faction. One of the reasons for this split was differential attitudes toward the problems in the Congo. Even more serious were the charges made by some political leaders that Ghana was actively supporting subversion against the political regimes of other African states. The leader of the anti-Nkrumah group within the OAU was Houphouët-Boigny of the Ivory Coast, solidly backed by the other Entente members. This conflict was magnified by the fact that the 1965 summit meeting was scheduled for Accra.

In May Houphouët-Boigny launched a "Peace Offensive" to gain support in boycotting the Accra meeting until Ghana would promise to stop encouraging exiles from neighboring states in their subversive activities. This maneuver was successful only in those ex-French states which had tended to follow Houphouët-Boigny's leadership in the past. In the months preceding the Accra Conference in October, various proposals were made to have Nkrumah and Houphouët-Boigny meet at a "little summit" and compromise their differences. All of these attempts were unsuccessful. Thus when the third general conference was held, seven states followed Houphouët-Boigny's guide and were not represented. These were the four Entente states and Togo, Chad, and the Malagasy Republic.

Nkrumah had done everything possible to impress the visiting heads of state. Thousands of banners and signs were erected in Accra. The city itself was cleaned thoroughly and the Ghana government had built a special facility to house the delegates. The main building in this complex was a twelve-story building with sixty presidential suites which cost a total of £10,000,000 to construct.

Despite these preparations, the Accra meeting was a general defeat for Nkrumah's policies. He had wanted the conference to create the machinery for an all-African government. The first step in this direction, he believed, should be the formation of an "Executive Council" to give continuing direction to unified political objectives. This proposal was referred to the heads of state for further study. Thus nothing could be done toward creating a stronger executive for at least one year. The Congo was another issue on which Ghana's position was not upheld. President Kasavubu attended the conference and made it clear that he would leave if the Congo question was made an issue. Perhaps because he had just removed Tshombe as premier and perhaps because of his own popularity, the Congo question was not discussed.

Although not represented, Houphouët-Boigny won a substantial victory when the conference, after lengthy debate, passed a strong resolution on subversion. This resolution was directed not only at non-African powers but also at African states which actively condoned movements in their territory designed to overthrow other African governments. This by implication struck directly at Ghana.

The issue which dominated the discussions was Rhodesia and Ian Smith's unilateral declaration of independence. The conference called upon Britain to use whatever steps necessary, including force, to bring down the white Rhodesian government. It also called upon all African states to utilize all their strength to put an end to the present Rhodesian state. In the resolution there was a veiled threat to Britain if the situation in Rhodesia was not immediately rectified. The resolution asked for African states to reappraise their economic, political, and diplomatic relations with Britain if Prime Minister Wilson's government did not act more speedily in ending the Smith regime.

In December 1965, at the foreign ministers' conference in Addis Ababa, the delegates returned to the question of Rhodesia and decided to implement the implied threat to Britain. In essence they delivered an ultimatum to Prime Minister Wilson to end the Rhodesian problem by December 15. If this was not accomplished, then the member states of the OAU would break off relations with Britain. The British government immediately replied that it would not be coerced into any hasty ill-conceived action. The Tunisian and Upper Volta governments repudiated within a few hours the OAU decision. The old Brazzaville bloc of states made no move toward a break in relations. Not even Rhodesia's closest neighbors, Zambia and Malawi, followed the OAU decision.

At the end of 1965, in reappraisal, the three-year existence of the OAU was a stormy one. It achieved certain of its objectives not the least of which was the phasing out of the Brazzaville and Casablanca groups. No matter how weak the OAU appeared or how divided its counsel, it was the only supranational political organ recognized by all African states. However, the OAU failed to achieve the status hoped for at its inception. There were two major reasons for this. One was a reflection of the immaturity of African statesmen. In two major African crisis situations the OAU failed to give constructive leadership. In both the Congo and Rhodesian questions the OAU was given the opportunity to react constructively in solving extremely complex problems. Instead, in each case, the delegates allowed emotion to govern their actions and assumed extreme positions which could not be maintained and which they later were forced to repudiate. The second reason for the continued weakness of the organization is more fundamental. However unpopular Nkrumah might have been, he had analyzed the OAU correctly when he said that it could never become the hoped for, positive force in Africa until its executive power was strengthened. Its ultimate success in securing the goal of Pan Africanism depends upon how much power the individual members are willing to give to the organization.

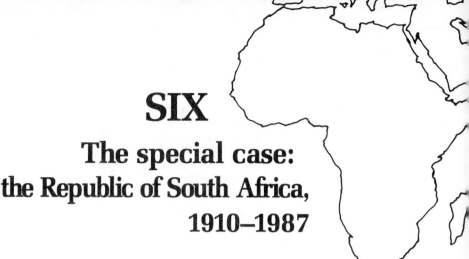

SIX
The special case: the Republic of South Africa, 1910–1987

Political developments to 1948

In 1910 the Union of South Africa was still predominantly rural. This was especially true for the Afrikaner people in each of the provinces. Electoral boundaries were drawn to favor the country vote and this was one factor in the initial success of the Afrikaners at the polls. Once in power a Boer-dominated government was not likely to alter the voting districts which helped give it power. This technical fact must be kept in mind in assessing the continued success of Afrikaner-led parties in all the parliamentary elections in the Union. The major area of political conflict for almost fifty years did not concern Africans or colored. Rather it was a continuation of the old Boer-British contest of the nineteenth century. Two of the chief political leaders, Louis Botha and Jan Christian Smuts, accepted the necessity for Afrikaners to function, in cooperation with the British population, within the context of the empire. Others such as J. B. M. Hertzog, N. C. Havenga, and Daniel Malan rejected the concept of continued cooperation. Their goal was Afrikaner domination of the political life of the Union and as soon as possible an independent republic free from British interference.

Botha and Smuts had created the South African party by blending their old *Het Volk* group with middle-of-the-road British supporters. Until the elections of 1924 this party dominated the political life of the Union. At imperial conferences, Botha and Smuts made clear their dedication to the empire and the necessity to forget the Boer War. During World War I, Union forces conquered German South West Africa and cooperated in the campaigns in East Africa. Botha led the South African army against many of his old comrades such as de Wet and de la Rey in the abortive Afrikaner uprising of 1914.

J. B. M. Hertzog, formerly minister of justice in Botha's first government, had resigned in 1911 to form the Nationalist Party which represented the separatist aspirations of Afrikanerdom. He

153

was joined by younger men like Dr. Daniel Malan who began to publish the influential Afrikaans newspaper, *Die Burgher*. So long as Louis Botha was prime minister, the Nationalists could hope for few gains even in the Transvaal. Botha, the stolid Boer figure, was still a great hero to most Afrikaners. With his death in 1919, Smuts became prime minister. Distrusted for his coldness and intellectual bent, "Slim Jannie" could not demand the same loyalty from the Afrikaners. Worsening economic conditions in the Union and Smuts' penchant for violent unilateral action alienated many. The killing in May 1921 of 163 Israelites, African followers of Enoch Mgijima, convinced many British supporters that they could not continue to support Smuts' government. This massacre at Bulhoek was soon followed by the repression of the Bondelswarts Hottentots in South West Africa. These Hottentots were pastoral people who supplemented their cattle tending by hunting. The government, in an obvious attempt to make them settle in one area, assessed a £1 tax per dog owned. The Bondelswarts refused to pay, whereupon in May 1922, Smuts, known to the outside world as one the architects of the mandate system, sent a column of 400 men and two airplanes against the Hottentots. The resultant loss of life exceeded one hundred and the incident indicated Smuts' readiness to use maximum force against his opposition.

The Rand strike, already referred to, was the final example of Smuts' use of force. However, on the Rand he was dealing with Europeans and his violent methods there alienated the minority Labor party whose support was crucial if Smuts was to continue in power. The election of 1924 gave the South African party fifty-three seats, the Nationalists sixty-three, and the Labor party eighteen. The Labor party refused to cooperate with Smuts in a coalition government and Hertzog and the Nationalists came to power for the first time. Hertzog was forced to compromise on his promise to create an Afrikaner republic for two reasons. One was the narrowness of his majority in parliament and Labor's opposition to the republican ideal. The other concerned changes then occurring in the institutional structure of the British empire. World War I and the Irish troubles combined with the growing sense of particularistic nationalism had led to granting de facto independent status to Commonwealth countries. Between 1926 and 1931, the leaders of British colonies worked out the details of the British Commonwealth. The Statute of Westminster of 1931 gave the Union of South Africa the best of both worlds—virtual independence with a continuation of the close economic links with Britain. Hertzog felt justified, therefore, in abandoning Afrikaners' dream of a Boer-dominated republic.

Hertzog's Nationalists retained control of parliament after the 1929 elections partially because they openly advocated the stripping of political rights from the Cape Colored. Thus his government was in power during the early, most stringent years of the depression. Undoubtedly the South African party could have utilized the depression to force an election and probably would have won. However, Smuts refused to use economic distress as a political issue and joined with Hertzog in 1933 to form a national government. The two political parties were fused to create the United party. Only a few Afrikaners refused to belong to the coalition and joined with Dr. Malan to form a new purified Nationalist party. Hertzog remained prime minister with Smuts as his deputy until September 1939.

The onset of World War II highlighted the differences between Smuts and his followers and those of Hertzog. Many of the latter group believed that the Union had no concern with Britain's war and wanted to remain neutral. After a lengthy acrimonious debate, Smuts and the interventionists won, South Africa declared war on Germany, the coalition was destroyed, and Smuts once more became prime minister.

Despite the South African army's distinguished record and Smuts' role in international politics, the war was not popular with the majority of the Afrikaner population. A number of Afrikaner organizations had developed in the 1930s such as the Broederbond, the *Afrikaanse Nasionale Studentebond* (ANS), and the *Ossewa Brandweg*. All of these were devoted to Afrikaner nationalism and the securing of more economic and political power for Afrikaners. Many Afrikaner leaders had become enamored of the Nazi message. J. F. J. van Rensburg, Oswald Pirow, and Johannes Vorster actively supported the Germans. Undoubtedly many other Nationalist leaders who were not as active had great sympathy with the ideas enunciated by the Germans.

At the close of the war the poor white Afrikaner of the late 1920s and early 1930s had been better assimilated into the industrial life of the nation. Their leaders had created a series of organizations to give form to Afrikaner ideals and there were more Afrikaans newspapers and periodicals. Many of the younger Boer politicians such as Dr. Hendrik Verwoerd, Johannes Strijdom, C. R. Swart, and Johannes Vorster were weary of attempts to conciliate the British-speaking population. Economic disturbances following the war, a series of strikes by African workers, and a belated recognition of the numbers of Africans in all the cities gave Dr. Malan's party an issue which in the election of 1948 dwarfed all others.

The position of Africans in the Union is discussed elsewhere, but it should be stressed that they had never been a real political issue between any of the white political parties. Dr. Malan, backed by all the Afrikaner organizations, provided with a philosophical and religious rationale by the South African Bureau of Racial Affairs (SABRA), decided to make the threat of African domination the chief issue in the election of 1948. His party for the first time openly enunciated the need for complete separation of the races. The United party was placed on the defensive on this issue and the aging Smuts never regained the initiative in the election. The results of the 1948 elections surprised everyone, including Dr. Malan. Although winning only forty percent of the popular vote, the Nationalist party of Malan won seventy seats and the smaller Afrikaner party of Havenga won nine. The United party could muster only sixty-five seats. In combination with smaller groups, the opposition to the Nationalists had only seventy-four seats. Thus Dr. Malan formed a government with a slim majority of only five seats. His government was pledged to carry out rigorously the campaign promises to establish apartheid as a way of life.

Economic developments, 1910–1948

The Union of South Africa's unique position in Africa is as much characterized by its economy as by its political development based upon European dominance. It was, even before the Boer War, a proto-industrial state. It possessed excellent harbor facilities, railroads, telegraph lines, and a firm financial base closely linked to the great banking houses of Europe. Gold and diamonds were the central features of South African wealth in the late nineteenth century, but diversified farming in row crops, vineyards, and orchards as well as cattle and sheep ranching undergirded the economies of all the provinces of the Union. Milner's reconstruction plans had restored the mining and transport industries of the Transvaal and Orange Free State. Spurred partially by the demands of World War I, South Africa continued its industrialization. In the half century after 1914 the mining industry assumed a greater role in South Africa. Platinum, iron, coal, copper, uranium, and chromate discoveries added to the wealth of an ever-developing gold and diamond industry. South African entrepreneurs were not satisfied with only an extractive economy. Smelters and fabrication plants were developed, the chemical industry begun, and food and packaging plants started. All these called for a myriad of service industries.

After 1910 the Union of South Africa was all but independent of British political control. Even the areas of political dependence were eliminated by the Statute of Westminster passed by the British parliament in December 1931. Thus the political system of South Africa, contrary to other British African territories, was vitally concerned with the rapid economic development of the country. There was a close relationship between government at all levels and business and banking interests.

The complex evolvement of each major industry in South Africa is beyond the scope of this work. It is sufficient to note that, by the time of the crucial election of 1948, it was an industrial and urban state. The seeming insatiable demands of the mines for more labor were early duplicated by other industries in centers such as Cape Town, Johannesburg, and Durban. Hundreds of thousands of Africans permanently left their home areas and became residents of the sprawling, unplanned towns which sprang up near every city. In the fifteen-year period following World War I, there was a mass exodus of Afrikaners from the farms to the cities. By 1936 almost forty-five percent of South Africa's population was resident in nine major cities. The poor unskilled white in the city, predominantly Afrikaners, came more into direct competition with the black laborer and this reinforced the earlier exclusivist attitudes of the white labor unions.

Although South African industry is highly diverse, the gold mining industry was the bellwether of the economy. Its position as the first support of the economy has waned in the period after World War II, but South Africa in 1969 still produced eighty percent of the world's gold. The historian C. W. de Kewiet reported that in the year 1935–1936, 26.95 percent of the entire government revenue of the Union was derived from the mining industry. Therefore, a brief survey of that industry is necessary to understand modern South Africa. The low quality of the ore of the Witwatersrand early dictated large-scale operations which, to be successful, had to utilize the most modern techniques available. Each producing mine needed in addition large amounts of cheap labor. Even before 1914 competition between mines was kept at a minimum by rationalizing common services. The Chamber of Mines through a series of offices provided a common approach not only to purchases and labor but also to medical research, health conditions, mining regulations, and taxation. A subsidiary of the chamber, the Native Recruiting Corporation, provides the bulk of native workers for all the mines, thus eliminating possible wage inflation. By utilizing this common approach and the latest in techniques and machinery, the productivity of an average African miner was raised from 500 tons per worker a year in 1914 to 1,600 tons a year in 1930. At the same time the cost per ton of the ore milled was reduced from approximately twenty-nine shillings to less than twenty shillings.

Labor had always been a critical problem. Most of the European miners who had held all the skilled and most of the semiskilled positions had left during the Boer War. There was not an adequate number of Africans trained in mining techniques available. The high commissioner, Lord Milner, in order to rapidly restore the mining industry, had imported Chinese workers. By 1907 there were 54,000 Chinese laborers in the Transvaal. Within a short time this policy was dispensed with and the mine operators began to use Africans for most of the unskilled work. Contract laborers were recruited from every nation and tribe in the Union. As industry expanded, Africans from Rhodesia and Basutoland also migrated to the Union to work in the mines. In 1901 and 1910, agreements were signed with the Portuguese for the importation of a maximum of 80,000 African workers per year from their territories. White miners were also used in unskilled as well as skilled positions, although they were from the beginning paid more for their work than Africans. The bulk of white miners before 1918 were of British origin. However, in the 1920s, Afrikaners began to be important in the European sector.

Tension developed very early between the mine owners and white workers. Needing cheap labor to reduce overhead, the mine owners were in favor of employing Africans through at least the level of semiskilled positions. White workers insisted not only upon higher pay for the same job but also that certain vocations be reserved exclusively for them. The government, despite its dependence upon the mines for working capital, has continually supported the concept of the color bar for certain occupations. The Mine and Works Act of 1911 was the first Union law to enshrine the concept that certain occupations were reserved for Europeans. This law was upset by the Supreme Court in 1923, but the industry continued to apply its principles until a new, more comprehensive act was passed. The Mines and Works Act of 1926 was Prime Minister Hertzog's way of paying off labor for its support after the election of 1924. Taken together with the Apprenticeship Act of 1922 which closed many occupations to potential African trainees, the new mines act gave white workers the special treatment which they demanded.

The Mines and Workers Act of 1926, with other mechanisms of control over white labor such as the Industrial Conciliation Acts, made the white unions in the 1930s a respectable part of the industrial scene. This had not always been the case. The first trade unions in southern Africa were modeled upon their British counterparts and in general were led by radicals. Syndicalism, the radical tradition, and after 1917, Communism propelled the early white unions toward direct action against their masters. The strikes on the Rand in 1913–1914 which spread to influence other workers were violent and the Botha government used police and troops to break the walkout. Better wages, better health facilities, and safety improvements were all delayed by World War I. By 1919 shrinkage in the price of gold on the world market necessitated cutting back operational costs. The Low Grade Mine Commission of 1920 recommended not only a reduction of wages but also the employment of Africans in certain positions and thus the removal of the color bar. The mine unions and associated organizations, infiltrated by radical leaders, reacted violently. In January 1922, strikes began in the coal mines and by March a general strike had paralyzed all mining on the Rand. Prime Minister Smuts reacted militantly as he had in 1914 by sending in troops and this time using airplanes against the strikers. The strike was broken, workers accused of being snipers were shot without trial, and others arbitrarily exiled.

The white unions had lost their short-term demands and were forced to accept the government and mine owners' dictates. The Labor party, although not in complete sympathy with the strikers, threw its support behind Smuts' opponents in the election of 1924. The new prime minister, Hertzog, early cemented this temporary liaison by granting the white unions their special position against native competition. The improved economy of the 1920s removed many of the economic demands of the unions from the imperative category. Although there continued to be labor problems, never again would the bulk of the white workers on the Rand confront the government with a potential revolution.

African workers have always suffered under almost insurmountable handicaps in their attempt to organize into effective unions. All the institutions of the state opposed strikes by Africans.. Government joined management and white unions in attempting to break any significant black union movement. The most important attempt to accomplish a general black union was the Industrial and Commercial Union of Africa (ICU) first organized immediately after World War I by Clements Kadile. By 1928, Kadile's union claimed over 250,000 members. However, the ICU was always relatively impotent. The Hertzog government used every means at its disposal to destroy its power. White workers were always available to break any black strike. In the latter 1920s the union became fragmented because of quarrels between Kadile and other leaders. The depression delivered the final blow to the ICU. No other African union has since had such appeal or success. Strikes and industrial disturbances by African workers, nevertheless, continued. Work stoppage became so serious during World War II that the Smuts' government, in 1942, passed War Measure 145. This made all strikes by Africans illegal. Despite this, there were continued disturbances on the Rand during the war. In 1946 a major strike involving over 74,000 workers closed almost half the mines. Utilizing War Measure 145 and the Riotous Assembly Act, the government sent in the police and drove the strikers back to work. Over fifty leaders were subsequently arrested and charged with a variety of disorders.

Prior to the election of 1948, the Union was already the industrial power of sub-Saharan Africa. Its preeminence was based not only upon capital and expertise but also upon the ready availability of cheap African labor. A series of laws and entrenched practices in government and industry had established firmly the principle of the subordination of the African worker. In a state where integration of the labor force was a key to continued success, the African had been segregated, his unions rendered ineffective, and his leaders proscribed. Long before apartheid became the official policy of the government, segregation had become the practice at all levels of industry and mining throughout the Union.

Developments in the non-European sector through 1948

Prior to 1948 there were few responsible officials who opposed the basic principle of separation between whites and blacks. Every government of the Union had made clear by significant acts of legislation its support of the white South African against the threat, real or imagined, of black predominance. These actions can be considered under four separate although interconnected headings of labor, land, urban problems, and political rights. In each of these categories the Bantu and to a lesser extent Cape Colored and Indians were relegated to the role of second-class citizens. Reference has already been made to the Mines and Works Acts of 1911 and 1926, the Apprenticeship Act of 1922, the Industrial Conciliation Act of 1924, and War Measure 145. All had been directed at curbing the Bantu's aspirations for better jobs and wages throughout industry. These acts had given the white laborer a superior, guaranteed position, in many cases to the direct detriment of economic establishment.

Despite the growing need for African workers in the urban areas, the majority of the Bantu during the first half of the twentieth century lived in rural areas. Beginning with the policies of Sir Harry Smith in the Transkei and Theophilus Shepstone in Natal, there had developed, in a haphazard manner, the concept of native reserves—areas of land guaranteed to the Bantu by the government in which, in theory, they could develop politically, socially, and economically in their own fashion and at their own speed. In these reserves indirect rule through chiefs or elected councils was the goal of administration. However, white officials could and did intervene directly in African affairs in the reserves. Major changes could also be instituted without consulting Bantu leaders which totally altered African traditions. The Glen Gray Act in the Cape in 1894 offers a good example of this since the act converted tribal ownership of lands to individual holdings and also instituted the rule of primogeniture.

The first comprehensive measure which established a standard reserve policy for the Union was the Native Land Act of 1913. This act demarcated areas on which various groups of Bantu had historic claims and made provision for later additions to the reserves by government purchase. This act did not of itself segregate the rural Bantu. It only recognized the de facto segregation which already existed. White public opinion in the next twenty years opposed any substantial appropriations to add to the size of the reserves although they were obviously inadequate for the growing Bantu population. In 1936 the Native Trust and Land Act finally provided for the purchase of an additional fifteen million acres of land to be added to the reserves. However, by 1961 only slightly more than ten million acres had been purchased. When the 1936 act is finally complete, the total area reserved for African occupation will be approximately 65,000 square miles or less than fourteen percent of the available land of the Union.

The African population increased from approximately seven and one-half million persons in 1936 to almost eleven million in 1961, indicating very clearly that population increase had outstripped the addition of new lands. Adding to the African dilemma is the condition of much of the land. Poor conservation techniques in many areas have converted previously fertile land to marginal land. Over ninety-four percent of African land is communally owned. Subsistence agriculture is the prevailing practice which prevents the utilization, even if funds were available, of most modern farming techniques. Thus the African population, notwithstanding government claims to the contrary, cannot live on the lands assigned to them. This is clearly seen by the fact that in 1961 only 3.6 million Africans were resident on the reserve land. The bulk of the adult male Bantu population were working outside the reserves either as farm laborers or in the cities.

The use of Bantu as workers in the cities caused the African urban population to increase dramatically. By 1961 almost three million Africans were resident in the urban centers with almost one million living in the Witwatersrand area. Such a concentration of population early brought severe problems related to housing. The Native Urban Areas Act of 1923 empowered local authorities to establish locations for African settlements with the understanding that these be segregated from white areas. Housing, sanitation, and control of the local population also became local responsibilities. Even before World War II, only about half the urban African population lived in controlled locations. The rest either lived with their employers or had simply "squatted" illegally on municipal and other unoccupied areas. There they built houses of scrap lumber, tin .cans, and galvanized iron. Needless to say, water, electricity, and modern sewage facilities were absent. These shanty towns were a feature of every large city and were a reflection on the government's inadequacy in solving the African's housing problem. World War II speeded up the movement of Africans to the cities and made an already bad situation much worse.

Most of the African population was rendered politically impotent by the South Africa Act. Instead of enunciating a common policy within the Union relating to African rights, the act enshrined the differences inherent in the four separate areas prior to unification. Only in Cape Colony was the African given theoretical rights equal to the white citizen. Even this was hedged by proscribing Africans from standing for election to the Union House of Assembly. However, if the Bantu and Colored met the educational and property qualifications of the Cape, they were guaranteed the franchise. The most important entrenched clause in the South Africa Act specified that in order to remove them from the common roll a two-thirds majority of both the House of Assembly and Senate was required. However, the South Africa Act did not provide for guaranteeing non-Europeans equal treatment if at some later date the franchise rules were broadened. Thus in 1931 when white women were given the right to vote in Union elections, it was decided that it was not necessary to include Bantu or Colored women in this reform.

In 1936 the Representation of Natives Act disenfranchised approximately 15,000 qualified Bantu in Cape Colony. Instead of being on the common roll with all other voters, they were given special representation. A twenty-two member Native Representative Council was created for the entire Union. It had only advisory powers in matters relating to African affairs. To replace the Cape Bantu's loss of political equality three special seats were created in the House of Assembly. Only whites could stand for these offices, but they were to represent the interests of the Bantu. Four senators were also chosen to watch over the rights of non-Europeans. Given the nature of these reforms and the relatively powerless position of the Senate, the arguments that the Bantu were given better representation had a hollow ring.

Thus in brief, the Bantu majority, long before 1948, were living in a society of apartness. There were two separate sets of rules governing whites and blacks in all important areas of life. However, the position of the Cape Colored and Indian, although affected by segregationist legislation, had not been seriously attacked before World War II. Since much of the thrust of Prime Minister Malan's program after 1948 concerned the Cape Colored, their peculiar situation within the Union should be briefly noted.

Numbering approximately one and one-quarter million by 1948, the Cape Colored are racially a very mixed group. Their historical antecedents date to the liaisons between slaves and Europeans in the seventeenth century. Later admixtures of Hottentot, Bushmen, Malay, and Bantu helped create the present population. Over eighty-five percent of the

Colored live in Cape Colony where they had been guaranteed theoretical equality before the law as early as 1828. The Colored population is more urban than the Bantu and because of the more favorable government attitude toward them, they hold positions normally closed to the Bantu. They are represented as artisans in the building and printing trades and hold semiskilled and skilled positions in industry. The majority of the non-European doctors, lawyers, and teachers in Cape Province are Colored. With the increasing race consciousness which began in the 1920s, many Afrikaner leaders looked hopefully to the time when the Colored would be put in their place. Standing between the Afrikaners and these desires was the entrenched clause of the South Africa Act. After Malan's election victory in 1948, a major goal of his Nationalist party was to remove the special privileges of the Colored.

There is another minority group in southern Africa, the Asian population, which is largely concentrated in Natal. Of the almost one-half million Asians, only approximately 20,000 live in the Cape and another 60,000 in the Transvaal. Indians were first brought to Natal in the 1860s as indentured servants to work the sugar plantations. Many chose the option of remaining in a territory which offered them more economic opportunity than India. They were later joined by their families and friends who also recognized the greater advantages of Natal, despite the color bar. Even before the Boer War there were many restrictions placed upon Indians. They could not even live in the Orange Free State. Although they could reside in the Transvaal, they could not individually own property. As soon as responsible government was granted to Natal, their right to vote was taken from them. Only in Cape Colony did the Indians continue to enjoy political freedom.

Mohandas Gandhi began in Natal to use passive resistance against discriminating legislation which would later become so much a part of the Indian scene. Before World War I, he was successful in removing some of the petty annoyances imposed on the Indians and also in preventing the enactment of more punitive measures against them. However, Smuts' government, responding to demands of white merchants and municipalities in the 1920s, introduced a Class Areas Bill which would have segregated Indians throughout the country. Smuts' government fell before this could become law, but in 1926 Hertzog introduced an even more severe measure. Extreme pressure from Britain and from the government of India prevented this from being enacted. By the Cape Town agreement, Indians were promised better treatment in South Africa and the Union government provided funds for repatriation of those who wished to return to India. Europeans remained unhappy with the Indians' way of life, their poverty, their aptitude in business, and their desire to own real estate. Finally in 1946, the Smuts government passed the so-called "Pegging Act" which attempted to restrict the sale of real estate to Indians in Natal. As a concession to the liberals within the United party, the Indians were granted the right to elect three European members to the House of Assembly. What was the political reaction of the three nonwhite sectors of the population to all the legislation which relegated them to inferior status within the Union? Their major problems in attempting to organize effectively to oppose any action of the government was lack of unity and weakness to implement any decisions. In 1902 the Colored formed the African Peoples Organization which reflected the hopes and aspirations of the professional, moderate middle classes. They believed in cooperation with the white governments and attempted to alleviate their problems by arguments, petitions, and persuasions. The consciousness of their special position prevented them from active cooperation with Bantu or Indian political groups. The Indian community also had similar problems of diffusion of aims. The South African Indian Congress created in 1918 was a development from Gandhi's earlier movement. It, too, was dominated by professional and upper-class businessmen whose methods were strictly within the law. Smuts' and Hertzog's class bills in the 1920s were defeated not because of the Indian Congress, but because of pressures from Britain and India. The Indian Congress by 1948, due to the desires of its leaders to please the white government, was almost powerless.

The traditional leaders of various Bantu tribes increasingly became government spokesmen since their continuation in office depended upon Pretoria. Even had they wished, they were not prepared to exercise leadership roles which transcended their own groups. There were few Western-educated Bantu and they found it difficult to communicate their ideas to the mass of tribal Bantu. Until 1912 there was no overall political organization through which they could express their hopes and fears. The early potential leaders of the Bantu were men of their times. They were middle class and believed in the efficacy of reason and peaceful petition. Perhaps as important were the jealousies between some educated Bantu. The career of John Tengo Jabavu is a good example of the pressures imposed on an educated Bantu. He was educated by missionaries, became a teacher, and edited a number of newspapers. The last was the very influential Xosa-English newspaper *Imvo*. In it he campaigned against the double standard of justice, pass laws, and general antinative legislation. In politics he supported a succession of white liberals who promised to alleviate the condition of the Bantu. When Jabavu's position as spokesman for the educated Bantu of the western Cape seemed to be threatened, he reacted against the imagined threat. Thus he opposed a Bantu, Reverend Walter Rubasana, for the seat to the provincial council from Tembuland in 1913, and this assured Rubasana's defeat and the election of a European. Jabavu was against the founding of the South African Native National Congress in 1912 and campaigned for the Land Act of 1913. These actions removed any influence he might have had over the form of the emerging Bantu political organization.

The South African Native National Congress was formed to oppose the Land Act of 1913. Its delegations to the governor-general, Lord Gladstone, and to the Colonial Office were ignored. This set the pattern for relations between the organization, renamed the African National Congress (ANC), and the government. Its leaders, such as John Dube of

Natal and Reverend Rubasana, could only petition the government. By the terms of the Act of Union the ANC could form no power base in the legislature, and the ANC rejected the radicalism and potential violence inherent in the program suggested by the Communists in the 1920s. The struggle to keep Communists and radicals from gaining control weakened the ANC further in the 1930s. Given that weakness and the attitude of the government, it is not surprising that the ANC opposition to the Cape Native Franchise Act of 1935, which removed the Bantu from the common roll, was ineffectual.

Perhaps the best example of the weakness of the ANC was the anti-pass agitation which began at the annual Congress in May 1944. Under Dr. Alfred Xuma, the ANC leadership confidently predicted that they would collect over a million signatures to a petition protesting the pass laws. Over a year later the petition was presented with only about 100,000 signatures, and it was ignored by the government. In June 1946, the ANC promised to continue the collection of signatures to indicate their disapproval of the passes. Partially because of government opposition, but also because of poor organization, the campaign was a failure.

In 1943 a number of younger educated Bantu under the leadership of Anton Lembede formed the Youth League. Its membership included Walter Sisulu, Robert Sobukwe, and Nelson Mandela. Because the Youth League had a definite coherent program of action, it was able to exercise a profound influence on the ANC in the immediate postwar years. This culminated in 1949 with the adoption by the ANC of a program of action designed to end "the idea of white domination or the domination of white over black." This more militant stand of the ANC, however, was too late because in 1948 the Nationalist party with its watchword of apartheid came to power.

South Africa since 1948

The election of 1948 represented a watershed in South African life. Heretofore the non-European had played a small role in the determination of elections. Dr. Malan's Nationalists, however, in all the campaign oratory, stressed that this was the major issue. They had been provided with a systematic theory of exclusion by the professors of Stellenbosch University and SABRA. Economic disorders following the war and the greater militancy of black workers and some Bantu intellectuals was also a convincing factor in the election. Afrikaner nationalism was focused by Malan on this one issue. Smuts' United party had no definite answers to the call for apartheid. He could not accept the full program of exclusiveness without alienating a large portion of the liberal electorate nor could he afford to adopt a meaningful liberal retort to Malan's program. Although the United party won fifty-three percent of the popular vote, it gained only sixty-five seats in the Assembly. The Labor party, allied to Smuts, won six seats. Together with the three seats guaranteed for Africans, the Smuts coalition could muster only seventy-four seats.

Countering this; Malan's Nationalists won seventy seats and Havenga's Afrikaner party won nine. Malan thus formed a government with a slim majority of five and a mandate to carry out his program of apartheid.

The factionalism within the United party and their lack of a suitable alternative program became more evident with every subsequent election. In 1950 Smuts died and was succeeded as party leader by J. G. N. Strauss whose leadership was so ineffective that he was replaced by Sir de Villers Graaf in 1956. In 1951 the Afrikaner party was absorbed by the Nationalists and the six representatives from South West Africa added to Malan's majority. The degree by which Nationalist control has been extended after 1948 can be seen by comparing the election statistics of that year with those of 1961. In 1961 the Nationalist party, although gaining less than fifty-five percent of the popular vote, won 105 seats in the Assembly. The United party could win only forty-nine.

Specific acts of the Nationalist government and a growing sense of frustration caused the creation of a number of small political parties in the 1950s. In 1953 Mrs. Margaret Ballinger, one member of parliament who represented Africans, became the leader of the Liberal party. Some of its members such as Patrick Duncan and Alan Paton gave the movement worldwide publicity. However, the party, because of its position reflecting the idea of one man–one vote, was never a threat to the Nationalists. Another group formed in 1953 which had little impact was the Federal Party mainly based in Natal which wanted to break up the unitary system. In 1954 a conservative revolt within the United party resulted in the short-lived National Conservative party. All the members of parliament who joined this group either lost their seats or joined the Nationalist party.

A more significant creation occurred after the United Party Congress in 1959. Twelve United party members of parliament resigned to form the Progressive party. Its platform was Rhodes' old concept of "equal rights to all civilized men." In the 1961 elections only one of these members of parliament, Mrs. Helen Suzman, was returned to office. Aside from the obvious fact that all the small new parties of the 1950s represented new approaches to the problem of race relations, their main effect was to further weaken the United party. There were, during this period, no serious defections from the Nationalists. Thus during the crucial phase of implementing apartheid, the only major opposition party was further divided and rendered almost impotent.

With this background of political development, one can better examine the policies of the Nationalists. Malan's major contributions to apartheid were the Suppression of Communism Act (1950), The Immorality Amendment Act (1950), The Population Registration Act (1950), The Group Areas Act (1950), and the Bantu Authorities Act (1951). The Suppression of Communism Act defined Communism in such a broad manner that the state could ban any organization which was remotely suspected of Communism. It was under the terms of this act that the long drawn out Treasons Trials of over 150 people were begun in 1956. The

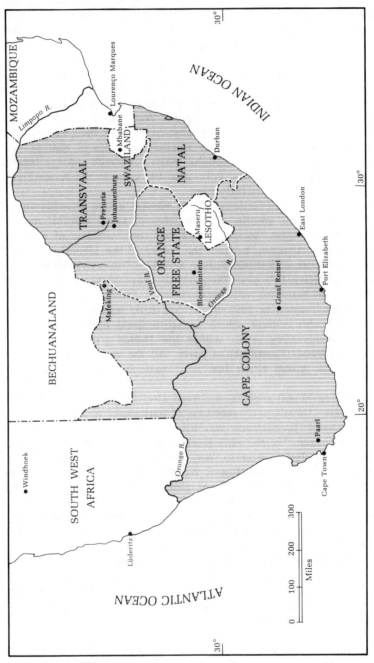

The Republic of South Africa

Immorality Act made any type of miscegenation a criminal offense.

The Population Registration Act provided for the registration of all persons according to race—based upon the 1951 census. An identity certificate was then issued. The definition of a white person was anyone who was obviously white by appearance or by general repute and acceptance. Anyone can object to the race classification of another person. A board operating under the jurisdiction of the interior ministry then hears evidence and can reclassify any person according to the evidence. A white classification carries with it all the economic and political preferences, so since 1951 the government has heard thousands of cases. Aside from the mental anguish caused by such classification, the terms of the act are so ambiguous that persons of the same family have been given differing classifications. However, the act did what the government hoped. It gave them a fairly accurate detailed breakdown of the population according to race. They could then proceed to other acts necessary to implement apartheid.

The Group Areas Act which Dr. Dönges, the minister of the interior, referred to as the "cornerstone of apartheid" restricted races to "full" areas already occupied. No member of one race could acquire property in areas reserved for another. It was the aim of the act eventually to restrict the residence of all persons to distinct areas and thus minimize contact between Bantu, Colored, Indians, and whites. A 1954 amendment gave the minister of native affairs power to expel Africans from zones declared white. Dr. Hendrik Verwoerd, armed with this authority, moved over 100,000 Africans from the immediate environs of Johannesburg to new group areas farther from the outskirts of the city.

The Bantu Authorities Act became the basis for the later Bantustan developments. It regularized the older system of indirect rule in the native reserves. Instead of assuming the economic interdependence of white and black in a growing industrialized South Africa, the Malan government made it clear that as soon as practicable all Bantu would have only one place of permanent residence—one of the native reserves. By 1955 the chiefs of the Transkei area had accepted the implications of the act. Chiefs from other areas reluctantly followed this lead. In 1960 the government removed the three special representatives of the Bantu from the House of Assembly.

In 1954 Dr. Malan retired from politics and was succeeded as prime minister by the even more conservative Johannes Strijdom. It was his government which devised the means by which the Cape Colored were removed from the common voting roll. In 1951 Malan had attempted to accomplish this by the Separate Registration Bill passed by a simple majority of the Assembly. In March 1952, the Supreme Court declared this act invalid since the procedure was not in accordance with the South Africa Act. In May parliament declared itself the highest court in the land when dealing with constitutional matters. This action was also negated by the Supreme Court in September 1953. In 1954 the Nationalists attempted three times to secure the necessary two-thirds majority and failed each time. Strijdom's government then reorganized the Appellate Court in 1955 by increasing its numbers from six to eleven members. In June the Senate Act reapportioned the seats in the Senate and increased the number of by increasing its numbers from six to eleven members. In June the Senate assured the necessary two-thirds vote for the South Africa Amendment Act of February 1956 which finally removed the Colored from the common roll in Cape Colony. The courts held that this action was legal as defined by the original South Africa Act, and thus the Colored lost the political rights which they had possessed for over a century.

Eight years after their victory in 1948 by means of these acts and a host of lesser supporting legislation and executive decisions, the Union had been converted into a state where segregation was the basis of political action. Hendrik Verwoerd who succeeded as prime minister after Strijdom's death in 1958 carried on the tradition of his two predecessors largely by administering the legislation already passed and thus made apartheid a working system. Mounting pressure from newly independent African states and other Commonwealth nations convinced Verwoerd in 1960 that South Africa could not continue to function within the Commonwealth. A referendum to decide whether it should become a republic was then conducted. Fifty-two percent of the voters agreed to the change and the Republic of South Africa was proclaimed May 31, 1961.

The African National Congress, although not completely converted to an action program, entered into an agreement of cooperation in 1945 with the Indian National Congress and the Colored Peoples Organization. This alliance called for brief work stoppages in 1948. In 1953 they collaborated with the Indian National Congress in an open campaign to challenge segregated public facilities. South African police reacted by arresting almost 9,000 of those involved in civil disobedience. In 1956 there was a long campaign by Africans against using buses in Johannesburg. In the following two years the ANC was involved in supporting a series of activities directed against government policies. In all these actions the leaders were dominated by Gandhian concepts of peaceful resistance. However, many of these protests were marred by bloodshed. In 1950 eighteen Africans were killed in Johannesburg and the 1953 campaign was finally cancelled because of the violence.

Traditional leaders of the ANC such as Chief Luthuli and Dr. Alfred Xuma were considered too moderate by some younger Africans. Led by Robert Sobukwe, a lecturer at Witwatersrand University, these radicals formed the Pan African Congress (PAC) in 1959. They favored direct action to create a situation which would force the Nationalists from power. Their first objective was the pass laws. They encouraged thousands of persons to refuse to show their passes to the authorities. Such a demonstration would thereby fill the jails and prisons. This type of passive resistance culminated in the Sharpeville Massacre in March 1960 where the police fired upon thousands of peaceful demonstrators, killing sixty-nine people. The outrage in the world press over Sharpeville played an important role in causing South Africa to withdraw from the Commonwealth. A state of emergency was declared in South Africa and both the ANC and PAC were declared illegal. Most of the leaders of the organizations were arrested or went into exile.

Verwoerd's government utilized every facet of its power to contain the protest movements. Chief Luthuli was placed under house arrest, Sobukwe was arrested, and later two other PAC leaders, Nelson Mandela and Walter Sisulu, were tried for sabotage. All nonwhite political organizations were proscribed and therefore their effectiveness was greatly limited. Verwoerd also announced his intention of proceeding with the Bantustan policy which would ultimately create a federal South Africa composed of black and white states. This ultimate in apartheid, however economically unrealistic, was advanced by the creation of the Transkei Bantustan under the leadership of Chief Kaiser Mantazima.

In September 1966 while addressing Parliament, Verwoerd was stabbed to death by a white assassin. It was feared that Balthazar Johannes Vorster who succeeded to the leadership of the country would pursue apartheid even more zealously than had Verwoerd. Although Vorster did not abandon the main principles of his predecessor, he did attempt to remove some of the more onerous aspects of that policy. In the early 1970s, his government desegregated some hotels and restaurants, opened the National Theater to all races, and allowed interracial sports contests. At the same time expenditures on economic improvements in the homelands and Bantu education were increased substantially. By the end of his twelve year tenure, Vorster was even prepared to accept separate parliaments for the Indian and Colored populations from which would be chosen cabinet members to help decide government policy and administer the state. Another area of relaxation was in the enforcement of the stringent rules which barred Bantu from certain categories of jobs.

The changing South African attitudes were most noticeable in the role Vorster played in altering the hard line policy of Prime Minister Ian Smith's government in Rhodesia. As early as 1974, South African representatives were meeting secretly with their Zambian counterparts to see if there was not some way out of the impasse created by Smith's recalcitrance to deal with moderate black leaders. The victory of FRELIMO over the Portuguese in Mozambique had left the Rhodesians very vulnerable to stepped up guerrilla action. This fact gave Vorster considerable leverage and in Feberuary 1975, he withdrew the bulk of the South African armed forces which had been helping man the Rhodesian frontiers. Thus Vorster added his direct support to the United States and Great Britain. His actions were probably crucial in forcing Smith to begin the talks that ultimately resulted in joint government with white and blacks comprising the executive and the guarantee of swift devolution of power to the Bantu majority.

South West Africa was another area where Vorster radically alterred the direction of South African policy although to a casual observer, it might appear that his government's attitude was unchanged from his predecessor's since he still refused to admit United Nations control. This huge, arid region, rich in minerals, had initially been turned over to South Africa to be administered as a class "C" mandate under the general guidance of the League of Nations. The Bondelswarts Massacre in 1922 was the first occasion of conflict between the League and South Africa over management of the mandate. However, the

League did nothing practical to enforce their rule and the Union government came to look upon the vast territory as theirs. In 1946 Smuts' government requested the United Nations to allow South West Africa to be incorporated within the Union. This was refused because of the past administrative history of the mandate. In 1950 the International Court of Justice gave a nonbinding decision that the United Nations had inherited the mandate responsibilities of the old League of Nations. South Africa disputed this, claiming that the mandate had lapsed. All attempts by the United Nations to implement their theoretical control have failed. The South West Africa Amendment Act of 1949 provided for six representatives elected by the white inhabitants to sit in the Union's House of Assembly. The International Court of Justice in 1966 refused to rule on the question of South West Africa brought before it by Liberia and Ethiopia. However, in 1971 the Court in an advisory opinion declared South Africa's continued presence there to be illegal.

The International Court's declaration gave South Africa's opponents in the United Nations the necessary legal underpining to step up their campaign against the regime. The issue of South West Africa was debated in the General Assembly and resolutions of censure were passed every year after 1971. Almost all African states recognized the South West Africa Peoples Organization (SWAPO) as the proper representative of the different peoples of the area. They renamed South West Africa Namibia. In early 1975 the Security Council set a deadline of May 30 for South Africa to comply with all the resolutions of the United Nations. Ten days before this date, Vorster announced that self-government for South West Africa and not absorption of the territory into the Republic was the eventual goal of his government. He again rejected United Nations supervision and denounced SWAPO as a terrorist organization which represented only one of the many different peoples of the territory. African states in the United Nations led the move to have South Africa branded as a threat to international peace. Only a triple veto by the United States, Great Britain, and France in June 1975 prevented such action. Once again in August 1976 these major powers had to veto a similar motion.

A constitutional conference met at Windhoek in September 1975. Although SWAPO refused to send delegates, there were representatives at the conference from eleven tribal and ethnic groups. This conference decided upon local autonomy and set three years as the target date for achieving independence. The debate continued between South Africa and the United Nations over how the elections for the legislature of this free state should be held. In April 1978, Vorster, SWAPO, and the United Nations seemingly had reached a settlement concerning United Nations supervision of the elections. However, difficulties over details of that supervision led Vorster in September 1978 to abrogate the agreement and press on for South West Africa's own internal settlement. Elections for a new Constituent Assembly of 50 members were held in December 1978 and the Democratic Turnhalle Alliance (DTA), a multi-racial party favoring continuing close ties with the Republic, won an overwhelming victory. Moderate parties were the multi-racial Namibian National Front and the SWAPO-Democrats, a breakaway party whose head, Andreas Shipanga, differed with the SWAPO leadership over escalating the violence. Neither party had any real power base in Namibia.

Continuing pressure by Britain, the United States, and the United Nations made Vorster reconsider his go-it-alone policy and in December 1978, his government once again accepted a United Nation's plan for a cease fire and supervised elections. However, continuing skirmishes with SWAPO insurgents along the Namibian border with Angola and Zambia caused yet again a change in the government's policy. Sam Nujoma, the SWAPO leader, declared in early March 1979 that SWAPO was less interested in winning the elections than in winning the guerrilla war. This attitude and the fact that the United Nations' plan allowed the SWAPO guerrillas to retain their arms during the election led Vorster to announce that South Africa would not agree to the United Nations' plan until it could provide better monitoring of SWAPO bases in Angola. The Namibian Constituent Assembly concurred in this action. The South African government then intensified their strikes against those bases and arrested a large number of persons in Namibia suspected of being associated with SWAPO.

South Africa in May granted the Constituent Assembly the power to enact certain laws for the territory. This was confirmed by an Act of the Republic's Parliament in August. By mid-1979, the Constituent Assembly's name had been changed to the Namibian National Assembly and its size was increased one-third by the appointment of new members. Following the recommendations of Administrator Gerrit Viljoen, the Assembly moved rapidly to remove the rules and laws which had made petty apartheid possible. This quick retreat from the theoretical concept of separation caused a reaction by the more conservative whites. Partially to placate them, Viljoen was removed and was replaced by Marthinus Steyn, a conservative and reputed head of the Broederbond.

A United Nations team visited Namibia in the fall of 1979. Partially because of their report which reflected the genuineness of South Africa's fears, negotiations related to a United Nations supervised elections were reopened. A new agreement for those elections was reached in August largely because President Neto of Angola promised to keep the SWAPO guerrillas out of Namibia during the elections. Further, the United Nations at this juncture accepted South Africa's suggestions for a demilitarized zone along the borders during this crucial period.

Although the South African government has spent over one billion dollars in South West Africa after 1975, it is probable that any independent Namibia which does not meet with United Nations approval is likely to suffer the same ostracism as that accorded the Transkei. The homelands policy of Verwoerd and Vorster was tested first in the Transkei. Upon the success of that experiment rested that fate of the announced goal of ultimately creating a federal South Africa composed of both black and white states. The plan was for the black areas, called Bantustans, to move slowly toward independence from Pretoria. If their independent governments so desired, they could continue close economic and ultimately political ties with the Republic. The Transkei in the decade after 1965 moved through all the steps determined by South Africa, and on October 25, 1976 was granted its independence. It had political parties, elections, and a loyal opposition to the responsible government headed by Chief Kaiser Mantazima. The majority of independent African states, many of which were poorer than the Transkei, denounced this independence as a front by which South Africa would still control the economically non-viable area. The General Assembly of the United Nations voted 134 to 0 to condemn the sham independence of the Transkei.

Unshaken by world opinion, the South African government announced its intention of continuing its homelands policy. On December 5, 1977, Bophuthatswana, the second of the Bantustans, was granted its independence, and this was followed by the third independent state, Venda, in September 1979. Bophuthatswana is far less cohesive than Transkei. Although much of its land is potentially rich, its 16,000 square miles is divided into six unconnected areas in the north-central portion of the Republic. Venda in the northeastern region is separated into only two parts, and is much smaller, having an area of only 2500 square miles. Bophuthatswana has a legal population of approximately 2½ million persons while Venda has only one-fifth as many. These population figures must be adjusted because most adult males are absent either temporarily or permanently in one of the cities of the Republic.

Although the specific problems differed, the generalized ones facing the new heads of state, Chief Lucas Mangope of Bophuthatswana and Chief Patrick Mphephu of Venda, were the same as those of the Transkei. These were under-capitalization, poor land, a lack of industry, and being surrounded and thus dominated economically and politically by the Republic. Despite their obvious dependence upon the Republic, there were indications that the new role designed to them by the Pretoria government was more than a facade. In April 1978, the Transkei government broke off relations with South Africa over the Republic's decision to transfer East Griqualand to Natal. Mantazima claimed that he had been assured before the Transkei was independent that parts of Griqualand would be assigned to the Xosa. Prime Minister Vorster expressed his regret over Transkei's action, but assured the Transkei that South Africa would continue its economic support.

South Africa's racial policies have resulted in defeating its aims in one direction—absorption of the High Commission Territories. In 1910, it appeared to British and South African statesmen that the logical development of these territories was toward incorporation within the Union. The evolvement of exclusive racial policies in the Union in the thirty-five years following the enactment of the South Africa Act postponed, but did not destroy, the possibility of reversion. However, the actions of the Nationalist government after 1948 combined with the devolution of political power to Africans elsewhere in Africa meant that no British government in the 1950s would seriously consider handing Basutoland, Bechuanaland, and Swaziland over to South Africa. The development of Britain's new attitudes toward the High Commission Territories has been detailed elsewhere. It is sufficient to note here that these territories, when they became politically independent, were still dependent economically on the Republic. Their future is still closely linked to South Africa. Lesotho (Basutoland), totally surrounded by the Republic, is particularly vulnerable. If the Republic feels threatened by events in the exterritories, it may well yet absorb them despite adverse world opinion.

Despite Prime Minister Vorster's efforts to improve the image of his government, world opinion became even more hostile during the latter years of his administration. One reason for this increasing hostility was South Africa's direct involvement in the civil war in Angola. The Portuguese departed their colony in haste, leaving the socialist MPLA party of Augostino Neto in control of Luanda and most of the larger cities. Two major factions refused to accept his leadership and fighting was endemic throughout the huge territory during 1975. The major anti-Neto force in southern Angola was led by Jonas Savimbi. Vorster's government supported the Savimbi controlled military forces in the Ovimbundu areas. In November 1975 South Africa sent its troops across the border to defend the Cunene River hydroelectric complex which had been jointly constructed with Portugal. In the months that followed South African armor pushed further north and was a significant factor in denying the MPLA the key urban centers of the south. It was not until the entry of Cuban troops into Angola and the collapse of United States opposition to Neto that South African forces were withdrawn in March 1976. Despite the direct involvement of troops from Zaire and Cuba into Angola at the same time, only South Africa was censured for its actions by the United Nations. On March 31 the Security Council voted to condemn South Africa as an aggressor in Angola.

The major cause of South Africa's worsening relations with the rest of the world was its domestic policy. This led to urban demonstrations directed against the government which began in mid-1976 and continued for over a year. The disturbances first began in Soweto, the huge black township adjacent to Johannesburg, and quickly spread to other major cities. There were a number of serious confrontations between the police and demonstrators, and by November 1976 the death toll had reached almost one hundred persons. Students at all levels were extremely important in dictating the time and type of demonstration. The students continued to put pressure on the government throughout 1977. At the beginning of the fall term of that year, over 200,000 students were out of school. The government met these mass demonstrations with force, and it banned eighteen organizations as unlawful. By 1978 the government had ended the immediate threat of the students, workers, and residents of Soweto. But the calm was one which covers up the latent unrest and hostility felt by most urban Bantu. Any minor occurrence could trigger a resumption of the summer days of 1976 and could even escalate into full scale revolt.

Another event which brought down world censure on South Africa was the Biko affair. Steven Biko, one of the most articulate anti-apartheid spokesmen, was arrested and died while in police custody on September 12, 1977. The official version of his death was challenged by friends and fellow activists. The failure of the South African government to appoint an investigating committee immediately brought about a major political crisis in the Republic and helped fuel the continued disturbances in Soweto. Although the police were later exonerated by the courts, the government settled $76,000 on Biko's family in July 1979, lending support to the anti-government critics who had maintained from the beginning that Biko had been murdered.

The Nationalist Party remains in firm control of the country. The November 1978 elections simply reiterated the trend of every election held during the past thirty years. The Nationalists increased their majority by winning over seventy percent of the popular vote and 135 of the 165 seats in Parliament. The United

Party has almost ceased to be a viable force in South African politics. Its place as the main opposition party has been assumed by the Progressive Federal Party which, however, in 1979 controlled only 17 seats in the lower house. Prime Minister Vorster at the crest of his domestic popularity decided in September 1978 to retire. The Nationalist party caucus chose as his successor a long time associate, former Defense Minister Pieter W. Botha. His selection had to be a disappointment for those who felt that South Africa was moving in a more liberal direction since Botha was generally believed to be more doctrinnaire and more prepared to use force than was Vorster. This, however, has not been the case, and Botha had been forced by circumstances to begin to dismantle the superstructure of apartheid.

Botha accepted the reality that South Africa must "adapt or die" and began to repeal the complex, interrelated laws which supported petty apartheid. Dual facilities were abolished and many of the theatres and restaurants in the major cities were desegregated. But the most emotion packed portion of Botha's reforms concerned the repeal of sexual restrictions. The Prime Minister indicated that in his policy of differentiation rather than discrimination, there would be significant changes in the Immorality Act and the Mixed Marriages Act. Further sweeping changes were made in the arena of labor policy. In May 1979, the government accepted the conclusion of the Wilhan Commission and by September had recognized the rights of black workers to join unions and participate in collective bargaining. Botha also indicated that he did not oppose qualified blacks from being employed in jobs from which they had previously been disbarred.

The comparative speed with which Botha undertook these reforms created a backlash within his own party. Some of the *verkrampte* group established a Reformed National Party. Connie Mulder, once a powerful figure in the government, was the center of a scandal involving a secret government fund and attempted influence buying. He charged that President Vorster, while Prime Minister, was privy to all the actions. A commission found that Vorster was innocent, and Mulder, refusing to withdraw his charges, was expelled from the party in April 1979. Still extremely popular with the conservatives, he and his associates in October created a new pro-Apartheid Action Front for National Priorities. The strength of the conservatives was shown in four by-elections in late 1979. The regular Nationalist Party candidate in each was defeated by his more extreme opponent.

Botha and the majority of the leaders of the Nationalist Party, convinced at last that the main elements of apartheid had to be dismantled despite growing criticism from the ultraconservatives, pressed on with their reforms. In 1980 the Senate was abolished and was replaced by a new multiracial, nominated consultative council of fifty-four members. There were no blacks on the council since the prevailing argument was that they were citizens of a homeland where they were adequately represented. Whites dominated the council and the Asians and Colored representatives were not necessarily recognized as leaders by their constituencies. Botha brought all his prestige to bear to deny those within the party who opposed his policies a secure power base. He shook up his ministry in October bringing in seven new ministers including Gerrit Viljoen, the former administrator general of Namibia who had only recently defeated A. P. Truernicht for leadership of the Broederbond. Botha's most significant move to stem the movement to the right was to call new elections in April 1981, one year before he was constitutionally required to do so.

The election proved not to be a total vindication of Botha's program as he had hoped. Although the Nationalist party won 131 of the 165 seats in the Assembly, this represented a loss of 7 seats. The relatively moribund official opposition, the Progressive Federal party which was very critical of Botha's actions since they did not go far enough in dismantling apartheid, increased its representation by 9 seats to a total of 26. Far more important to Botha than this was the fact that the *Herstigte Nasionale Party* (HNP) led by Jaap Marais, although not gaining a seat, won fifteen percent of the total popular vote. The HNP was further to the right than even the *verkrampte* group within the Nationalist party. The election results were a clear signal that a significant minority of his constituents were in complete disagreement with his program. Perhaps because of this, Botha decided to slow down the rate of reform. It became clear that he could not avoid an open breach with Truernicht and his *verkrampte* followers. As a vote of confidence in Botha the Transvaal branch of the Nationalist party in February 1982 removed Truernicht from its executive board. The following month Truernicht and fifteen other members of Parliament resigned from the party and established the Conservative Party.

Although slowing down the dismantling of the most obvious elements of apartheid, Botha pressed on with his plan to reorganize the government to admit Asians and Coloreds to some participation in decision making. In July 1982 he convened the first National Congress of the ruling party which approved his plan of reorganization. Despite criticism from the right wing and liberal parties, all the black leaders and many Asian and Colored, Botha's ideas became the basis for the new constitution introduced into Parliament in May 1983. It was approved by sixty-six percent of the voting population in a referendum in November. The Constitution provided for an executive president elected by a multiracial electoral college for a five year term. President Vorster had died in September thus making it even easier for Botha to be chosen the first state president when the Constitution went into effect. The most significant change in the government was the creation of a three-house legislative system. The 4.5 million whites were to choose a 178 member House of Assembly, the 2.5 million Colored would vote for members of an 85 seat Asian House, and the ¾ million Asians would have their own 45 member legislature. The majority black population was not represented, the government maintaining the fiction that these people were represented in the homelands. Differences between the three legislatures were to be adjudicated by multiracial committees. If no consensus could be obtained then the President's Council would decide the issue. In August 1984 elections were held for the Asian and Colored legislatures. Dr. Allan Boesak, leader of the most important Colored party, the United Democratic Front, organized a very effective boycott. An estimated seventy-five percent of the eligible Asian and Colored voters refused to vote in the elections. Despite this clear rejection of the scheme, it went into effect on September 14, 1984. Botha, the new state president, included in his ministry two nonwhites. The Reverend H. J. Hendrickse of the Labor party and Amichand Rajibansi of the National Peoples' Party were appointed ministers without portfolio.

It would have been fanciful to imagine such revolutionary changes in the government structure and apartheid program only a scant decade earlier. Nevertheless, Botha's government was given little credit at home or abroad for dismantling petit apartheid and attempting to accommodate the conflicting desires of a half-score of interest groups. He was attacked by the ultraright and the liberals within South Africa and international pressure for a speedy end to apartheid was growing. All this coincided with increased activity of the outlawed ANC and escalating protest movements and violence in the black townships. Operating from bases in neighboring states, the ANC leadership ordered attacks upon police stations, banks, and particularly vulnerable rail lines. One of the boldest actions by the *Umkhonto we sizuie*, the Spear of the Nation, the guerrilla arm of the ANC, was the June 1980 raid on a major synthetic fuel plant. No major city was free of bombings. The worst occurred in Pretoria in May 1983 when a car bomb exploded outside Air Force headquarters in Pretoria killing 18 persons and wounding 217.

The ANC also pursued a soft line attempting to align itself with more traditional African organizations without renouncing violence as a means of securing its goals. This became easier as violent protests against the government erupted in the townships which were met with harsh punitive actions by the police and army. South African raids on ANC headquarters in Mozambique or Zambia were offset by the linkage of the ANC with the legitimate goals of students and workers. In Europe and the United States the ANC was increasingly viewed not as a terrorist organization but as a legitimate political party denied participation in the nations affairs by an unyielding white dominated government. The United Nations also ignored the violent aspect of the ANC, supporting any group pledged to end apartheid. The growing legitimacy of the ANC was evident when three of its senior leaders met in August 1986 with the United States ambassador to Zambia. The ANC leader, Oliver Tambo, also had numerous meetings with members of the British Foreign Office. United States Secretary of State, George Schultz, also appeared to give his blessing to at least the stated aspirations of the ANC. Even within South Africa as the internal situation worsened there were many important business leaders who were willing to discuss the future with the ANC. Sixty-one white moderates flew to Dakar in 1987 to engage in discussions with ANC leaders.

Although a major contributor to the unrest in South Africa, the ANC was only one factor in the anti-apartheid movement in the 1980s. Many of the leading religious leaders had courageously spoken out against the system for more than thirty years. This opposition gained international recognition and support when in 1984 Anglican Bishop Desmond Tutu received the Nobel Peace Prize in recognition of his nonviolent efforts to end apartheid. He used his visit to Europe and later the United States to castigate the regime in dozens of speeches. The government was in a dilemna concerning Tutu. If the government arrested him as had been done to so many others he would become even more a symbol, and despite all attempts to prove to the world that it was rapidly changing the face of apartheid the government would appear to be even more repressive. Thus Tutu and some other ministers such as Dr. Boesak were allowed to continue their anti-apartheid activities even in the worst days of the emergency. Tutu's position became even stronger when in 1987 he was named Archbishop of the Archdiocese of Cape Town. However important Tutu was in rallying the world to his cause, events simply overtook him and he, like Mahatma Ghandi a half-century before found that although nonviolent himself, he was involved in a situation where proponents of violence on both sides had gained the upper hand.

The universities, particularly the four predominantly English speaking ones, had long been opponents of the many repressive decrees of the government. Students at the African Universities of Ft. Hare and the University of the North were even more outspoken. As a result of their protests the African Universities were closed in 1980 just when the first wave of militant opposition by young people was noticeable. In October 1986 the government moved even further to control embarrassing activities of university students and faculty. A new decree tied the granting of state subsidies to the universities to their efforts to police and control anti-apartheid activists. This brought an immediate reaction from over 15,000 protesters from the English speaking universities. However, there was hardly a ripple of protest from the five Afrikaans universities whose students and faculty apparently could not see this decree as politicizing the universities or as a further attack upon freedom of speech or action.

The seething unrest in the black townships exploded in early 1980 ignited by Colored student protests in the Cape Town area over poor conditions and mediocre teaching. At first confined to only a few schools, the disturbances spread rapidly and by May affected over 100,000 elementary and secondary students joined by students from the black universities. After 3,000 students occupied shopping centers in Cape Town in May, the government banned all meetings of more than ten persons and the police broke up student marches and meetings. By the opening of the fall term a majority of the students returned to school but over 50,000 stayed away. By this time the disruption of the townships had become a way of life for so many unemployed, disenchanted young men. There were also labor walkouts protesting low wages and poor working conditions. The most serious of these was at the West Rand Mining complex where workers clashed with the police. Ten persons were killed there, 300 arrested, and thousands of workers were dismissed. Combined with the urban guerrilla actions of the ANC, these disturbances caused great embarrassment to the Botha government which was planning its major change in the method of governing the Republic. Although these activities damaged the government's credibility, they did not seriously threaten the regime nor did they provide sufficient propaganda to sway the attitudes of foreign governments, particularly the United States, enough to alter their policies.

The event that triggered the most serious crisis in the history of Nationalist party rule was the reform of the Constitution which gave at least token representation to Colored and Asians but left the majority black population with no voice in the government. This action combined with the other grievances over unemployment, low pay, rent increases, and bad schools caused thousands of blacks in the township surrounding Johannesburg to take to the streets in September 1984. The government's reaction was predictable. Over 7,000 police and defense force troops moved into the most disturbed areas conducting house to house searches and ultimately arresting more than 350 persons for various violations. Despite the arrests and show of force, the protests continued in 1985. The government responded by using more troops and bringing in armored vehicles to the troubled black townships. The crowds numbering in some cases thousands of persons threatened at times to overwhelm the security forces who then used water hoses, guns firing rubber bullets, tear gas, and in the last resort shotguns. By mid-1985 there was a coalescense of black opposition movements. The ANC was already deeply involved in urging the demonstrations. Oliver Tambo called for activists to make South Africa ungovernable. Moderates such as Bishop Tutu and Dr. Boesak, while condemning violence, used their positions to influence foreign opinion against what they saw as an evil system. The labor unions, only recently recognized as legitimate by the government, were also active in the anti-apartheid movement. The largest, the Congress of South African Trade Unions (COSTAU), organized strikes and orchestrated boycotts. The United Democratic Front with an estimated 1.5 million members was also active in a variety of ways.

Faced with a vocal, potentially violent opposition which appeared to be growing, President Botha on July 21, 1985, declared a state of emergency in thirty-six townships. This was the first such official state of emergency since 1960. It gave the police and army broad powers in the affected areas. They could declare curfews, search people and houses at any time, and were released from any indemnity claims resulting from their action. By the end of the year there had been over 5,000 arrests and detentions. Many of those arrested were the political, labor, or educational leaders in the black communities. Without them the leadership roles in many cases fell to more radical young men who led the people into confrontations over and over again with the authorities. At year-end, the violence had claimed over 1,000 lives. Funerals for those killed were turned into public fetes, attended at times by thousands, where political activists could denounce the government. Eulogies became polemics leading to further violent action. Finally the government banned all outdoor funerals and stipulated that only one person could be buried at a time. In June 1986 the state of emergency was extended throughout the country.

Not all the deaths were caused by government action. Within the townships lived persons from all the different national groupings in South Africa. Many of these had a long history of antipathy toward one another, particularly the Zulu and Xosa. Most of the Zulu, naturally conservative under normal circumstances, tended to follow the advice of their leader, Chief Mangosuthu Gatsha Buthelezi. The Xosa leaders were much more militant. This difference led to a number of violent incidents in the townships surrounding Johannesburg and Durban. Far more disturbing for the authorities was the rise of young militant leaders within the townships which in many cases had indeed become ungovernable; the authorities responded there only when there was a major threat to peace and order. The youths aged fourteen to twenty-two organized gangs who struck at anyone suspected of aiding the government. It was these "comrades" who made popular the execution of their fellow blacks by the "necklace." The victim would either have his hands chopped off or tied behind him; then an automobile tire would be placed around his neck . . . gasoline would be poured over it, and it would be set afire. So dominant had the youth gangs become by 1987 that older men began forming their own vigilante groups called the "fathers" to combat the spread of the mindless violence of the "comrades." Even the ANC ultimately disavowed their tactics. It was estimated that by 1987 over 2300 people had been killed in the violence; an estimated three-fourths of these had been the result of blacks killing blacks. One of the complaints registered by the government against the media was that only very seldom did the newspapers or television report black against black violence, stressing instead what appeared to be the unfair contest between armed white soldiers and police and unarmed blacks. This situation was a major reason for the government in December 1986 establishing strict guidelines for reporting the news. The following year the journalists were further restricted.

Nelson Mandela, the ANC leader convicted of sabotage in 1962, emerged during the disturbances as the symbol of African resistance to apartheid. Even moderate leaders such as Bishop Tutu and Chief Buthelezi supported his release from Pollsmoor Prison. It became apparent that the preface to any lasting settlement between the government and black leaders would be the release of Mandela. President Botha in 1986 indicated that he would consider releasing Mandela if he publically rejected the use of violence to gain his goals. Mandela's refusal to acquiese made him appear to the world as someone larger than life, a martyr to the cause of liberty. Demand for his release came from political leaders around the world. Mandela's imprisonment became a concrete symbol of the immorality of apartheid and was one important factor in convincing the United States and the European community to impose sanctions. The release in November 1987 of his associate, Govan Mbeki, who had served twenty-four years for the same crime as Mandela was viewed by some as a prelude to Mandela's eventual release.

By mid-1987 the worst disturbances in the townships were over. Government force, at least temporarily, had prevailed. Tambo's injunction to make South Africa ungovernable had failed. In August 1987, however, there were serious labor troubles in the mines near Johannesburg. Walkouts and subsequent violence had more to do with economic problems than in supporting those who were demanding a share in the political future of South Africa. Black miners were caught up in the results of the fifteen percent annual inflation rate and they wanted more money for their labors. The National Union of Mineworkers was not demanding parity with white workers but rather an across the board thirty percent increase which would have amounted to an average increase of approximately $50 a month. The Chamber of Mines which represented the six largest mining operations were prepared to grant increases of between fifteen percent and twenty-three percent. Over 300,000 miners, approximately half the nation's miners, then went on strike. A great deal of property was destroyed and some violence occurred at a few mines between the strikers and those blacks suspected of acting with the owners. The government dispatched police to the affected areas and in some cases used tear gas and rubber bullets to break up large crowds. The mine operators refused to give in to the strikers; thousands were fired before the Mineworkers Union capitulated. Once again the readiness of the government to counteract black demands with force had won.

Despite the many pressures from opponents within South Africa and throughout the world, Botha's government continued slowly to dismantle much of the superstructure of apartheid even during the state of emergency. In 1983 five judges of the Appeals Court ruled that migrant workers who had jobs in South Africa for ten years were entitled to permanent residence with their families in the black townships instead of a homeland. Although this policy struck directly at the heart of the Bantustan concept, the government decided not to challenge the decision of the High Court by introducing legislation to counter the decision. The government clarified its position on black South African citizenship in July 1986 by the Restoration of Citizenship Act. This specified that after written application, homeland citizens who qualified could be granted South African citizenship. This could ultimately affect as many as 2 million persons. Another significant move in 1986 was the Abolition of Influx Control Act which restored freedom of movement to black South African citizens. Botha had announced earlier that year that South Africa had "outgrown the dated concept of apartheid." This latter act, however, illustrated how cautiously he had to move in the area of black freedoms. It did not apply to citizens of the homelands who remained under the constraints of the Alien Act.

There was considerable evidence by 1987 that the old, hard line, immovable white supremacy concept was being abandoned by many Afrikaners who, like Botha, had perceived that change of some type was inevitable. The leaders of the business community, many of whom had lost capital and could see the possibility of the violence in the black townships spilling over into the white areas, wanted some type of rapprochment with black leaders, even with the ANC. This was shown clearly when sixty-one white moderates flew to Dakar to meet and discuss issues with representatives of the ANC. Although the majority of the black leaders in the townships might have favored the radical leadership of a Tambo or Mandela, the bulk of the Zulu who number over 3 million persons were loyal to Chief Buthelezi. Almost alone of the important black leaders, he called for a more evolutionary approach to reform, recognizing that the white minority could not accept immediately a concept as radical as one man, one vote. He was one of the proponents of the "Kwa-Natal Option" which was considered for nine months by representatives of thirty-nine black and white groups in 1986. The final report of the conference recommended a merger of the Kwa-Zulu homeland and Natal. The proposal called for a multiracial government with a two house legislature elected by all who qualified for the vote. Despite the fact that the recommendation was rejected by the Minister of Home Affairs in December the plan was certainly a viable one and showed that despite the government's intransigence, white representatives from Natal had concurred that power sharing with the black population was ultimately the only way out of South Africa's dilemma.

South African citizens, already partially isolated from international competition and the government, and castigated generally in the world media, had to contend increasingly with another serious threat in the 1980s. Anti-apartheid spokesmen had long argued that an economic boycott by major investor nations would be necessary to end apartheid. This argument gained more support as pictures of the violence in the townships reached the world's television stations. The United States government was the bellwether for the imposition of sanctions and ultimately the United States proved particularly vulnerable to anti-apartheid pressure. The Reagan administration, while protesting apartheid, had argued that continuous political pressure would help bring about evolutionary change in the white dominated government. However, protest movements against this policy became common in the United States. Many representatives in Congress with a large black or liberal constituency could no longer ignore the South African problem and ultimately they made it clear to the administration that harsh sanctions should be imposed. At the same time pressure was brought to bear on companies with major holdings in South Africa to divest. In September 1985 in response to public opinion and the threat of harsh sanctions then being debated in Congress, President Reagan imposed limited sanctions. Canada and France had already taken action to cut off most trade with South Africa. Great Britain and West Germany at that time opposed sanctions and Japan continued its profitable $3 billion a year trade. As the situation in South Africa worsened the United States Congress debated and in September 1987 passed a punitive action measure. President Reagan vetoed the bill but the veto was overridden. The European Economic Community also agreed to a weaker set of sanctions but even these could have helped damage South Africa's economy. Although questioning the value of sanctions in ending apartheid, Britain's Conservative government acquiesced to the European plan.

Sanctions and disinvestments struck at a weakened South African economy. In 1980 South Africa had one of the world's healthiest economies because of the extraordinary rise in the price of gold, South Africa's major export, as well as the growing demand for its other minerals. During the previous decade its economy had grown an average of 7.5 percent annually and the GNP in 1980 had reached $54 billion. South Africa's currency, the rand, was worth $.75. All these conditions changed very quickly. The price of gold which provided half of the nation's export earnings had fallen to $400 per ounce from a high of $875. Then in 1983 southern Africa was struck with the most devastating drought in 100 years which lasted for 3 years. The rivers dried up, reservoirs fell to less than one-half of capacity, crops burned up, and livestock died. Although the drought affected traditional black farmers most, their white counterparts who provided the bulk of South Africa's agricultural exports also were hurt. The crop loss for 1983 alone was estimated at $800 million. By the following year the nation was suffering its worst recession since the depression of the 1930s. There was a negative balance of payments and inflation had by mid-decade reached seventeen percent.

It was at this time that the violence in the townships focused world attention upon South Africa. Work stoppages and the disruption of normal services in the urban areas damaged the economy further. Then sanctions were applied and disinvestment by foreign firms escalated. By 1985 the rand had fallen to a low of only $.35. In August the government suspended trading in the stock and currency market for several days. Strict exchange controls were put into place and a two-tiered system was introduced creating a financial rand which was available at a lower rate only for foreign investors. In reply to the refusal of foreign bankers to make new loans or renew old ones, the government in September placed a freeze on the repayment of debts over $10 billion in value. Foreign exchange reserves stood at $2.5 billion. Disinvestment which was advertised by the more radical opponents of the government as a certain way of forcing political change further damaged the economy. By the end of 1985, thirty multinational corporations had either left South Africa or reduced their involvement. In 1987 General Motors, IBM, and Coca Cola announced termination of their involvement and Barclays Bank of England sold out its operation as did a subsidiary of ITT.

As critics of disinvestment had argued, the combination of sanctions and disinvestment, although troublesome, did not dangerously undermine the system. The people who bore the brunt of economic readjustment were the black workers who did not have a social security net to rely on. The number of unemployed blacks was estimated in 1987 to be ¾ million. The government, although threatening retaliation against alien workers in South Africa, only began a serious cutback in the number of foreign workers in late 1986. This involved many from Mozambique who, before the economic crisis, had been almost assured of work in the mines. There are an estimated 1.8 million foreign workers in South Africa from the so called "front line" states which have been most vociferous in opposing apartheid. If South Africa expelled all these it would seriously affect the lives of an estimated 10 million persons in neighboring Botswana, Lesotho, Zimbabwe, Mozambique, and Zambia. Disinvestment may have damaged the situation of employed South African black workers because most foreign firms followed guidelines which allowed for advancement of blacks on a scale comparable to white workers. Disinvestment did not mean the closing down of the plants or banks involved. They were simply sold to other investors, most of whom were South Africans not committed to the guidelines. Many of these welcomed disinvestment since it gave them a chance to acquire valuable property which otherwise they could not obtain. Frequently they acquired these foreign holdings at bargain prices. For example, the South African firm of Anglo American purchased Barclays Bank shares at $8.06 per share while they were valued at the time at $10.30. With the two tiered monetary system this actually meant that Anglo American paid only one-half the current market price for Barclays stock.

President Botha made it clear that economic pressure would not alter his plans for gradual change. His government was prepared to accept a projected growth rate of three percent rather than that higher rate which had prevailed in the 1970s. Disinvestment and sanctions may even in the long view have strengthened South Africa since it forced them to be even more self-sufficient. Already the industrial giant of Africa, South Africa, had its own nuclear generating plants, an advanced hydro-electric system, and manufacturing and agricultural sectors which could provide most of domestic needs. Oil from coal by the mid-1980s produced seventy percent of the country's liquid fuel needs. Its own armament industry also was sufficient for most of the needs of the armed forces, and more sophisticated weaponry could be obtained abroad, particularly from Israel. Most of South Africa's export earnings came from hard to sanction minerals such as strategic metals, diamonds, and particularly gold. All the Far Eastern markets were still open to South Africa. Japan, the most important Far Eastern trade partner, showed no signs of interrupting its profitable trade links. Foreign Minister R. F. Botha in assessing the impact of sanctions was therefore probably correct when he said, "It will harm us but will not kill us."

A further indication that classic apartheid as envisioned by Strijdom and Verwoerd had not met the challenge posed by the realities of South Africa was the failure of the Bantustan policy. One example of this failure was the government's capitulation with regard to granting South African citizenship to blacks. Another was its willingness to consider the report of a multiracial committee investigating the possibility of allowing Natal and Kwa-Zulu to merge on the basis of one man, one vote. But the final evidence of the Bantustan plans shortcomings was the performance of the independent states which were expected to provide the final step in that policy. Instead, they have been generally an embarrassment to South Africa. The four "independent" states—the Transkei, Venda, Bophuthatswana, and Ciskei—although not recognized by any other nation, have exhibited many of the least desirable attributes of black African states north of the Limpopo. Government overspending, an inflated bureaucracy, an expensive lifestyle for a select few, inefficiency, and misgovernment have been the norm in all. Most operating expenses of the states were financed by the taxpayers of South Africa who spend $1 billion a year to maintain them. An additional $1 billion is invested in the six homelands, not yet considered ready for or who refuse independence.

The oldest and largest of the independent states is the Transkei which was to be the showpiece of the Bantustan plan. Instead the first Prime Minister, Kaiser Matazima, quickly established an authoritarian regime. Kaiser changed his title to president in 1979 and installed his brother, George, as heir apparent. Together they amassed a fortune while controlling the political life on the Transkei. In 1978 Kaiser even broke off relations briefly with South Africa in a quarrel over territory bordering the Transkei. In early 1987 Mantazima's counterpart in the Ciskei, Lennox Sebe, accused the Transkei of sending commandos to assassinate him. In 1979 George Manatazima succeeded his brother but little changed in the mechanism of government. In 1987 in a power struggle between the two brothers, Kaiser, using the pretext of corruption, tried unsuccessfully to remove George from office. Finally in September 1987 a coup led by General Bantu Homolisa deposed George and replaced him as prime minister with a woman, Stella Sigcau. Later in December charging her with corruption and bribery, Homolia, backed by the army, ousted the prime minister and assumed that position himself.

Although not as notorious as the activities in the Transkei, the other governments have provided their share of embarrassment for Pretoria. In Venda, President-for-Life Patrick Mphephy lived ostentatiously in a palatial home and was driven around his poverty stricken country in an expensive foreign bullet proof limousine. Ciskei's president gained brief notoriety by beginning construction on an unneeded international airport. The most successful and most efficiently operated state is Bophuthatswana which has become well known for Sun City, its Las Vegas style gambling casino and recreation center which attracted some of the world's most famous entertainers. This and other similar spas provided for affluent South Africans the type of entertainment illegal in Calvinist South Africa. In addition, Bophuthatswana has a very healthy mining industry which provides thirty percent of the world's platinum.

Despite the relative success of Bophuthatswana, President Botha decided that the excesses in these states could not be allowed to continue. Although fully aware of the consequences, South Africa in September 1987 decided to reassert control over the "independent" states. Several committees were created which were charged with the responsibility of controlling public spending in the four states. In addition the government indicated that it was not prepared to grant independence to a fifth state, Kwa Ndebele, which comprises a number of noncontiguous settlements northeast of Pretoria. The Chief Minister of Kwa Ndebele, Majozi Mahlangu, claimed a mandate on the basis of a 1984 election where one percent of the voters took part. The government's reassessment of the homelands policy could become a major breech in the structure of apartheid and confirm the position of Chief Buthelezi who had from the beginning condemned the philosophy and practice of "independent" homelands.

South Africa's major foreign policy problems obviously were closely related to the attitude of foreign governments toward the domestic policies of the Nationalist government. The actions of the United States and Britain particularly were damaging to South Africa. However, the state's basic foreign policy directives remained unchanged. There was first the need to minimize damage done by hostile world opinion and to postpone indefinitely, if possible, political action which would have an adverse effect on the economy. Despite the imposition of sanctions by the United States and European countries, South Africa still maintained good relations with many important trading partners. Even Zimbabwe, Zambia, and Mozambique whose leaders were publically vociferous in condemnation of apartheid continued their open and clandestine trade with the republic. The second goal of Botha's foreign policy was to minimize the actions of guerrilla forces based in neighboring states and if necessary to destabilize those governments whose actions might prove detrimental to South Africa. Although the generalized goals were the same, the actions taken against Mozambique, the SWAPO forces in Namibia, and in Angola were determined by the individual threat posed by each development.

South Africa's goal with reference to Mozambique was to counter any type of hostile action by the Marxist government of Samora Machel by both direct and indirect action. A cornerstone of that policy was to make certain that the ANC did not have a safe base from which to operate. A South African strike force in January 1981 responding to several urban guerrilla actions in Durban, Pretoria, Port Elizabeth, and East London raided ANC headquarters in Maputo killing 13 persons. A similar raid was staged in May 1983. The most successful action, however, was indirect. Botha's government actively supported the Mozambique National Resistance Movement (RENAMO) which sought the overthrow of the Marxist government. RENAMO forces were supplied with all types of equipment in order to prolong the civil war and divert Machel's attention from South Africa. The devastating three year drought combined with RENAMO's success brought Machel's government to the conference table. On March 16, 1984, the Nkomati agreement was signed on the banks of a river 300 miles east of Johannesburg. By this nonaggression pact South Africa was to desist from aiding RENAMO and Machel would cease his support of the ANC. Eight hundred ANC members were immediately expelled from Mozambique leaving only a ten man diplomatic mission in Maputo. The continued success of RENAMO within Mozambique brought charges that South Africa was breaking the Nkomati agreement by continuing its aid to these antigovernment guerrillas. The Mozambique government also accused South Africa of causing the death of Machel in a plane crash in October 1986, an accusation vociferously denied by South African officials. South Africa's innocence was confirmed by an international investigative panel in July 1987 which found that pilot error was the cause of the crash. The new President of Mozambique, Joaquim Chissano, lacking the prestige of Machel was even less able to aid in the subversion of the Nationalist government.

The Nambian situation was even more complex as it involved not only the future of the territory but South Africa's policy toward the Marxist government of Angola. The 1978 agreement in principle on having elections supervised by the United Nations came to nothing because the South African government would not accept the arrangements for providing security. Pretoria's attention was then directed toward strengthening the position of whites in the multiracial political assembly. Once again in 1981 it appeared that South Africa was ready to accept the Security Council Resolution 435 of 1978. Sam Nujoma leader of SWAPO, also indicated his willingness to take part in an all parties congress. This seemingly promising environment soon faded because of the presence of an estimated 30,000 Cuban troops in Angola. South Africa supported by the United States made the removal of the Cubans a prerequisite for any meaningful discussions on the future government of Namibia. This was a demand that President dos Santos of Angola could not afford to accept. The linkage of Namibian independence with the removal of one of Angola's main military supports meant that the impasse over Namibia would continue.

Angola presented a dual problem to the Pretoria government. The threat to South African security would increase if dos Santos and his communist allies ever won total control over all of Angola. Therefore South African aid to Jonas Savimbi and his UNITA forces within Angola continued. This covert assistance was one major factor in the success of Savimbi's army in their Ovimbundu strongholds. As long as the civil war continued the Angolan army and its Cuban allies could not afford much direct support to the SWAPO guerrillas who had been granted sanctuary by dos Santos. The SWAPO bases were the second set of problems for President Botha. If he respected Angola's boundaries this would give the SWAPO leaders not only bases from which to attack into Namibia but also would give them safe haven to attract other dissenters and thus build up their forces. There had never been a question as to South Africa's response. In the mid-1970s units of the army cooperating with Savimbi had penetrated hundreds of miles into Angola. This active, military policy was continued into the 1980s. In June 1980 a three week long action deep into southern Angola resulted in the destruction of a number of SWAPO bases. Again in August 1981 two South African columns with air support struck at newly established sites and this time they had brief engagements with the Angolan military. In January 1983 there was a further incursion into Angola.

In February 1984 representatives from South Africa and Angola signed a disengagement agreement. The Angolan government promised to monitor and control SWAPO activities and in return South Africa would stop aiding the UNITA forces. The success of this agreement given the relative weak position of the Angolan government in southern Angola depended upon whether Sam Nujumo and the SWAPO leaders wanted to come to terms. In July 1984 there were direct talks between SWAPO and South African representatives. South Africa proposed to recognize an interim government in Namibia under SWAPO leadership if the key ministerial appointments were determined by South Africa. This plan was vetoed by the SWAPO leadership and the unstable conditions returned to the southern regions of Angola. Violation of the borders became a continuing process as SWAPO tried to construct a viable guerrilla organization within Namibia and the South African army tried to thwart SWAPO both within Namibia and Angola. That the 1984 pact was a dead issue was shown by the May 1985 commando attack against Cabinda, the vital petroleum producing region far to the north of the troubled Namibian border. In November 1987 units of the South African army supported by aircraft were directly engaged with Cuban and Angolan units to help counter the Angolan major offensive against Savimbi's UNITA bases. This development indicated that South Africa probably would commit major units of its army in the civil war if Savimbi's position was seriously threatened.

Despite the manifold foreign and domestic problems faced by South Africa during the 1980s, the hold of the Nationalist Party on the government remained unshaken. President Botha and his advisors were convinced that the evolutionary approach to dismantling apartheid was the only viable way of reform, criticism from the liberal and ultraconservative parties notwithstanding. This seemed confirmed by the election for the white House of Assembly held in May 1987 after a three month long campaign. The Nationalist Party generally stressed a law and order theme and this in combination with the gradual approach toward reform taken by Botha appeared to many English voters. The PFP in partial disarray after the celebrated resignation of its charismatic leader, Frederick van Zyl Slabbart, won only fourteen percent of the popular vote and lost 6 seats, retaining only 19. The far right Conservative Party polled twenty-six percent of the vote and increased its representation from 17 to 22 seats. Some observers saw the increase in the popular vote for Conservatives as a threat to Botha. If so, it was a distant one since the Nationalists claimed 123 of the 166 elected seats. This appeared a clear indication that Botha's policies in spite of urban violence, sanctions, and a wounded economy was popular with most white South Africans. It was also a clear message to the international community that the government would not be moved from the policies enunciated by President Botha.

SEVEN
Troubled independence:
West Africa

In the latter years of the 1950s there were two diverse, extreme attitudes held by observers of the African scene. One view held that Africans were not prepared technically, philosophically, or psychologically to manage their affairs as independent entities. These critics pointed to the small number of persons with a university education even among the politically elite. Most of them had never exercised political power and were completely unfamiliar with the mechanisms of government. Even more critical was the extreme shortage of competent, well-trained personnel who could staff the mid-range white collar positions and perform competently as technicians for the railways, telegraph services, port facilities, and other vital services. These critics pointed to the dichotomy between the small, politically active, and now dominant urban political elite and the traditional rulers of the African masses. With the manifold health, educational, and economic problems of almost every area, the new, untried naïve political leadership seemed an invitation to disaster.

At the opposite extreme were the European liberals who saw independence for Africa as the logical continuation of the anticolonial struggles for liberty and self-determination. They believed that African statesmen would continue the development of Western-style political democracies. Such free governments based upon an expanding African middle class would be able, with disinterested outside assistance, to guarantee civil liberties for all and guide their states peacefully through the transition from traditionally based rule to a new, viable African synthesis. This optimistic attitude was shared by the largest numbers of African politicians.

In the decade after independence was gained by most African states, the liberal attitude was shown to be unrealistic. Kwame Nkrumah and the CPP in Ghana showed the way for others to move toward the negation of parliamentary democracy. After less than three years, Ghana had ceased to have an actively functioning legal opposition party. The good of the party became synonymous with the good of the state. Disagreement with the CPP was tantamount to disloyalty. Other polities, not all for the same reasons, soon after gaining independence became one-party states where deviation from a preestablished party position could mean prison or exile for the individual. In states such as Guinea, Mali, and Ghana mechanisms of domination associated with European totalitarian states were used very efficiently to make certain that the party program was carried out with a minimum of opposition.

The omnipresence of the ruling elite was noticeable even in polities such as those of Senegal, Ivory Coast, Kenya, and Nigeria. Less ideologically committed than the members of the Casablanca group, politicians in these states nevertheless sought to protect their position and tended to consider criticism of their policies as threats to them and their programs. The variety and complexity of the reactions of political leaders to real or imagined threats will be described in detail in the following chapters. However different the responses were, one factor emerged very clearly by 1965. Politicians in power had come to view their high positions as a type of reward for previous services. They and their political parties had, in a short period, become entrenched and much of their energy was devoted to protecting themselves. By making disagreement and dissent either illegal or dangerous, they were assured that their most implacable political opponents could only resort to violence to change the structure of the state. Violence in some form became the only way to secure a change in a corrupt, moribund government.

The manifold problems of each independent nation would have been difficult enough had all the politicians involved been as honest and idealistic as they appeared during the anticolonial struggle. By 1965 it was obvious that a larger number of high-placed politicians were using their offices for personal profit and many showed little interest or aptitude for doing their jobs well. Where there were elections, corruption of all forms existed to assure that the dominant party would stay in power. In many independent states the life of the ordinary African was little, if any, better than it had been when the Europeans ruled. The rising expectations of millions of Africans were succeeded by growing frustration. The great majority of the people were helpless to change the political situation. Only those who could command a coercive force superior to the government had the potential to overthrow the entrenched political machines. Once this was realized, the military throughout Africa were quick to take advantage of their special position within the state structures to oust moribund, unpopular, or ineffective civilian governments. The depth of estrangement between the people and their elected governments can be measured by the immediate popular support given to most new military regimes.

As previously noted, the military reacted in many different ways once they had ousted the politicians. In some cases the army announced that it was playing only a caretaker role and would withdraw once certain deficiencies had been corrected. Some of the military regimes such as in Ghana and Sierra Leone actually followed through with these promises. In other areas such as the Congo and Mali, the military leader gave a sense of civilian legitimacy to his rule by issuing a new constitution and continuing on as the civilian head of state while elsewhere the military ruled openly with no apparent plans ever to return to a form of civilian rule.

It seems clear that in most cases the assumption of control by the military, far from being a setback, actually marked an advance in the fortunes of the state. The military replaced political regimes which had either been discredited or could not solve the pressing problems of their polities. Thus the extreme pessimists who expected Africa to disintegrate once European leadership was removed have also been proved wrong. Economics seem to be the key to the future. Those states such as the Ivory Coast, Gabon, and Tanzania, where there was either great economic potential or where the government was deeply involved in providing the people with a more promising future, have avoided military take-overs. If military regimes can minimize corruption and utilize better the resources of their states, then they will be able to survive, no matter what constitutional form they assume.

Much of western Africa comprises either marginal grazing or agricultural land. Even during the best years life was hard for the sedentary farmers and pastoralists. During the 1966 season there was a marked decrease in rainfall. This pattern was repeated for the next seven years with disastrous results for the human and animal populations. By mid-1974 an estimated 100,000 persons had died of starvation and disease in West Africa despite heroic efforts of public and private agencies to save them. An additional 100,000 were reported to have died in Ethiopia. The states most affected were Ethiopia, Mali, Niger, Upper Volta, Mauritania, and Senegal. Those suffering to a lesser degree were the Gambia, Ghana, and Nigeria. Over one million persons in the Sahel zone were kept alive by food distributed by the Food and Agriculture Organization. Over one-half of the food and general supplies were provided by the United States.

The pastoral way of life for some people was permanently ended by the drought. The Tuareg and Fula lost most of their cattle, goats, and camels. An estimate placed the livestock losses in West Africa during the drought at eight percent of the total. In Niger alone over four million cattle died. Many of the people who survived did so by abandoning their lands and moving into the shanty towns which sprang up on the margins of the main towns. Food distribution was hampered in many cases by poor intra-state distribution systems. Feeding the people became tied into local political questions which impeded the efforts to aid. Lack of appropriate response by the government agencies were directly responsible for overthrowing the regime of Emperor Haile Selassie in Ethiopia and President Hamani Diori in Niger.

A brief survey of political developments in each geographic area of Africa since 1965 may help to underscore the very tentative generalizations made in this introductory section.

English Speaking West Africa

GHANA

The most significant phenomenon noted in West Africa in the period after 1965 was the new role assumed by the military. In Ghana early in 1966 the long-time one-party regime of Kwame Nkrumah was overthrown by a portion of the military led by junior officers. The subsequent regime of General Ankrah provided the necessary conservative leadership to stabilize Ghana's economic drift. True to its promise, the military in November 1968 appointed a constituent Assembly to create new constitutional instruments for a return to civilian rule. General Ankrah resigned in April 1969, and his place as head of government was taken by a triumvirate led by Brigadier-General Afrifa. In 1969 political parties again began to function in Ghana. The two most important were Dr. Kofia A. Busia's Progress Party with its main strength in Ashantiland and the National Alliance of Liberals based upon the Volta regions and headed by Komla Gbedemah. In the August 1969 elections for the legislature, the Progress Party won 105 of the 140 seats and Dr. Busia became prime minister of the new Ghana government on October 1.

The most troublesome problems confronting all governments after the ouster of Nkrumah were not ideological but economic. Cocoa was the major export and income from this crop was not enough to meet recurrent expenditure and still pay Ghana's debts. Inflation, particularly after the rise in petroleum prices in 1973, became a major factor in the instability of Ghanian politics. President Busia attempted stringent cutbacks in government spending. His proposed measures would have adversely affected the army and they acted to protect their interests. In a bloodless coup on January 13, 1972, Colonel Ignatius Acheamapong ousted Ghana's second attempt at responsible civil government. Achempong and the military modified Busia's austerity program and renegotiated some of the more pressing debts. Good cocoa crops masked for over five years the fundamental instability of Ghana's economy. However, by 1978 the economy was at a standstill and inflation had risen to over 30% per year. The military government of Acheampong was unable either to stimulate economic development or halt the disastrous inflation. In late 1976 Acheampong proposed a union government comprising both civilian and military elements, but the military leaders still refused to allow the return of political parties. Increasing dissatisfaction with the performance of Acheampong's regime led to a number of minor disorders in 1977 and 1978. Most civilian leaders, the media, and students wanted a return to genuine parliamentary government, a point that Acheampong was reluctant to concede. In July 1978 a reaction against Acheampong within the military estab-lishment resulted in his displacement as head of state. The new leader, General Sam Akuffo, moved quickly to devalue the currency, cut government spending, and promised a return to full civilian government by the end of 1979.

To this end a Constituent Assembly was formed and made its report in November 1978, and on the basis of that, the military announced that it would allow the creation of political parties. In May 1979 the Constituent Assembly with the approval of the military presented Ghana's new constitution which called for a directly elected functional, rather than ceremonial, president and a 120 person elected Assembly. Amnesties were granted for many accused of political offenses, and boards were established to certify all potential candidates for office. Despite the liberalization of the military regime, there was still widespread corruption among government officials at all levels, and the economy continued to worsen. This was fuel for increasing discontent which showed itself in an overt way first in May when Flight-Lieutenant Jerry Rawlings and a few followers attempted a coup. This failed and Rawlings was imprisoned, but his actions had made him a hero with the lower ranks of the military and the poor. On June 4, a new rebellion against the Akuffo regime began in Accra and quickly spread throughout the country. Rawlings was released from prison and soon became the spokesman for the rebels. After two days of fighting in the capital, Rawlings and his followers were firmly in control of the government.

Rawlings announced that his regime was to be corrective and temporary, and that the elections would proceed as planned. The fourteen man Armed Forces Revolutionary Council (AFRC) stated its intention of punishing corrupt officers of previous regimes and beginning the redistribution of wealth. The first high ranking official to be sentenced to death by the Peoples Revolutionary Court for malfesance was General Acheampong. After his execution, another group of fifty were immediately brought to trial. Most were given long prison sentences, but six were sentenced to death. Among these were General Akuffo and General Afrifa, chief of state in the late 1960s. They were shot at the Accra firing range before a cheering crowd of thousands. Throughout Ghana there were less newsworthy, but nevertheless effective purges of officials charged with corrupt practices. Pleas to end the executions poured into Ghana from all over the world. Some of Ghana's neighbors immediately retaliated against the AFRC and cut off trade. The most effective such action was by Nigeria which ceased to send petroleum products to Ghana. The AFRC relented, and the sentences of other major figures were limited to prison terms.

Elections for the Assembly and for president took place during this time of stress. The Peoples National Party (PNP) led by a northerner, Dr. Hilla Limann, won fifty-six of the Assembly seats to only thirty-nine for its nearest rival, the Popular Front Party (PFP) headed by Victor Owusu. In the presidential elections, no one candidate won a majority of the votes and a runoff was necessary. Limann won the runoff by more than 300,000 votes over Owusu and was declared the president. The key question related to Rawlings and the AFRC. They controlled the military power. Would they be willing in such a short space of time to turn over control of the government to civilians? In an action unique in Africa, Rawlings and his associates indeed gave up power only 124 days after seizing it. In late September, Dr. Limann became president of the Third Republic of Ghana.

Despite Rawlings's gesture, he remained one of the most popular men in Ghana, and the civilian leaders had to realize that what he had engineered once could happen again. The problems facing President Limann's government in late 1979 were immense. Ghana was bankrupt, its world credit shattered. It had proved in the period after Nkrumah's overthrow that an export monoculture could not meet the heavy obligations incurred during his half-decade of extravagance. The inflation rate by mid-1979 had reached 200% and many Ghanaians were hungry and still very angry. The success of the Third Republic depended upon Limann's ability to convince those people that his government was honestly attempting solutions to the worst of their problems.

Perhaps the people expected too much too soon from this civilian regime. Dr. Limann, like Busia before him, had to placate a number of factions within the state while at the same time attempting to correct the economic problems which had bedevilled his predecessors. The Gross National Product continued to fall, real income declined, the inflation rate even by conservative estimates stood at over fifty percent, consumer products became increasingly scarce and there was an almost total breakdown in the transportation system leaving over 100,000 tons of cocoa, the nation's leading money crop, stranded in the interior. The balance of trade ledger showed imports exceeding exports by almost $200 million each year. To add to the woes of the government was the almost cavalier acceptance of official corruption as a necessary way of life.

The performance of Dr. Limann's government was not acceptable to the mass of Ghanaians who could not see any hope for substantial changes in their lives with what they considered the inept actions of the civilian authorities. Even more critical were the leaders of Ghana's military forces then numbering over 17,000 men. Their accepted leader and spokesman, Rawlings, used that influence and his well known popularity to engineer a second coup on December 31, 1981.

In many ways Rawlings and his supporters acted as they had after his first takeover of the government in 1979. The constitution was set aside, high government officials including President Limann were arrested and a central government authority, the Provisional National Defense Council (PNDC), made up of soldiers and civilians was established. Rawlings became the chairman of the PNDC and as such the functional head of state. By mid-1982 People's Defense Committees had been formed and were operating throughout the country acting as overseers to check on public and private excesses. People's courts from which there were no appeals were created to mete out sentences for those accused of wrong doing before and after the coup. The press was closely monitored, a curfew from midnight to 4:00 A.M. was established and checks were imposed upon individual exercise of free assembly and speech. At first Rawlings's dictatorial regime was welcomed, but as the economic conditions worsened there were growing protests particularly from students and from the Trade Union Congress.

Rawlings promised the people a real revolution, one that was more than just a change of leaders, but a socialist state which built on the strength of the people. However, he found the economic conditions so bad that the first year of his rule was simply a struggle to meet the conflicting demands of the various sectors of society. He was confronted with double digit inflation, high unemployment in the cities, wages were so bad that the unions were demanding raises of up to 1000%. Cocoa production had fallen and serious drought conditions prevailed in the north and central parts of the country. The normal food distribution system had broken down and hundreds of thousands of people were kept alive by international agencies. The PNDC efforts to put a ceiling on prices was at first a failure since entrepreneurs simply ignored the rulings. Closing the borders with the Ivory Coast and Togo, slowed down smuggling, but did little to improve the supply of food in the urban areas. The International Monetary Fund representatives signalled their willingness to help only if the PNDC began to put into effect some basic improvements in government management. Specifically they wanted the Cedi, Ghana's currency, devaluated to a reasonable level. Although not happy with the pressure, Rawlings agreed in October 1983 to a ninety percent devaluation.

Resistance to Rawlings's authoritarian regime and austerity program was slow in developing because many of those in opposition were either jailed or in exile. Nevertheless, by mid-1983 students and workers were bold enough to take to the streets in Kumasi and Accra demanding more freedom and better wages. The police were able to control the disturbances with little difficulty. Far more dangerous have been the attempts to overthrow Rawlings's regime. On November 23, 1982 one group of dissidents had tried a coup but the army soon crushed the uprising. Some of the leaders of that attempt fled to Togo from where they organized an invasion of Ghana. On June 19, 1983, while the government was busy dealing with the students and trade unionists, they crossed the border and attacked three prisons in Accra and Nswam. At first the dissidents met with considerable success. They freed fifty-two prisoners and seized the Ghana Broadcasting Company buildings. Within hours, however, loyal troops crushed the uprising. Those captured were tried and twenty conspirators were sentenced to death.

One result of this action was the worsening of relations between Togo and Ghana despite both states having signed a quadripartite agreement with Benin and Nigeria in December. Ghana accused President Eyadema's government of openly supporting those elements in exile who sought to bring down the Rawlings regime. Relations deteriorated after March when another small incursion from Togo was checked. In the fighting the army killed seven of the invaders and later three of those captured were executed. The government of Togo retaliated by accusing Ghana of complicity in the placing of bombs which exploded in Lomé and further of supporting an attempted coup against Eyadema. Despite the war of words exchanged between Lomé and Accra, Rawlings approved the reopening of the border with Togo and also with the Ivory Coast.

The attempts to overthrow Rawlings took on an even more international flavor with the arrest in December 1985 of Ghanaians in the United States for conspiring to purchase $250,000 in weapons to arm a 100 man force. One of those arrested, John Henry Mensot, had been Finance Minister during President Busia's tenure and was one of Rawlings's more vocal opponents. Another plan to invade Ghana was uncovered in early 1986 when the Brazilian government arrested 8 Americans and 10 Argentines off its coast and charged them with plotting Rawlings's overthrow by force. The plan supposedly was to pick up 100 armed men in the Ivory Coast and these would spearhead the invasion. Four of the American mercenaries escaped after ten months in prison and their story implicated elements in the American government with the abortive invasion.

Thus it is obvious that Rawlings and his government are in some danger from influences outside Ghana. Presumably he was not popular with a considerable number of persons who viewed his regime as dictatorial and by those within the state who believed he had not kept his immediate post-revolution promises. Nevertheless, there has been very definite progress during his regime. Ghana was no longer the economic disaster it was during the latter stage of the Limann tenure. Agreements with creditor nations took some pressure off the government. Three devaluations of the Cedi brought the currency closer in conformity with IMF suggestions and the World Bank has underwritten plans to increase gold production. Most important, easing of the drought combined with changed government priorities which now stress agriculture has brought a situation where Ghana's exports exceed its imports in value. The production of maize in 1985 was so good that one-third of the harvest was exported to Mali and Burkina Faso. The cocoa harvests improved steadily and with a stable world market price, the PNDC was able to reward the farmers with a considerable increase per ton for their crop. The outlook for any significant change in the government's autocratic control does not seem hopeful. However, Rawlings and his associates in the PNDG have halted the disastrous economic decline and their policies appear in 1987 to be popular with the great mass of the Ghanaian people.

SIERRA LEONE

In Sierra Leone the government of Albert Margai did not measure up to the standards established by his brother, Sir Milton Margai. In the elections of early 1967 the ruling Sierra Leone Peoples Party was challenged by Siaka Stevens' All People Congress. The elections, marred by corruption and violence, was extremely close. Governor Lightfoot-Boston declared the All Peoples Congress the victor and called upon Stevens to form a government. However, the head of the armed forces, Brigadier-General Lansana, and a small number of adherents overthrew the government on March 21 and arrested Stevens and Governor Lightfoot-Boston. Two days later a counter-coup organized by junior officers deposed Lansana. The new junta or National Reformation Council eventually invited Lieutenant-Colonel Juxton-Smith to act as head of state. The military immediately launched a series of investigations into alleged mismanagement of the previous regime. One report of the disputed election confirmed that Stevens had indeed won. Juxton-Smith repeatedly promised a return to civilian government as soon as possible and he appointed a committee to study the full range of problems connected with the transfer of power. Many Sierra Leoneans did not believe these promises. Among the disbelievers were junior officers who in April 1968 staged another military coup and thus forced a return to civilian control. They jailed Juxton-Smith, Lansana, and other members of the former military regime and invited Siaka Stevens to return. After conferences between the two major parties, Stevens was chosen the leader of a national government. Widespread disorders followed and a state of emergency was declared in November 1968.

The deep divisions between country and city and between Creole, Temne, and Mende continued well into the 1970s. In 1970 a new party, the United Democratic Party (UDP) was organized to reflect northern hostility to the APC. The government acted to halt any open signs of disaffection. In July Juxton-Smith was executed and in October the UDP was banned and two senior and six junior military officers were arrested, charged with plotting to overthrow the government. Despite such strong counter measures against the possibility of a coup, there was an effort organized by the army commander, Brigadier John Bangura, on March 23, 1971 to overthrow Stevens. The bulk of the army remained loyal, but Stevens was not convinced and invoked a clause in the mutual defense treaty with Sekou Touré and troops from Guinea entered the country and remained until all overt actions of the anti-APC groups was contained. Meanwhile in April 1971 parliament had acted to convert Sierra Leone into a Republic and Stevens became president. At first Stevens allowed some political activity on the part of the rival SLPP. Then in 1978 the constitution was changed so that Sierra Leone became officially a one-party state. All political parties other than the APC were forced either to disband or go into exile. Stevens was elected president for life and soon became recognized as one of the most astute politicians in Africa. Although his control of the state was near absolute, he allowed for considerable participation in decision making, seldom resorting to a show of force to obtain his ends. Despite the poorness of Sierra Leone and its many economic problems, the "Old Man" as he was known during his seventeen years as head of state managed to give the country a stable and relatively efficient government with only a minimum of corruption on the highest levels.

The worsening economic conditions brought on largely by the increase in petroleum prices in the late 1970s combined with falling world prices for cocoa and coffee plagued the latter years of President Stevens's administration. It was necessary to cut back sharply on development programs and government subsidies and put a ceiling on wage increases. As was true elsewhere in West Africa, the government program brought protests from student organizations and the trade unions. In 1981 there occurred the first general strike in Sierra Leone's history. The government responded by briefly closing Fourah Bay College and arresting eighty union leaders. Inflation, smuggling and food shortages continued to plague the government and brought opponents of the APC regime closer together. Despite the rescheduling of a major portion of the foreign debt and agreement with the IMF which at one time had suspended all dealings with Sierra Leone, the economics of the country continued to deteriorate. Many who otherwise supported the government turned hostile as it tried to implement the stringent economic reforms suggested by the IMF. Students at the various colleges took to the streets in 1985 and again in January 1987. The latter demonstrations over food costs were the most violent as government buildings were attacked; looting was widespread, especially in Freetown and Kenema.

In the midst of the economic crisis in 1985, President Stevens who was over eighty years of age decided to retire. At the APC convention in July his hand picked successor, Major General Joseph Momoh was confirmed as the APC candidate for president. It was necessary to modify the constitution since Momoh had not resigned from the army within the limits imposed nor did he meet the age qualification. Nevertheless, in the election of October 1985 he was elected president and on November 28 there was a peaceful transferrence of power. Although Monoh promised major reforms in the economy designed to benefit the consumer, he like Stevens was a prisoner of Sierra Leone's relative poverty and world economic conditions beyond the control of his government. By following the demands of the IMF in allowing the currency to float, he has caused additional distress to the ordinary citizen. It was obvious that Momoh's popularity in 1987 was less than when he was elected and this could coalese the heretofore weak opposition groups. The small army, quiescent since 1968, could nevertheless be a factor in the future government of Sierra Leone. The possible worsening of the political situation in Sierra Leone was shown by the discovery in March 1987 of a plot involving forty persons including some senior police officers who had stockpiled over one million dollars worth of arms to use to assassinate the president and overthrow his government.

NIGERIA

In Nigeria, after the second military coup, Colonel Yakuba Gowon replaced the assassinated Major-General Ironsi on August 1, 1966. He retained the old structure of military rule and kept the governors of the four regions, including Colonel Odemegwu Ojukwu in the East. Gowon promised a speedy return to civil rule and appointed a constitutional conference to facilitate this. His plans were upset in September by the killing of thousands of Ibo in the Northern Region. Within a month a flood of Ibo refugees inundated the East.

Ojukwu ordered northerners out of the east for their safety and openly questioned whether one Nigeria could exist when over seven million citizens could not travel freely in any part of the country. After that time, Ojukwu began to govern the East with little reference to the government at Lagos and started to build up that portion of the army under his command. He stated that for reasons of safety he would not meet with the other military leaders outside of the Eastern Region.

After many attempts, a conference between the military commanders including Ojukwu was finally convened at Aburi, Ghana, in January 1967. Agreement was reached at Aburi on a number of salient points. Chief among these was that the future structure of the federation should have a weaker central government and more power should be devolved to the regional authorities. However, Gowon made no attempt to put the agreement into effect and, in early March 1967, Ojukwu announced that he would do so on a unilateral basis.

From this point on, Nigeria edged toward civil war. Both sides increased their military forces and attempted to create a feeling of patriotism in their people. On May 27, Gowon announced the government plans for a new federation of twelve regions with the central government retaining supreme authority. The Ibo would be restricted to one landlocked region. Ojukwu had not been consulted before this declaration and he considered the plan a negation of the Aburi agreements. Therefore, the Eastern Consultative Assembly declared its secession from Nigeria on May 30, 1967 and took the name Biafra for their new state.

Actual hostilities began on July 6 when federal troops invaded Biafra on two fronts. The initial numerical superiority of approximately three to one remained constant throughout the war although the Nigerian army grew, by 1969, in excess of 80,000 men. Early in the conflict the Biafran ports of Bonny, Port Harcourt, and Calabar were captured, thus preventing Ojukwu from receiving large quantities of war material and food supplies. Except for the August 1967 Biafran offensive which resulted in the occupation of a part of the Mid-West, Ojukwu's forces were always on defensive. Enugu was lost to the federal army in October 1967, and despite heroic efforts, the Biafran forces were driven from Aba, Okigwi, Owerri, and Onitsha in 1968. Biafra was thus reduced to only a small fraction of what had been Eastern Nigeria. Despite its inferiority in numbers, supplies, and equipment, the Biafrans refused to surrender. To Gowon and his chief advisers this was an embarrassment since almost everyone had believed that the war could be quickly won. Instead it had become a nightmare, killing thousands of federal troops and draining the credits of a once prosperous state.

Biafra's only hope by mid-1968 lay in gaining recognition from a significant number of other states. However, only Tanzania, Zambia, the Ivory Coast, Gabon, and Haiti recognized Ojukwu's regime. The United States maintained a neutral position while Britain and Russia supplied Nigeria with war materials. France, although refusing to alienate Nigeria by supporting Biafra diplomatically, did allow its nationals to provide arms to Biafra. All such aid had to be funneled into one bad, temporary airstrip at Uli. Attempts by various nations and the OAU to mediate the dispute proved fruitless. Meetings at London, Kampala, Niamey, and Addis Ababa had no influence toward ending the conflict. In addition to combat casualties, untold thousands of Biafran civilians died in the conflict. Many of these were children, most of whom died of starvation despite the efforts of national and international relief agencies to abate the suffering. When Biafra finally capitulated on January 12, 1970, Nigeria was once again a united state, but the once rich Eastern area had been thoroughly devastated.

Nigeria, like so many African states, was plagued throughout the 1970s by economic problems. The inflation rate which in the earlier decade had been manageable rose steadily following the decision in 1973 by the petroleum producing states to raise their prices. The successive military governments were not able to control the upward spiral and by 1979 the annual increase in the cost of living index was almost thirty percent. Two domestic factors complemented the worldwide causes for inflation. Nigeria in the years after 1966 became one of the world's largest producers of petroleum. The tremendous influx of capital had not only a positive effect, but also a negative inflationary one. In 1975 the decision to raise the salaries of all government employees, while necessary, also helped fuel the inflation of the late 1970s. Thus despite Nigeria's great newfound wealth, individual citizens discovered that the cost of living was increasing at a greater rate than their incomes. Petroleum profits have, however, enabled Nigeria to remain solvent, finance its own recovery program from the devastating drought in the north, and to undertake major construction projects far beyond the dreams of most African states. Overspending, corruption, and the finiteness of Nigeria's petroleum reserves were major problems which the proposed civilian government had to solve if Nigeria was to continue its political recovery from the civil war.

On July 29, 1975 just nine years after the second military coup, troops were on the move again securing the key cities for a new group of conspirators. General Gowon who was in Kampala for a meeting of the OAU was quietly supplanted in office by General Murtala Muhammed, a Hausa who had distinguished himself in the Biafran war. The reasons given for this coup were that the government on all levels was corrupt and many of the military governors were totally unresponsive to the needs of the people. One reason for the quick shift of the people's allegiance away from Gowon was the stand he had taken on a return to a government run by civilians. Gowon at first had promised full civilian government by 1976 and then had recanted because he did not believe the country could be ready by then for such a drastic change. Muhammed promised the nation reforms on all levels, honesty in government, and a systematic return to civil control by 1979.

General Muhammed's reforms and promises brought a negative reaction from a powerful minority in the military who attempted to overthrow the new government on February 13, 1976. Although the coup was unsuccessful, General Muhammed was assassinated in Lagos. General Olusegun Obasanjo, the ranking military officer and chief advisor to Muhammed, became head of the Federal Military Government. The most important of the conspirators were soon arrested and executed. General Obasanjo's government devoted much of its time in the following two years in preparing the nation for civil government. In late 1976 the first elections for a redesigned system of local government were held. The following year a

Constitutional convention made public its plans for a civil government with a directly elected president possessing considerable power who would not be responsible to the legislature. As the necessary prelude to election, in mid-1978, General Obasanjo dismissed from government many of the leading army officers, ordering them back to strictly military duties. The new constitution was approved, a Federal Elections Committee (FEDECO) appointed, and general elections scheduled to begin July 1979. FEDECO employed over 400,000 persons for the elections, screened the qualifications of over 8700 candidates, and banned over 1000 persons from standing for election.

Five political parties were formed to contest the elections. The three northern based parties were the National Party of Nigeria (NPN) led by Alhaji Shehu Shagari, the Great Nigerian Peoples Party (GNPP) headed by Alhaji Ibrahim, and the Peoples Redemption Party (PRP) of Alhaji Amino Kano. The two southern parties were led by old opponents. Chief Obafemi Awolowo led the United Party of Nigeria (UPN) while Dr. Nnamdi Azikiwe headed the Nigerian Peoples Party (NPP). All the leaders proposed to run for president, but FEDECO banned Alhaji Kano from the elections. The elections for local governments, state governments, the Federal Assembly and Senate, and president were held between July 7 and August 11. There was a heavy turnout of voters for each election and very little violence. The NPN won substantial victories on all levels and in all sections of Nigeria. It held 168 of the 494 seats in the national Assembly, 36 of the 95 seats in the Senate, seven state governorships, and Shehu Shagari won the presidential election over his closest rival, Chief Awolowo, by more than 700,000 votes. Having no clear majority at the central level, the NPN was forced into a coalition government, but this did not present difficulties since two of the other parties were northern oriented.

The military played a supportive role during the entire complex process of developing once again a civilian government. General Obasanjo at the inauguration ceremonies of Shehu Shagari on October 1 announced his retirement from the army, but pledged that the army would continue to sustain the new government. Nigeria's wealth in petroleum had masked the economic weakness of the state. Once nearly self-sufficient in food production, Nigeria had become an importer of food for its burgeoning population. This alone cost over 1 billion Niara each year. The military regimes had been more interested in high cost extremely visable projects rather than a concerted effort to improve both subsistance and export agriculture. The result was that the nation was dependent for over ninety percent of its export earnings on petroleum production. These profits had enabled all governments in the 1970s to be extravagant and give a continued appearance of prosperity. All this ended with the glut of petroleum on the world market and subsequent fall of prices and the end of the OPEC nations' ability to dictate to the more developed countries. Unfortunately the depressed state of petroleum sales occurred in about the same time that the new civilian government of Shehu Shagari took office.

The NPN government did not at first recognize the seriousness of the economic downturn. Wage and price controls were established and a ceiling was placed on incomes. However, the income from Nigeria's "sweet" petroleum continued to be good. Thus expensive projects were continued, the armed forces remained at an inflated 140,000 men and the government began to implement plans for the purchase of vast acreages of land to begin its green revolution. An agreement to share power at the center had been reached with all the rival political parties except Chief Awolowo's UPN. After the first eighteen months, the civilian regime appeared to be settling in. The army was back in barracks, corruption and urban crime seemed no greater than before, and the general public was quiescent.

By mid-1981 Shagari's government was confronted with a series of problems which it could not easily solve. The first was the extreme cutback in petroleum production necessitated by the world surplus. A low point had been reached when production fell to only 500,000 barrels a day. By the end of the year the total production had decreased by one-third and this problem was compounded by the decline of the price per barrel. Undoubtedly the worsening of the economy contributed to breaking up Shagari's political coalition, but there were other factors as well. Religious differences between north and south had obviously blocked Shagari's dream of making the NPN into a strong, permanent national party. Personality clashes among politicians as was true throughout Nigerian history also played an important role in the political disturbances that rocked the country.

The breakup of his coalition at the center was caused by differences between the president and members of the House of Representatives over retention of government revenues. In July four NPP ministers resigned from the government. Later the NPP joined the other parties in creating a more united opposition. Political differences were also apparent in the government of many of the states. In June violence between supporters of the UPN and NPN flared in Ijebu Ode and students at Ife and Owerri took to the streets. Shagari's government arrested the editors of four of Nigeria's major newspapers for stories allegedly unfavorable to the regime. The most serious outbreaks against public order occurred in the states of Kano and Kaduna. There elements loyal to the leader of the People's Redemption Party (PRP), Alhaji Aminu Kano, engineered the expulsion of the governors of those states. Governor Balarbe Musa of Kaduna was impeached. Later rumors that the governor of Kano state had insulted the Emir led to violence in that large northern city. A fanatical Muslim leader so inflamed many of his followers that they began a series of indiscriminate attacks on persons and property in Kano. The government was forced to send in troops and in the fighting that followed an estimated 1000 people were killed before order was restored.

In February 1982 the government discovered a planned coup and arrested those responsible. Evidence throughout the country of growing dissatisfaction with the inability of the NPN government to solve the economic problems was apparent. But these were mainly feelings; there was little overt opposition to the continued civilian regime. Shagari was confident as the Federal Election Committee (FEDECO) in 1982 began preparations for the elections scheduled for the fall of 1983. The meticulous preparations by FEDECO and the campaigning accomplished with a minimum of violence appeared to most observers to be a vindication of moderate constitutional government. There were four separate elections held in August and September. As predicted Shagari was returned to office defeating his old opponents, Azikiwe and Awolowo, winning almost fifty percent of the popular vote. His party, the NPN, won 264 of the 450 seats in the House, 55 of 85 in the Senate, and 13 of the 19 governorships. It appeared that the NPN was assured of another long tenure in control of the government. Shagari's opponents could not agree with each other and none could present as cogent a plan as the NPN for governing the country.

The leaders of the armed forces, true to Obasanjo's promise, had been closely monitoring the performance of the civilian government. Not surprisingly, they found much that did not please them. Finally despairing of any significant change, they acted. The second civilian regime during Nigeria's short independence was ended by a military takeover on December 31, 1983. The constitution was suspended and many executive and legislative bodies were replaced by the Federal Military Government (FMG). The position of head of state was taken by Major General Mohammad Buhari who had been the minister in charge of petroleum production under Shagari. Most civil servants at all levels were retained, but all elected governors were removed and were replaced by military men appointed by the central authority. The takeover was quick, efficient, and bloodless. Only three months after the general elections, the Nigerian electorate was prepared to accept military rule once again.

In a series of speeches General Buhari and his associates laid out their objectives. These were generally laudable, but such promises had been made before and many of the civilian leaders of Nigeria adopted a wait and see attitude. Buhari soon discovered that the economic malaise was worse than the army leaders had imagined. The external debt stood at over $20 billion, much of which had to be paid or rescheduled. A loan application to the IMF made by the Shagari government had been refused because of the chaotic state of Nigeria's finances. Buhari believed he could not put into effect all of the IMF's stringent suggestions. Nevertheless in March 1984, the FMG passed a series of harsh decrees regulating exports and imports and foreign exchange. All old currency was recalled and new, less valuable, naira was issued. In an attempt to halt smuggling, the borders with Nigeria's neighbors were closed. There were drastic cutbacks on government expenditures and thousands lost their jobs, joining the ranks of the millions of urban unemployed. These measures combined with better harvests of cocoa and palm oil and increased petroleum production gave a brief uplift to the economy and allowed the government to refuse to comply with the IMF demands. One action popular with many Nigerians but which alienated the governments of neighboring countries was the expulsion in May 1985 of more than 700,000 aliens, the majority of whom were from Ghana.

Buhari discovered that while all the cutbacks and controls might have been necessary, they did not make him popular. The unemployed, students, workers who had taken pay cuts, and businessmen forced into bankruptcy were all unhappy. General Buhari did not have the charismatic personality to make his "war against indiscipline" popular. There was some indication by early 1985 that Buhari's harsh economic program was having an effect. However, in March the government issued two decrees after much debate within the FMG which further eroded support for Buhari. One made criticism of public officials a criminal offense; the other gave government the right to imprison anyone without trial who was considered a subversive. The implementation of these in connection with the "war against indiscipline" convinced many within the FMG that Buhari would have to be replaced. Chief among Buhari's critics was Major General Ibrahim

Babangida, an important figure in two previous coups. Finally on August 27, 1985 while Buhari was absent from Lagos, his colleagues acted and brought to an end his twenty month regime. His replacement as chief of state was Babangida.

Two factors favored Babangida. He was able to project himself and his proposed program more skillfully than his predecessor. In this he reminded many observers of Murtala Mohammad. The second point in his favor was the slight improvement in Nigeria's economy brought on in part by the Buhari program, but primarily by the upturn in world petroleum prices. Babangida promised more leniency toward dissent, he released over 100 political prisoners in January 1986, and repealed the two offending decrees of March 1985 against dissent. Babangida also continued to cutback on government subsidies and true to his promise diverted funds toward rural development. He imposed a two tier system on the value of the currency, which allowed for stringent controls in certain areas but gave more flexibility in purchasing needed overseas goods. The FMG was also able to obtain a debt moratorium, new credits from European bankers, and a promise to reschedule all debts.

Despite the success enjoyed by Babangida, the old problems remained although somewhat attenuated. Lack of profitable exports, corruption at all levels, overpopulation, particularly in the cities, foreign debts amounting to over $25 billion, dozens of opposing, hostile ethnic groups, and two religious systems at odds with each other are some of the most critical. The expectations of many Nigerians are beyond the economic realities; they demand too much of any government. When those expectations are not achieved they are ready to support any alternative. Two examples show how tenuous is Babangida's hold on government. In December 1985, his old friend, the poet Major General Maman Vatsa, and other ranking officers attempted a coup. It was unsuccessful and Vatsa was subsequently executed. Then in July 1986 student disturbances began at Ahmadu Bello University and the protests were soon joined by students throughout the country. Troops and police eventually put down the disturbances but only after forty persons had been killed and twenty colleges and universities had been closed. In addition to his charisma Babangida will need a steadily improving economy, the support of the army, and continuing good government if his regime is to survive and avoid chaos.

GAMBIA

The Gambia, once believed to be a nonviable entity, has proved to be one of the surprising success stories of Africa if success is measured by political stability. From its independence on February 17, 1965 until the attempted coup of July 30, 1981, the Gambia was one of the few states in Africa where a multiparty political system operated within a democratic form of government with a minimum amount of coercion by the dominant People's Progressive Party (PPP). The leader of the PPP, Sir Dauda Jawara, was a staunch defender of the concept of free elections. The only major change from the Westminister model provided at independence was the establishment of a republican form with an elected president in 1972. Jawara merely exchanged titles from prime minister to that of president. The continued dominance of the PPP in every election held after independence was due less to government attempts to subvert the opposition than to the ineptness of the leaders of the United Party (UP) which at first provided the main alternative party. With the failure of the UP, younger politicians then created the National Convention Party (NCP) in 1977 which although never winning more than one-quarter of the popular vote nevertheless has continued, even after the coup, to function in opposition to the PPP.

For over a decade the government was able by its strict austerity programs to avoid the massive foreign debts that so plagued many larger and richer African states. Then in the late 1970s world wide inflation, drought, and falling world market price for peanuts, its major export, forced the Gambia to begin to borrow in order to continue government operations. Rising unemployment resulted in the creation of a number of radical movements in Banjul which were supported by dissidents. Some of these radicals financed in part by outside agencies attempted a coup against the PPP government on July 30, 1981. They were briefly successful since many members of the Gambia Field Force joined the rebellion. President Jawara invoked the 1967 mutual defense treaty with Senegal whose President, Abdou Diouf, dispatched enough regular troops to crush the uprising. With more than 600 persons dead in Banjul, Jawara within a few days was once again in power. There was no massive violent retribution against those arrested. Instead special courts were created to mesh into the regular judicial system and judges were brought in from other West African territories. Although the procedures were lengthy, the government wanted to show that the rule of law still prevailed. The popularity of President Jawara and the PPP was confirmed by the 1982 elections and in subsequent years the memory of the terror in the capital city faded.

One lasting legacy of the failed coup was the Confederation of the Senegambia. Some type of closer association had been assumed by Britain and Senegal at the time of Gambian independence. However, the success of the Gambians in governing themselves combined with their deep fears of being dominated by their larger neighbor had postponed any meaningful political agreement. In the aftermath of the 1981 rebellion, Jawara found he could no longer resist Senegalese pressure. He and President Diouf soon agreed upon the basic framework of a confederation and it was approved by the legislatures of both states on December 29, 1981. The agreements envisioned a federation where a central legislature and executive would have the authority to make common economic and foreign policy. The head of state of Senegal was to become president of the federation while the vice president would be the president of the Gambia. Very soon all the old fears of Senegalese domination returned and the half-decade since the confederation was formed saw very little movement toward full implementation of the agreements. The framework for the confederation exists but both states remain practically separate entities.

LIBERIA

Despite the obvious stability of President Tolbert's government, there were signs that economic problems could change this. The most serious disturbance in recent Liberian history was occasioned in April 1979 when the government announced a seventeen percent increase in the price of rice. Farmers and young people took to the streets in many Liberian towns to protest the increase. In Monrovia, the protest could not be controlled and there were very serious riots. President Tolbert declared an emergency and the police and army put down the demonstrations by force, killing 41 and injuring over 500 persons. The Progressive Alliance of Liberia (PAL), a banned radical political party, was blamed for the riots, although the obvious cause was the huge increase in the price of the staple food of most Liberians. The University was closed, and three members of the Soviet Embassy were expelled. In June the government announced that it was cancelling the price increase and instead was lowering the price of rice by ten percent. The crisis was thus surmounted amidst indications that the Liberian population was not as docile as once believed. During the crisis, President Tolbert invoked a mutual aid pact with Guinea which sent more than 100 soldiers to help restore order.

Criticism of Tolbert's regime mounted after the riots and some of his opponents were quite vocal in their attacks upon the oligarchy. One such was Baccus Matthews, leader of the Progressive Peoples Party. He was arrested on March 9, 1980, and jailed, charged with treason. This action convinced a number of enlisted men in the army to take action against the tyranny of the government. On April 12, a small section of the Monrovia garrison seized key points in the capital. Master Sergeant Samuel K. Doe's seventeen men invaded the executive mansion and killed Tolbert and subsequently twenty-seven other government officials. These were thrown unceremoniously in a common grave. In the following days with the apparent support of the citizens throughout the country hundreds of persons with ties to the previous government were arrested. Most were accused of participating in the rampant corruption which had characterized the government by the Americo-Liberia oligarchy. Five member military courts tried some of the most influential of those accused. On April 22, thirteen former officials including the chief justice, the foreign minister, and the brother of the former president were machine-gunned in front of a festive, cheering crowd. Doe promised that all who were guilty would be found and dealt with quickly and efficiently. However, there was such an international outcry over the operations that a week later he announced the suspension of the killings. The new government legitimized itself of April 26 by suspending the 133 year old constitution and vesting all power in a seventeen member Peoples Redemption Council (PRD) with Doe as its chairman.

Instead of conditions improving in the aftermath of the coup, they worsened. The ferocity of the army's actions alienated world opinion. Liberia's delegates were at first refused admission to the West African Economic Community meetings. Liberian troops stormed the French Embassy in Monrovia to seize ex-President Tolbert's eldest son. The French government recalled its envoy. In many ways Sergeant Doe had come to replace Idi Amin in the minds of observers who considered him a buffoon albeit a dangerous one. Throughout the early stages of the new government the United States continued to support Doe with economic aid while trying to mitigate some of the excesses of his regime.

There were a number of reasons why Liberia's economy continued to falter in the half-decade after the coup. The PRD had inherited a nation already plagued with economic woes. Another factor was the lack of confidence in the new government shown by potential investors and foreign states. Despite Liberia's position as an exporter of rubber and high quality iron ore, there was little interest shown in putting money into a state whose leader was so mercurial and inexperienced in government. The last and perhaps most important factor was this inexperience. Although most of the civil servants accommodated themselves to the new regime they were generally not in a policy making position and thus could do little to prevent disastrous decisions. One of these was when Doe accepted the tempting solution to his currency problem by deciding to mint Liberia's own money, a seven cornered dollar, to circulate along with the old United States currency. By 1986 there were at least $30 million in Liberia's new currency which had by then depreciated to only fifty percent of its issued value. United States dollars became increasingly difficult to find even on the black market.

The economic picture for Liberia had not improved even after the 1985 elections. The treasury was almost empty, inflation was double digit, and some government workers had not been paid for months. Liberia owed $90 million to the IMF and $1.4 billion to the World Bank. The interest on the latter debt alone exceeds government revenues. Only additional loans from the United States, Liberia's "special friend," allowed for the servicing of the foreign debts. The excesses of Doe's administration were overlooked because of the historic, economic, and military ties between the two governments.

The PRC was in many ways no more oppressive than the Tubman and Tolbert regimes. They, too, had controlled the press, limited public criticism, maintained a one-party state, and meted out outrageous jail sentences to their opponents. These policies continued under Doe. All persons suspected of opposing the government found Liberia a difficult place in which to live. Journalists were a favorite target of the PRC; many were jailed after their newspapers were shut down by government order. Then in 1985 Decree 88A was issued which gave the police sweeping powers to "arrest and detain any person found spreading lies and misinformation against any government official either by writing or public broadcast." This decree which remained in force, by 1987 allowed the new civilian regime to continue the repressive policies of the PRC.

Under pressure from within and from the United States, Doe announced the return of civilian government under a new constitution. The four year ban on political parties was lifted in 1984 and the constitution based largely on the model of that of the United States was promulgated. Although the elections scheduled for the fall of 1985 were supposed to be free, the parties opposing the National Democratic Party of Liberia (NDLP) dominated by Doe and the ruling group were harassed. Three leaders were briefly imprisoned in the maximum security unit of Bella Yella prison less than two months before the scheduled election in October. The United Peoples Party (UPP) of Doe's one-time foreign minister was banned. This prohibition was not lifted for thirteen months. The UPP leader, Dr. Amos Sawyer, one of those imprisoned in August, was prohibited from running for president. Given the power and the attitude of those who controlled the NDPL, the election results appeared a foregone conclusion. Surprisingly there was considerable opposition to Doe's regime as reflected by the popular vote. Many observers concluded that Doe had lost the presidential election. However, a special election committee recounted those ballots and declared Doe to have won 50.9% of the vote.

Amidst charges of election fraud, another of Doe's former associates, Brigadier General Thomas Quiwonkpa, who had been in exile, decided to act. His supporters in the army on November 12 seized important buildings in Monrovia and he broadcast to the nation an end to Doe's control of the government. However, forces loyal to Doe smashed the coup and Quiwonkpa's bullet riddled body was found a few days later. Attempting to minimize the seriousness of the uprising, the government announced that only eleven persons were killed. Others pointed to the evidence of heavy fighting and labelled the government's casualty figures as ridiculously low. In the aftermath of the coup attempt once again the United States using its economic leverage moderated the government crackdown on alleged conspirators. The reality of the Liberian situation in the second decade of Doe's government was continuing poverty alleviated only in part by the inflow of assistance from the United States. Between 1980 and 1986, the United States provided $434 million in economic and military assistance to Liberia. Then in 1986 the General Accounting Office in Washington could not account for over $60 million. This fact combined with the resistance of the Doe regime to implement suggested reforms caused the United States to suspend all aid to Liberia. Without such assistance the debt ridden government could not long survive. Doe was forced to yield to this pressure and agree to put the economic future of Liberia in the hands of seventeen financial managers from the United States. Technically Doe would have the final say in such matters but the reality of control of all phases of the economy including preparation of the budget would be controlled by these experts for an indefinite period. The agreement was denounced by Doe's political opponents as a surrender of Liberian sovereignty and propping up a corrupt inefficient government. Just how much of an effect this economic interference would have on the admittedly autocratic regime of the PRC remains to be seen.

French Speaking West Africa

Most of the independent states of what had been French West Africa were even more volatile after 1965 than their English-speaking counterparts. Even the most stable, the Ivory Coast and Senegal, witnessed some plots against the government and confrontation with students and labor. A crucial fact in the recent history of the states of the Sahel was the drought of the early 1970s and the return of similar if less devastating conditions a decade later. Many of the independent nations of what was formerly the AOF were already desperately poor with little of economic value to earn the necessary funds even to meet ordinary expenditures. The French government, unlike the British, maintained close economic and military ties with its former colonies and provided the capital necessary to keep states such as Mali, Upper Volta (Burkina Faso), Niger, Togo,and Dahomey (Benin) solvent. However, the drought was responsible for the deaths of thousands of people despite the best efforts of international aid agencies. The bulk of the livestock on which the majority of the population of the Sahel depended also died. There was a mass exodus of people into the already overcrowded towns and cities. With the return of normal rainfall some of the pastoralists resumed their old ways but for a majority that life was irretrievably lost. They remained in the towns adding another set of problems to those already confronting the impoverished governments.

Another factor in the complex of problems for some of these states was the war in the Western Sahara and Chad. Even if this war did not directly affect some states, it caused the governments to be alert to a spill-over effect and on a larger scale divided the Organization of African Unity. One of the states most directly involved in the long, costly conflict in the Western Sahara was Mauritania.

MAURITANIA

Mauritania was a state long considered to be a bastion of stability. Mokhtar Ould Daddah was a model, skilled politician who had successfully gained the support of both the modern and traditional elements in the state. Nevertheless, he was overthrown in July 1978 by the military who disagreed with his handling of the escalating guerrilla warfare in the Western Sudan.

In the mid-1970s the final dissolution of Spain's African empire appeared to be favorable for both Morocco and Mauritania since the Spanish government agreed to divide its possession between these two claimants with Morocco gaining the northern two-thirds of the territory. However, even before Spain withdrew in 1975, there were demonstrations against this settlement. The politico-military group, the Polisaro, ostensibly representing the Saharan people, demanded independence. In this they had received considerable support from Algeria which had allowed them to operate military bases in the area adjacent to the Western Sahara. The Polisaro, which formed a government called the Saharan Arab Democratic Republic, escalated the hit and run raids after 1976. Most of the military activity was in the north against the more heavily populated region near the phosphate mines of Bou Craa. Nevertheless, the guerrillas were able to move freely throughout the country, even shelling the Mauritanian capital of Nouakchott.

A stalemate had been achieved in the fighting by 1978 because a large section of the Moroccan army was concentrated in the Sahara and Mauritania had increased its army to 17,000 men. This unexpected strain on the Mauritanian government proved costly and led directly to the assumption of control by the military under the leadership of Colonel Mustapha Ould Salek, who in addition to being chief of the Military Committee for National Rectification also assumed the position as President of Mauritania. However, by early 1979, Colonel Ould Boucief, the Premier, had emerged as the strongman of the government. He had decided just before his death in a plane crash in May to begin discussions with the Polisano. He believed that Mauritania could not afford to pursue the war and therefore was prepared to give in to the Polisano demands. This policy of accommodation was followed by Bouceif's successor, Lieutenant-Colonel Khouna Ould Haidala, and on August 9, normal diplomatic relations were restored with Algeria. King Hassan II of Morocco denounced Mauritania's new policy and removed the last of its 6,000 troops which had been stationed at Nouakchott. The radical change in Mauritania's attitude left President Ould Salek without the necessary support, and he resigned in early June. His replacement, Lieutenant-Colonel Mohammad Ould Luly, was much more at ease with the new directions undertaken by Premier Ould Haidala.

Despite the recognition by Haidala of the Polisaro, Mauritania's participation in the war had drained money from its already limited funds. Little could be done to reduce the size of the army since Morocco posed a threat. King Hassan's government believed that Mauritania was providing bases for the Polisaro. The drought had killed vast herds of cattle, sheep, and goats and had forced thousands of pastoralists into the few urban areas creating unforseen problems which the government could not solve. Then in 1982 a plague of grasshoppers destroyed a large portion of the crops. Thus Mauritania was forced to import over ninety percent of its food. This litany of problems appeared to the army leadership to be beyond the ability of the civilian government to solve. In Decmeber 1985 Colonel Moauia Ould Sidi Mohamed Taya seized power in a bloodless coup, suspended the constitution, banned political parties, and created the Military Committee for National Recovery as the main governing body of the state. Charging the previous government with mismanaging the economy, Taya promised a more enlightened, honest administration. The key to providing this lies as much with nature as with the capability of the military and civilian rulers of this new regime.

THE SAHARAWI ARAB DEMOCRATIC REPUBLIC (SADR)

Although recognized by 1986 as a legal government by sixty-six states, the SADR remained a questionable entity. The government remained in exile in Algeria throughout the period of struggle with Morocco. Although controlling most of the territory of the Western Sahara, particularly after the 1979 agreement with Mauritania, its guerrilla forces numbering more than 3,000 men could not dislodge the Moroccans. The Polisaro held no towns of any consequence and the land they dominated had few, if any, resources. The SADR government in the area it controls is a loose political system reflective of desert pastoralism. The 600 representatives at the Fifty Party Congress in 1983 elected a president, a nine member executive, and twenty-one member poliboro. The shadow government and its military branch continued to operate because Algeria supplied it with arms and allowed the Polisaro to use Algerian territory as a safe base for its actions against first Mauritanian and then Moroccan forces.

King Hassan II of Morocco backed by diplomatic and military support from the United States showed no signs of compromise with the Polisaro. His troops had withdrawn into the "useful triangle" in the north from whence they could make sorties into the desert in pursuit of the guerrillas. Within this triangle guarded by 50,000 men and sophisticated modern equipment is El Ayoum, the only town of consequence in the huge territory. Aside from historical, nationalistic reasons, the major factor in Morocco's tenacity is also in this region. That is the phosphate deposits which make the area the sixth largest exporter of this mineral in the world.

The question of control of the western Sahara has serious international overtones. Sekou Touré of Guinea, reacting to the recognition of the SADR, claimed it was a "baptism of a child before its conception." Nevertheless most African states quickly recognized the SADR claims. The United States supported Morocco and most western European countries either remained neutral or found some reason to agree with Morocco's historic claims. The decision to admit the SADR to the OAU in 1982 caused the breakdown of the summit conference that year. Further dissention was avoided the next year by the withdrawal of the SADR representative from the summit meeting. A peace plan was proposed which envisioned a referendum in the western Sahara by the end of 1983. This never occurred since King Hassan refused to deal directly with the SADR. The following year the question of the SADR position within the OAU continued. Nigeria finally recognized it as a legal entity but in the debates the Moroccan delegates became so incensed that Morocco withdrew from the OAU. Zaire also withdrew. Despite its general recognition by most third world states, the Polisaro by 1987 was far from its goal of occupying the mineral rich north and the issue of the SADR is one that will continue to divide the OAU and both armies will continue to gain their ends by force. There exists the possibility that the rivalry between Algeria and Morocco could flare into a large scale war. Indicative of the potential for the spread of the conflict was the failed assassination attempt in February 1987 of SADR President Mohamad Adelazziz in the Algerian town of Tindouf.

SENEGAL

Senegal is one of the few states in Africa where there has been a minimum of internal conflict since independence and which returns a civilian regime that allows for political dissent. Much of the credit for the maintenance of a stable political climate must go to the long-time President Leopold Sedar Senghor. He kept firm control of the government and during his long tenure made certain that no opposing party could build a base strong enough to challenge his rule: his party, the *Parti Socialiste* (PS) dominated the legislature. Senghor's successor, Abdou Diouf, reversed his mentor's policy, allowing opposition to come out of the back rooms into the open. He recognized the need for transferring opposition into legal channels. Although there is a law against coalitions there were in 1987 fourteen political parties, seven of which proclaimed themselves Marxist-Leninist in philosophy. The inability of the government's opponents to forget their differences, many of which related to leadership, has been a major factor in the domination of the PS.

There was no difficulty in approving Diouf, who had served as prime minister, to succeed Senghor as head of state in 1980. Upon his retirement, the poet-president had decided that Diouf should be the next president; the party and the legislature meekly acquiested. In many ways the choice was an inspired one. Lacking the prestige and charisma of his predecessor, Diouf has skillfully maneuvered his way through or around the numerous problems which he inherited. As with most African states, the most pressing of these was the economic situation. Fifteen years of recurrent drought had impoverished the rural population. Many farmers had responded by cutting back on planting peanuts, the nation's major export product, in favor of subsistance crops. The peanut harvest for 1984–85 was the lowest since 1960. Smuggling across the border to the Gambia where prices for peanuts was higher was another reason for the failing national income. Imports in 1984 exceeded exports by $300 million per year and the foreign debt stood at $1.6 billion.

Diouf's government has not been able to convince farmers to plant more peanuts. Until the weather reaches a satisfactory plateau and the farmers themselves decide to invest their time once again in peanut cultivation there is little that can be done to offset the balance of payments deficit, high costs, and shortages. Thus Diouf's government remains vulnerable. One way of offsetting the high cost of government would be to reduce the number of civil servants. In 1985 there were 61,000 persons employed by government, a figure almost as large as that of the Ivory Coast with twice the population. Yet Diouf can do little to remedy this situation since he must depend upon these employees and their families for much of his support and he is concerned about the political implications of strikes and possible riots.

After some difficulty with the IMF in the early 1980s, Senegal was able to meet some of that agency's demands and in 1984 was granted $75 million in standby credits. The consortium of creditors, the Paris Club, rescheduled the payment of Senegal's debts four times since 1981. The World Bank at the end of 1984 pledged $500 million per year for seven years in hopes of revitalizing the economy. These measures reflect the confidence the lenders have in the moderate stable government of President Diouf but there are indications that the creditors are growing impatient with the moribund economy and Diouf's seeming inability to launch any schemes to alleviate the stagnation.

Politically there are a number of problems which could disturb Senegal's balance. One is the power of the Mouride brotherhood which in many ways continues to be a state within a state. The Mouride leaders have tremendous influence over the ordinary Senegalese. In addition, they control one-third of the annual peanut crop. Like Senghor before him, Diouf must retain their goodwill even if it means shelving some plans for agricultural improvement. Then there is the growing separatist movement in the Casamance, that part of Senegal south of the Gambia. Citizens there have felt that the central government in Dakar has largely ignored their needs. In 1983 the leaders of this movement staged demonstrations in the major city of Ziganchour and in some smaller towns. The army was sent in and put an end to the overt protests resulting in many citizens being killed. with its leaders jailed, the movement went underground but it still exists.

Diouf has managed so far to survive all these problems while giving the appearance of a dedicated democrat. In 1984 there was a major reorganization of the government with the abolition of the position of prime minister. Thus the power residual to that office passed to the president. As Diouf looks forward confidentially to the presidential and legislative elections in 1988, he has perhaps one more important triumph which can be used against his opponents. This is the Confederation of Senegambia. Responding to President Jawara's call for military assistance, Diouf sent Senegalese troops into the Gambia to crush a rebellion in July 1981. Using this assistance as a lever, Diouf was able to achieve what his predecessor had failed to do—to bring the Gambia into a confederation with Senegal. The agreements between the two states called for a confederation legislature to be elected in the future, the President of Senegal became the president of the confederation while the Gambian president became vice-president. Although the agreement is more than half a decade old, little has been done practically to bring about a political union. Gambians are still afraid of being dominated by their larger neighbor. If Diouf can make a reality of the confederation then all the other problems of the state could be brushed aside in future campaigns.

MALI

President Modibo Keita, secure in the election victory in 1964 of the only recognized political party, the *Union Soudanaise*, proceeded with his plans to make Mali a socialist state using China as a model. State enterprises were increased, collectivization of farms begun, and large numbers of Chinese were brought in to advise the government on forwarding its plans for state socialism. Controlling the government and the sole political party, Keita then made the mistake of giving more power to the party's private militia in order to secure compliance with the economic reforms. This was viewed by many officers as a threat to the position of the army. Keita who was aware of the rising tide of opposition to his policies surprisingly did nothing to quell it and on November 19, 1968 a group of young officers led by Lieutenant Moussa Traoré overthrew Keita's regime in a bloodless coup.

Traoré and the other conspirators set up the Military Committee for National Liberation which began a slow movement away from Keita's strict socialism. The ending of farm collectives saw an increase in crop production. Ties with China and Russia were maintained while at the same time the government provided incentives for foreign investment. France was particularly helpful in aiding the transition to a mixed economy despite the fact that Keita had taken Mali out of the franc zone. This situation was remedied in June 1984 when Mali was readmitted to the Monetary Union of West Africa (UMOA) which reintroduced the CFA currency once more as the legal tender of the state.

During the first years of Traoré's rule it was discovered that cotton grew very well in the loose sandy soils, thriving on the high temperatures. By 1984 it had become the major export product, the harvest that year reaching 152,000 tons. However, nothing could mask the disaster of the fifteen years of low rainfall. Mali had been one of the states hardest hit by the drought of the early 1970s. The loss of livestock and the resultant abandonment of traditional grazing and farm lands had been one of the reasons for the overthrow of Keita's government. After a short period when the rainfall was normal, the drought returned with a vengeance. The worst drought in its history killed seventy percent of the cattle, and grain production in 1985 was only fifty percent of normal. Timbuktu, once a small town, grew with the influx of refugees to more than 20,000 persons. Elsewhere almost 100,000 refugees flooded the towns and almost a million persons faced starvation, particularly those in the semi-desert areas. The deficit in grain production for that year was almost 500,000 tons. Despite the lack of a domestic food distribution infrastructure and poor roads, the United Nations Disaster Relief Organization and private agencies kept the majority of refugees alive. Although the drought receded, most of Mali is a prisoner of its geography and as its population increases the fragile land is unlikely to be more productive. An entire way of life for most of the pastoral people such as the Tuareg has ended.

Considering the magnitude of the natural disasters which struck Mali, it is remarkable that Traoré, young and inexperienced in government when he engineered the coup, has been able to survive. There have been surprisingly few conflicts between the government, students, and workers. In 1979 Traoré converted the military regime into a civilian government complete with an eighty-two member National Assembly. There was only one political party, the *Union Democratique de Population Malian* (UDPM) which was allowed to contest the election. Traoré, the only candidate for president, was elected for a five year term and subsequently reelected in 1984. The party and state elections of 1981–82 introduced the matter of choice among various candidates although there was still only one legally recognized party.

Mali's relations with Senegal, once so poor that all rail communications were halted, have remained remarkably good as Traoré recognized the importance of the rail and road links to Dakar. The relations with neighboring Guinea improved remarkably after the death of Sekou Touré. Both governments signed an agreement in March 1983 which projected for the future a unification of the two states. Although little has been done to make this union a practical reality the agreement indicated the harmony existing between Mali and Guinea. Unfortunately this peaceful condition is not the case with Burkina Faso (Upper Volta). A boundary dispute over the Agacher region, reportedly rich in uranium and natural gas, escalated in 1974 into a full scale conflict. After both armies of these poorest of states had suffered a number of casualties the war ended and an unquiet truce prevailed while the border question was submitted to arbitration. Violence in this region flared again on Christmas 1985 and before the fighting was ended by the intercession of Houphouët-Boigny of the Ivory Coast, a reported 30 persons had been killed. The rivalry and hostility between the leaders of the contending states continued in the diplomatic sphere where Burkina Faso's allegations of Malian corruption in the *Communanté Economique de l'Afrique de l'Ouest* threatened for a time to break up this customs union.

GUINEA

Guinea, under the tight control of Sekou Touré and the PDG, nevertheless experienced one invasion attempt and a number of attempted coups. In November 1970, a small invasion force comprising Portuguese, mercenaries, and Guinean exiles put ashore. The invaders were quickly captured and ninety-two sentenced to death. The details of the invasion remain unclear because Guinea banned Western reporters from the proceedings and official accounts were contradictory. Even the United Nations' investigating commission reached no conclusion but simply reported the allegations. According to Radio Conakry, Sekou Touré was the target for a number of assassination attempts, but it was difficult to know how many were serious plots to overthrow the government since certain events in Guinea were often exaggerated for purely political reasons. One major plot in 1976 ostensibly involved Diallo Telli, the respected former secretary of the Organization of African Unity. Despite this type of evidence confirming dissatisfaction with the socialist regime, Touré after two decades remained firmly in charge of his party and the country. The mineral resources of Guinea and considerable foreign aid from both Western and Communist bloc have been major stabilizing forces. The settlement in 1977 of the long time problems with France brought more international political support to the regime as well as considerably more Western investment.

Touré's government was an excellent example of how one man could shape the definition of socialism, control the only political party in the state, and foster economic programs which were pragmatically harmful. To Touré, anyone who opposed him and the PDG dictatorship was a traitor. More than 2,900 persons who were detained during his tenure simply disappeared. In 1982 Amnesty International confirmed what many had suspected of the many human rights

violations which had taken place. Touré had persisted in his peculiar interpreta-
tion of socialism despite evidence that the economy was faltering. Although parts
of Guinea had been affected by the drought in the Sahel zone, the country was
potentially rich. Under normal circumstances there was a balanced agricultural
economy and there were rich deposits of bauxite, iron ore, and gold. However, the
radical politics of the PDG had alienated Guinea's immediate neighbors and
relations with France, its most important European source of assistance, had
deteriorated. Even Touré by 1980 could see that some changes were needed in
order to bolster the economy. Domestically the government began to allow more
free trade and in foreign policy to repair the damage done by two decades of
strident criticism and accusations launched against its neighbors. Most important, Touré mended the breach with France. President Giscard d'Estaing paid a
state visit to Guinea and later Touré's friendship with President Mitterand had all
but returned the relations of the two states to normal. An indication of Touré's shift
to the West was his official visit to the United States in June 1982, following his
unanimous reelection to another seven year term as president, where he discussed
with government officials, bankers, and businessmen ways to help the moribund
economy of Guinea.

The economic and political conditions in Guinea spawned open opposition
to Touré's policies. Even the women's groups which had at one time been the
strongest supporters of the PDG became more vocal in their demands for change.
The people of Guinea were ready to admit that something more had to be done.
They were prepared to accept change when Sekou Touré who had come to the
United States for medical reasons died after emergency heart surgery on March 26,
1984, in Cleveland, Ohio. Touré's ministry was caught by surprise with seemingly
no definite plans even to the naming of a successor. Then on April 3 the army
acted. Led by Lansana Conté, the thirty-nine year old commander of the Boké
garrison, it took over the state in a bloodless coup. Two days later the Military
Committee for National Recovery (CMNR) announced the formation of a new
government with Conté as President, Diarra Traoré as Prime Minister, and thirty
ministers. Included in the later were six civilians. Conté also tried to balance his
government by seeing that men from the four ethnic groups were included. During
Touré's tenure the Malinke had become dominant and the jealousy between
differing ethnic groups was and continues to be a latent threat to stability. Political
prisoners held by Touré's government on a variety of charges were released as soon
as possible.

Conté's rule was welcomed by most. He assured the people that his government would be only a transitional one, staying in power only long enough to
abolish the evils of "racism, religionism, sectarianism, and nepotism." However
honest this statement might have been at the time, the manifold problems the army
inherited precluded any sudden return to civilian control. The treasury was
empty, the bureaucracy large and inefficient, agricultural production at an all time
low, and the nonconvertible currency, the syli, grossly overvalued. The new
government announced the abolition of many of the state run projects and that as
soon as possible a capitalistic infrastructure allowing free enterprise would be
implemented. The condition of the economy when Conté assumed power was
such that there could be no sudden improvement in any of the economic sectors.

The IMF called for a 600% reduction in the value of the currency, reduction of the inflated bureaucracy, and stimulation of the mining industry which provided over 90% of Guinea's earnings. Devaluation posed certain threats to the government since the ordinary citizen would be damaged by any severe reduction. The bureaucracy inflated to almost 200,000 persons who felt their positions secure would take considerable time to effect significant cutbacks. In addition to the size of the bureaucracy the work habits of many had been developed over twenty years of Touré's system. Almost any officer's efficiency was drastically affected by tardiness, ignorance of procedure, and a general attitude of not caring. Then, too, there was the corruption; bribery had become one of the best ways of getting anything accomplished.

The CMNR slowly attacked these various problems. In October 1985 there was a massive devaluation of the currency. A new franc was issued roughly equivalent to the CFA franc. At first there was a dual exchange rate, but as the new franc maintained its value this system was dropped. Guinea appeared to be moving in the direction of rejoining the franc zone. Three new banks were created and were supported by a large French institution. The French by the mid-1980s were involved in what some critics called "neo-colonization" where they were active as advisors to government, business, and agriculture as well as being participants in the various economic enterprises. France, West Germany, Italy, and the United States also had contributed to the various development plans of the Conté regime. It was apparent that the government had begun to manage its foreign debts very well. The $400 million debt to the Soviets was being repaid by the bauxite profits from the Kundia mine. By early 1986 the IMF had granted a $33 million standby loan, the World Bank had extended a $42 million loan, and the so-called Paris Club of lenders had rescheduled $200 million of Guinea's debts.

Unlike many of its neighbors, Guinea with proper management could work its way out of its maze of foreign commitments because of the actual and potential wealth of its mines. Guinea has the largest bauxite reserves in the world and is currently operating three mines. In addition there is the potential for petroleum, and the iron mines at Mt. Nimba contain ore estimated to be worth $1.5 billion. However, expansion of Guinea's economy under Conté has been slow. There are many reasons for this aside from the conservatism of the government. Private investors have not regained enough confidence in the new regime to bring in the sums necessary to fully exploit the iron, gold, or even the bauxite deposits. The plan to open a fourth bauxite mine was still on hold in 1987 for lack of funds. Another reason for the relative slowness in developing Guinea's ample agricultural potential is the lack of trained personnel. The educational system of Sekou Touré was responsible for creating a lost generation of young men inadequately prepared for the modern technological society. Guinea's literacy rate is approximately twenty-five percent.

Nevertheless significant changes have occurred in the country's economy and in the political realm. Two major reorganizations of the central government have strengthened Conté's dominant position. In December 1984 the number of ministers was reduced from thirty-two to fifteen and the number in the CMNR to only twenty. The most important reform abolished the post of prime minister. Traoré in the months after the coup had been the most visable of any of the leaders. His foreign visits and public appearances in Guinea indicated to Conté and others in the CMNR that he was building his own political base from which to challenge the president. The reorganization struck directly at such ambitions and he was demoted to Minister of Education. In early 1985 while Conté was attending an ECOWAS meeting in Lome, Traoré and others dissatisfied with the regime, acted. They seized Radio Conakry and a number of important buildings in the capital and broadcast that a new government was in power. The rebellion collapsed because the conspirators had no firm base of support throughout the country and the army remained loyal to Conté. Details of the aftermath of the attempted coup were shrouded in mystery, but it was later discovered that Traoré and many of his most important supporters including the brother of Sekou Touré were shot.

Conté did not immediately demand any change in the central government but waited for over six months before reorganizing it. Some observers believed that Conté might follow the Malian example and convert the government into a pseudo-democracy, standing for election as the single candidate for president in a civilian regime. He rejected this idea since it was obvious that the economy had not recovered and the jealousies between Malinke, Fulbe, and Susu would make it difficult for any elected regime to succeed. Thus the reform of December 1985 was a half-way measure. He reduced the power of the army by appointing more civilians to head ministries and he brought expatriates into the government. Many of those persons in the army who could be considered potential rivals were sent off to less prestigious posts far away from the capital. Thus Conté the pragmatist had by 1987 assumed more direct control of the government and by moving slowly with his reforms had not alienated any significant segment of the population.

NIGER

Niger was once a state synonymous with poverty because so much of its land was desert or semi-desert where the major occupation was a pastoral one. It was landlocked, there were no railroads, the road system even in the more developed southern section was poor, and the nearest port was Cotonou in Dahomey (Benin). The drought of the early 1970s had catastrophic results. Herders lost over sixty percent of their animals and in 1974 relief agencies estimated that over two million persons depended in some fashion on relief supplies. With the return of the rains and government subsidies the agricultural sector improved in the late 1970s but pastoralism as a way of life was much slower to recover. One casualty of the drought was the government of President Hamani Diori who was held responsible for the slowness with which relief efforts were extended to those in need. In 1974 Lieutenant Colonel Seyni Kounteché led the southern units of the small army which deposed Diori, banned all political parties, and created a twelve man Supreme Military Council. Diori and many of the most important politicians of the old regime were imprisoned.

In general Kounteché continued the policy of state socialism begun by his predecessor. This meant an increase in the civil service and state monopolies controlling much of the economy. Fortunately for Kounteché the drought ended soon after the coup and the uranium mines in the north began producing. The first of these at Arlit had cost a European consortium over $60 million before it began operations in 1971. Later a second mining complex was opened in the Akouta district and rich deposits were discovered near Agades. Niger soon became the second largest exporter of "yellow cake," semi-refined uranium, on the continent. The world price of uranium escalated reaching a peak in 1979. The military government launched an ambitious development program in that year aimed at bettering the communication, road, and irrigation systems in addition to paying for the inflated government staff. Then the world price of uranium declined sharply. In 1982 the price per pound of "cake" was $24. By 1987 it had declined to only $17. In addition the demand for uranium had slackened. Italy and West Germany ended their agreements and the United States sharply cut back on its purchase. This led to serious financial trouble. The development program could not be completed and Kounteché was forced to appeal to the IMF for assistance and had to agree to its guidelines. That meant a reduction in the size of government and a phasing down of state owned companies and allowing more private business. The service on the $11 billion foreign debt by the mid-1980s was $70 million a year. Despite such immediate problems, Kounteché could depend upon reasonable returns from uranium and if judiciously managed many of the projects for agricultural improvement and a better road system outlined earlier could be achieved.

Kounteché promised a new constitution at some future date and began quietly phasing out the military predominance in the government. To further his concept of the "Development Society" he allowed a 150 person National Council to be chosen by consensus voting and his ministry by 1987 did not contain any military representatives. His National Charter proposal, the centerpiece of his plan to return the state to constitutionality, was approved by referendum in June 1987. Kounteché's confidence in his ability to continue to rule was reflected in these measures. Another example of this reform is the release of more than three dozen political prisoners on the tenth anniversary of his coup. Included in this group were the former President Hamani Diori and the prominent political leader, Djibo Bakary. One reason for such confidence was the economic and political support his regime received from France. France has been very active in providing funds for Niger. Perhaps as important is the French military presence and the guarantees given by President Mitterand of support against Libya, Niger's troublesome neighbor to the north which according to Niger sources was responsible for supporting Tuareg dissidents and was implicated in the failed coup of 1983.

The plans for change in Niger received a temporary setback when Kounteché died of a brain tumor in a Paris hospital on November 10, 1987. Almost immediately his place as head of state was taken by a cousin, Colonel Ali Seibou, who was unanimously elected by the Supreme Military Council. Seibou, like Kounteché, a Djerma-Songhai which dominated the officer corps, promised in his first public statements as head of state to carry out the program of his predecessor.

BURKINA FASO (UPPER VOLTA)

This small landlocked state is one of the poorest in West Africa with a per capita income estimated in 1985 at approximately $150 per year. Unlike some of its neighbors in the former AOF, there have been no mineral discoveries of consequence to shore up the government services or to allow for any significant development programs. There are a few service industries in the major cities, but most Burkinabe follow traditional agricultural or pastoral pursuits. The major export crops are peanuts and cotton, the bulk of which must pass through the Ivory Coast. Conversely most of the imports including vital petroleum products must also come by road from Abidjan. The twin scourges of Africa in the 1970s— the drought and inflation—raised havoc in Burkina Faso. As elsewhere in the Sahel zone there were crop failures and many pastoralists lost all their livestock. Traditional life was disrupted, for some for only a few years, for others forever. The continuance of the drought in the early years of the 1980s once more brought relief supplies from the United Nations World Food Program and other independent agencies and a continuing exodus from the country districts to the cities. By mid-decade both Ouagadougou and Bobo Dioulasso had populations in excess of 200,000. The drought, poverty, and the overcrowding had political ramifications which aided in the toppling of several different regimes.

One factor present in Burkina Faso to a greater extent than elsewhere in French speaking Africa is the power of the various labor unions. Approximately 10,000 persons in the civil service and teaching form a solid phalanx which in the past has sought to maintain the unique power of the educated elite. Lieutenant Colonel Sangoule Lamizina had depended heavily on union support when he overthrew the government of Yameogo in 1966. Massive strikes before the takeover had weakened his authority to such an extent that there was no point in resisting the coup. Lamizina on taking power promised a quick return to civilian control. Like most such promises in Africa, it was only partially kept. In 1970 a new constitution was finally adopted which provided for an elected assembly and a prime minister to function with the guidance of Lamizina and the military. In part because of the worsening economic conditions, Lamizina in 1974 suspended this constitution, dismissed the prime minister, and banned all political parties. He reconstituted the ministry by keeping or appointing new military men. After less than two years he was forced by the opposition led mainly by union heads to dismiss most of the army men from his ministry and to appoint civilians. He also promised a return to the elective principle in determining who should rule. In 1977 the ban on political parties was lifted and a new constitution providing once again for an elected assembly was approved. The proposed form of government was to be the presidential system. The following year more than a decade of military rule came to an end. A National Assembly was elected and Lamizina, ostensibly now a civilian, was elected president.

The onset of the drought once again and the seeming inability of Lamizina and his associates to check inflation, with a near bankrupt treasury and failure to solve the country's other pressing problems led the unions once more to act. There was a strike every three weeks in the period before the army led by Colonel Saye Zerbo decided that Lamizina's regime was paralyzed and once more in a bloodless coup in 1980 ousted the President and placed him and many of his associates under arrest. Zerbo's short tenure is attributable to the many problems connected with the continuation of the drought and the opposition of the unions. Under-standing their latent power, he tried to curb its exercise. Zerbo also had to contend with divisions among the ruling army oligarchy and personal ambitions of some of his subordinates. All these difficulties culminated in another bloodless coup in November 1982. Major Jean-Baptiste Ouedraogo, an army doctor, seized power from his associate and reconstituted the military government. One of his supporters, a young idealistic captain, Thomas Sankara, was named prime minister. It soon became apparent that Sankara and Ouedraogo differed greatly in their approach to solving the short-term and long-range problems of the country. Ouedraogo was more inclined to continue with the basic approach of his predecessors while Sankara wanted to break the power of the elite and mobilize the people in a way not heretofore attempted. Specific differences between the two allowed Sankara to gain the support of most of the union leaders and he undercut Ouedraogo's base in the army. The first test of strength between the two occurred in May 1983 when Sankara was arrested. His supporters rallied over 1,000 students to march in protest in Ouagadougou and he was released. Finally in August, the differences between the two resulted in another coup and Ouedraogo and his supporters were ousted from government.

Sankara promised the union leaders that he would protect the unions since they had been a force acting for democracy in the country. Nevertheless the organization of local government authorities and his other public statements contrasted sharply with this promise. The central government dominated by the Military Council remained unchanged in form and there were no political parties allowed. Sankara called for a dedication of all citizens to help improve the economy and root out corruption on all levels. He acted as the role model and was ostentatiously honest and the poorest of any of the West African heads of state. Soon after his assumption of power the government created the Revolutionary Defense Committees (CDR) composed of both men and women to take over local government functions previously left to traditional chiefs. The committees were also mandated to ferret out corruption and to carry out agricultural and construction development throughout the state. As a part of Sankara's drive for honesty and rededication he declared a new name for the state on the first anniversary of his coup, August 23, 1984, a further symbolic break with the past. The name of the state was changed from Upper Volta to Burkina Faso meaning the "land of honest people." The government also adopted at this time a new motto, anthem, and flag.

Sankara's dealings with his neighbors were not smooth. Most of them within the *Entente* feared his approach to government. Houphouët-Boigny especially has used his considerable influence to isolate Sankara's brand of revolutionary socialism. However, he did not threaten to block Burkina Faso's lifeline to the ocean, being content to oppose Sankara diplomatically and politically. The most dangerous situation for Burkina Faso exists on the northern disputed border with Mali. In 1974 there was a military confrontation in the disputed territory. Sankara paid a state visit to Bamako in September 1983. The result was the joint decision to submit the dispute to the arbitration of the International Court of Justice at the Hague. Despite this measure there was a major clash on Christmas day 1985 resulting in the deaths of thirty people. This volatile situation was not improved by Sankara's allegations in late 1985 of corruption within the CEAO that the previous Malian authorities skimmed money from the organization. In early 1985 a bomb exploded in the hotel suite reserved for Sankara while on a diplomatic mission in the Ivory Coast. Then in June another bomb exploded in an ammunition dump in Ouagadougou killing three soldiers and injuring a number of others. Sankara considered these incidents and the attempt to sabotage French President Mitterand's visit in November 1986 to be the work of dissidents supported by Togo or Mali. President Eyadema of Togo in turn charged Sankara with complicity in the spate of bombings in Lomé. An attempt to patch over these problems within the *Entente* failed in late 1985 when Sankara refused to sign the report of the meetings even accusing Houphouët-Boigny with trying to sabotage his government. During this period Sankara was moving closer in relations with another young, revolutionary leader, Flight Lieutenant Rawlings of Ghana. The crucial quarrel with Burkina Faso's neighbors continued as evidenced by the failure of the parties to meet in the so-called reconciliation summit meeting which had been scheduled for January 1987.

Sankara's government which seemed secure although in economic difficulties was overthrown on October 15, 1987. As in coups in other parts of Africa, the ringleader and new head of state, Captain Blaise Compaoré, was a friend and close associate of Sankara whose support had been vital in the earlier coup of 1983 and who had served as a minister of state and justice. According to an early communique, the conspirators feared that Sankara was planning to arrest and execute his opponents in government and Compaoré and his associates in the so-called Popular Front for the 15th of October acted to prevent a bloodbath. The coup was certainly bloody. Sankara and eleven high ranking members of his government were shot and buried immediately outside Ouagadougou. Compaoré announced the freeing of all political prisoners and stated that representatives from the country's thirty provinces would meet to decide on the new form of government and to elect a president.

CAMEROON

The Cameroon is one of the few states in western Africa with a solid economic base. Most of the land, measured by African standards, is good and there is adequate rainfall in all areas; the coastal reaches near Mt. Cameroon receive over 200 inches a year. These conditions enable most of the traditional farmers to raise a variety of food crops. The distribution system is adequate so there is no hungry season. In addition a variety of products such as coffee, cocoa, cotton, bananas, peanuts, and timber are exported. Exploration of offshore petroleum deposits proved successful in the 1970s and production of this vital resource had by 1985 reached 120,000 barrels a day. In contrast to its neighbors, the Cameroon exports on a yearly basis have exceeded imports by one-third. Its close ties with France were supplemented in the 1980s by better trade relations with Great Britain and Japan, and in late 1986 the Cameroon became only the fourth African state to reopen diplomatic relations with Israel. This latter move portends even more foreign investment and increased trade. The health of the economy with an average growth rate of approximately nine percent removes from the government one of the most destabilizing factors that exists throughout much of the continent.

The Cameroon has been known as one of Africa's quiet countries, not only because of the stability of its government but by the design of its government. Ahmadou Ahidjo, President of the Cameroon for twenty-two years, made it a policy to steer clear of Commonwealth and Franco-African summits and cautioned his representatives not to take the lead in either the United Nations or the OAU. Although his successor moved from that semi-isolationist position, the Cameroon is far less known than many smaller, more troublesome African polities. Much of the energy of the government in the 1960s was taken up in the civil war begun by disagreements with the radical UPC which had launched a guerrilla war against the French in 1956 and continued its activities against the independent government. By the time that this internal conflict had been ended in 1970 more than 80,000 persons had died. At the same time the government was attempting to make work a federal system encompassing two significantly different territories which had previously been ruled by Britain and France. This federal experiment ended in 1972 when the constitution was altered to provide for a unitary state with a strong executive and an elected 120 member National Assembly. Ahidjo's powers as president were extended by the new governmental system. The constitution also provided for a prime minister to assist the president in managing the ministry. In 1975 Paul Biya was picked by Ahidjo for this post. At the height of his popularity in 1982 Ahidjo stunned observers by resigning as President, ostensibly for reasons of health. He retained his position as chairman of the party and obviously believed he could continue to run affairs from behind the scenes.

Biya became the new president and moved slowly but definitely to create what he claimed to be a more open political climate. He brought young technocrats into the government. After the first year in power it was obvious that Biya had become president in fact as well as name. Ahidjo's idea of controlling the government from afar was not happening. This fact was the major cause of the coup attempted in August 1983. It failed completely and the government accused Ahidjo of complicity. He resigned from the party and went into exile in France. He was later charged with treason, tried in absentia, and sentenced to death. Biya then commuted the sentence to life in prison. Many in the Cameroon, particularly senior army officers, questioned the linkage of Ahidjo with the plot and resented the verdict. One of these was Colonel Ibrahim Saleh, a close friend of Ahidjo who on April 6, 1984 led units of the army against the government. At first the rebels appeared to have been successful seizing key points in the capital. However, reinforcements loyal to the government were flown in and after heavy fighting, particularly in Yaounde, the coup was crushed by the evening of April 7. There were heavy casualties, mostly civilians caught in the crossfire. Estimates of the dead varied from 500 to 1000. In the aftermath more than 1000 persons were arrested. Under the state of emergency more than 400 were tried in secret by military tribunals and by mid-1984, 46 people had been executed. The failed military takeover resulted in Biya and his associates establishing a regime which in many ways was more authoritarian than Ahidjo's. The party was reorganized and given the task of mobilizing the people behind Biya. Reflecting this action, the party's name was changed to the *Mouvement Democratique du Peuple Camerounais* (MDPC). New press laws were passed and the right of criticism of th government officials was severely curtailed.

Although Biya's regime dealt harshly with any appearance of opposition, it did give the state relatively efficient government. The favorable balance of trade which in normal times was over $500 million a year came from a variety of agricultural resources and most recently from petroleum. New investments were openly solicited by Biya on his official visit to Britain in 1985 with some success. Recognition of Israel was also designed in part to supplement the considerable French business interests already in place. Biya has managed the state budget very well, keeping corruption in check and in the period after 1983 he replaced several inefficient managers of state owned industries and banks. The health of the economy is reflected in major development projects completed and projected, particularly in the Yaoundé, Doula, and Bamenda areas.

IVORY COAST

Under the leadership of Felix Houphouët-Boigny, the Ivory Coast has been a model of stability in an otherwise disturbed continent. Houphouët-Boigny, the doyen of French African leaders, has been in complete control of the government and the only recognized political party, the *Parti Democratique de la Côte d'Ivorie* (PDCI), since before independence. He has been unchallenged in all six presidential elections since 1960 and has managed to keep political friction at a minimum. Surprisingly for one who led the earliest, communist associated, successful French African political party, he showed no signs of wanting to end the close ties with France. Although fiercely maintaining the political independence of the Ivory Coast, he depended upon French teachers, government advisors, and economic experts to a much greater extent than any of the other formerly French West African states. In part this dependence combined with a steady inward flow of French capital and over 50,000 French expatriates called *culs blancs* was a major reason for the continued growth of the economy.

The Ivory Coast has avoided the economic disasters of so many African states in part because of the moderate political and economic position taken by the stable PDCI government. Houphouët-Boigny and his advisors created a system of state managed capitalism whereby investors are welcomed but the economy functions within parameters established by the government. There was a healthy trade surplus even during the early 1980s when prices for the Ivory Coast's exports declined. The inflation rate was a manageable four percent. The Ivory Coast has few mineral resources, its wealth comes from its export agriculture. It is the world's leading cocoa producer and among the top five in the export of coffee. Timber is also a major source of income, both to private firms and the government. All produce is purchased by government agencies and then resold to overseas buyers at considerable upgrading in price. For a time in the late 1970s the government was receiving nine times the price per kilogram of coffee over what was paid the producer. Although the price differential had narrowed by the mid-1980s, the lower producer price was one of the criticisms of the government. However, the PDCI government generally used its income well, pumping money into the agricultural and industrial sector as well as into the communications infrastructure. The road system is one of the best in Africa and six large dams on the Sassandra River provide cheap power for the eastern areas of the country.

Inevitably there have been economic and political problems, particularly during the period after 1980 as world market prices for cocoa and coffee declined. There have been scandals concerning illicit enrichment by some high ranking members of the elite. One of the worst of these offenses was when the mayor of Abidjan, Emmanuel Dioulo, fled the country after the activities of one of his companies and the Agricultural Bank were disclosed. Increasingly the intellectual community has demanded a larger share in governing the country. Houphouët-Boigny was also criticized for the considerable sums he expended transforming his home village, Yamoussoukro, into a show place. Students and professors particularly have been critical of the corruption in business and government and they were responsible for one of the most serious demonstrations against the PDCI in February 1982 which resulted in the closing of the university briefly. Another point of contention has been Houphouët-Boigny's commitment to "globalization" meaning the employment of Europeans, mostly French, to what many believed the exclusion of equally well qualified Africans. The worsening of the economy in the 1980s has partially alleviated this situation since the Ivory Coast in 1983 was unable to pay its share of the costs for technical assistance. Consequently 450 French technicians were terminated in 1984 followed by an equal number the next year. This action reduced the Ivory Coast's costs in this sector by half.

Throughout the decades Houphouët-Boigny maintained firm control of the state. During the past decade the most serious political problem had nothing to do with the government's policies but rather concerned succession. Houphouët-Boigny is the oldest head of state in Africa and for reasons best known to himself he did not in any fashion indicate a preference as to which of his supporters he favored to assume the reins of government when he is gone. Bending to some criticism, the government in 1980 allowed relatively free elections for the first time. Although the PDCI remained the only party, there was not merely an official slate of candidates. In all, 647 persons contested for 147 seats in the Assembly. Only 27 of the 80 incumbents running for office were returned. This freedom within the party continued in the 1985 elections with over 500 would be assemblymen standing for election. During both elections Houphouët-Boigny was uncontested for president. Ostensibly reacting to worries about succession, he sponsored a change in the constitution in 1980 which created the office of vice-president who, instead of the president of the Assembly, would succeed in case of the president's death or retirement. At first seen as a way of providing orderly change, it later became obvious that it was a means by which Houphouët-Boigny could dampen the aspirations of his long time lieutenant, Philippe Yacé, the Chairman of the PDCI and then President of the Assembly. The office of vice-president was not to be filled until 1985 and a 9 member Executive Council was appointed to aid the President until then. Yacé lost his influence within party and government circles and although he regained some of his prestige, by mid-1980 he was no longer as certain as before that he would eventually become president. The constitution was amended once again before the 1985 elections to do away with the office of vice-president and return the succession to the president of the Assembly. Thus the issue of whom Houphouët-Boigny favored remained as much of a mystery in 1987 as it had been a decade earlier. The lesson of the Cameroon showed that this was not an academic issue. Whether the comparatively rich Ivory Coast continues its pragmatic economic and political programs would in the future depend largely upon the man chosen to lead after Houphouët-Boigny is gone.

TOGO

The apparent unity of the four political parties evinced by the coalition government in December 1965 was short lived. The basic north-south split led in the following year to further political bickering. This seeming failure of the civilian government gave the small army led by Lieutenant Colonel Gnassingbé Eyadéma to seize power on January 13, 1967. Eyadéma had been one of the leading conspirators in the overthrow and assassination of Togo's first president, Sylvanius Olympio, in 1963. He now became head of state. He promised a return to civilian rule as soon as conditions warranted. Direct army rule continued until 1979 when a new constitution went into effect calling for an elected president and a sixty-seven member national assembly. Eyadéma, by now a general, was uncontested and became President while the Assembly was composed of members elected from the only recognized political party, the *Rassemblement du Peuple Togolais* (RPT).

The early years of Eyadéma's rule was made easier by the relative health of the economy. Phosphate mining provided the bulk of export earnings and the world price was excellent. The comparative resultant wealth led the government to embark on ill conceived, costly development projects. Much of the private sector was taken over by the government adding to the numbers in an already inefficient bureaucracy. The phosphate boom ended in the late 1970s and the market had only partially recovered by the mid-1980s. Consequently Togo was left with a huge foreign debt, estimated in 1985 at over $1 billion, and large yearly budget deficits. The foreign debt was rescheduled several times and Eyadéma's government was forced to seek aid from the IMF which demanded a policy of stringent austerity whose central aim was privatization allowing the government to rid itself of unprofitable government run businesses.

Eyadéma's control of all facets of public life made it difficult for any who opposed his plans to be heard in Togo. He reshuffled his ministry a number of times to minimize opposition and to bring into the government young, loyal technocrats. His political opponents within Togo were neutralized or jailed. Two of the most important, Colonel Koffi Kongo and Grunitzky's vice-president, Idrisson Méatche, suffered fatal heart attacks while in prison. More important were those who voluntarily went into exile. There were two opposition parties, one dominated by ex-army personnel and the other by disgruntled politicians. Neither party posed an immediate threat to Eyadéma's government but the latter led by Sylvanius Olympio's two sons has been accused of participating in coup attempts and bombings. Three coup attempts occurred during the 1970s, the most serious occurred in 1977 and its failure resulted in a general roundup of opponents. Thirteen persons were convicted of conspiracy including the Olympios who were tried in absentia. The opposition to Eyadéma continued. In 1980, forty opponents of the regime briefly occupied the Togolese embassy in Paris. Then in July 1985 a plot to blow up the United States embassy and the central market in Lomé was discovered and the government alleged that the conspirators had connections with Libya. In late autumn a series of bombings shook downtown Lomé and a plot to assassinate President Eyadéma was uncovered. This time the government accused Ghana of orchestrating the failed coup. For some months the border with Ghana was closed before Eyadéma's government admitted it had no direct evidence linking Flight Lieutenant Rawlings to the plot. In 1987 Eyadéma, by now an elder statesman of African politics, celebrated the twentieth anniversary of the overthrow of the Grunitzky regime. Despite the various minor attempts to displace Eyadéma, his position at the time of the anniversary celebrations, reinforced by a quickening economy, was stronger than at any time in the past decade.

BENIN (DAHOMEY)

One of the poorest states in West Africa with a per capita income of less than $150 a year, Dahomey had also been politically one of the most unstable. Between 1960 and 1972 there were eleven different governments. The major reason for such instability was the jealousy among various ethnic groups. Each of these had its own political party and dominant leader. Hubert Maga's strength was in the north while Serou Apithy's base was the coast and Porto Novo and Justin Ahomadegbe's support came from the Fon areas in Abomey. None of these leaders was ever powerful enough to end the selfish ambitions of his rivals and their political organization. This balance of political power assured instability in all the civilian governments after independence. The small army led by General Christophe Soglo intervened three times in the 1960s. Contrary to the actions of other military strong men, Soglo genuinely did not want to hold on to control of the state but twice turned power back to civilian authorities. Each time that experiment failed. Finally in 1965 Soglo seized control again and it appeared that this time he was not going to relinquish the position as head of state. However, factionalism within the army itself defeated Soglo when a group of younger officers in 1967 in a bloodless coup overthrew Soglo's technician government.

The military junta once again attempted to compromise with the various factions and tried to retire from governing the impoverished state. Thus a new civilian government was constructed in 1968 under the leadership of Emile Zinsou. However, the return of Maga and Ahomadegbe from exile upset this hastily constructed government and an agreement was soon reached to modify the constitution to attempt to reconcile the differences among the political factions. This new instrument of government which went into effect in 1970 called for a presidential commission to aid the president in running the country. The office of president was to rotate among the three dominant political leaders, each serving for two years. Hubert Maga was the first of the three to hold this position and in May 1972 he turned the government over to his old rival Ahomadegbe. The political infighting during the decade of independence could not conceal the poverty of the state which had no mineral resources and very little export agriculture. The political instability had only added to the economic problems. In reality there was little that the civilian government could do to reverse these conditions even under the best of circumstances. Nevertheless dissatisfaction with the civilian regime caused the army to act once again and on October 26, 1972, it toppled the Ahomadegbe government. This was another movement of junior officers led this time by Major Mathieu Kérékou who established an eleven man military executive. That government followed Kérékou's suggestion and in 1975 the country's name was officially changed from Dahomey to Benin.

The new government declared itself to be in the Marxist-Leninist mold and in the decade that followed banks, many industries, insurance companies, and schools were nationalized. The media was brought directly under government control. However, no change in government focus could alter the reality of poverty. The major exports were palm oil, cotton, and cocoa, a large part of which was smuggled across the border into Nigeria. There was a continued imbalance in trade which in 1985 amounted to over $200 million a year. The government was kept afloat by loans and by aid especially from France. There was evidence of some petroleum offshore and in the early 1970s a contract was signed with a Norwegian company to explore and exploit this possibility. In late 1984 this contract was abrogated and the rights granted to another company with the hopes of increasing the per day flow of petroleum from the modest level of 7,000 barrels a day.

Not surprisingly, unrest continued after the 1972 military takeover. In 1975 a coup led by the Minister of Labor was crushed and two years later a more serious rebellion occurred which included some exiles aided by European mercenaries. This latter attempt implicated Morocco and Gabon and left behind a fear on the part of the government of opposition and criticism. The 4,000 man army remained loyal to Kérékou and in 1979 he felt strong enough to allow a restructuring of the government. The new constitution provided for an elected National Revolutionary Assembly of 336 members although the only legal political party allowed was the *Parti Revolutionaire du Peoples Benin* (PRPB). Kérékou, the only candidate, was elected president. Civilian in form, the new government was still dominated by the president and his closest military advisors. However, more civilians did begin to participate in the legislative process and in the 1980s many were appointed to some of the most important offices in the state. Kérékou managed to contain criticism of his regime by acting firmly when it appeared that the criticism could escalate into action. Thus he used the army to crush student demonstrations in mid-1985 with the orders to "shoot on sight" any demonstrator. He closed the university and all schools for a month. The long-range problem for Benin is a moribund economy combined with a population growth rate of more than three percent.

EIGHT
Troubled independence: Central and Southern Africa

Central Africa

GABON

Most states of what had been the French Equatorial African Federation have been unstable since independence. An exception is Gabon. The Gabon, one of the richest areas in Central Africa, which has since independence maintained extremely close relations with France, had only one serious crisis. This was in the period immediately after the death of long-time President Leon M'ba in December 1967. M'Ba's chosen successor, Vice-President Albert Bongo, became president with only minimal opposition. President Bongo's tasks have been made easier by the compactness of the country, the homogeniety of its people, and its wealth. That wealth comes largely from petroleum, Gabon being the second largest producer in sub-Saharan Africa. Manganese ore also is a major source of income. Gabon is estimated to have one fourth of the world's known reserves of manganese. Okoueme timber taken from the tropical inland forests is another important export. There is also iron ore as well as very rich deposits of uranium. All these resources have given the Gabonese the highest per capita income in sub-Saharan Africa. Estimated at $5500 per person, it is forty times greater than in many African states.

In general the Gabonese have shown their appreciation of President Bongo's government which seemingly was responsible for the economic health of the state. There have been few disturbances and those such as that of the university students demonstrating for a multiparty system have been harshly dealt with. Although difficult to corroborate, rumors of torture and summary executions of some considered enemies of the regime continue to circulate. As a gesture showing his forgiving nature, Bongo in 1985 on the anniversary date of his assuming power released most political prisoners. The reality of Gabon's government is that the healthy economy simply reinforces Bongo's control of the machinery of government and the 1900 man army.

President Bongo and his associates have spent large sums on symbols of wealth and by analogy, power. Examples of this are the presidential palace, the new, magnificent buildings constructed for the 1977 OAU summit and the president's special railway car rumored to have cost $750,000. The most extravagant expenditure was the Transgabonais Railway, the showpiece of Bongo's regime. At first glance the project begun in 1975 and almost completed twelve years later appears to be an excellent idea. Four hundred miles long with forty-nine bridges and one tunnel, it links Libreville with Franceville in the southeast. It gives the interior access to the coast and makes it easier for timber to reach port as well as providing better transport for the manganese ore at Moanda. However, the project cost $4 billion and the government has admitted that there is no chance of the line producing a profit. Rather it will demand a yearly subsidy of approximately $60 million each year.

One of the reasons for the continuing economic success of Gabon is the maintenance of a close association with France. There is tacit agreement that French troops stand ready as they had with M'Ba to support President Bongo. French experts, as in the Ivory Coast, are noticeable in every facet of Gabon's economic life and French capital has been available to develop the nation's resources. The primary petroleum producer, Elf-Gabon, for example, is seventy percent French owned. President Bongo was not averse to using the critical French investment to his own advantage such as in 1984 when he reacted to negative stories about his regime which had appeared in the French press. He accused the French of trying to destabilize his government. There were also implications that he would nationalize Elf-Gabon. The response was immediate. French Prime Minister Pierre Mauroy paid a state visit to Libreville to reassure Bongo, and later the French promised to aid the president in another of his pet projects, the building of a nuclear reactor.

CENTRAL AFRICAN REPUBLIC

Gabon's land-locked neighbor to the northeast, the Central African Republic, is not blessed with similar riches. It is large, ethnically divided, and poor. In January 1966 the army seized power and its head, Colonel Jean Bedel Bokassa, became president. The single political party, MESAN, became less important as Bokassa was able to dispose of most of his rivals. He was forced to call for French troops in 1967 to help thwart a planned coup, and his government survived another abortive takeover in May 1968. Colonel Alexandre Banza, a close friend of Bokassa, attempted in April 1969 to get other army officers to support his attempt to overthrow the government. This power play failed and Banza was publically beaten to death in the streets of Bangui by Bokassa's guards. Bokassa instituted very harsh penalties for ordinary crimes and sanctioned even greater coercion by the soldiers. Periodic sweeps through Bangui kept the streets clear of beggars and unfortunates with physical deformities. It was later confirmed that some of these were taken upriver and drowned. Bokassa's reactions to opposition both real and imagined was violent and psychotic. Many suspected opponents simply disappeared; the main prison was filled and its commander, Joseph Mokwa, carried out even the most violent orders given by Bokassa. The most serious threat to Bokassa's life came in February 1976 when his son-in-law, Fidel Obrou, attempted to blow up the president with a hand grenade. Obrou and ten others implicated in the attempt were executed. Bokassa felt secure supported by a loyal army of more than 1,500 men, and the close friendship of President Giscard d'Estaing of France who visited at least once a year and whose government provided over $5 million a year to make up the government deficit. Nevertheless he endangered his friendship with France by attempting to gain money from Libya. After a visit by Qaddafi he announced his intention of becoming a Muslim and took the name Salah-Addin Ahmed Bokassa. His flirtation with Islam was short lived because to achieve a further grandiose plan he needed the cathedral at Bangui. This action was no less than declaring himself emperor. Enamored of Napoleon, he sought to duplicate Napoleon's coronation. The coronation in December 1977 cost the impoverished state over $25 million. To his surprise no European or African leader attended the ceremonies in the renamed Central African Empire.

Bokassa's excesses including charges of cannibalism had by this time become an embarrassment for France and its representatives discreetly tried to influence Bokassa without success. His downfall was swift because he personally went beyond what even a tolerant French government would countenance. In late 1978 he decreed that all schoolchildren should wear uniforms. This rule was resisted and a demonstration against the edict was staged on January 9, 1979, by several hundred schoolchildren in Bangui. Bokassa commanded soldiers to be given ammunition and they fired into the crowd, killing an estimated dozen persons. The next act in this tragedy was when children on April 19 in one district of Bangui threw rocks at his car. The soldiers, acting on orders, rounded up 180 children of elementary school age and forced them into three small cells at the notorious Ngaragba prison where some suffocated. The Emperor visited them in the evening, had the children brought before him, and personally split open the heads of a half dozen with a heavy cane. He then told Mokwa to finish them off. Only 27 children survived. Amnesty International reported this horror and it was confirmed by Bokassa's ambassador to France just before he resigned and sought asylum in Paris. The immediate reaction of public opinion around the world left Giscard d'Estaing little choice. In early September while Bokassa was in Libya, the French flew in a thousand paratroops from their stations in Gabon and Chad. These soldiers quickly negated Bokassa's poorly trained units and occupied the key positions in Bangui and throughout the countryside. David Dacko who had ruled the nation thirteen years before was awakened by French authorities in Paris and told he was once again the head of state. He was quickly flown to Bangui to make the French planned and executed coup legal. Bokassa at first attempted to move with his entourage to France but was denied sanctuary. He later was accepted by Houphouët-Boigny and spent four years in the Ivory Coast. In the meanwhile he was tried for certain of his crimes *in absentia* in Bangui and sentenced to death. Surprisingly the Ivory Coast made no move to return Bokassa to the Central African Republic. Houphouët-Boigny finally forced Bokassa, his staff, and fifteen of his children to leave the Ivory Coast only because an attempt to restore the ex-emperor involved mercenaries who landed at Abidjan, thus seeming to implicate the Ivory Coast in the affair. Bokassa was this time allowed to enter France and lived in a chateau outside Paris until October 1986. Inexplicably, considering his crimes, Bokassa wanted to return to Bangui. In 1984 he attempted to leave France but was stopped. Two years later, despite police precautions, he escaped to Belgium and from there flew to Bangui where he was promptly arrested.

French support for the successor regimes in the Central African Republic continued in the form of trade and direct assistance. More than fifty percent of recurrent budget of the state came from France. Dacko, who had little to do with his return to power, had difficulty rallying support, particularly from the army. Thus the coup of September 1, 1981 was no surprise to most observers. The head of the small force, General André Kolingba, simply assumed power and ousted the civilians from their positions. Instead, he appointed a military committee which under his direction had both executive and legislative powers. Like many leaders of military coups, Kolingba also promised a return to civilian government as soon as practicable. He moved this plan closer to reality in 1985 when the military committee was dissolved and a new council created which included civilians, and early in 1986 a committee was formed to study the problem of further democratization. The Kolingba regime has not been free of opposition. There have been two serious attempts to overthrow him and some of his former ministers formed a government in exile. The first of these occurred in March 1982 and implicated Ange Patasse, a political rival, and Dr. Abel Goumba, the rector of the University of Bangui. The main result of this failed coup was the worsening for a brief period of the relations with France since President Mitterand gave asylum to Patasse. Then in November 1983 mercenaries were employed by Kolingba's opponents to fly to Abidjan, take Bokassa from the Ivory Coast, and presumably restore him to power. This plot was thwarted by Houphouët-Boigny. There have also been disturbances in the northwest where guerrilla forces called the *Codas Rouge* led by a former minister operated. Joint military action in 1985 with neighboring Chad kept this movement from spreading.

World attention was once more focused upon Bangui as a result of Bokassa's almost inexplicable decision to return. There was never a chance that he could gain enough support from the populace after what he had done, even among the M'Baka, his own people, to overthrow Kolingba. Arrested almost immediately, Kolingba resisted executing him as the court in 1980 had decided. Rather he put on a show trial and allowed Bokassa to bring in two extremely competent French lawyers to defend him. The proceedings were broadcast by radio throughout the country. Most observers agreed that the trial was fair. The testimony of many witnesses only confirmed what had been brought out in the earlier trial and confirmed the many rumors concerning Bokassa's complicity in torture, murder, and perhaps even cannibalism. In June 1987 the court again found him guilty and reimposed the death penalty.

EQUATORIAL GUINEA

Another area whose rule has been synonomous with poverty, terror, and irrational rule was Equatorial Guinea. It comprises the mainland territory which during the Spanish period was called Rio Muni and the Island of Fernando Po. The Spanish in the late 1960s cooperated fully with the embryo nationalist movements in both areas and Equatorial Guinea, despite its divisions, its extreme poverty, and small population, became independent in 1968. Its first president, Macias Nguema Biyogo, with the use of the police and his small army, soon converted both provinces into the equivalent of private fiefs. By the time he was chosen president for life in 1972, European technocrats had left, Nigeria had ordered out her nationals, and most African nations had ceased to even maintain diplomatic relations with Equatorial Guinea. Because of its isolation, it was difficult to discover what was indeed occurring to the 300,000 people over whom Macias held sway. But there were stories of terror circulated by people who had escaped which placed Macias in the same company as Bokassa and Amin. No accurate count of the numbers who died during Macias' misrule can ever be made. It appears that some areas were virtually depopulated, Macias's forces killing between fifty and sixty persons a day in those places for imaginary crimes. On the small island of Annobon a cholera epidemic broke out in 1973. Macias refused to allow international medical and relief agencies on the island. The island's depopulation continued in 1976 when all able bodied men were removed and joined 20,000 forced laborers from Rio Muni to work the plantations on Fernando Po. Macias also changed the place names of the islands. Fernando Po was given the name Macias Nguema Biyogo Island, an accurate if not compelling name. Annobon was renamed Pagalu and the capital city of Santa Isabel was called Malebo. Only the latter name has survived Macias. The successor regime changed the name of Macias Nguema Biyogo to Bioko.

Macias's murderous regime was brought to an end on August 3, 1979, by a revolt of his own military without which he could not have perpetrated his crimes. The coup was led by the chief of the small army, Macias's nephew, Lieutenant Colonel Teodora Obiang Ngeuma Mbasogo. The new Revolutionary Council immediately declared an amnesty for all political prisoners and exposed the brutal excesses of the previous regime to world scrutiny. Macias was tried for his crimes by a special tribunal at Malebo, found guilty, and executed by the soldiers he once controlled. A new constitution was later promulgated by the ruling military government which provides a Bill of Rights but reports from exiles continued to circulate regarding human rights violations. However earnest Mbasogo might have been about charting a new course for his small impoverished state, he and most of his associates could not escape the fact that they had been a part of the previous government.

Equatorial Guinea's major problems as with so many African states are economic which have been exacerbated by the insane policies of the Macias years. The cocoa and coffee plantations on the mainland and Bioko slowly returned to productivity. The timber and plywood industry also revived, but there is little else to attract much foreign investment. In 1984 the total exports amounted to only $13 million while imports, mainly food, amounted to $37 million. It was imperative that Mbasogo attempt to show potential investors the stability of his government. In part he was successful. Not until 1986 was there any concerted attempt to overthrow his government. Then in mid-July a plot was discovered which was led by a deputy in the National Assembly, Eugenio Abeso Mondu. Before he could put into effect his plans, he and thirty other civilians and military men were arrested. Included was Mbasogo's uncle, the deputy prime minister. Mondu was tried by a military tribunal and immediately executed. The others were given prison sentences. The recent history of Equatorial Guinea has done little to negate the idea that the state was one of the best examples of the faults of rapid decolonization which led to Balkanization and misrule.

CONGO

In the Republic of the Congo (Brazzaville) the factors which had created instability before 1965 continued to cause problems. In mid-1966 Marien Ngouabi and other junior officers failed to unseat President Massamba-Debat. Their power base was such that most of the would-be rebels were able to continue in their positions without retribution. In early August 1968, Ngouabi and his associates were finally able to overthrow Massamba-Debat. Until January 1969, Ngouabi was content to be the power behind the new military-based regime. Then he replaced Major Alfred Raoul as president, crushed a counter coup in February, purged the army and police, and established a hand picked Council of the Revolution to aid him in ruling the Congo. By 1972 Ngouabi could afford to become more moderate since he had rid himself of much of the competition from his army associates and had survived a number of plots against his government. Despite all precautions, he was assassinated in 1977. The Revolutionary Council struck out against a number of past opponents of the previous regime. One of the victims was Massamba-Debat. After some weeks Brigader-General Opango was named the new president of the Congo. Although Opango performed reasonably well within the limits imposed by the poorness of the Congo and the factionalism within the ruling Congolese Labor Party, he resigned in February 1979. His successor was Colonel Denis Sassou-Nguesso.

For many years the Congo was more fortunate than most African states because of its economic situation. Until the mid-1970s its major exports were timber and a variety of tropical agricultural products. As important as its own exports, was the fact that the Congo was a crossroad for trade in Central Africa. Its 800 miles of railroad and river systems made it indispensible for trade for the entire region keyed to Pointe Noire, its major port. By 1973 the search for offshore petroleum deposits proved successful. Within ten years the Congo had become Africa's fifth largest producer of petroleum, pumping up to 120,000 barrels a day, which generated over two-thirds of the state's revenue. This wealth, however transitory, because the petroleum reserves are small, enabled Colonel Sassou-Nguesso to proceed with his socialist plans for the Congo until the world petroleum glut and concommittant decline in prices forced a reconsideration of the government's far reaching development program.

It was not merely the loss of revenue which caused problems. As elsewhere in avowed Marxist-Leninist states, many of the government supported schemes failed due to inefficiency of operation and lack of experience of the managers. State farms proved to be costly ventures and the ever growing bureaucracy took an inordinate share of state revenues. The $4.1 billion development plan begun in 1982 proved far too ambitious even though the credit of the Congo when it was begun was excellent. However, by 1984 the public debt stood at more than $1 billion and the money necessary just to service it had grown to fifty-five percent of the recurrent budget. Sassou-Nguesso turned to the IMF for aid which tied any monetary support to basic reforms in the economy. These conditions he was unwilling to accept. Instead, the government embarked on its own Structural Adjustment Plan (SAP) which went almost as far as the IMF demands. It placed a cap on the government payroll and cut back on hiring recent university graduates, limited government investment, and put on hold the implementation of the central village scheme which would have grouped the bulk of the rural population around 157 central villages. More than anything else, SAP sought to bring the inefficient state corporations under more knowledgeable management. Europeans were brought in to run some of these. State farms were supplanted by state supported peasant production. Further, the government tried to bring in more foreign investment by advertising the relaxed economic controls and increased private enterprise. These measures tended to curb the worst excesses of the socialist experiment but they did little to ease the problem of servicing the debt. The major creditors would not reschedule payments until the government accepted the IMF conditions. Finally in 1986 Sassou-Nguesso reached an accord with the IMF. This agreement combined with the upswing in petroleum prices assured him that he could begin what he called the "post-oil" era of development stressing the communications infrastructure and agricultural development.

In contrast to the political infighting which plagued the country prior to 1979, Sassou-Nguesso and the government dominated by the *Parti Congolaise du Travail* (PCT), has given the Congo stability even during the trying period of economic readjustment. Participatory government through a series of regional and local congresses and a National Assembly has existed since 1972. Representatives were chosen on all levels from a list of candidates who were approved by the high ranking party officials. At the third general congress of the party on July 30, 1984, Sassou-Nguesso was unanimously reelected president. The Political Bureau, the ruling council of the PCT, was enlarged. Most important, a presidential form of government was established making the president the head of government in all matters. The position of prime minister was downgraded; his task became merely to coordinate ministerial actions. With improving economic conditions, a single party which was now amenable to his wishes and with the new found international prestige gained after being elected Chairman of the OAU, Sassou-Nguesso appeared in 1987 to be firmly in control of the state.

CHAD

Chad with a mixed population of Semitic nomads in the north and black agriculturists in the south has been the scene of a series of crises. President Tombalbaye in 1966 and early 1967 was confronted with a number of raids across Chad's eastern frontier from the Sudan. No sooner had this problem been diplomatically resolved than Chad army units in the Tibesti area mutinied (in March 1968). Some joined the nomads who were already hostile toward the government. Unable to check the growing rebellion with his own forces, Tombalbaye, in August, requested France to honor its defense treaty with Chad and send troops to the Tibesti area. The revolt spread to other areas of northern and eastern Chad despite the actions of French troops. The main political force behind the uprising was ostensibly the Chad Liberation Front led by Dr. Abba Sick with its headquarters in Libya. By the close of 1969, the French had over 2500 troops including elements of the Foreign Legion operating against the rebels. Nevertheless, the rebels continued to control much of the northern area.

President Tombalbaye decided to institute certain fundamental changes in Chad's society. At the center of this reform was the reinstitution of the harsh initiation practices of Yondo. This unpopular decision combined with Tombalbaye's extravagance, lack of leadership in the face of civil war, and drought convinced the leaders of the army, mostly men from the dominant Sara tribe, to overthrow the government. On April 13, 1975, they moved violently to supplant the premier. Most of the fighting was concentrated near the premier's residence and Tombalbaye was killed. General Felix Malloum then assumed the position as president. The change of government did not alter the civil war where the guerrillas led by Hissene Habré controlled most of the north. These rebels received direct aid from Libya whose troops in 1977 occupied a 100 kilometer strip of Chad's territory. A rift in the Liberation Front resulted in Habré losing his leadership to a rival, the son of the traditional ruler of the Toubou. The French increased their technical and military aid and a new government offensive was begun in 1977. This was no more successful than previous attempts, and soon Malloum's control of even the central areas had been lost. Some measure of unity was gained by naming Habré premier while Malloum remained president. But the truce was short lived, and by the end of 1978, the insurgents controlled most of the countryside around the capital, Ndjamena.

Early in 1979, Habré moved to oust Malloum and thus gain total control of the government. Although nearly successful, the coup failed and Ndjamena became the scene of serious fighting. During the three days from February 12–15, an estimated 500 persons were killed in the street fighting. A cease fire was finally arranged by French authorities who had previously committed over 3000 troops to aid the government in its struggle against the insurgents. The truce was broken by FRONILAT guerrillas in the north supported by Libya, and by the massacre in early March of a reported 1000 Moslems at Moundou in the south. Finally the Nigerian authorities' offer to mediate was accepted and on March 16, a more permanent agreement was reached between the Habré-Malloum factions at a meeting held at Kano. This called for a cease fire, a general amnesty, and the withdrawal of French troops. A second provisional government was formed on March 23 comprising an eight member executive headed by Goukouni Oueddei, a former leader of one of the FRONILAT factions. Habré had lost much popularity with the guerrillas because of his earlier decision to cooperate with the Malloum group, and the new government reflected that loss of power. President Malloum, recognizing that Ndjamena was under the control of his enemies, left Chad for Nigeria. In an attempt to placate all nine political factions, Oueddei reorganized his government again in August. He appointed Lieutenant-Colonel Wadal Abdel-kader Kamougue, a southerner, as vice-president, hoping that this would soothe the fears of the non-Muslim south. He also promised free elections for a new government sometime in 1980.

This third coalition was from the beginning unstable. Each of the rival leaders maintained his own private army. It was inevitable that there would be a confrontation despite an international peacekeeping force, the largest segment of which was a 1200 man French force at Ndjamena. On March 22, 1980, a major battle began in Ndjamena between Oueddei and Habré's troops. Both sides used artillery and rockets and the casualties reached over 700 in the three days of intense but indecisive fighting. Attempting to avoid deeper involvement the French and Congolese troops were withdrawn. During the following months the Red Cross and a number of African states attempted to end the fighting. Five separate cease fire agreements were negotiated: all were broken. Later in the year intense fighting began again. This time Libyan troops supported by tanks entered Chad to support Oueddei's faction. Habré fled first to the Cameroon and later to the Sudan where he began reorganizing those units loyal to him who had been operating in eastern Chad.

Libya's involvement focused international attention on the Chad civil war because it was obvious that Qaddafi hoped to use his power base there to further revolutionary activities elsewhere in West Africa. In January 1981 he announced the merger of Libya and Chad. As with earlier federation schemes of Qaddafi, this one did not last long. Libyan participation in Chad was denounced throughout Western Europe and North America. This attitude, particularly that of the French government, convinced both Qaddafi and Oueddei that the federation was not a good idea and it was abandoned. Qaddafi began removing his troops from Chad in July. By November they were all gone. The internecine warfare had left the already impoverished country, still reeling from the effects of the Sahel drought, in desperate condition. The capital, Ndjamena, was in ruins, its population reduced by two-thirds, the refugees fleeing to neighboring Nigeria or Cameroon. Continued drought-like conditions in conjunction with the fighting which disrupted normal planting cycles had by 1982 reduced agricultural production to only fifty percent of the level two years previously. Much of the population lived by the largesse of French and international aid.

Oueddei's position as Libya's favorite ultimately did him little good. He reformed his government in 1982 but could not hold that fragile coalition together. His Vice-President Kamougue left the capital and retired with the bulk of his army, *Forces Armeés Tchadienne* (FAT), into the populous southern part of the country. The Foreign Minister, Acyl Ahmat, also kept his smaller army intact and separate from that of Oueddei. Most important for the success or failure of Oueddei's regime was the attitude of the French and Sudanese governments. The Mitterand government halted the supply of arms to Chad. President Niameiry of the Sudan allowed Habré a safe base from which to rebuild his army, the Forces Armees du Nord (FAN), and Niameiry and President Sadat of Egypt provided supplies and equipment. By May 1982 Habré had assumed the offensive in eastern Chad and by early June they had advanced within fifty miles of the capital. There the FAN troops defeated the government forces without much difficulty. On June 7 Habré's army took Ndjamena. Oueddei fled the country, first to the Cameroon and then later he went to Libya where he began to reconstruct his government and with Qaddafi's support an army. Habré's position was strengthened greatly by the death of Acyl and successful negotiations which brought Kamougue briefly into the government. Habré's new government was recognized by France and the United States, both of which began to funnel more military and nonmilitary supplies to Chad. The area appeared to be so secure that the peace keeping forces sent by the

OAU were withdrawn in the fall of 1982.

However, Oueddi and his ally Qaddafi had not given up. In April 1983 he reopened hostilities in the northeast. His troops backed by Libyan ground units with Soviet built tanks and supported by a portion of the Libyan airforce swept aside Habré's army. They took the important town of Faya-Largeau and swept on toward the Sudanese border. Once again Chad became the focus of international concern. Zaire sent in troops to help police Ndjamena, Nigeria declared its support of Habré, and the United States increased its aid. The key question for Habré was how far the French were prepared to go in support of his regime. President Mitterand was reluctant to have France become heavily involved again. However, the reality of the military situation convinced him finally in August to commit French air and ground forces. Within a month more than 1,000 French troops were in Chad. Ultimately there would be three times that many. Included in the French support were attack helicopters, jet fighters, and bombers. The French military presence combined with diplomatic pressure halted the advance of the Libyan units. President Mitterand, much to Habré's chagrin, announced that French forces would not be used to recapture the north. This left Oueddei with Libyan support controlling that area. Neither Mitterand or Qaddafi wanted an escalation of the fighting and agreed upon the so-called "red line" along the 16th parallel which divided Chad.

After a number of small scale confrontations on the ground and in the air, both the French and Libyans seemed ready for a mutual withdrawal of forces. In September 1984 President Mitterand flew to Morocco for talks with King Hassan. With Hassan as an intermediary, an agreement was reached whereby both states would pull their troops out of Chad. Although France removed a large portion of its forces, Libya did not significantly reduce its troop strength in the north. Despite the *de facto* division of the country, the economic conditions of Chad had improved considerably during the two years of relative peace under Habré in the productive southern area. The return of normal amounts of rainfall also aided the traditional sector's production of foodstuff, and the harvest of cotton, the main export of the state, by 1985 had reached the 1979 levels. United States and French aid continued and large parts of Ndjamena were rebuilt.

Meanwhile Habré's opponents, instead of uniting against him, were busy tearing each other apart. Oueddei's Transitional Government of National Unity (GUNT) in exile was no stronger than previous coalitions. Kamougué who had rejoined Oueddei and had become Vice-President of GUNT defected in early 1986. The Chadian Liberation Front (FRONILAT) also broke with GUNT in September joining Acheikh Ibn Omar's Revolutionary Democratic Council (CDR) in opposition to both Habré and Oueddei. In late August fighting broke out in the Faya-Largeau region between troops loyal to GUNT and the CDR forces. Libyan troops maintained strict neutrality in the fighting which left thirty dead and more than fifty wounded. More important even than the conditions of the opposing Chadian factions was the cooling of relations between Qaddafi and Oueddei. Certainly one factor in Qaddafi's reexamination of his policy toward Chad was the attack in March by United States aircraft which had dared cross his "line of death" in the Gulf of Sidra. A reconciliation meeting between Oueddei and Habré in Brazzaville in March never materialized because Oueddei did not choose to attend. Oueddei later in the year, perhaps realizing how vulnerable and isolated he was, came to an agreement with Habré after breaking with Libya.

By December 1986 most GUNT troops in the Tibesti area had joined Habré's forces to attack their former ally Libya, particularly in the vicinity of the town of Zour. The United States had increased its military support, and the French maintained 1400 men south of the 16th parallel and numerous fighters and bombers. Thus emboldened, Habré ordered a resumption of hostilities against the estimated 10,000 Libyan troops in northern Chad. The first major objective was the oasis of Fada, Libya's strongpoint in northeastern Chad. In a one day battle on January 1, 1987, the outnumbered and outgunned Chadian troops drove out the Libyans who left behind millions of dollars worth of sophisticated electronic equipment, tanks, and artillery, many of which were never brought into action. Habré also announced that the Libyans lost over 1000 men killed. More than 100 prisoners were paraded in triumph through the streets of Ndjamena. Habré's next objective was to drive the Libyans from the Aouzou strip, a 44,000 square mile area reportedly rich in minerals which Qaddafi had annexed in 1973. Units of Habré's army in August launched an attack on the town of Aouzau near the Libyan border and drove the Libyan troops out, thus taking over practical control of the strip and temporarily at least ending Libya's occupation of any part of Chad.

President Habré, however, took note of the presence of 10,000 Libyan troops near the border and announced his belief that the border war would continue for some time and decided to carry the war into Libya despite opposition to such a plan from his French advisors who did not wish to become further involved in a war with Libya. Chadian army units met and destroyed a Libyan column headed toward Ounianga Kebir and then invaded Libya for the first time in the war. Driving swiftly inland, they took the airfield of Matan as Sarra sixty miles north of the border on September 4 after very heavy fighting. Against losses of sixty-five dead and twelve wounded, the Chadians killed an estimated 1700 Libyan troops, captured a number of large caliber guns, late model tanks, and eight SAM missile sites. They destroyed thirty aircraft before retreating back across the border. Libya attempted a weak retaliation by sending bombers over Ndjamena the next day only to have one destroyed by a ground to air missile provided by the United States. The escalation of the conflict with Libya meant that the Chad war had ceased to be a local affair and had assumed openly international ramifications. Certainly Libya's defeats had at least temporarily removed it as a potent threat to Habré's government and bolstered his claim to the Aouzou strip. The French, however reluctantly, honored their defense agreements with Chad and the United States continued to send aid of all types and its government could only be pleased that Libya had suffered such crushing defeats.

ZAIRE

The former Belgian areas, which had been the scene of so much warfare and bloodshed in the early years of the decade, had become relatively quiescent by 1970. In the Republic of the Congo (Kinshasa), General Mobutu, who had earlier seized power from Tshombe and Kasavubu, was able to restore peace throughout most of the Congo. Potentially the most serious threat to Mobutu was the action in

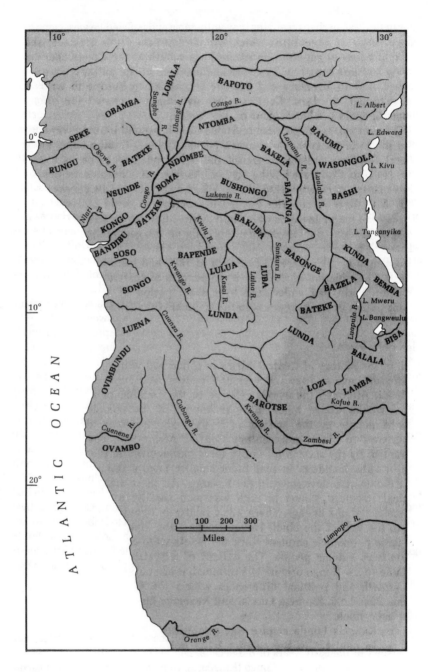

Peoples of the Congo Basin

1967 of approximately 150 white mercenaries and 900 Katanga gendarmes. For over six months they held a large portion of the eastern Congo based upon their control of the town of Bukavu. Eventually the mercenaries crossed into Rwanda where they were repatriated. Mobutu's rival for power, Kasavubu, died in March 1969. Moise Tshombe, who had been detained in Algeria for two years, died the following June. Mobutu had executed Pierre Mulele the year before. Thus the most important Congolese leaders who could have rallied support against Mobutu were removed from the political scene. Even before the mercenary threat ended, Mobutu had renegotiated, for the new Congolese government company, favorable terms with Belgian mining concerns in the Katanga. With the return of peace throughout the Congo, the economic position of the state rapidly improved and this as much as any other factor solidified Mobutu's regime.

During the calm era of the early 1970s, President Mobutu began a program designed to break down tribal loyalties and the half-century of Belgian control. He decreed the change of name of the country to Zaire. Most of the major cities and other geographic features were also renamed. Individuals were forced to give up European names, and an attempt was made to dictate modes of dress. In this period Mobutu also invested heavily in grandiose, expensive projects such as an airline, a billion dollar hydroelectric complex, and an equally expensive new copper smelting facility. Then the price of copper declined by more than one-half from 1974 to 1976. The government defaulted on over $400 million in foreign loans and was forced to devalue the currency by forty-two percent. By 1977 the inflation rate stood at over forty percent and there were even shortages of food in some regions.

Mobutu's domestic problems were compounded by his foreign ventures. Holden Roberto and the FLNA were not only provided sanctuary but direct military assistance, particularly in their abortive attempt to seize power in Angola. Soon after Zaire's defeat in Angola there was an invasion of Shaba Province (formerly Katanga) by anti-Mobutu forces. These largely Lunda insurgents were refugees who had been loyal to Moise Tshombe and had been driven out of Shaba by the military actions of the late 1960s. In March 1977 over 2000 invaders representing the National Liberation Front of the Congo (FNLC) drove into this richest of all Zaire's provinces from their bases in Angola. Despite massive military aid from the United States, the Zaire army proved to be little better than its counterpart a decade before. Mobutu pled for direct aid from other African and Western states. In response King Hassan of Morocco dispatched 1500 troops in April. France airlifted the troops, Uganda, Sudan, Egypt, and China also gave aid, and the United States sent special grants of money and equipment. The Moroccans supported by some of Zaire's forces stopped the invaders twenty miles from the provincial capital and major industrial center of Kolwezi. Most of the insurgents then retired to sanctuaries across the Angolan border.

In May 1978 the rebels launched a new invasion of Shaba. Zaire's army, caught by surprise, once again proved no match for the invaders who this time captured Kolwezi. The situation was again stabilized by foreign intervention. On Mobutu's invitation, 1,200 French Foreign Legion paratroopers and a like number of Belgian paratroopers were flown into the province, and later 1,500 Moroccan troops were sent by King Hassan. Many of the estimated 3,000 European civilians were evacuated from the province. As the attempts to retake Kolwezi reached a peak, the rebels began to execute hundreds of blacks and whites in the city. After severe fighting, European paratroopers liberated Kolwezi and within a short time had driven the invaders once again into Angola. Zaire charged, with considerable truth, that not only had Angola harbored the dissident forces, but that these forces had been trained by Cuban instructors.

The fighting shut down copper and cobalt production for months, thus worsening Zaire's financial position. Although approximately 200,000 refugees returned to war-torn Shaba, industry was slow to recover largely due to the shortage of skilled technicians. In 1978 the inflation rate had reached seventy-five percent, the state owed $36 billion, and the government was defaulting on over $100 million in debts every year. Zaire's economy could not be left to fail because of Zaire's vast mineral resources and its long standing Western orientation. In June 1978, representatives of five Western nations met together and formulated an economic rescue plan for Zaire, and the International Monetary Fund attempted to aid the government in controlling speculation and illegal transfers of funds. Despite the application of some of the measures suggested, Zaire continued throughout 1979 to be a deeply troubled state faced not only with bankruptcy, but with the failure even of its agriculture. There was widespread famine in western Zaire and food riots in Kinshasa. Mobutu had weathered many other storms in his long tenure, and with outside aid there was every chance that despite mismanagement, he would also survive the ongoing economic crisis.

The invasion of Shaba Province by the *Front National la Libération du Congo* in 1977 and again in 1978 focused world attention upon Zaire and showed clearly how mismanaged was this large and potentially wealthy state. President Mobutu's control of Shaba, the mineral rich southern part of the country, was secured only by the dispatch of a large contingent of the French Foreign Legion to Kolwezi. Later the Belgians, Moroccans, and Senegalese sent troops to bolster the obviously incompetent ill-trained Zairian soldiers. After the rebels had been driven out of Shaba, elements of the foreign units stayed behind, partially to insure that a further invasion could be contained and also to train the shaky Zairian army units also on guard there. Mobutu spent a considerable amount of time in Shaba in the two years after the rebels had been negated as if to reassure the workers in this vital area of his continuing concern. In 1980 he reached an agreement with the Angolan and Zambian governments whereby each promised not to aid revolutionary groups seeking to overthrow the regime in each state. The betterment of relations with Angola continued and was capped by a meeting between Mobutu and President José dos Santos in July 1986. At this meeting Mobutu promised to help interdict the supplies reaching UNITA forces from Zaire.

Zaire is an excellent example of the contention that political stability alone does not assure success in government. President Mobutu and the party he leads, *Mouvement Populaire de la Revolution* (MPR), the single legal political party, have controlled Zaire for over two decades. During that period members of the elite have systematically looted the state either by direct expropriation or by enriching themselves by managing state run industries. Corruption in government as elsewhere in Africa became a way of life and mismanagement became so pronounced that this richest of all sub-Saharan states was bankrupt by the mid 1970s. The road and river systems had been allowed to deteriorate, inflation in 1980 was estimated at 200% per year, and the real wages of workers was only one-tenth of 1960 levels. Once a major exporter of tropical agricultural products, Zaire by 1980 was importing food and there were even cases of local famines. The decline of agricultural productivity was aggravated by the rapid increase in population and the migration of vast numbers of relatively destitute people from rural areas into the cities.

Some of the reasons for Zaire's economic condition was not the fault of its corrupt leaders but was due to the depressed market for copper and cobalt, the two major export minerals. The decline in demand and reciprocally the fall in price struck very hard at Zaire's currency earning potential. This economic fact did not halt the annual increase in the civil bureaucracy or result in a cutback of the armed forces of 100,000 men. Nor did it slow down the expensive development projects such as the powerline from the Inga Dam to Shaba. Over 1100 miles long, it was completed in 1982 after seven years work. The powerline was designed to provide electricity for a major increase in cobalt and copper production, but due to the decline in demand for these, it currently does not earn enough to pay the interest on the loans which financed it.

Finally in 1979 in the face of drought, severe food and fuel shortages, runaway inflation, and an inability to service its $5 billion external debt, Zaire appealed for help from the IMF which responded by providing $150 million in credit. This loan was followed later by guarantees of $350 million in 1983 and $165 million in 1986. However, the IMF dictated stringent conditions for the government to follow. An officer of the IMF became the director of the Central Bank and immediately began the Herculean task of cutting back on loans to a score of companies and refusing outright large, unsecured loans to high government officials. A cap was placed on expanding the bureaucracy and Mobutu promised to be more aware of corruption on all levels. Most important, the value of the zaire, the basic currency, was cut by fifty percent. The continued fight to make the zaire conform to the reality of the exchange market is shown by its further devaluation by thirty percent in 1980 and by another eighty percent in 1983. Although Zaire could not conform totally with the IMF guidelines due in part to the continued depressed markets for its major exports, those efforts resulted in a lowering of the inflation rate by 1986 to only fifty percent. The number of inefficient government run companies was reduced by turning them over to private enterprise and the external debt problem was brought under control. The creditors rescheduled payments five times in the 1980s.

The major reasons why Mobutu's corrupt, inefficient government did not collapse economically in the early 1980s was because of the value of its resources of cobalt, copper, zinc, iron, gold, and diamonds. Further the United States government and to a lesser extent those of Western Europe considered Zaire strategically important — "the hub" of Africa. Mobutu for all his failings had been staunchly pro-Western and there were fears that if his regime collapsed the successor government might eventually be a Marxist one such as in neighboring Angola. Finally there was no opposition group either in Zaire or in exile which could guarantee stability in this once factionalized region. No reasonable Western official, banker, or industrialist wanted to see Zaire lapse into the chaos of the early 1960s.

Throughout all the difficulties Mobutu remained in firm control of the mechanisms of the party and state. In 1984 he was reelected President for his third seven year term. One of the methods used by Mobutu to make certain that no rival can carve out a power base within the government is to constantly reshuffle his ministry. His control of the army remained secure. Criticism of Mobutu and the government was curbed by use of the state's police powers and Amnesty International has noted a number of human rights violations. Strikes by workers were against the law and student activity was closely monitored as witness the closing of Kisangani University in 1985. Most internal opposition to the government was fragmented and that coming from those in exile have had little success in gaining support even from their hosts let alone from within Zaire. The largest of the three main opposition groups was the Conglese Front for the Restoration of Democracy whose headquarters is in Brussels. Its leader is Nguza Karl-I-Bond, a former prime minister who broke with Mobutu in 1981.

Mobutu has attempted to better his image by assiduously courting the leaders of nations on which he depends for continued economic support. Mobutu visited Washington in 1983 and 1987 and paid a state visit to France in 1984. He has aligned Zaire with the more conservative African states. Thus he supported Morocco in its claim to the Western Sahara, going so far as to pull Zaire out of the OAU in 1982. Mobutu dispatched over 2,000 troops to Chad to help support Hissène Habré. Following the dictates of economic pragmatism, he allowed a subsidiary of de Beers Corporation of South Africa to market Zaire's diamonds. In this same sense Mobutu's government in 1982 was the first sub-Saharan state to resume relations with Israel, broken after the Six-Day War. The border difficulties with Angola dating to the MPLA takeover there have been eased if not ended by a series of meetings with President José dos Santos, the last occurring in July 1986. The agreements reached there call for both governments to prevent dissident elements from building up their military strength in safety. Zaire also promised to interdict the aid designated for Jonas Savimbi's UNITA forces from Zaire.

RWANDA AND BURUNDI

These two landlocked highland countries bordering Zaire historically have much in common. The population of each comprised a majority of agricultural Bahutu people ruled by a pastoralist aristocracy of Watutsi. The political and social systems of these traditional kingdoms were left relatively undisturbed by first the Germans and later the Belgians who dominated each after the scramble for Africa. When Belgium reluctantly granted independence to the two dependencies in 1962 they were very similar not only in political and social structure but demographically and economically. Each was and remains one of the poorest states in Africa with a per capita income estimated in 1984 at less than $150 per person. Despite the richness of some of the volcanic soils, there were few crops of export value and the conservative way of life of the traditional Watutsi ruling class inhibited any substantial diversification of crops. Population pressure also played a part in the relative poverty of Rwanda and Burundi. Their population density is the highest in Africa. Events since independence have significantly changed each state, especially Rwanda. By the mid-1970s the political systems of the two states had become radically different because of the diverse responses to the demands of the Hutu majority in each. In Rwanda this majority gained power by the ballot box and drove out the ruling Watutsi nobility and during the early 1960s killed thousands of Watutsi. In Burundi, although there have been important changes in the government since independence, the Watutsi minority has held on to power and the Bahutu people remain basically without political voice.

In Rwanda the Bahutu political party, PARMEHUTU, under Belgian protection won the early elections and its leaders deposed the king, Mwami Kigeri V, and seized the opportunity to form a government with minimal Watutsi input. When Rwanda became independent in 1962, Gregoirē Kayibanda was named the first president. The attempt by the Watutsi to reverse the situation proved disastrous. The brief civil war of 1963–64 resulted in the deaths of more than 15,000 persons and for all purposes meant the end of Watutsi domination. Kayibanda's government during the decade of his rule concentrated upon improving the domestic sector and attempted, without much success, to moderate the hatred between the rival Watutsi and Bahutu. More than twenty-five percent of the national budget during those years was devoted to education. In 1970 Rwanda signed a friendship pact with Belgium and with foreign aid began to improve its road system, particularly that portion which linked it to Uganda. Stresses within Kayibanda's government in July 1973 led to a bloodless coup orchestrated by the head of the 5,000 man army, Major General Juvenal Habyarimana, a Bahutu from the north. The previous constitution was declared void and a military council dominated until a new constitution came into force in 1978. Kayibanda and seven other high officials in his government were tried for their alleged crimes and sentenced to death, but their sentences in 1974 were reduced to life imprisonment.

The constitution of 1978 provided for a legislature, the National Development Council of fifty members, and a presidential type executive. The military government recognized only one political party, the National Revolutionary Movement for Development (MRND). Voters were allowed some choice since they could select from a list of candidates prepared by the provincial governors. Union activity was also allowed although the parameters of their actions were circumscribed. General Habyarimana, the only candidate for the office of president, was, not surprisingly, elected for five year terms by an overwhelming majority in the elections of 1978 and 1983.

President Habyarimana attempted to secure the basic goals established by his predecessor. Most pressing was the problem of Bahutu-Watutsi hatred. The government established an informal quota system for jobs and schooling. Tension between the groups nevertheless remained and was the basis of an unsuccessful coup attempt in 1982. Thousands of Rwandans who fled to neighboring states during the troubles of the 1960s remain there and although posing no immediate threat to the Bahutu dominated government, could at some future date be an important factor in the politics of Rwanda. The government has tried to diversify agriculture, attempting to find in tea or pyrethrum an export of equal value to coffee, the primary foreign currency earner. Considerable foreign aid has flowed into the country making possible the extension of the road network and some improvement of the amenities of the capital city, Kigali. One of the main supports to the Habyarimana regime is the Catholic Church. Almost sixty percent of

Rwandans are Christians and most all of these are Catholic. Until 1985 the Archbishop of Kigali was a member of the MRND Central Committee. This close association was one reason for the government's attack after 1984 on Protestant missionary activity. In 1986 a mass trial in Kigali found that nearly 300 persons of four religious groups were guilty of fostering civil disobedience, holding illegal meetings, and distributing subversive literature. Although the sentences were generally light, the leader of the Jehovah's Witnesses was sentenced to twelve years in prison. It is doubtful that the Protestant groups posed any threat to the government. Rather, the Catholic Church which controlled eighty-five percent of the secondary and one-half of the primary schools was assuring that there would be no undermining of its authority in these areas which might lead to secularization as was occurring in Burundi during the mid-1980s.

The political history of Burundi since independence has in many ways been exactly opposite to that of Rwanda. The presence of an active functioning king enabled the Watutsi minority to continue its control of all the important state offices after independence. Although Watutsi opponents of the monarchy overthrew Mwami Ntare V in November 1966, they had no intention of sharing power with the Bahutu who made up eighty-five percent of the population. Colonel Michel Micombero simply declared himself president and his ministry was composed of those Watutsi whom he appointed. Most of these were from the south. The legislature which was dissolved in 1965 was not revived. Opposition to Micombero's government came from northern Tutsi who believed themselves shut out from a share of power by the southern aristocracy. Their dissatisfaction caused him to dismiss his ministry on April 29, 1972, and he planned to include more northerners in the future. Complicating matters for Micombero was the presence in the country of Mwami Ntare V who still could claim support from the more traditional Watutsi. He had returned to Burundi the previous month after being assured of his personal safety. Nevertheless he was immediately arrested and accused of plotting an invasion of the country. More serious than any other factor was the Bahutu resentment at being continued as second class citizens. They had been politicized by the events leading up to independence and were encouraged by the events in Rwanda. On April 30 they began a concerted attack on the government. Violence was centered in the southern provinces and in the capital. Thousands of Tutsi were massacred before the army checked the rebellion. In a separate action, monarchial supporters attempted to rescue Ntare who was imprisoned in the northern town of Gitega. They failed and the former ruler was quickly executed. The Watutsi reaction to the Bahutu uprising was merciless. Spearheaded by the army, the Watutsi minority began a systematic liquidation of the Bahutu, particularly any who had some education. Whole villages were wiped out and some of the streams were choked with bodies. No worse case of genocide has occurred on the continent in the past half-century. In all at least 100,000 Bahutu lost their lives and to many observers this was a conservative estimate. An additional 50,000 Bahutu fled the country. Thousands of homesteads were destroyed and this in future years would present further problems to the government as it tried to mend an already ailing economy.

The challenge to reconcile the Bahutu to a regime tainted with the blood of thousands of their tribesmen proved too much for Micombero. Despite the issuance of a new republican constitution in 1974, he found that he could not even dominate the leaders of the Watutsi as he once did. In November 1976 the army led by a Belgian trained officer, Lieutenant Colonel Jean-Baptiste Bagaza, deposed Micembero in a bloodless coup and banned all political activity. Bagaza became the head of the Military Council, all of whom were Watutsi. Bagaza himself was a Hima from the south, the dominant Watutsi subgroup. His government also faced the twin challenges of reconciliation of the Bahutu and a need to diversify the export agriculture to find a product to augment coffee, the main crop which provided over eighty percent of the earnings. In neither problem area was he very successful. Most of the Bahutu who had fled the country chose to stay in their places of exile and those who remained were not eager to forget the massacres and their subservient position. The Watutsi leaders, both modern and traditional, upon whom Bagaza's control of the state depended, did not wish to surrender any of their traditional rights and privileges. The five year plans first instituted in 1978 emphasizing rural development by 1987 showed few positive results although Burundi escaped the drought of the 1970s and 1980s. One of the major reasons for this relative failure was the old Watutsi-Bahutu client relationship which satisfied the dominant landowners and made modernization extremely slow.

Burundi received a large amount of foreign aid partially because Bagaza provided a stable government which was pro-Western and definitely within the confines of a Francophone Africa. In 1987 the aid totalled $150 million, enough to make up the deficit in foreign trade and allow the government to operate. Twenty percent of this aid came from France which maintained a joint Franco-Burundi Committee on Economic Cooperation and had sent 160 technical advisors to Burundi.

In 1981 Bagaza issued a new constitution which provided for an elected executive president and an elected National Assembly of 52 members. There was to be universal suffrage for those over nineteen years of age. Only one political party, UPRONA, controlled by upper class Watutsi, was to be allowed. On October 22, 1982, the first elections in seventeen years took place for members of the National Assembly. Voters chose 52 deputies from a list of 104 persons selected by UPRONA. Even this minor concession proved that the voters were not completely happy. Three of Bagaza's ministers and three UPRONA high officials failed to win their contests. However, the constitution allowed Bagaza to choose 13 additional deputies. Nevertheless there was a major reshuffling of ministerial posts in early 1983. Very few of those elected were Bahutu. The election for president was not scheduled until 1984. Not surprisingly Bagaza was the only candidate approved at the Second National Party Congress and in August won the approval of ninety-nine percent of the 1.7 million eligible voters.

The major internal problem in Burundi concerned the role of the Catholic Church. Dominant in education and many health and social services, its position within a society that was sixty percent Catholic seemed unassailable. The government disturbed by the potential political influence that foreign priests might have with the Bahutu decided in 1985 to curb the power of the church. Noting the high rate of absenteeism on the farms and offices, the government placed a ban on all church services between 7:00 A.M. and 5:00 P.M. on weekdays. Ostensibly many missionaries ignored this decree. The government then detained 150 local priests in August. By the end of the year more than 100 foreign missionaries had been deported. The minister for External Affairs reflecting the fear that the foreign priests were injecting politics in their work declared that the Catholic Church was the sole force of opposition in Burundi. The attack on the church's position continued in 1986 with the decision to nationalize small and medium sized seminaries, to outlaw Catholic youth movements and instruction based on religious texts. Bagaza continued his secularization program despite pastoral letters by Burundi's bishops and irate statements from Pope John Paul II. By the end of 1987 the number of foreign priests had been reduced from a high of 500 in 1982 to only 30. Undoubtedly the furor attendant upon these reforms added to the continuing economic and political problems was a factor in the bloodless military coup of September 3, 1987. President Bagaza was in Quebec attending a meeting of French speaking countries when the army led by midrange officers took control in Bujumbura. The borders were closed temporarily and a short-lived curfew was imposed. The constitution of 1981 was declared void; instead the governing agency was to be a Watutsi dominated Military Council headed by Major Pierre Buyoya.

Southern Africa

ZAMBIA

The three areas which comprised the old Central African Federation were stable in their internal politics in the period after 1965. Zambia, the largest and potentially wealthiest of the three, was firmly ruled by Kenneth Kaunda's United National Independence party. In the December 1968 elections UNIP candidates won control of 81 of the 105 seats in the Assembly and Kaunda was reelected president, soundly defeating the leader of the opposing African National Congress, Harry Nkumbula. In 1967 in the wake of the Rhodesian crisis, Zambia disassociated itself from the joint railway and airline company. The following year Kaunda began a cautious policy of nationalization when the state took control over twenty-five smaller companies and renegotiated a new royalty formula with others. This policy was extended by the general nationalization of the copper industry in 1969 with the state taking over control of fifty-one percent of the stock of the companies. Finally in July 1975, the government nationalized all privately owned lands, theaters, hospitals, and newspapers. Despite such activity, the country was in financial difficulty caused mainly by the fall off of copper prices. By 1977 Zambia's imports were double the value of its exports. The cutting of the Benguela railway during the Angolan civil war and the closure of the borders with Rhodesia also damaged the economy. These setbacks were only partially compensated for by the opening of the Tanzam railway in 1975 which linked the copperbelt to the port of Dar es Salaam. Politically Zambia has been operating under a new constitution adopted in 1973 and is a one party state.

    The greatest direct danger to Zambia in the latter 1970s was from Rhodesia which considered Kaunda's support of guerrilla forces tantamount to active participation in the struggle. Rhodesian air and ground forces struck across the border a number of times seeking to destroy the sanctuaries for Nkomo's troops. These attacks escalated after the Muzorewa-Smith accord of early 1979 and the number of insurgents training on Zambian territory increased. Four major attacks were launched into Zambia by Rhodesian forces during the year. One raid in April brought the war directly to Lusaka when strike forces seized and burned Nkomo's house in the capital city. In October the Rhodesian army cut the Tanzam rail line and blew up the last remaining bridge of the railroad which linked Zambia with Rhodesia and South Africa. Zambia's road communications with Zambia's neighbors had already been interdicted. President Kaunda ordered the nation and his 12,000 man army on war alert status on November 20. Zambia's difficulties with Rhodesia were matched on a smaller scale in the southwest in the region adjacent to the Caprivi Strip. There SWAPO irregulars had been granted sanctuary by the Zambian government and South African ground and air forces had struck at the military camps a number of times. Kaunda obviously welcomed the results of the Lancaster House Conference of late 1979 since it brought a cease fire to his troubled border between Zambia and Rhodesia and a possibility that any new black government in the south would remember Zambia's sacrifices and quickly restore normal economic relations with his troubled state.

The independence of Zimbabwe, Zambia's neighbor, did bring security to that troubled border, but the nation's economic problems which had begun in 1974 with the decreasing world price of copper and cobalt continued. Copper prices fell from a high of $1.40 per pound in 1973 to only half that amount a decade later. Kaunda's role in opposition to South Africa did not help since the destabalization policy of the Botha government also had detrimental effects on Zambia's economy. To these factors must be added the mismanagement of economic affairs by Zambian officials described by some observers as chaotic. Zambia's international debt by 1987 stood at over $5 billion, dictating that a disproportionate amount of the government's time and energy had to be devoted to attempts to reschedule it. A major rescheduling occurred in 1984 after Kaunda agreed to follow the guidelines laid down by the IMF. The currency, the *kwacha*, was devalued forty percent, there was a cutback in government spending, and food subsidies were drastically reduced. The IMF immediately made available $225 million in extra credits.

Zambia became a good example of how detrimental the foreign debt was and how it was nearly impossible for a government to operate with such a millstone. The 1984 adjustments made in conformity to IMF suggestions resulted in more unemployment, an increase in the inflation rate and labor costs, as well as an immediate increase in food prices for the forty-five percent of Zambia's population who live in towns or cities. Nor did the corrections end Zambia's poor economic situation since this is ultimately tied to the price paid for its mineral exports. A fact which most Zambian planners tried to ignore was that the known copper reserves will be exhausted in less than twenty years. They were more concerned with the ongoing present problems which meant installing in October 1985 a system of weekly auctioning of foreign currency. This had the effect of devaluation of the currency by approximately sixty percent which struck further at the Zambian citizens' standard of living. In the short term this move had one salutory effect by providing a stimulus to the industrial sector which had been operating at only thirty percent capacity. The IMF and World Bank provided more funds to shore up the sick economy. Later in 1987 a further readjustment in the auction scheme took place as Zambia fell behind in its obligations to the IMF by over $200 million. Under the best of circumstances, servicing the huge external debt would claim over forty percent of Zambia's yearly export earnings. Never happy with the strictures imposed, President Kaunda announced in September 1987 that Zambia was abrogating its agreement with the IMF. Instead, his government would follow its own economic plan. He announced that Zambia would not devote such a large percentage of its earnings to paying off the external debt. Instead, only ten percent maximum of the country's import earnings would be devoted to paying the creditors. The auction system was abolished and the *kwacha* was fixed at eight to the dollar. This aggressive stance of Kaunda's could have important ramifications for other African states unhappy with the IMF guidelines. These might follow Zambia's example. However, Kaunda's decision was fraught with danger since this action damaged Zambia's credit position and there was every possibility that potential investors or lenders would simply refuse to risk their capital in Zambia.

Throughout these years of economic crisis, President Kaunda was never seriously challenged for his economic or foreign policy. He continued in the forefront of the African opposition to apartheid in South Africa even if this meant providing bases from which guerrilla forces could operate against the Botha government. As chairman of the OAU in 1987 he became even more vocal. There has been only one threat to Kaunda's domination of the only legal party, the United National Independence Party (UNIP), and the government. This occurred in 1981 when a number of important men hatched a plot to kidnap Kaunda and force his resignation. The plot was discovered and thirteen persons were tried for treason; five were sentenced to death in 1983. There were indications that Kaunda was tiring of his responsibilities. In 1985 he broached publicly the idea of retirement, fuelling speculation that his successor was likely to be the young Prime Minister, Kebby Musokotwane. However, the president has made no concrete moves to assure a peaceful succession in his economically troubled state.

MALAWI

Hastings Banda in 1966 presided over the conversion of Malawi to a republic. As president, his major problem remained the lack of resources and relative poverty of its four million citizens. Banda has negotiated trade agreements with South Africa and communications agreements with the Portuguese in Mozambique. He has also maintained friendly relations with Israel. Because of Banda's foreign policy, Malawi has been viewed by many other African leaders as a betrayer of the cause of black Africa. Banda replied that Malawi, landlocked and poor, needed the aid and trade with Rhodesia and South Africa in order to progress. President Banda continued to dominate all phases of Malawi's political life and was declared president for life in 1970. He had no trouble with opponents until 1977 when a plot against his government was uncovered. This, however, was not a serious threat and the aging president emerged with even greater power than before. Although Banda became the oldest head of state in Africa after the retirement of Siaka Stevens of Sierre Leone, he showed no signs of losing his grip on every facet of Malawi's politics. He continued to rule with an iron hand to maintain law and order. There have been no strikes, rebellions, or large scale migrations from the country since independence. This latter fact indicated that however inflexible Banda was with regard to opposition, the policies of his government were popular with the mass of the citizens.

By shifting the personnel in his ministry around, Banda did not allow any one member of the ruling Malawi Congress Party (MCP) to build a popular base from which to challenge the leader. His autocratic rule spawned three opposition groups which operate from outside Malawi. These are the Malawi Freedom Movement (MAFREMO), the Socialist League of Malawi (LESOMA), and the Congress for the Second Republic. Tanzania and Zambia allowed members of these organizations to operate within their borders and this has been one factor in the poor relations between Malawi and these states. None of these organizations has posed a serious threat to the MCP partially because Banda's police were very active in arresting potential activists. There were also a number of accidents to some of those who criticized Banda's policies and bombings of opposition members' houses in Dar es Salaam and Lusaka. In one celebrated case in 1981, former Justice Minister Orton Chirwa, his wife, and son were kidnapped from Zambia. Chirwa and his wife were subsequently charged with treason, tried, and sentenced to death. Later in 1983 in celebration of his birthday, Banda commuted their sentences to life in prison. With such methods it is not difficult to imagine that the aged president will hold his office for life.

The Banda government for all its faults in the areas of individual and political liberty has been one of the most pragmatic and efficient governments in Africa. Malawi has no minerals of commercial value and also has a large and dense population. Therefore Banda from the beginning of his rule stressed financial aid to the agricultural sector. Standing against the tide of opinion, Banda has maintained good relations with the Republic of South Africa and Israel even paying a state visit to the former. The result was financial assistance and technical aid from those two advanced states in addition to that forthcoming from other European countries and the United States. The transportation infrastructure of Malawi has been greatly improved. Good water at considerable cost to the state has been piped from the mountains to many of the agricultural villages. The target date for good water supplies to be available for all villages in the country is the mid-1990s.

Most of the soils of Malawi are good by comparison to many areas of Africa and the MCP government has expended considerable sums to upgrade both village and plantation agriculture. Banda resisted the temptation after independence to break up the large cotton, tea, and tobacco plantations, and these provide a large portion of Malawi's export earnings. Malawi was fortunate to escape the droughts of the early 1980s which devastated the agriculture of its neighbors. Also the world market price of its major exports, particularly tobacco, remained high. Although affected by the worldwide recession and an inflation rate of approximately eight percent per year, Malawi by the mid-1980s was in relatively good condition. There was almost an eight percent growth in the Gross Domestic Product during the 1985–86 year. The Marketing Corporation had decided in the year previous to raise the price paid to the farmers for maize. This resulted in a six percent increase in the output and enabled Malawi to export grain to its less fortunate neighbors, Zimbabwe, Zambia, and Mozambique.

ZIMBABWE

The territory which offered the most potential for violence and instability was Rhodesia (after 1978 Zimbabwe-Rhodesia). The actions of members of the United Nations and the OAU, after Ian Smith's government declared its independence in November 1965, was an open invitation to activists. The economic boycott of Rhodesia did not support British Prime Minister Wilson's contention that this would bring the Rhodesians into line. It has damaged the economy of the breakaway state and made Smith's followers in the Rhodesian Front party more convinced that their actions were correct. All attempts by Britain to negotiate the problem foundered on its demands that the four million Africans be given a larger share in the government. The militant attitude of Kenneth Kaunda of Zambia who pressed the British to crush Rhodesia militarily did nothing to ease tensions in Central Africa. From May to August 1967, there were several guerrilla raids into the northern areas of Rhodesia. In the largest action in August, Rhodesian police killed over eighty guerrillas. This hit-and-run action continued well into 1968 but was eventually contained by the Rhodesian armed forces. The feeling of being assailed by the world led to a hardening of white Rhodesian attitudes. The new constitution of 1969 approved by a referendum confirmed this. Rhodesia became a republic with a two-house legislature. The new instruments provided for complex voting procedures to choose black and white representatives, but the white minority arranged to retain ultimate political authority in the foreseeable future. In 1966 the United Nations at the urging of British Prime Minister Harold Wilson voted economic sanctions against Rhodesia. These adversely affected Rhodesia's economy but not enough to bring the breakaway state again into the British Commonwealth. Petroleum products, heavy machinery, spare parts, and the thousands of items needed to maintain a modern state continued to reach Rhodesia from South Africa, Mozambique, and even Zambia. Rhodesia was able to find markets for its agricultural products, particularly tobacco, in a dozen different states. The effectiveness of the mineral embargo was severely damaged by the Byrd Amendment of 1971 which allowed the United States to continue its purchases of chrome. Despite extreme criticism, the Byrd Amendment was not withdrawn until March 1978. Economic factors eventually played a role in softening the attitudes of the Rhodesian Front government but not until the collapse of the Portuguese in Mozambique altered the entire geopolitical balance in southern and central Africa.

Successive British governments, stung by criticism from African leaders for not acting forcefully in 1965, continually sought some formula by which Ian Smith's government would be reconciled once again to British control. The Rhodesian Front leaders made clear that such a development was unlikely unless the British leaders gave up the demand for speedy enfranchisement of the Bantu majority. In March 1969, further emphasizing the break with Britain, the qualified voters of Rhodesia approved a new republican constitution. This new instrument of government provided for a two house legislature. Election to the important lower house was by a complex voting procedure by which fifty seats were allocated to the white community, eight to biracial constituencies, and eight members were chosen by tribal councils. At the first election Ian Smith's Rhodesian Front won all fifty of the seats alloted to the first roll. The party continued to hold all the white allocated seats in the subsequent elections of 1974 and 1975.

British Prime Minister Heath attempted further negotiations with Rhodesia in 1971. In November, Foreign Secretary Douglas-Home brought to his conference with Ian Smith a plan to phase out white control gradually over a period of years. Although Smith rejected this, he did agree to allow a British fact finding commission to come to Rhodesia and query both black and white Rhodesians on their desires for the future. The Pearce Commission sampled opinion in Rhodesia for three months beginning in January 1972. This polling was the cause of many demonstrations and clashes between police and Bantu. There were over fourteen deaths reported and the government detained more than 1500 persons including ex-Prime Minister Garfield Todd. The activities of the African National Council (ANC) and its leader, Bishop Abel Muzorewa, were sharply circumscribed. The report made public in May ended any hopes the Heath government might have had that the Bantu leaders would accept a slow devolution of power. It also indicated that the majority of Bantu rejected any education and property qualifications for the vote.

Guerrilla attacks from Zambia upon frontier areas were endemic throughout the late 1960s. These escalated sharply in 1972 as world pressure on Rhodesia increased. Rhodesia was condemned twice in 1970 and Rhodesian athletes were barred from participating in the 1972 Olympic games. In January 1973 Rhodesia closed its border with Zambia and although Smith's government later indicated a willingness to reopen it, President Kaunda refused and with a great loss to his state rerouted Zambia's copper shipments either to Angola or Tanzania. He also allowed the guerrillas to use Zambian sites as training and supply bases for their attacks into Rhodesia. There was an immediate buildup of guerrilla bases in Mozambique after it had become independent. It was along this 600 mile border that Rhodesia proved particularly vulnerable. The increasing insurgent activity caused the government to call up more reserves, develop special anti-insurgent teams, and get added police reinforcements from the Republic of South Africa. White farmers in the troubled zones either closed down or fortified their farms and transformed their workers into guards. In 1974 over 60,000 Africans were moved away from the border areas with Mozambique and resettled in fortified villages in the interior.

After the breakup of the coalition of black parties in 1976, guerrilla opposition became more organized. Those based in Zambia came under the direction of Joshua Nkomo while those in Mozambique were led by Robert Mugabe. Bolstered by world opinion and assured bases in friendly neighboring states, these insurgent forces had come to control much of the borderlands of northern and eastern Rhodesia. The Rhodesian forces struck back across the borders attempting to destroy the guerrilla sanctuaries. In late 1977 and again the following spring, Rhodesian units penetrated deep into Mozambique in hot pursuit of insurgent forces. The biggest raid into Zambia occurred in October 1978 when twelve base camps were raided and over 1,500 guerrillas killed.

The collapse of Portugal in southern Africa brought a profound change to the foreign policy of the Republic of South Africa. Prime Minister Vorster ceased his complete support of Ian Smith's policies and began to seek ways of getting moderate black leadership peacefully into power in Rhodesia rather than a completely hostile radical group. This change of attitude forced Smith in 1974 to agree to negotiate with the black politicians. Soon afterward three of the major African leaders met at Lusaka and developed an expanded working group under the leadership of Reverend Muzorewa. This, in turn, led to a brief cease-fire on the northern frontier. The peace offensive pushed by the unlikely tandem of Vorster and Kaunda continued throughout 1975. Vorster even met with the president of Zambia in a railway car on the Zambesi bridge and also conferred with Smith and his representatives a number of times. Despite all the effort, the talks failed partially due to the recalcitrance of Smith but more from the demand of the black Rhodesians supported by the OAU for immediate complete control of the country. After the breakdown of the diplomatic offensive, Reverend Muzorewa and another major Bantu leader, Reverend Ndabaningi Sithole, went into self-imposed exile and Joshua Nkomo was elected head of the ANC. His selection placed him in the forefront of further negotiations with Smith. Nkomo could do no better than his predecessor in gaining concessions from the Rhodesian Front and he grew increasingly radical in his demands.

The United States had become more involved in the affairs of central and southern Africa because of the Angolan crisis and in April 1976, Secretary of State Kissinger proposed a ten point program to solve the Rhodesian problem. In combination with continued pressure from Vorster of South Africa, he managed to get all parties to agree on a basic plan for future political development. Details were to be decided upon by a general meeting of the protagonists at Geneva. Differences between the Bantu leaders had split the black coalition and Muzorewa, Nkomo, Sithole, and Mugabe all represented differing points of view and constituencies by the time the Geneva Conference opened in October. The talks eventually ended in January 1978 because neither side would compromise on certain items. Smith was particularly adamant against turning over the defense forces to new Bantu commanders during any interim period. Later in the year he rejected another British and American plan because it called for sharing power with guerrilla leaders.

A shift of attitude took place after 1977 when Nkomo went into exile in Zambia and took direct charge of the insurgents there. He formed a loose coalition called the Patriotic Front with Mugube and his guerrillas in Mozambique. Muzorewa and Sithole, however, proved more tractable. In August when Smith announced that with guaranteed safeguards the white government was willing to grant the Bantu population control of the government, these leaders decided to cooperate. A four man executive council was established to act as a transitional government and the goal of full majority rule was set for early 1979. The members of this council were Smith, Muzorewa, Sithole, and an African appointed to represent traditional interests. Undoubtedly Smith and his white constituency had been forced to accept moderate black rule as an alternative to radical control. In October Smith and Sithole visited the United States and attempted to convince the State Department to accept the new coalition and stop giving support to the Patriotic Front. Few opinions were changed by this maneuver, and the new coalition regime prepared a constitution without the outside support they so desperately wanted. The new instrument of government provided for elections for a responsible government based upon a 100 member legislature.

The bulk of criticisms leveled at the compromise agreement was aimed at the special provisions for the protection of the white minority. The constitution reserved twenty-eight seats in the legislature and five ministerial posts for the whites. They also retained certain complex veto provisions over changes in the judiciary, civil service, and security. During the ten week election campaign for the new government, the guerrilla forces stepped up their activities and hundreds more died in the border fighting. Nkomo and Mugabe's threats, however, failed to discourage the voters. In April, over sixty percent of the 2.8 million qualified voters turned out to give Muzorewa's UANC party a resounding victory. Some of the lustre was taken from this victory by charges of corruption leveled by Sithole, Muzorewa's erstwhile partner in the executive. The United States and Britain remained adamant in their opposition to any government which did not represent the guerrillas and the economic boycott against Rhodesia was not lifted. The Patriotic Front forces in Zambia and Mozambique grew to over 50,000 by mid-1979 and they escalated their attacks, certain that they could bring down Muzorewa's government.

Bishop Muzorewa hoped that the new conservative government in Britain would move quickly to redeem its pre-election pledges and recognize his regime. However, Prime Minister Margaret Thatcher refused to do so and instead offered the good services of her government in mediating between the various factions. She proposed a general conference of all interested parties. African leaders, particularly Nyerere and Kaunda, were very important in persuading Mugabe and Nkomo to agree to the proposed open ended meeting to be held at Lancaster House in London. The British Foreign Secretary, Lord Carrington, moderated the six week long conference, and despite the acrimony, fundamental agreement between the factions was reached in late October 1979. Muzorewa agreed to the phasing out of his government, unilateral declaration of independence would be repealed, and the British would once again assume executive responsibility until free elections for a new government under a new constitution could be held. Major stumbling blocks to a final solution concerned integration of guerrilla forces into the regular defense force, and Mugabe and Nkomo threatened a number of times to break up the conference. After agreement was finally reached in November, Muzorewa's government was disbanded and Lord Soames, the new governor, officially reassumed British control over the territory on an interim basis. A British election commissioner was designated to organize the elections for the future government of Zimbabwe-Rhodesia. A small peacekeeping force of British troops was sent in to help police the cease fire. There were indications that not all the guerrillas were willing to abide by the agreement, and sporadic raids continued during the first months of Lord Soames's temporary government. It was obvious that the main obstacle to an ultimate settlement—the last ditch opposition of many of Ian Smith's followers—had been removed. Once the guerrilla leaders understood this they cooperated with Lord Soames and the election commission knowing that in time they would be recognized as the power in Rhodesia-Zimbabwe. The constitution as approved called for an elected legislature of 100 members and a responsible ministry headed by a prime minister. The special position of the 200,000 whites was entrenched by allowing them one-fifth of the seats in the House. White representatives were to be elected on a separate roll. The constitution guaranteed that no major alterations in the form of government could be undertaken until 1987.

The work of organizing the critical election went on with cooperation between the temporary government and Mugabe and Nkomo's forces with surprisingly few violent conflicts between the competitive groups. In these elections held on February 27–29, 1980, over ninety percent of those qualified voted. Mugabe's Zambia African National Union—Popular Front (ZANU-PF) gained sixty-three percent of the vote and won 57 seats. Surprisingly Reverend Muzorewa's UANC won only 3 seats. The rest of the elected seats were claimed by the Ndebele based Zambia African Peoples Union (ZAPU). At midnight April 17, the Union Jack was lowered, the last of the events which gave independence to this deeply troubled region, and Mugabe, the avowed Marxist, and his party thus controlled the still divided state. Mugabe proved to be more a pragmatist than an idealogue, being content at first with only cosmetic changes. One of those changes was to eliminate Rhodesia from the name of the state. Henceforth it would be Zimbabwe. Perhaps Mugabe had the example of Mozambique in mind whose economy had been all but destroyed by blindly following socialist schemes carried out by inexperienced administrators. He tried to assure the white population that the war was past and their rights and property would be safeguarded. Mugabe understood that he desperately needed to hold on to the educated whites who had the technical expertise in all fields. In particular he needed those 5,000 white farmers whose modern farms provided the bulk of profitable agricultural production. To further mollify the whites he included the head of the Rhodesian army during the war, General Walls, in his ministry and continued him in his military position.

The efforts of Mugabe's government in reconciling the white population to his regime were only partially successful. Many other black leaders were not as forgiving as he. Edgar Tekere, the Secretary General of ZANU-PF and Minister of Manpower was one of these. He led a group of ex-guerrillas in an attack on the farm of a sixty-eight year old white who was killed. In a celebrated case which embarrassed the government, Tekere was arrested in August 1980 and charged with murder. In December he was acquitted with two black judges overruling the guilty opinion of the one white judge. The subsequent removal of Tekere from the cabinet and later from leadership of the party did not convince many whites of the government's good intentions. The resignation of General Walls in July and his banishment for statements made about the war also seemed to indicate that Mugabe would not honor his promises. Then there was the ongoing problem of disarming the guerrillas and phasing them once again into civilian life either by providing them with jobs or land. This procedure was complicated by the state of the economy as well as the enmity between Nkomo and Mugabe's followers. However, armed bands of blacks in the countryside did not reassure white farmers. By February 1981 it was estimated that clashes among guerrillas had accounted for hundreds of fatalities. The final disarmament and integration of some of these men into the armed forces took well over a year. The result of all these factors was that by the end of 1980, approximately 2,000 whites were leaving the country every month. Despite all of Mugabe's efforts, this drain would continue. By 1986 there were only about one-half the number of whites as had been in the country at independence. Some observers believe that the white population will eventually stabilize at approximately 70,000 persons.

Far more disturbing immediately to the equilibrium of the state was the Shona-Ndebele rivalry which was reflected in the two major political parties. Nkomo, disappointed in the elections results, nevertheless accepted a post in the new government. This uneasy truce between the parties was broken in 1982 when Nkomo was accused of hoarding arms on his property in preparation for a coup and giving active support to guerrilla forces still operating in Matabeleland. Nkomo resigned from the ministry and accused Mugabe of trying to destroy ZAPU. There was an escalation of violence, looting, and robbery in Matabeleland and in June guerrillas directly attacked Mugabe's residence in Harare. The following month six European tourists were kidnapped and held hostage in western Matabeleland. A major airbase was attacked and thirteen planes, one-fourth of the airforce, were destroyed. In July Mugabe extended the state of emergency first proclaimed by Ian Smith's government and capital punishment was reinstated. The generalized unrest and sporadic violence continued through-out the rest of the year. Then Mugabe decided to act to end the problems in Matabeleland. Nkomo was stopped from leaving the country for a European conference and his passport was confiscated. Later he fled to Botswana and accused the government of planning his death. In January 1983 Mugabe sent the North Korean trained elite Fifth Brigade composed mainly of Shona into Matabeleland. Apparently this unit had *carte blanche* to root out dissidents and the soldiers took full advantage of their power. Church leaders and relief workers in Matabeleland later claimed that in the nine months the Brigade was posted there, it was responsible for 2,000 civilian deaths. Reverend Muzorewa in October was also arrested and charged with criticizing the government and sponsoring members of his party in secret military training. In August the six white officers of the airforce charged with complicity in the destruction of aircraft were acquitted by the High Court because their confessions were obtained by torture. They were subsequently rearrested on orders of the home affairs minister under the emergency regulations. Pressure from Great Britain and the United States eventually obtained their release. The government also moved against the press making it a criminal offense to report acts of terrorism or sabotage by security forces who were combatting terrorism.

It appeared in 1983 that the worst fears about the regime were about to be realized. Then Mugabe did an about face and moderated his tactics. In large part this reversal was due to the economic situation and the recognition that he had to depend for aid on those states that he was alienating by his harsh policies. The United States particularly resented Zimbabwe's condemnation of the Grenada operation and its abstention from the censure vote of Russia concerning the Korean airliner incident. United States aid which had not met Mugabe's expectations was decreased further. South Africa in response to Zimbabwe's position toward apartheid had already crippled the railway system by withdrawing its twenty-six locomotives which had been on loan. Permits for more than 20,000 Zimbabweans to work in South Africa were also cancelled. These specifics taken with continued weak commodity prices, inflation, three successive years of drought, and inflation meant that Zimbabwe was in deep economic distress. The situation worsened in 1984 when in addition to all other problems the government had to provide for more than 100,000 refugees from Mozambique. The low point in Zimbabwe's economy was 1983 when the government was forced to negotiate with the IMF, cutback government expenditures, and devalue the dollar. Although still in financial difficulties, the return of the rains after 1984 meant a rapid recovery for the agricultural sector.

Zimbabwe's relations with South Africa presented a study in pragmatic duplicity. Mugabe was as vocal as any African leader in denouncing apartheid, but he closely monitored the all civilian staffed office of the African National Congress in Harare. In August 1986 Mugabe went a step further in his war of words with South Africa. In a meeting with five other Commonwealth leaders he agreed to impose economic sanctions against the Republic. Despite the rhetoric of "paying the price," it was doubtful that Zimbabwe would depart from its policy of keeping political diplomacy separate from economic reality. The harsh fact remained that ninety percent of Zimbabwe's exports must pass through South Africa. Despite efforts to help Mozambique protect the alternate railroad to Beira, this line was subject to continued raids by Renamo guerrillas and was no substitute for the South African transport link. Just to emphasize the point of Zimbabwe's vulnerability, the South African government beginning in late 1986 ordered a slow down in the border inspections of all Zimbabwean goods in transit.

The announced decision by the ZANU-PF party congress in 1983 to move as quickly as possibly toward a socialist state was not welcomed by potential foreign investors. Through 1984 there was only one major investment in Zimbabwe undertaken by a large private firm. Relations with the United States, strained at best, reached a low point in mid-1986 when the American ambassador resigned. Before his replacement could arrive, the acting ambassador and visiting ex-President Jimmy Carter were treated to a speech filled with invective at an Independence Day celebration. Although Mugabe later apologized, the harm had been done. In September the United States government announced that it would provide no more financial aid to Zimbabwe and cancelled $13.5 million already provided for.

During the first five years of the 1980s, Mugabe had pursued the goal of a one party state only to be thwarted again and again by opposition from Nkomo and ZAPU. Nkomo who had resumed his seat in the legislature in August 1983 had no intention of submerging his and the interests of the Ndebele in a party whose leaders had sanctioned the excesses in Matabeleland in 1983 and again in 1984. However, Mugabe's position was strengthened slightly by the first postindependence elections which took place in June and July 1985. There was considerable evidence of government intimidation of Ndebele voters as Mugabe hoped to win the majority of seats in Matabeleland. ZANU-PF increased their number of seats in the House to sixty-four but was not able to break Nkomo's hold on the Ndebele areas. Although Bishop Muzorewa's party lost all three of their seats, Mugabe did not gain the seventy seats necessary to force a change in the constitution to recognize only one party. Mugabe, nevertheless, planned other major changes in the constitution. It had been agreed in 1979 that 1987 was the earliest date for any structural changes. Mugabe and the other ZANU-PF leaders looked forward to that date when they could rid themselves of the white minority separate roll which provided for inordinate white representation. The election of 1985 had confirmed the Conservative Alliance of Zimbabwe (CAZ) as the majority party of the white minority. This party led by Mugabe's old opponent, Ian Smith, which won fifteen of the twenty seats also gained the right to appoint ten whites to the forty member Senate. Mugabe swore that he would eliminate this special treatment of the dwindling white population. One step in that direction was the suspension of Smith from Parliament for twelve months for alleged inflamatory statements he made in South Africa. This move effectively brought to an end Smith's tempestuous twenty year political career. White political priviledge appeared to be near an end. The key question was whether this action would spur the flight of more badly needed white experts from the country. The other major political question concerning Zimbabwe in mid-1987 was whether Mugabe could achieve a peaceful acceptance of one party rule or whether this would begin a new cycle of violence in Matabeleland. He accomplished his goal by the approval of a new constitution providing for an executive president instead of the older responsible government format. Mugabe, chosen as the first such president, assumed that office on December 31, 1987. Earlier that month his chief rival, Nkomo, agreed to set aside past differences and to merge ZAPU into ZANU, thus practically assuring Mugabe's goal of a one party state.

LESOTHO, BOTSWANA, AND SWAZILAND

The one common factor which links together all the independent states of southern Africa is their dependency upon the Republic of South Africa. Despite the denunciations of the apartheid regime made by their political leaders or their well wishers in Africa, the United States, or Europe, the fact remains that each in some way is tied economically to the only industrial African state. This applies more to the former High Commission Territories—Lesotho, Botswana, and Swaziland—than any to the other neighboring states because of their proximity and poverty. However distasteful, they must depend upon the Republic. All are landlocked and must use the ports, roads, and railroads of South Africa. Despite the adherence of all to reviving Mozambique's rail system, the bulk of the imports and exports of each has to rely on South Africa's facilities. Capital poor Lesotho and Swaziland have in the past obtained a large portion of their private investment from their more affluent neighbor. Botswana, more fortunate because of mineral discoveries, nevertheless has seen substantial South African investment in the more habitable eastern regions of the country. Each state also receives a cash flow from its workers who are employed in South Africa.

Lesotho is the most dependent upon South Africa; its position is scarcely if any better than the independent areas of Bophuthatswana, the Ciskei, or Transkei. It is the poorest of the three former High Commission Territories having almost no mineral resources. Its once considerable timber stands have all but been eliminated. Only thirteen percent of the land of this highland kingdom is arable and much of it is rapidly being eroded. Traditional agriculture practiced by a majority of the population becomes less productive each year. Most of the capital in circulation comes from the 160,000 persons, one-half of the adult males, who work on the farms or in the mines in South Africa. Since Lesotho belongs to a customs union with the Republic, it received some rebates and there was also foreign aid which helped keep the state solvent. The value of imports normally exceeded Lesotho's exports by a factor of three to one. Lesotho's economy was obviously very fragile and vulnerable, a fact which its political leaders should have recognized at the beginning of its independence in 1966.

Lesotho is theoretically a constitutional monarchy with King Moshoeshoe II as head of state. However, the real power in this small enclave was, for almost twenty years, the Prime Minister, Lebua Jonathan, the leader of the Basuto National Party (BNP). There were few areas in Africa more controlled by one man. During the first election held after independence in 1970 when it became apparent that the rival Basuto Congress Party (BCP) would win, Jonathan declared the election and the constitution void. This act set the tone for much of the domestic violence which troubled Lesotho over the next fifteen years. An uprising against the BNP government in 1974 failed. Leaders of the opposing political parties fled the country, receiving sanctuary either in Mozambique or South Africa, and they campaigned against Jonathan's dictatorial regime. Young militants of the BCP created the Lesotho Liberation Army (LLA) and began a campaign of sabotage. In September 1981 the LLA claimed responsibility for a series of bomb explosions that damaged several commercial buildings in the capital city of Maseru as well as its airport facilities. Jonathan accused South Africa of supporting and encouraging the LLA which in all probability was correct. Lieutenant General Coetzee, chief of South Africa security, in response to Jonathan's policy of aiding the ANC stated that two could play the game of giving sanctuary to rebels. After 1981 there was an escalation of low level guerrilla action to force the prime minister to hold elections. The government responded by kidnapping opposition leaders still in the country. Jonathan's political enemies charged that the special paramilitary troops were responsible for murdering some of his key opponents.

Jonathan's autocratic rule was ended not by the actions of his Sotho opponents, but by his aggressive policy with regard to South Africa. Despite Lesotho's economic dependence, Jonathan aligned his government with the goals of the "front line" states, spoke out against apartheid, and allowed the ANC to establish bases in Lesotho. This posture called forth intermittent South African retaliation. In 1974 South Africa cut back on oil deliveries and over 10,000 Basuto were not rehired. This example of South Africa's power was sufficient to stop most anti-South African activity for half a decade. In the fall of 1983 at the main crossover point, the Maseru Bridge, South African customs officials staged a slowdown. They diligently searched every car, backing up traffic for miles. They also briefly cut off Lesotho's supplies of fresh food. Despite such examples, Jonathan's government continued its dangerous game of annoying South Africa.

By 1980 the ANC had built a substantial base in Maseru under the protection of the BNP. Warnings from South Africa were ignored. The ANC was not expelled and in 1982 and again in 1985 South African forces raided the ANC holdings in Maseru. In response to South African pressure and the growing unpopularity of his government, Jonathan in 1983 promised that national elections would be held by the end of the following year. His opponents claimed that he had no intention of carrying out this promise because a necessary census could not be completed before 1986. The election was finally scheduled for 1985 but the rules were such that opposition candidates found it almost impossible to be nominated. All seven of the opposition parties ultimately refused to participate and as a result only BNP candidates were nominated for the sixty elected seats in the legislature. Jonathan then declared the election unnecessary and cancelled the voting.

South African officials decided to act decisively to bring an end to Lesotho's open and clandestine support of the ANC. In December 1985 they imposed a crippling total economic blockade which lasted for only three weeks because Major General Justin Lekhanya, head of the 1500 man army, decided to act and brought Jonathan's two decade rule to an end. He, as head of the Military Council, immediately ordered the expulsion of all ANC members and this action led to a normalization of relations with South Africa. The result was that the needed supplies of all types could begin to flow into Lesotho again and South Africa once more began seriously to consider funding of the Highlands Water project which would bring water and hydro-electric power to Lesotho and, more important, to South Africa. Despite the presence of a pragmatic instead of a doctrinaire regime, Lesotho's long-term future could only be described as desperate. The land is wearing out. In 1970 there were only 2000 landless families. Ten years later there were 35,000 and the flight from the land continued in the 1980s. This factor made the prospect of employment in South Africa even more crucial. However this source of work was also threatened. If international sanctions against South Africa have any significant impact, this will affect the employment of Basutos. Even more threatening is the increasing mechanization of South Africa's mines. In 1981 the mines employed almost 124,000 persons. This number had fallen to 102,000 two years later and continued to decline slowly in the ensuing decade. It is doubtful that Lesotho could long survive without the funds supplied by its itinerant workers.

Swaziland shared some of the problems of Lesotho. It, too, was landlocked, surrounded by South Africa and dependent to a large extent on the good will of the Republic. There were, however, many significant differences between the two states. The most important was the relative prosperity of Swaziland. There are minerals present in exportable quantities of which asbestos and iron ore are the most valuable. The real wealth of Swaziland lay in its agricultural productivity. Foreign investment and management, mainly from South Africa which began long before independence, resulted in expansion and diversification of agriculture. Plantation crops such as rice, cotton, sugar, as well as timber, account for most of the $350 million in exports. Tourism became very important in the 1970s when the first casinos and nightclubs were opened in the capital, Mbabane. These gave weekend tourists a chance to indulge themselves in activities forbidden in Calvinist South Africa.

Another contrast to Lesotho has been the political stability of Swaziland. King Sobhuzu II during his long reign first as the paramount chief under British tutelage and later as king had the undivided loyalty of most of the citizens. He created a political and economic atmosphere which welcomed much Westernization while retaining traditional Swazi values. The *Imbokodvo* party, formed to contest the first elections for the Legislative Council after independence, represented the royal views and dominated that election as well as those in 1967 and 1972. In 1973 he dissolved the legislature which from its inception had been none too popular with the Swazis. He claimed that the Westminster style system was not based upon Swazi traditions, and not until 1979 was there a replacement. Then the king provided a new, nonpartisan parliament, some of whose members were chosen by indirect elections and some appointed by the king. Although this system did not dispense with political parties, it did strengthen even further the position of the king and his council, the *Liqoqo*. Sobhuza died in late 1982 and this occasioned an internal power struggle which, however, never spread far beyond the palace. The *Liqoqo* appointed a new Prime Minister, Prince Bhekimpi, and a Queen Regent, Ntombi. During the period before the coronation of a new king, Ntombi removed a number of imagined opponents from positions of power, particularly those with modernizing views. In April 1986 after much ceremony, the new eighteen year old King Mswati II was crowned. Soon after he showed that he intended to rule on his own by dissolving the *Liqoqo* and reconstituting it.

Sobhuza and the new king realized how vulnerable Swaziland was and how important it was to maintain stable relations with South Africa. Consequently, there was little official opposition to a nonaggression pact when it was first proposed by South Africa. The ANC had established itself in Mbabane as early as 1965 but its position in the early 1980s had become tenuous. Swazi security forces, partially because of South African pressure, moved against the activists. Eighty-six members of the ANC were arrested and deported to Tanzania. Another example of the good relations between the two states was South Africa's abortive attempt to return lands claimed by Swaziland. If this move had been successful the transfer of land to the north and west of Swaziland would have given it access to the sea. It would also have rid South Africa of almost one million black inhabitants of the Kwa Ngwane and Ingwavuma territories. However, the furor raised by natives of those areas was so great that the plan was eventually abandoned. To underscore the ongoing good relations the South African Foreign Minister, R. F. Botha, in March 1985 opened a trade mission in Mbabane which was duplicated soon after by Swaziland in Johannesburg despite the OAU rules forbidding member states from having diplomatic relations with South Africa.

Botswana, the largest of the three former High Commission Territories, although much of its land area is desert or semidesert, has been the most prosperous. Although the drought of the 1980s following quickly an outbreak of hoof and mouth disease, struck the cattle industry very hard, other sectors of the economy continued to flourish. Thousands of citizens of Botswana work in South Africa but the state does not depend as heavily on their earnings as does Swaziland and Lesotho. The discovery of high grade diamonds soon after independence combined with quantities of nickel, copper, potash, and coal gave Botswana products in demand on the world markets. South African capital became readily available for the exploitation of these resources. A stable and frugal government held inflation in the 1980s to less than ten percent per year and insured that the currency, the pula, remained one of Africa's strongest. Realizing its vulnerability because all of its imports and exports must pass through South Africa, Botswana's government belonged to the customs union with South Africa, Lesotho, and Swaziland. The government's plans for rural development were set back by the drought and the country needed foreign aid in foodstuffs, mainly grain, during the worst of the drought years. Despite such problems the first twenty years of independence witnessed many basic improvements in the life of most of Botswana's 1¼ million people. In spite of the drought, the clean water program benefitted most of the villages of eastern Botswana. In 1966 there were only two miles of tarred road in the entire nation. Twenty years later there were more than 1,500 miles of such all weather roads linking together every major village. The government also developed a very ambitious elementary and secondary school program.

Botswana has been one of three African areas previously controlled by Great Britain which continued to function the way the framers of the early constitutions had envisioned. It remained a parliamentary republic with an elected president and thirty-six member National Assembly. Although the Botswana Democratic Party (BDP) under the leadership first of Sir Seretse Khama and later Quett K. J. Masire who succeeded him as president, has dominated the government, there was no attempt to make Botswana a one party state. The Botswana National Front (BNF), Botswana People's Party (BPP) and Botswana Independence Party (BIP) were allowed to contest each election without the coercion so noticeable elsewhere in Africa. The government has encouraged the restoration of the *kgotla*, a traditional decision-making process whereby judicial and political decisions were made in open forum in local communities. Plans have been made to integrate this traditional practice into the more formal system. Relations with South Africa had remained generally harmonious until the Republic in 1984 began pressing for a nonaggression treaty similar to those signed by Swaziland and Mozambique. President Masire resisted, claiming that Botswana had never harbored South African rebels so there was no need for such a formal treaty. South Africa was nevertheless convinced that the ANC had an operating headquarters in Gaborone and in May 1986 their commandos attacked a suburb of the capital killing fourteen alleged ANC members. President Masire protested this invasion and continued to deny that Botswana was a base for the ANC. During its period of emergency, South Africa was prone to strike at all suspected ANC sanctuaries and the attack was in all probability a warning to Botswana of its military and economic vulnerability.

NINE
Troubled independence: East and Northeastern Africa

East Africa

TANZANIA

President Julius Nyerere's government in Tanzania has been involved in a far-reaching political and economic reorientation of the state since 1967. This plan was announced after a high-level conference between government and TANU party leaders at Arusha in February 1967. The government subsequently took over all banks, the food processing industry, and many businesses to assure the continued socialization of the economy for the good of all the people. Foreigners were to be eased out of jobs which Tanzanians could hold. Swahili was also to be utilized wherever possible in government, business, and the elementary schools. However revolutionary these government actions were, there was little obvious opposition. There were only two examples of a potential deep-seated dissatisfaction with Nyerere's regime. In 1968 Oscar Kambona, the minister of local government, resigned and fled to London where he accused Nyerere of dictatorship and dogmatism. Far more serious as an indication of future trouble was the arrest in September 1969 of Abdullah Hanga and the former Tanzanian ambassador to the United States, Othman Shariff, along with sixteen others. They were executed in October with two others who also had been charged with conspiracy against the state. Although Nyerere and Vice-President Karume announced in April 1969, on the fifth anniversary of the Tanzanian union, that the merger was working well, Zanzibar continued as a possible source of division to Tanzania.

The government of Zanzibar continued to be far more harsh and doctrinaire than that of the mainland. There have been no elections on the island even though the mainland has had a number of general elections. In 1970 the entire judicial system of the island was reorganized with power given to three-man political courts. No defense attorneys were permitted. In May 1971, Vice-President Karume announced that nineteen persons had been executed for treason. In the following year Karume was assassinated and the Zanzibar Revolutionary Council detained hundreds of suspects. Eventually in 1974 thirty-four persons were sentenced to death for the assassination. The mainland government reacted differently to the crisis. It refused to hand over eighteen accused persons to the People's Courts because there was no assurance that they would have a fair trial. The two areas seemed no closer to an actual union of their politics in 1978 than they had at the beginning of the union despite the merging in 1977 of TANU and the Afro-Shirazi Party into a single entity entitled *Chama cha Mapinduzi* or Single Revolutionary Party.

President Nyerere announced on the tenth anniversary of the Arusha declaration that Tanzania was far short of reaching its goal of agricultural self-sufficiency. This was partly due to resistance by traditional Africans to the *ujamaa* village concept and relative inexperience of Tanzanian managers of the nationalized firms and industries. More crippling than all else was the rise in the price of all imported goods in the late 1970s. The oil producing nations treated developing areas in the same manner as more highly developed states. For Tanzania the increase in the price of petroleum meant wiping out its small budget surplus and forcing the state to go into debt despite budgetary stringencies. The Chinese in October 1970 began construction of the 1,116 mile railway connecting Dar es Salaam with Zambia. The railway was completed and formally turned over to Tanzania in July 1976. A combination of low prices for copper and inefficient management of the railway has meant lower profits to the railway than at first expected.

Julius Nyerere was one of the major spokesmen for the liberation movements in Africa. He granted use of Tanzania territory to the FRELIMO guerrillas and has given some aid to those who opposed the white government of Rhodesia. It was somewhat ironic that this champion of the nonviolent approach to Tanzanian problems would give unequivocal backing to the revolutionaries. Even more surprising to some observers has been the hard line taken against his neighbors, particularly Uganda. He opposed the Amin regime since its inception, and in 1971 gave sanctuary to the ex-president of Uganda, Milton Obote. In 1972 there was a brief flurry of fighting with Ugandan troops along the northwest border. More serious attacks from Uganda occurred the following year before a general agreement was signed at Addis Ababa in October. Ill feelings persisted and Tanzania was one of three states to boycott the OAU summit meeting in 1975 when it was held at Kampala. In early 1977 Tanzania, angered at Kenya for its actions in helping to close down East African Airways, decided to close its borders with its northern neighbor. This action effectively brought to an end the East African Community which had at one time held such promise for regional cooperation. Underscoring this breakup was the decision of President Amin of Uganda to invade Tanzania again in the fall of 1978. After some sharp fighting, the drive was blunted and Tanzanian and rebel Uganda forces invaded Uganda. Tanzanian forces bore the brunt of the fighting which resulted in the capture of Kampala and the overthrow in mid-April of Nyerere's old adversary. The Ugandan provisional governments of Yussuf Lule was a reflection of Tanzanian support and even after his resignation, Nyerere continued to have considerable influence over the new government of Godfrey Binaisa.

Nyerere's plan for remedying Tanzania's ills despite some limited success, notably in education, was largely a failure. It resulted in the growth of a bureaucracy generally out of touch with the reality of life in the countryside. One major reason for the lack of success of the *ujamaa* village scheme for the reorganization of agriculture was that it was dictated and run by these bureaucrats with little input from the villagers who conformed to the plans only when necessary and then in a half-hearted manner. The rise in the price of petroleum products which cost the state over fifty percent of foreign exchange and subsequent high inflation in the 1970s undermined the ability of Tanzania to keep from going more deeply into debt to foreign creditors. The drought years from 1979 to 1984 created near economic chaos in some areas, particularly in the more arid southern sections. Nationalization of production placed politicians and unskilled managers in charge of the financial and manufacturing sectors of the country with a general fall of productivity. In a capitalistic world market environment Tanzania was chronically short of capital either to develop its own industry or even to purchase the necessary raw materials or spare parts. The result was that Tanzania's already inadequate industrial sector was by the mid-1980s operating at approximately twenty-five percent of capacity. The black market flourished and the nation's transportation system was in shambles.

Nyerere and his government were aware of the many problems but because of their doctrinaire commitment to the socialist schemes, were unable to correct them. In many cases all that was done was to issue proclamations from Dar es Salaam urging the people to support those plans which had already been proved to be inadequate. Tanzania appealed to the IMF and World Bank for assistance but balked at putting into effect the stringent guidelines necessary before any substantial help would be forthcoming. Nyerere was particularly vocal in stressing that these guidelines were in direct conflict with the aims of his socialist state. Nyerere's realistic enunciation of Tanzania's problems caught the attention of the world and he was praised for a wise, far-seeing statesman, but generally without reference to the fact that Tanzania was one of the twenty-five least developed countries in the world and its economic production had declined at an average rate of six percent every year after 1982.

The approach to tourism was illustrative of Nyerere's attitudes. He understood that Tanzania was not receiving its fair share from tourism since most of the wild animal safaris originated in Nairobi. Tourists who visited Serengeti or Ngorongoro left behind in Tanzania only a fraction of what they had spent in Kenya. Nyerere's solution was typically destructive. In 1977 he closed the border with Kenya. All tourists to the great game parks in Tanzania would be forced to deal with the Tanzanian Tourist Corporation and begin their visit at Dar es Salaam. In addition the state spent large sums on developing tourist facilities, and where there was only one national park at independence, there were sixteen by 1985. However, tourists did not flock to the new facilities. In the first year after the border was closed there was a fifty percent reduction of visitors and it was not until 1985 that the number once again reached the 1976 level.

The political system, although plagued by inefficiency and some corruption, was without the internecine quarrels that so characterized many African states. Nyerere as head of state and party chief attempted, in general successfully, to allow political debate within the ruling *Chama Cha Mapinduzi* party. The system allowed challenges to incumbents within the one party system. For example, in the 1980 election more than one-half of the incumbent legislators were voted out of office. A new party constitution provided a secret ballot for election of all major offices and the powers of the party and government were separated and more clearly defined. This did not mean that there was no political infighting. Although noticeable on the higher levels on the mainland, it was much worse on Zanzibar. The island had most of the same problems as the mainland compounded by a strong Islamic movement and the belief of many that Zanzibar should declare its independence. The leader of the Zanzibar Revolutionary Council and Vice-President of Tanzania, Aboud Jumbe, was forced to resign his office after the discovery that he was deeply involved in the separatist movement. He was succeeded by Hassan al Myini, a mainlander committed to making the strange union work.

Nyerere had informed an incredulous party in 1980 that he would soon retire as president. He was persuaded by his associates and also the realities of Tanganyika's economic situation at that time to continue in office. However, in the spring of 1984 he announced that he would not stand for reelection, resulting in rivalry among various senior members of government. The leading candidate, Edward Sokoine, the prime minister, was killed in an automobile accident which left the field to Salim Ahmed Salim, the foreign minister, and Myini. Nyerere finally retired as president on November 5, 1985, retaining his position as party chairman. In the elections of the previous month Myini received ninety-two percent of the votes largely based on his record as president of Zanzibar.

There was an almost immediate change in the attitude of the government. Myini was not as doctrinaire as Nyerere. He had shown this on Zanzibar when he returned part of the economy to private ownership and attempted to secure outside aid to expand a clove oriented economy. Myini as president of Tanzania moved to ease some of the socialist schemes. Although *ujamaa* remained the core of agricultural development he allowed some of the large sisal plantations to pass into private hands. He recognized the short-term need for *ulanguzi*, the unofficial economy which allowed the low paid government servants to spend their free time in other sideline businesses and on their own small farms. Cooperatives were reestablished and farmers urged to increase food production. There was a dramatic increase in village based production after 1985 because rainfall returned to normal amounts.

The most dramatic change was the turnaround with regard to the IMF. The Tanzanian shilling by 1985 was officially pegged at eighteen to the dollar whereas it has been eight in 1979. The inflation rate was nearly forty percent and service on the $2 billion external debt took thirty percent of the recurrent budget. Myini was prepared to accept the IMF suggestions resisted by Nyerere for seven years. That meant cutting back on agricultural subsidies and reducing real imports by fifty percent and trying to cut the size of the inflated bureaucracy. The shilling was also devalued by two-thirds and a foreign currency auction similar to that in Zambia was established. The agreement with the IMF in mid-1986 resulted in the IMF immediately extending credit to help service the debt and support the proposed $4.5 billion Economic Recovery Program. At a meeting of the donors in Paris, $130 million was pledged and the World Bank provided $100 million in loans.

Another example of Myini's more pragmatic attitude was the improvement in relations with Uganda and Kenya. At a March 1985 meeting at Arusha of economic ministers of the three states, an agreement was reached to build a new powerline from the Owens dam in Uganda into power hungry northwestern Tanzania. Rail and maritime services with Uganda were restored. The open border with Kenya allowed normal trade between the two countries to resume. Myini's pragmatic approach, although opposed in part by Nyerere and other senior officials of the party, appeared to have halted Tanzania's economic decline. Like other African states which had attempted a total socialistic system, Tanzania was leaning in the direction of privatization and more economic freedom for its citizens.

KENYA

Kenya was, until mid-1969, a model of decorum and stability in East Africa. In 1966 at President Kenyatta's urging, the two-house parliament was converted into a 168 seat unicameral legislature. The government's handling of the Indian question was popular in Kenya. Britain's limit on immigration forced Indians to decide within two years whether to become citizens of Kenya. Kenyatta's firmness caused Somalia in 1967 to call off the guerrilla attacks in the northern territories. Another KANU triumph was the constitutional reform which provided that upon the death of the president, the vice-president would automatically succeed to that office until a general election could be held. Kenya's economy, more balanced than any of its neighbors, provided Kenyatta with a firm base on which to frame more moderate policies than those followed in Tanzania or Uganda.

Kenya's stability is fragile. The Luo-Kikuyu rivalry, although masked, is real. The dismissal of Oginga Odinga from KANU and the government and his subsequent exile showed Kenyatta's fear of the radical Luo. Those concerns were further confirmed after the assassination of Tom Mboya, the young Luo minister of economic planning, in July 1969. Government apprehension and execution of the guilty Kikuyu did not end Luo dissatisfaction. On October 25, there was a major riot in Nairobi which caused the deaths of eleven persons. Kenyatta immediately proscribed the Luo-based Kenya Peoples Union and arrested a number of its leaders. By the close of 1969 the overt dissatisfaction with Kenyatta's government had passed. However, in 1975 Kenya's internal order was again disturbed. This time it was the mysterious death of a vocal critic of Kenyatta's regime. The government did not act quickly enough to allay the rumors of KANU complicity. This Kariuki affair showed how vulnerable even Kenyatta was to divisive rumors. Only the speedy jailing of many of his critics ended the agitation.

Kenya's relations with its neighbors in the 1970s were stormy. Early in the decade President Amin of Uganda lost no opportunities to insult Kenya. This antipathy reached its height after Kenya gave permission to Israel to use the Nairobi airport after their raid on Entebbe in July 1976. Amin accused Kenya of being privy to the plot and initiated border incidents. Kenyatta retaliated by cutting off Uganda's oil supply and demanding immediate payment in advance for transit costs for all Uganda's imports. This hostility continued for almost a year before Amin agreed to Kenya's terms and oil shipments were resumed. In February

1977 Tanzania closed its border to Kenya. Although the move hurt Tanzania more than Kenya, there were still some adjustments which had to be made in the tourist industry.

On August 22, 1978, Jomo Kenyatta, one of the most respected of all African leaders, died at the age of eighty-eight. Many observers feared that this would signal a struggle for power between the leaders of the two dominant groups in Kenya. Although still a possibility, the immediate fears did not prove warranted. His long time vice-president, Daniel arap Moi, acted as the interim head of state until being sworn in as Kenya's second president in mid-October. His close association with Kenyatta and the fact that he was a Kalenjin, not one of the major tribal groups in Kenya, presumably gave him a chance at the beginning to avert a major confrontation between the Kikuyu and Luo. At first Moi was conciliatory to potential rivals within the party, knowing that he had succeeded one of the legendary figures in modern African history. He made no radical changes in the government's attitude in economic or foreign policy. In 1980 Kenya was viewed by many as the model African state. Foreign investment had created considerable wealth. The new industrial centers were thriving as was the agricultural sector. Nairobi had been transformed by the influx of foreign money. Much of the investment came from United States firms and agencies. A fair amount came also from Israel whose technicians in a variety of fields had helped the economic development of Kenya. Moi continued to court these two powerful friends. An agreement in 1980 granted the United States the right to use Nairobi airport and also Mombasa as a base for its navy. Moi in 1982 also gained a significant victory when he achieved the normalization of relations with the Tanzanian government which led to the opening of the borders to its less prosperous southern neighbor.

However, beneath the calm surface there were deep social, economic, and political problems. The new wealth which flowed into the country was not evenly distributed. Forty percent of Kenya's wealth was controlled by only ten percent of the population. Corruption and inefficiency in the bureaucracy were apparent everywhere. Kenya's birthrate was one of the world's highest, the population increasing by an estimated four percent each year. The unemployment rate was very high, particularly in the capital city whose population had reached 1¼ million persons and whose streets were crowded with the poor. Nairobi, the hub of East African tourism and once viewed by foreign visitors as one of the safest cities in Africa, had by the mid-1980s gained the opposite reputation. Roving bands of thieves operated openly in various parts of the country. Of more immediate consequence than all other problems was the fact that the economy, once so robust, was failing. In the 1970s the growth rate was a fairly constant six percent per year based largely upon profits from a wide variety of exports including coffee, tea, sugar cane, rice, pyrethrum, and cattle. The decline of world demand for some of these products and generally falling commodity prices were responsible for this recession. By the mid-1980s there was a serious foreign exchange problem. In 1984 there was an imbalance of imports over exports of $300 million and Kenya, once self-sufficient in grain, had to import 1.5 million tons and there were food lines in some urban areas.

The government reacted to the economic problem by devaluing Kenya's currency, prohibiting the export of any grain, and borrowing from European and

United States agencies. The worsening economic situation, however alarming to Moi and his associates, was not of the same order as the problems faced by most African governments. By comparison Kenya remained wealthy, but the economic situation undergirded the growing opposition to Moi and his harsh reaction to such criticism. University students were at the forefront of much early vocal criticism. However, they were relatively powerless and Moi reacted to their complaints by closing the schools, particularly the University of Nairobi, a number of times. Student leaders were arrested or discovered that exile was preferable to jail. Some of them became involved in the Mwakenya clandestine movement. The one event which perhaps changed Moi's political stance more than any other was the abortive coup of August 1982. Organized by disgruntled members of the Kenya airforce, it was swiftly contained by army units hurried to Nairobi. Although parts of Nairobi suffered heavy damage from the fighting and more than 250 persons were killed, the coup never seriously threatened the government. However, it conditioned Moi to fear further coups and to rid himself of potential political rivals within KANU.

The five years after the coup witnessed Moi securing his position by ousting potential rivals and closing the gap between government and party. The most celebrated object of Moi's aggressive policy was that of Charles Njonjo, the minister for constitutional affairs and former attorney general. Njonjo, a Kikuyu and former close associate of Kenyatta, was recognized as a major power within the government and a man well known for his pro-British attitudes. This was turned against him by Moi and his associates who in early 1984 accused him of conspiring with a foreign power to overthrow the government. Pro-Moi groups circulated the rumor that Njonjo was implicated in the assassination of Tom Mboya. After much public discussion Njonjo was indicted. After seeing Njonjo thoroughly discredited, Moi pardoned him in December. By this time Moi had engineered the expulsion of fifteen heretofore important members of KANU including two former cabinet ministers. The jails were filled with those who were accused of opposing the government. The Preservation of Public Security Act gave the authorities the right to detain any person without trial for an indefinite period. The president also consolidated his power base in the party. All civil servants were required to join the party by January 1, 1986, and in August a decision was made that in all future elections the secret ballot would be dispensed with. Voters would have to declare publicly their choice, thus opening the way for further intimidation.

Despite the economic situation, it appeared on the surface that Moi's position was unassailable, but there was growing opposition to the dictatorial domination by the party and president. Moi had alienated people from both ends of the political spectrum. The most important opposition to the government was from a clandestine organization calling itself Mwakenya (Patriotic Front for the Liberation of Kenya). Similar to the earlier Mau Mau, it was a secret organization where oaths were administered. It was suspected of being a continuation of the Twelfth of December Movement which had been very active before the 1982 coup attempt. Its main function through 1987 was to provide propaganda to the masses of people in order to undermine the government. Its newspaper *Mpatanishi* (the Arbiter) appeared everywhere, even in government offices. The full weight of the government's coercive power was directed at stamping out Mwakenya. Moi denounced it as a subversive organization run by the educated to the detriment of the country. Dozens of persons were arrested including nineteen who were either students or instructors at the University. Given the economic and political climate of Kenya where Moi's government appeared to be moving toward a one party police state, it is likely that Mwankenya or some other secret organization would, despite police actions, continue to function. The border difficulties with Uganda which first surfaced in 1987 appeared to some observers as staged partly to draw public attention away from President Moi. If so, it could prove dangerous. The small scale fighting which occurred in mid-December which resulted in Kenya's expulsion of Uganda's ambassador could very easily escalate into a full scale war.

UGANDA

In neighboring Uganda, the question of the relationship between the rights of sovereignty of the kabaka of Buganda and the power of the central government prevented any real political stability. In May 1966, Prime Minister Obote sent the army into Buganda and forced the kabaka, Sir Edward Mutesa II, to flee the country. A state of emergency was proclaimed throughout Buganda which enabled the central government to dispense with the usual formalities of democratic rule. In September 1967, a new constitution was issued which gave Uganda a republican government with an executive president. The traditional kingdoms of Bunyoro, Buganda, Toro, and Ankole were abolished. The existence of large numbers of supporters of the kabaka in Buganda kept the state of emergency in force until the beginning of 1970. In September 1969, former Prime Minister Benedicto Kiwanuku was arrested and charged with sedition and libel. The death of the kabaka in London in November increased the tension within Uganda. On December 18, President Obote was seriously wounded in an attempted assassination. Dissatisfaction with Obote's consolidation plans continued to develop and on January 25, 1971, the army led by Major-General Idi Amin took control of the government. Tanzania granted the deposed president asylum.

General Amin was immediately given full executive powers. To this was added legislative authority when the National Assembly was dissolved. The coup at first was very popular. Amin promised fundamental changes in the government which would benefit all segments of society. The central government attempted to ameliorate the dissatisfaction of Buganda, corrupt officials were dismissed, and there was a rollback of Obote's socialist program. However, the army was also trebled in size to a force of over 20,000 and Amin later asked for and received sophisticated arms from Libya and the Soviet Union. The first concrete indication of a substantial change in the military regime's attitude was the expulsion of the Asians. In Uganda as in the other East African territories, Asians controlled most of the mid-level business establishments. They were disliked by most Africans and posed a very real economic and political problem for all the governments of East Africa. Amin, without reference to individual injustice or the damage to Uganda's economy, ordered the 60,000 resident aliens to leave the country within ninety days. Uganda also broke relations with Israel, expelled the British High Commissioner, and moved to improve relations with the Arab bloc states. Libya in particular lent considerable financial and military aid to Uganda. General Amin's public statements became more bombastic and aggressive. These were accompanied by forcing border incidents upon Tanzania and Kenya, continued nationalization of foreign firms, and irrational acts such as the brief detention of 112 Peace Corp volunteers who were in transit to Zaire.

By the time of the OAU summit at Kampala in 1975 where Amin was to be chosen titular president, it was obvious that the Amin regime was dictatorial, cruel, and quixotic. Stories of false imprisonment, torture, and murder began to gain currency throughout Africa. Some agencies estimated that by the close of 1978 over 100,000 persons had been killed by Amin's soldiers. The groups which bore the brunt of this oppression for a long time were the Buganda. Then in 1977 Amin began a purge of the Lango and Acholi people. Even worse was the killing of the educated, many of whom had originally supported the regime. Cabinet ministers, university professors, army officers, the Anglican archbishop of Uganda, and even members of Amin's family all disappeared under mysterious circumstances. Amin, by now named president for life, enjoyed baiting the British. In 1975 he arrested a British lecturer, Denis Hills, who was subsequently sentenced to death. Before releasing him, Amin publicly humiliated Hills and forced the British Foreign Office into a subservient position in order to save the life of their national. Amin later created a new award called the Highest Order of the Conqueror of the British Empire and presented it to himself. In 1977 he made preliminary moves threatening United States citizens still resident in Uganda. He ordered them all to Kampala. Diplomacy and the presence of the aircraft carrier *Enterprise* off the Kenya coast made him reconsider.

President Amin gained the most notoriety from his role in the hijacking of an Air France plane in June 1976. The plane, after its capture by Palestinian nationalists, was landed at Entebbe airport. There the crew and 258 passengers, many of them Israeli citizens, were kept in the main building while the terrorists' demands were passed on to Israel. During this time Amin made a number of appearances and assured the prisoners that he would handle the problem and assure their safety. However, he gave the impression not only that he condoned the hijacking, but was an active spokesman for the terrorists. This situation led to the famous Entebbe raid by Israel forces on July 3–4 which resulted in the liberation of most of the passengers. The commandos destroyed the bulk of Uganda's modern airforce on the ground and the Uganda army suffered considerable casualties. His prestige dealt a harsh blow, Amin broke relations with Kenya which had allowed the Israeli planes to land at Nairobi. One British national, Dora Bloch, a Jewish passenger on the plane, had been hospitalized before the raid. After the raid she disappeared from the hospital and was reported to have been murdered by Ugandan soldiers. Britain then severed diplomatic relations with Uganda on July 28.

Precise details are unavailable, but Uganda's economy by 1978 appeared to be in a shambles. No suitable group of entrepreneurs had taken the place of the Asians, and the depradations of the soldiers had sharply restricted agricultural production. Some observers believed that Amin staved off disaster because of large loans and grants made by Libya and communist bloc states combined with the increased world wide demand for coffee which had taken all of Uganda's stockpiles by 1978. Amin's troubles nevertheless continued to mount. The United States placed a boycott on Ugandan coffee.

Late in 1978 Amin decided to use a time honored method of diverting attention from his failures and he attacked Tanzania once again. This invasion appeared to have been ill-conceived for the Tanzanian forces aided by Ugandan guerrillas loyal to Obote threw back Amin's forces and then launched an attack directed toward Kampala. To the surprise of most observers, the Ugandan army crumpled. Even the Libyan troops which had been provided by Amin's benefactor, Qaddafi, fell back before the two invading columns of Ugandan exile guerrillas and Tanzanian troops. Mityana fell in late March, severing western Uganda from Kampala, and after two weeks of skirmishing, the capital fell in mid-April. Those few troops loyal to Amin made a last stand in the Acholi area the following month, but by that time the self-styled president for life had fled the country. A provisional government was immediately formed by the Uganda National Liberation Front, and Yusuf Lule, a former chancellor of Makerere University, was named as president. Lule resigned less than ten weeks later and Godfrey Binaisa, a former attorney-general under Obote, became the new head of state. Uganda's problems were severe—the results of years of maladministration by the murderous Amin regime.

Binaisa inherited a nation in shambles whose economy had been all but destroyed and whose many tribes and nations had retreated into their own ethnic particularism. Crime and violence of all types was rampant, particularly in the capital, Kampala. Binaisa's government could do little to reverse the country's downward spiral without consulting the senior military officers in the small, ill trained Ugandan army and the leaders of the Tanzanian military. Charges of favoritism for the southern tribes in government appointments and financial aid combined with the army's opposition finally brought down Binaisa's impotent regime in May 1980. Paulo Muwenga, the labor minister in Binaisa's cabinet, was chosen to head the government. He was a Ganda and his selection by the military was due in part to a desire to mollify that powerful nation. The real power, however, rested with the Military Commission which after postponing promised elections, finally allowed them to take place in December. The commission had decided to allow any political party to participate. The two strongest parties which emerged were the Democratic Party (DP) and the People's Congress Party (PCP). The latter was headed by the former president, Milton Obote. The proposed civilian government comprised a legislature of 126 members, a president, and an appointed ministry. The PCP won 63 seats in the legislature and Obote returned as head of state.

The DP leaders with some justification claimed that the PCP had won because of widespread fraud and intimidation, and they demanded new elections. However, a Commonwealth Observation Group accepted the results. Almost immediately fighting began among the factions in Kampala. There was a further breakdown in law and order which the police and 5000 man army could not control. In many cases they simply contributed to the turmoil. The economy, already in desperate condition, grew worse. The official rate for the shilling was 7.5 to the dollar but exchanges in the black market were as high as 30 to 1. For a time in the eastern areas Kenya currency became the recognized, if unofficial, medium of exchange. There were no funds available in the treasury to pay for necessary imports. Starvation was widespread, particularly in the north where among the Karamojong an estimated 100 persons a day were dying. Despite United Nations relief efforts, over 20,000 persons died in the last six months of 1980.

A number of resistance movements began to operate. In the north, elements still loyal to Amin raided across the Sudan border and in the south and White Nile regions the National Resistance Movement (NRM) began to take form. The Democratic Party in the legislature continued its vocal opposition to Obote. He, in return, revived the dreaded State Research Bureau and gave its members the right to detain and execute people without warrant. The police force was corrupt and the army ill trained and there were manifold cases of their active participation in the epidemic violence. Armed opposition groups controlled large sections of the state and lawlessness became a fact of life. Ordinary citizens in Kampala did not dare venture out after dark. Then in June Julius Nyerere, whose Ugandan venture had cost over $700 million, withdrew the 10,000 man Tanzanian force, leaving only the inadequate Ugandan army and police to attempt to maintain order. The situation in Uganda became worse than during the latter stages of the Amin regime. The economy, such as it was, ground to a halt and hunger and starvation became commonplace for hundreds of thousands, and Ugandan refugees poured across the borders into neighboring Zaire and Sudan.

Surprisingly amidst this near chaos, the general economy improved in 1982. Obote devalued the shilling by 1000% and raised the guaranteed price for coffee which normally provided 95% of export earnings. The IMF provided $200 million in immediate aid and a promise of more. In those areas where order could be maintained the production of foodstuffs was increased largely due to the excellent soils of much of the country. The civil war and banditry continued. A raid on Kampala army headquarters in February 1982 led to mass arrests. Many of those arrested were tortured by the police and hundreds of the detainees were executed. There was even a brief border conflict with Sudan at mid-year whose main result was the killing of huge numbers of animals in Kidepo Park. In November 1982 the government forcibly expelled more than 60,000 Rwandans from southern Uganda, many of whom had lived in Uganda for years.

Obote's government, while approving of the mass arrests, killings, and general intimidation of all who seemed to oppose it, nevertheless struggled to restore the health of the economy. Export earnings for coffee and cotton enabled the state to show a $51 million trade surplus in 1983. This was partially due to the government's tight control over imports. Nevertheless, with direct aid from the United States and international agencies the economy was slowly improving. Even manufacturing on a low level had resumed. Obote, understanding how important Asians had been to the economy, attempted to rectify Amin's error and invited the 45,000 who had been expelled to return and reclaim their confiscated property. Although few had returned by the end of 1983, more took advantage of the invitation in the coming years. Their presence as shopkeepers and mid-range businessmen helped the revival of the economy. Obote wanted a more professional and disciplined army and to this end he employed North Korean instructors whose year stay did have an impact on a segment of the army. Reacting to the armed opposition, Obote also increased the size of the army.

Despite all the problems attendant on a civil war, the economy continued to slowly improve in 1984. A two tier system was established to regulate foreign exchange, and coffee, tea, and cotton exports improved. With added security in the capital, even some places of entertainment were reopened. All of these gains were more than offset by the rise in violence throughout many country districts. Members of the NRM raided a government arsenal at Masindi in February and removed many sophisticated weapons. The Ugandan army reacted in a random violent manner against any village suspected of being loyal to the rebels. By the end of the year an estimated three-quarters million persons had been displaced and one-half million had fled the country. The Karamojong and the Pokot in the north were particular targets and a special campaign of internment was launched in Buganda where thousands were imprisoned. The excesses of the government increased the popularity of the NRM whose leader, Yoweri Musaveni, could by this time claim control over most of western Uganda. The abuses of the Obote regime were ended by the action of the army, some of whose leaders had become concerned with Obote's preference for his own tribesmen, the Lango. One of the factors relatively unnoticed in all the violence and killing was the internal stresses within the army in large part due to the rivalry between Lango and Acholi. The overthrow of Obote on July 27, 1985, by Brigadier General Basilo Okello, an Acholi, commanding the Northern Brigade, was merely a culmination of this rivalry. Obote fled to Kenya, bringing to an end a regime as murderous, if not as internationally well known, as that of Idi Amin.

The army created a Military Council which named seventy year old Lieuten-ant General Tito Okello head of state. Paulo Muwanga, Obote's vice president, was named prime minister and functioned as such until replaced in mid-August by Paul Ssemoqerere, a Ganda and leader of the sadly depleted Democratic Party. The new government released 1400 political prisoners and ultimately arrested over 1000 police charged with various crimes. The Military Council announced its intention of returning the government to civilian control by July 1986. Obote's overthrow did not mean an end to the civil war. Musaveni, although welcoming the coup, made it clear that the NRM should have a prominent role in the military government. The fighting continued until late December 1985 when a cease fire was agreed to which promised the NRM what it wanted. The agreement never took effect since fighting resumed in early January 1986. Musaveni charged Okello's regime with carrying out a reign of terror against his enemies. After a week of hard fighting, the better disciplined army of the NRM captured Kampala on January 26 and Musaveni was sworn in as head of state two days later.

The new ruler of Uganda, an Ankole with a degree in economics, had served Obote before the Amin coup and was later, very briefly, defense minister in 1979. The following year he broke with Obote, fled into the bush, and launched the NRM. By early 1986 he was in control of Uganda at the head of a loyal army of more than 30,000 men. He announced the creation of a thirty-six member National Resistance Council to act as an interim parliament until a constituent assembly could be formed. During 1986 the new army confiscated weapons, ammunition, forbade roadblocks, and sought a reconciliation with much of the Ugandan army. Musaveni understood that if peace could be assured, the agriculture of Uganda with its good soils would soon revive. He also entered into agreements with Kenya and Tanzania to expedite trade between the states. Rail cargo service was resumed with Kenya for the first time in nine years and Kenya agreed to aid in extending the oil pipeline to Uganda. Lake service with Tanzania was restored. International agencies were also quick to assure their economic support to Musaveni if he could maintain order without the terrible excesses that marred Uganda during the Amin and Obote regimes.

Although the portents for Uganda's future in early 1987 were good, there were signs that Musaveni's government could still be in great difficulty. The newly established good relations with Kenya were threatened by a series of small incidents which together caused name calling and threats on the highest level. Kenya had expelled illegal aliens, many of whom were Ugandans, then a Ugandan teacher was arrested and allegedly tortured and killed by Kenya police. Kenya border guards tightened their security which led to charges that Kenya was planning to close the borders. Musaveni threatened to reroute all trade through Tanzania and relations between the states worsened until a high level Ugandan delegation in June was dispatched to Nairobi to bring to an end the petty differences and prevent the possibility of long-term conflict. The discussions did not end the tension and in December 1987 the dispute escalated into a number of firefights near the border town of Busia. On December 18, President Moi of Kenya ordered the Ugandan ambassador to leave the country within twenty-four hours after accusing the Ugandan government of preparing for war.

Ultimately not as serious as the potential rift between Uganda and its eastern neighbor, the rise in popularity of a prophetess, Alice Lakwena, in northern Uganda showed how volatile the social situation remained in parts of the country. Unless halted, her anarchistic movement could have seriously compromised the government. Her followers of the Holy Spirit Movement estimated at more than 4,000 persons marched southward toward the capital in early October singing hymns as they went. Perhaps the government overreacted, but Musaveni believed that the poorly armed group could easily be dispersed by the military. Instead, Lakwena's followers who believed her magical powers would protect them repeatedly charged the troops and were shot down by the hundreds before being driven into a papyrus swamp just north of the main highway to Kenya. Following the final government offensive in late October, the remnants of the Holy Spirit Movement numbering only a few hundred persons dispersed into the hills. Lakwena fled to Kenya where she was arrested and imprisoned for entering the country illegally. However futile the Holy Spirit Movement may have been, it was an indication that the legacy of two decades of corruption, robbery, and mass murder had left behind serious wounds in Ugandan society which would take a very long time to heal.

Northeastern Africa

SOMALIA

The pattern of unrest and violence so noticeable throughout the continent was continued in northeastern Africa. Somalia which had earlier in the decade followed an active expansionist policy was forced to abandon the dream of uniting all Somalis under one state. The closing of the Suez Canal, which had an adverse effect upon Somalia's economy, along with the firm stand of Haile Selassie and Jomo Kenyatta, meant that President Abdirashid Ali Shermarke and Prime Minister Muhammad Ibrahim Egal's government had to become more moderate. The more militant Somalis opposed this and created a minor crisis within the ruling Somali Youth League in 1968. Egal, nevertheless, retained control. In the election of March 1969, the SYL was challenged by sixty-three different political parties, but nevertheless won seventy-three seats in the 123 man National Assembly and Egal formed a coalition government. On October 15, President Shermarke was assassinated and six days later Egal's government was overthrown by the army and police. A Supreme Revolutionary Council was formed headed by army chief Major-General Muhammad Said Barre. The council promised to restore trust in a purified Islamic government and the state was renamed the Somali Democratic Republic.

The Supreme Revolutionary Council moved rapidly to implement its socialist program with the nationalization of the banks and foreign firms. Said Barre's government almost immediately alienated the West by its recognition of East Germany and opening of trade with North Vietnam. The United States terminated its aid program and West Germany recalled its diplomatic representative. Any decrease in aid from the West was more than compensated for by Somalia's closer relations with the Soviet Union and other Communist bloc states. The Somali army was increased in size and refitted with Russian equipment. The Soviet Union was granted the right to maintain its naval forces in Somalia ports and they sent hundreds of experts to the horn of Africa. Said Barre's programs were accepted by most of the Somalis. However, plots against the government were discovered each year from 1970 through 1972. The major events in Somalia's history concerns continued Somali irredentism and its attempts to take advantage of the unrest in neighboring Ethiopia. Said Barre's stated objective of incorporating the Haud and Ogaden provinces of Ethiopia into Somalia led to a major reversal of alliances and one of the most serious wars to rock Africa since independence.

The Western Somali Liberation Front operating within eastern Ethiopia precipitated one of Africa's major wars by instigating a rebellion in mid-1977. The Somali government, taking advantage of a perceived confusion in the Ethiopian government and the fact that a large part of its army was tied down in Eritrea, moved to aid the rebels. Most of the Somali army supported by its Soviet built tanks crossed the Ethiopian border. Despite international condemnation for the invasion, the Somalis continued their advance and by late 1977 controlled most of the Haud and Ogaden Provinces. The planners, however, had not adequately assessed certain factors. One oversight was the increasing difficulty of keeping their troops supplied as they advanced across the semidesert terrain. Another and more important factor was that Ethiopia's new-found allies, the Soviet Union and Cuba, responded to Mariam's request for aid. The Eritrean campaign was halted and the bulk of the Ethiopian army backed by an estimated 15,000 Cuban soldiers took the offensive. The outnumbered and outgunned Somalis gave up their conquests and hastily retreated across the border. There was no invasion of Somalia. The beleagured government of Mariam did not wish to add to its already

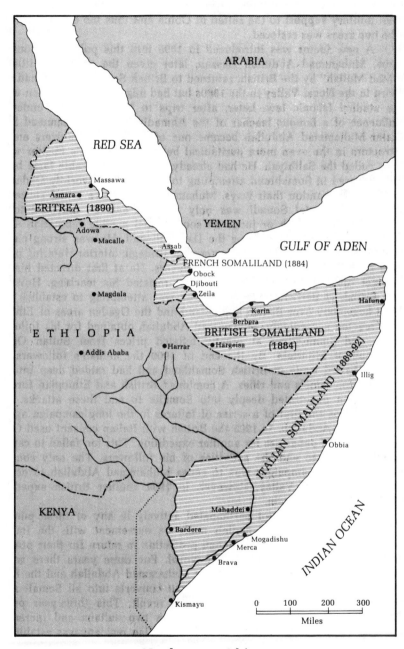

ARABIA

RED SEA

Massawa

Asmara

ERITREA (1890)

Adowa

Macalle

Assab

YEMEN

GULF OF ADEN

FRENCH SOMALILAND (1884)
Obock
Djibouti
Zeila

Magdala

Karin

Berbera

Hafun

BRITISH SOMALILAND
(1884)

E T H I O P I A

Harrar

Hargeisa

Addis Ababa

ITALIAN SOMALILAND (1889-92)

Illig

Obbia

KENYA

Mahaddei

Bardera

Mogadishu
Merca

Brava

INDIAN OCEAN

Kismayu

0   100   200   300
Miles

Northeastern Africa

difficult problems by continuing a major war which would bring even more criticism of his harsh government. The war simply stopped although border skirmishes continued necessitating the posting of a significant part of the army in the border regions. In 1982 Ethiopian troops occupied two Somali townships, Balambule and Guldogob, which they continued to hold five years later. In another area of the frontier in February 1987, an Ethiopian armored column crossed the border only to be driven back by the Somali army.

The abortive war was not only costly in men and material but it was directly responsible for the flood of refugees into western Somalia which threatened to engulf Said's government. Even before the war the Somali government was almost bankrupt and the cost of caring for approximately 150,000 refugees was beyond its capacity. Most of these were victims of the killer drought which struck the northern savannah zones of Africa in the mid-1970s. Western relief agencies had provided most of the care. After the war, Ethiopia expelled many Somalis, and others, fearful for their lives, elected to leave. By 1981 there were almost two million refugees in Somalia and there was widespread starvation. That there were not more deaths and suffering was due to the efforts of the United States, Western European governments, the United Nations, and many private relief agencies. Camps were established. Thousands of tons of food and medical supplies were offloaded at Mogadishu and transported hundreds of miles into the interior. With the return of rains and with government assistance hundreds of thousands left the camps, some even returning to Ethiopia. However, the camps became permanent fixtures. There were still thirty-six of these in 1986 and the various relief agencies were still taking care of approximately three-quarters of a million people. There appeared little hope that there would be a substantial reduction in the numbers of refugees given the economic situation in Somalia after the return of the drought in 1983. The traditional way of life for these many thousands of Somalis had simply ended.

Even before the drought years Somalia was one of the poorest countries in Africa. In the decade after the war with Ethiopia the economy continued to decline. Cattle was the only significant export. Over 1½ million head a year were normally exported to Middle Eastern countries. Thousands of Somalis were employed by Saudi Arabia and their earnings aided the generally stagnant economy. However, Somalia continued to exist primarily on the largess of its friends. The Saudis provided petroleum products at a fraction of the normal cost and the massive injection of relief funds had some positive economic results. Most clearly the military accord of 1980 which gave the United States Navy the right to use Mogadishu and Berbera as staging ports has been of greatest benefit. Somalia became the third largest recipient of United States aid in Africa. Despite such assistance, Somalia's economic problems continued to mount. There was rampant inflation averaging over thirty percent per year, the currency in 1984 was devalued by seventy-five percent and the state could not even meet the service charges on its huge external debt.

To compound Somalia's problems, the government dominated for so long by Said Barre and his associates from the Marehan tribe were being weakened by internal rivalries. Much of this was caused by the president's condition. Barre, who had created a personality cult to bolster his power, was seriously injured in an automobile accident in May 1986. The vice president, Lieutenant General Muhammad Ali Samatur, declared a state of emergency and emerged as the possible successor to Said. It had become apparent that although Said, in his late seventies who had been reelected president for another seven year term in November 1986, had lost much direct authority. This seemed confirmed by the government reorganization of January 1987 which created the position of prime minister and two associate prime ministers. Samatur was designated prime minister. However, the other posts were filled with possible rivals for head of state when Said either is permanently incapacitated or dies.

Two small active opposition movements developed in the 1980s. One, the Democratic Front for the Salvation of Somalia, was headquartered in Addis Ababa. The other is the London based Somali National movement. Each had guerrilla forces operating in the troubled areas adjacent to the border and they received support from Ethiopia which viewed this as another means of gaining the upper hand in the frontier regions. The United States and the governments of the European Economic Community persuaded both governments to try to end their differences by promising substantial economic aid to each if an agreement could be reached. Discussion toward this goal began in Djibouti in January 1986 between representatives of Somalia and Ethiopia and continued in a desultory fashion. The major stumbling block to any agreement was Ethiopia's demand that the present frontier line be guaranteed, a concession that the Somalia government could not make due to opposition from the Western Somali Liberation Front and its strong supporters within Somalia. This would be a far greater concession than that given to Kenya in 1984 and would mean a total abandonment of its pan-Somali policy.

ETHIOPIA

Since the abortive coup of December 1960, Haile Selassie, by utilizing his great power, had been able to keep internal opposition to his regime in Ethiopia to a minimum. Difficulties with the Sudan occurred in 1967 over the border area near Falasha. In the same year Ethiopia was forced to rush troops to the Somalia border to counter subversive activities there. In the following year tensions with both parties were eased due largely to a change of policy by the new governments in Somalia and the Sudan. Haile Selassie was not able to assuage the hostility of many Eritrean Muslims and their demands for a separate state. In 1967 the Eritrean Liberation Front, coordinating the efforts of guerrillas, temporarily closed road traffic in Eritrea. The Ethiopian army swept through a number of villages and forced several thousand inhabitants to flee into neighboring Sudan. The guerrilla raids nevertheless continued throughout 1968 and 1969. The separatists attacked Ethiopian air facilities in Germany and Pakistan and attempted to steal an Ethiopian airliner in December 1969. By the end of the year, guerrillas had managed to shut down, by attacking road convoys, a large portion of normal road traffic in Eritrea. Another source of trouble for the emperor was student unrest. Ostensibly demanding educational reform, the student groups were also demonstrating against a broad range of government policies. At one time in mid-1969 the university and all secondary schools in Ethiopia were closed and the government arrested or detained thousands of students.

Despite the outward semblance of continued order, Haile Selassie's hold on his government was not firm when the drought of the early 1970s struck the country. The central government's slow reaction to the crisis was one of the major factors in the emperor's downfall. By 1973 an estimated 50,000 persons had died. There was practically no assistance given to the people in the devastated regions. Inflation was another major cause for urban dissatisfaction with the emperor's regime. These generalized factors affected Ethiopia's 42,000 man army. The army wanted pay increases and many of the younger officers were deeply committed to ideologies totally at variance with Ethiopian government practices. Dissatisfaction became open in March 1974 when teachers and taxi drivers struck for more money. Very soon they were joined by other workers and the strike became general. Even some of the Coptic priests demanded more support from the government. As the strike spread, violence in Addis Ababa and Asmara escalated and after two weeks of this, the Second Division took control of Asmara. The military leaders demanded pay increases, better housing and medical care, and the dismissal of most of the ministry. Haile Selassie capitulated, shuffled his ministry, and granted all the army's demands. The new prime minister, Endalkachew Makonnen, promised further economic and social reforms. The army returned to barracks and it appeared that the emperor had ridden out the storm. However, by the end of summer it was obvious that the military was assuming more control. A new prime minister, Michael Imru, was appointed and an Armed Forces Coordinating Committee created.

The military leaders moved quietly behind the scenes to strip the emperor of his power. In August the commander of the Imperial Bodyguard was arrested and the four major offices through which Haile Selassie ran the state were abolished. A new constitution was created which made the emperor a figurehead without power over the church or the judiciary. Finally in September the emperor was deposed and imprisoned. The constitution was suspended and legislative and executive power was assumed by a 120 man Provisional Military Council (Dergue) with representatives from all ranks through that of major. The ostensible leader of the Dergue was a respected professional officer, Lieutenant-General Aman Andom, who was known to be a moderate both in foreign and domestic affairs. A split soon developed in the ruling council between Andom and the more doctrinaire followers of Major Mengistu Haile Mariam. The major area of disagreement related to how the Eritrean rebels should be handled. The leftists wanted to use more coercion and Andom who had been born in Eritrea was accused of being a traitor. In late November 1974 there was a military clash between the factions. During a two hour fight near his headquarters, the army chief was killed. The majority of his most powerful supporters were arrested and fifty-eight of them were immediately shot at Akaki prison in Addis Ababa. The number included two former premiers, twelve ex-governors of provinces, and eighteen generals.

Brigadier General Teferi Benti replaced Andom as head of the council. He immediately escalated the war against the Eritrean Liberation Front by ordering 7,000 more men to reinforce the Second Division already operating there. It was, however, apparent to most observers that the strongman of the government was Major Mariam. This was confirmed in January 1975 by the government's

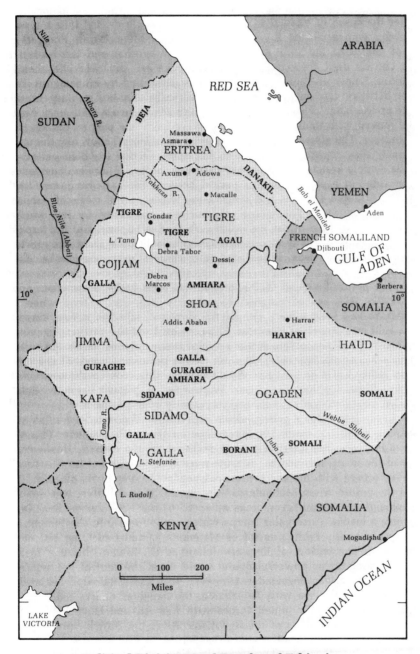

Political Divisions and Peoples of Ethiopia

announcement of a policy of state socialism followed by a decree nationalizing banks, insurance companies, and there were increasing media attacks upon foreigners. The government's offensive in Eritrea stalled despite very heavy fighting, and by the close of 1975 over half of the army was directly involved in the attempted pacification. There were also revolts in Tigre by Ethiopians still loyal to the imprisoned emperor. Compounding the government's many difficulties was the continued drought in the Ogaden which affected over one-quarter million persons. However, one of the Dergue's major problems was solved when on August 27, 1975, the emperor died in his sleep.

In February 1977 Major Mariam and his followers in the Dergue staged a repetition of the shootout of two and one-half years before and deposed General Benti. General Benti and eight of his high ranking supporters were immediately executed. The reasons given for the overthrow of Benti were the same as the charges against Andom, namely that he was a secret supporter of the Eritrean revolutionaries. The Dergue had been reduced by purges to only sixty members and Mariam was finally openly in control of the government. Abitrary arrests, imprisonments, and executions which had become the trademark of the regime in 1976 continued unabated after the Benti execution. Despite the new leader, the war in Eritrea continued to drain the country's resources and Ethiopian troops held only the major towns; the countryside belonged to the rebels. It was at this juncture that the war with Somalia began.

One factor involved in beginning the conflict was the French desire to be rid of the responsibility of administering the small enclave around the port of Djibouti. The French had conducted a plebicite there in 1967 to determine whether their presence was still wanted. The result was a positive vote and as a concession to a small group of urban nationalists, the name of the area was changed to Afars and Issas. Somalia had made clear that it expected to annex the area when the French left and Ethiopia had stated that under no circumstances would it allow the rail terminus at Djibouti to fall under Somali control. The West Somali Liberation Front's guerrillas supported by Somalia were active in the country areas and in 1976 they increased their hit and run raids against the French. The chances of getting caught up in another African war convinced the French to leave the territory and Afars and Issas became independent in June 1978.

The leaders of the new state were not eager to give up their independence so soon and Somalia did not want to risk a confrontation with France. Said Barre's government then turned to eastern Ethiopia, an area which promised quicker success. Russia which had been sending weapons and advisors to Ethiopia pressed on the Somalis a plan to create a large powerful socialist state in the horn by federating Ethiopia and Somaliland. Somalia's leaders refused to consider this seriously and also made this known to Fidel Castro when he visited Mogadishu in May 1977. In the following months regular Somali army units crossed into Ethiopia ostensibly to support the guerrillas of the West Somali Liberation Front.

Ethiopia had only one division in the Ogaden at the start of the conflict and was still involved in the drawn out struggle with the Eritreans. The Somali army aided openly by the pastoral peoples of the Ogaden advanced rapidly and took the major town of Jijiga. They were thwarted by the reversal of Soviet and Cuban attitudes. These states now decided to support Ethiopia and began to send massive amounts of aid to Mariam's hard pressed forces. By December 1977 almost one billion dollars in arms had been received. The Somalis turned to the West for support but were cooly received. The United States maintained a hands off policy although Said Barre repudiated his earlier alliance and forced all Russians to leave Somalia in November. Somalia was reduced to receiving supplies and arms clandestinely from the Middle East. Cuba did more even than the Russians. Castro dispatched thousands of his well trained troops to reinforce the Ethiopian regulars and militia. In February 1978 the Ethiopians and their allies operating with some of the latest Russian tanks and aircraft launched a counter-offensive. Jijiga was swiftly retaken and the Somalis pursued to the border. Ethiopia was content to assume the role of the injured party and did not attempt an invasion of Somalia because this would have risked direct Western intervention.

Although the regular Somali army had been beaten, those Somalis resident in Haud and Ogaden did not give up the fight against Ethiopian control. Mariam and his advisors have had to deal with large scale guerrilla activity in both provinces. Many of the reported 14,000 Cubans were used in early 1979 to help pacify the eastern regions. In the aftermath of the war and continued fighting in eastern Ethiopia, a reported 300,000 persons had fled the country for refuge in Somalia. Far more serious than the Haud and Ogaden rebellions was the continuing war in Eritrea. In July 1979 Mariam deployed most of his army regulars against Nahfa, the last large rebel town in Eritrea. The competitive Eritrean Liberation Front and Eritrean peoples Liberation Front had just before this offensive decided to combine their efforts against the Ethiopians. Despite being backed by Soviet built tanks, artillery, and aircraft, the attack against Nahfa was unsuccessful. Mariam's poorly trained troops suffered very heavy casualties. By the close of 1979 the Ethiopian army held all the major towns in Eritrea, but they had failed to secure the countryside, and the threat of Eritrean secession remained as real as in the first years of the new Ethiopian revolutionary regime.

Mariam's regime which had proved to be one of the most murderous in Africa continued in the 1980s to pursue the twin goals of suppressing all opposition and converting Ethiopia into a communist state. In pursuing the first objective the police monitored any suspected subversive activities and arrested all who might pose a threat to the government. The United Nations Human Rights Commission in August 1982 cited the Ethiopian government as a major violator of human rights which carried on a campaign of repression against various Christian churches operating in Ethiopia and particularly against the Falasha, the black Jews. The threat to them was so menacing that many fled to neighboring states and the United States had by 1985 flown over 10,000 Falasha to Israel. Forced resettlement of hundreds of thousands of persons in the midst of the famine from Tigre and southern Eritrea to locations in the south also resulted in thousands of deaths and unimagined hardship.

The greatest threat to Mariam's regime was from various liberation groups. Almost every section of northern Ethiopia had some type of resistance movement. The most successful was the Eritrean Peoples Liberation Front (EPLF) whose guerrilla forces had opposed Ethiopian domination since 1961. By 1987 they controlled over three-fourth of the Eritrean countryside and their army, grown to more than 20,000 men, manned trench lines over 300 kilometers long. The

Liberation Front had, behind the lines in the mountains, constructed a network of hospitals, schools, and transport centers. The ongoing war forced the government to resort to conscription and the size of the Ethiopian army grew to almost one-quarter million men, many of whom, however, were poorly trained and poorly motivated. Many young men joined the flood of refugees to other countries rather than serve in the army. Nevertheless the Ethiopian army was well equipped with weapons acquired from the United States and the Soviet Union. There were also 11,000 Cuban troops backing up the regular Ethiopian army. These forces were not withdrawn until 1984 when Ethiopia could no longer pay for them. MIG jets controlled the air over the battlefront in Tigre and Eritrea. Despite eight offensives against the Eritrean rebels, the Ethiopian army even with superiority in numbers and equipment was not able to break through the lines. Only the heavily guarded seventy mile road between Asmara and the port of Massawa was relatively safe. Even the towns were no longer immune to attack by the EPLF.

The rebels attacked heavily guarded areas on the outskirts of Asmara, and in January 1987 a commando group penetrated the airfields defenses and spent thirty minutes blowing up airplanes. An attack on a convoy of twenty-three long-haul trucks operated by the United Nations World Food Program in October 1987 indicated how little protection the Ethiopian government could offer even the relief agencies in rebel held territory. This action which destroyed the trucks and 450 tons of wheat destined for famine victims marked a change in the attitude of the Liberation Front leaders who obviously believed that famine relief, however noble its objectives, strengthened Mariam's regime. The bloody stalemate in Eritrea seemed likely to continue as long as the Ethiopian government tried to suppress the Eritrean's desires for separation and will continue to drain the scarce resources of an already impoverished state.

Mariam also had to maintain a significant part of his armed forces near the border with Somalia. The Western Somalia Liberation Front continued to be active in parts of the Ogaden and it was directly supported by Somalia. The small unit border war with Somalia continued with Ethiopian aircraft intermittently bombing villages in northwest Somalia. Ethiopian funds and equipment were also channelled to various groups opposing Said Barre. The major recipient of such assistance was the Democratic Salvation Front. In July 1982 Ethiopian troops aiding this subversive organization invaded Somalia, capturing two villages which they refused to surrender. Then again in February 1987 an Ethiopian armored column crossed the frontier but was turned back by Somali army units. There appeared a chance to settle this long-standing disagreement when talks began between representatives of Somalia and Ethiopia in January 1986 in Djibouti and continued throughout the year. There was the added inducement of $40 million to each side promised by the European Economic Community if a solution could be reached. Although the talks marked an advance over fighting, it was not likely that Said Barre and his associates could afford to surrender their claims to the Ogaden.

The plans of the Dergue to establish, at first, state socialism and later a communist state received major setbacks because of the political infighting in the 1970s between power factions in the government and then the war with Somalia and the Eritrean civil war. Most devastating to Mariam's plans to recreate a Soviet styled state was the return of the drought that earlier had devastated Ethiopia and had precipitated the downfall of Haile Selassie. Rainfall was below normal in the northern areas before the first disastrous results of the lack of rainfall became known in 1983 when United Nations and European relief workers reported that millions of persons could starve if massive efforts were not immediately launched. All subsequent aid attempts were hampered by the ongoing war in Eritrea and Tigre and the sometimes hostile attitude of the government toward the relief work. Although linked by treaty and by philosophical conviction to Ethiopia, the Soviet Union provided only a small amount of direct humanitarian aid while continuing to supply the government with sophisticated weaponry. The United States, although its relations with the Ethiopian government were almost nonexistent, provided the bulk of famine relief. In 1983 it provided $6.7 million and this aid swelled to more than $250 million in 1985. This latter sum was matched by relief funds from Western European governments and relief agencies. By the onset of the 1987 drought, the United States had given over one-half billion dollars in aid. Eight of Ethiopia's districts were declared disaster areas by the United Nations and at one time as many as 11 million Ethiopians were at risk. Although the rains returned in 1985, there were still millions of Ethiopians either in camps or in their own villages who were being kept alive by the largess of various relief agencies. During this drought period an estimated million persons died and more than one million migrated into neighboring states where their presence strained the poor resources of Somalia, Djibouti, and the Sudan. The permanent feeding camps established by the United Nations, however necessary, were the indirect cause of hundreds of thousands of deaths. Weakened by the lack of food, the refugees were an easy prey to the rampant infectious diseases which spread rapidly through the camps.

The rains returned in 1985 and were also good the following year, leading to the belief that the drought was over. The majority of the people in the feeding camps left to return to their villages. In June 1987 the rains came on schedule, but no rain fell in the following months and the crops burned up. Eritrean farmers lost eighty percent of their crops while over forty percent were destroyed in Tigre and Wollo Provinces. Ethiopia was once again faced with the possibility of hundreds of thousands starving. By the end of the year an estimated six million persons were at risk. Estimates made by the Food and Agricultural Organization indicated that Ethiopia would need 1.3 million tons of relief grain while only forty percent of that amount had been pledged. The United States, as it had in the earlier crisis, was providing most of the grain and transport vehicles. In August approval was given for 115,000 tons valued at $43 million to be sent immediately. Delivery of the relief food to Ethiopia under the best of circumstances took four to six months after the initial pledge. Once it arrived, relief workers had to deliver it to the affected areas. Poor roads and semidesert conditions made it difficult for the truck convoys to move needed food quickly into the interior. The attack by the EPLF in late October 1987 on an unguarded convoy of twenty-three trucks on the way to Macalle in Tigre showed that the rebels were no longer going to allow unrestricted passage along the Eritrean roads. The destruction of that one convoy lost enough grain to feed 30,000 people for a month. The government reaction made the situation worse because they closed off all roads in the Eritrean-Tigre hinterland for over a month.

While millions of Ethiopians were near starvation, the government began to implement its plans for resettlement. Against the protests of many relief officials, a massive shift of population began in 1985 particularly from the worst famine areas of Tigre and parts of Eritrea. By the end of 1986 an estimated 500,000 persons had been moved south and relocated in central villages. The government's explanation was that it was necessary to move the people from the most famine prone areas and to begin seriously once again the process of agricultural socialism delayed by the natural disaster. This was in line with the ten year development plan adopted by the Central Committee of the Workers Party of Ethiopia in 1985. Other observers believed the major reason was to depopulate those areas already in rebellion or most likely to revolt against the central government. An estimated 100,000 persons died as a result of the government's forced resettlement program.

The Soviet Union provided the hardware for Mariam's armed forces and also maintained military advisors in Ethiopia and developed a naval base in the Dahlak Islands. Despite the apparent closeness of this relationship, the Soviet leaders were perturbed at the slowness with which Ethiopia had acted to establish legally a communist state and pressed Mariam on his visit to Moscow in 1984 to reorganize the government. This was done in September. The Workers Party of Ethiopia was recognized as the sole political party. An eleven member Politburo, a 136 member Central Committee, and a party general-secretary were also created. Despite the change, there were no major realignments within the government. Those who possessed power before simply took on new titles. Mariam became the secretary-general in addition to being chairman of the council of Ministers and chairman of the forty member Dergue. It appeared that as long as the army leadership remained loyal, despite the problems with the Eritrean rebels, Somalia, and a bankrupt, chaotic economy, Mariam would survive as leader of his stricken country.

DJIBOUTI

During the early stages of the scramble for Africa the French government understood the need for a Red Sea port as a stopover and repair station and they secured first the port of Obock and later Djibouti. From the beginning the port was primary, the hinterland was mostly desert or semidesert. For a variety of diplomatic reasons the French did not contest with the Italians for a larger share of the coastline or with the Ethiopians for more of the inland areas, particularly after their stunning defeat of the Italians at Adowa in 1896. The division of the Red Sea littoral between the European powers divided the population. In the south lived the Issa, a Muslim group closely akin to the Somalis in the British dominated area near the horn of Africa. The Afars lived in the northern section of French Somaliland, a people related by intermarriage and custom with the coastal Ethiopians in Eritrea. This division did not assume any major importance until the clamor for independence began in the 1960s. The port of Djibouti continued to prosper until the closing of the Suez Canal in 1967 and the advent of the super tanker lessened its importance. One major factor in the role Djibouti played and still plays is the railway, completed in 1917, which links the port with Addis Ababa. The continuing civil war in Ethiopia which has closed off Eritrea from the hinterland has given Djibouti a strategic importance it had never previously enjoyed.

Following World War II, Djibouti became an Overseas Territory of France and its inhabitants were declared French citizens. By the early 1960s France's other African territories had become independent and British and Italian Somaliland united to become an independent republic. Nevertheless, few observers imagined that Djibouti with no resources and a population of less than 300,000 could ever be a viable state. However, a nationalist movement centered in the capital did develop. In part this was neutralized because of the polarity of its population. Somalia wanted to annex the territory and many Issa agreed while some Afars wanted union with Ethiopia. The French conducted a plebicite in 1967 to determine whether the people still wanted their presence. The result was a positive vote and as a concession to the small group of urban nationalists the name of the territory was changed to Afars and Issas. French administrators had favored the Afars in employment and in government offices generally as a counter to Somali irredentism. The devastating drought of the early 1970s coinciding with the revolution in Ethiopia changed the balance of power in Djibouti. The Issa leaders, no longer enamored of any union with Somalia, demanded independence and the French complied. On June 27, 1977, the Republic of Djibouti, one of the more improbable states in Africa, came into being. Hassan Gouled Aptido, an Issa, became president and Ahmed Dini, an Afar, the prime minister. The sixty-five member unicameral legislature was almost equally divided between representatives of the two groups.

The 1977 war between Ethiopia and Somalia could have had destructive ramifications for the ministate. Fortunately the government remained neutral. Nevertheless the war did affect Djibouti negatively. Over 50,000 Somalis crossed the border into an already near destitute country. The United Nations established camps to handle the flood. As in Somalia many of these camps believed at first to be temporary would become permanent. The state of Djibouti, for the most part rocky and arid, cannot support even its own population and requires massive outside aid. The continuing problems in the Middle East has refocused attention on the Red Sea region and the horn of Africa and this concern has made Djibouti important for strategic reasons. The port had a revival in the 1980s illustrated by the construction of a new international cargo container terminal. France contributed the most in direct and indirect economic aid. The presence of 3,500 French troops, many of them legionnaires, not only helped bolster the urban economy but provided support for the 4,800 man Djibouti force whose size was determined by the threats to Djibouti's independence from its more powerful neighbors.

SUDAN

The two salient facts in the recent history of the Sudan have been religious and political factionalism and the ongoing civil war in the south. The government of Sadik al Mahdi, which had seemed so powerful in 1966, had broken apart by May 1967 primarily because of opposition to his policies by the ultraconservative wing of the Ansar sect. Muhammad Ahmed Mahgoub replaced al Mahdi as premier to head a coalition government which attempted to associate members of the Southern Front party with its rule and thus bring an end to the hostilities in Equatoria. Although elections had been held in the southern Sudan in March 1967 for the first time in ten years, the recognized political parties did not represent the rebels and the war continued. In February 1968, Mahgoub asked for the dissolution of the National Assembly rather than face a vote of confidence. A major conflict between the government and the followers of al Mahdi who streamed into Khartoum to protest Mahgoub's action was barely averted. In the general elections of April, Mahgoub continued as prime minister because his party won 101 of the 218 contested seats. The war in the south continued to be a constant drain on resources. A revolutionary southern Sudanese government in exile led by Aggrey Jarden was formed in Uganda and all attempts at pacification seemed to fail since the rebels controlled most of the countryside in the three disaffected provinces. Finally on May 25, 1968, young army officers led by Colonel Jaafar Muhammad al Niameiry, despairing of improvement in the political future of the Sudan, over-threw the civilian government. A revolutionary council and a twenty-one man cabinet was created to aid al Niameiry in ruling the country. People's military courts were established to try persons accused of crimes against the state. Press censorship was imposed and in October al Niameiry was named prime minister as well as head of the council. The new government, attempting to reconcile the southerners, extended the 1968 amnesty provisions and promised a number of political and educational reforms for Equatoria. The southern rebel leadership did not appear impressed by the new regime and the fifteen-year civil war continued.

The 1970s witnessed a series of bloody confrontations between Niameiry's government and those who were committed to its overthrow. In March 1970 the disgruntled Imam al Hadi al Mahdi attempted a revolt and was killed. Sadik al Mahdi was accused of being a part of the conspiracy and was deported. The most serious of all the various coup attempts was that of July 1971 when the Sudanese Communist party led by Abdul Mahjub which had been cooperating with Niameiry tried, with the support of left-wing officers, to seize power in Khartoum. Niameiry and all the other members of the revolutionary council were taken prisoner. Fortunately for Niameiry, the revolt did not extend beyond the capital. Most of the army remained loyal and the officers scheduled to head the government were arrested on their way to Khartoum. The Sudan Brigade returned from the Suez Canal area and after very heavy fighting the rebels were defeated and Niameiry was rescued. This revolt was the beginning of Niameiry's disenchantment with the Soviet Union. He arrested large numbers of known Sudanese communists, expelled over 1000 Soviet advisors, and forced the recall of the Soviet ambassador. Niameiry sought to counterbalance this loss by improving Sudan's relationship with the West and by seeking closer relations with the Arab world. For over a year he pursued the possibility of a political union with Egypt, Libya, and Syria.

On February 26, 1972, Niameiry was able to bring an end to the long drawn out costly civil war. His representative signed an agreement with the Ana Nya in Addis Ababa which restructured the government of the Sudan. The three affected provinces were grouped together to form South Sudan. A regional executive and a regional council were given charge of all affairs of the South Sudan with the exception of defense, currency, and foreign affairs. Members of the Ana Nya army were phased into the Sudanese military and their leader was given the rank of general. The southern council and executive composed almost entirely of southerners was given the option of conducting its business in English. It has functioned well for a number of years and there were no serious conflicts with the central government at Khartoum.

The entire governmental structure of the Sudan was again revamped by the approval of a new constitution in May 1973. This document gave further support to the self rule of the south and ended Niameiry's plans to amalgamate the Sudan with other Arab states. Despite Niameiry's obvious popularity and the banning of all political activity except that of the Sudanese Socialist Union (SSU), there were a number of other attempts to overthrow his government. These plots were hatched by two disparate groups—the Communists and the Muslim Brotherhood. In January 1973 there were student riots in Khartoum and a railway strike. This emboldened some of the military to plan for another coup. The coup never got far beyond the planning stage and collapsed with the arrest of the leaders. A similar weak attempt was made by the Muslim Brotherhood in September 1975. The most serious threat was the abortive coup of July 2, 1976 which once again pitted army units against one another in Khartoum. Niameiry was once again saved by the support he received from the outlying areas. During the fierce fighting over 800 were killed. Later ninety-eight of the rebels were executed. Niameiry blamed Libya's leader, General Qaddafi, and the exiled Sadik al Mahdi for fomenting the rebellion. He broke relations with Libya and then signed a new mutual defense pact with Egypt.

Niameiry launched a number of major agricultural improvements which, added to what had previously been accomplished, allowed the Sudan to survive the drought in relatively good condition. In 1975 gas and petroleum were discovered and thus gave the Sudan greater potential for financing its agricultural and industrial base. Money from oil rich Arab countries was committed to a long range two billion dollar investment for further agricultural improvement in the Sudan. By the end of 1977 Niameiry felt that the state and his regime was strong enough to grant a general amnesty to over 1,000 persons previously implicated in the various coups. As a part of this reconciliation program, Niameiry allowed Sadik al Mahdi to return to Khartoum and the two men apparently decided to bring an end to the differences which had fueled a number of the coups against the government.

Politics in the Sudan nevertheless remained volatile and Niameiry's control of the state continued to depend upon his considerable skill of combining force with compromise. In August 1979 there were student led riots in Khartoum and Omdurman to protest the sharp rise in the cost of basic foodstuffs. These forced Niameiry to reorganize his government, dismiss the vice-president, and announce a reduction in the price of corn and meat. Niameiry also handled the Ugandan problem extremely well. In the wake of the war which overthrew President Amin, thousands of Ugandans crossed the border, many of them armed soldiers loyal to their former leader. These were disarmed and Niameiry began to cement better relations with the new Ugandan regime by refusing Amin's request for asylum. Niameiry's government also followed a policy of conciliation with regard to Egypt's detente with Israel. Although Sudan's representatives reluctantly voted with the majority in May 1979 to ban Egypt from the conference of Islamic states, Niameiry made it clear that he supported Sadat's peacekeeping attempts. One reason for Sudan's conciliatory attitude was the proximity of Egypt, but another was the government's fear of any long term close cooperation between the conservative Saudi Arabian leaders and the unstable radical, General Qaddafi of Libya.

Sudan's economy had long been maintained by foreign loans and grants. Its exports had always lagged behind imports. The rise in price of all petroleum products in the 1970s combined with the fall in world prices for its exports meant that Niameiry's government should have radically curtailed spending in the early 1980s. He could not do this. Believing his regime to be threatened by invasion from Libya and facing a resumption of civil war in the southern Sudan, he had to maintain a relatively well equipped army in excess of 50,000 men. As with most African states, the government bureaucracy was far larger than necessary. Yet Niameiry could not make substantial cuts because he needed their support. The labor unions in Khartoum were particularly strong. Costly projects such as the development of the Jonglei Canal in the north were continued even though the government was near bankruptcy. By 1982 the external debt of Sudan amounted to almost $5 billion, $500 million of which was rescheduled by the Paris Club of thirteen creditor nations. The IMF in that year also approved $250 million more in credits. The government at that time was counting largely on the future profits from the newly discovered petroleum deposits in the southern and western Sudan. Chevron Oil was in the beginning stages of exploiting those discoveries and Standard Oil was planning a 900 mile pipeline from the oilfields to Port Sudan.

Although troubling, the economic problems appeared to be the least of Niameiry's worries. In 1983 Libya appeared to be preparing an invasion. The United States and Egypt responded with warnings to Libya and the United States dispatched four of its advanced Airborne Warning and Control planes to Egypt and increased its military aid to the Sudan to $60 million that year. The following year a Soviet built aircraft bombed Omdurman. Although there were serious doubts that Libya planned an invasion, Egypt invoked its 1976 treaty and sent troops into the Sudan to bolster Niameiry.

The volatile population of Khartoum was deeply divided among supporters of the regime, radical Muslim fundamentalists, radical labor union members, and students who had been affected by communist and Libyan propaganda. Consequently Niameiry tried to retain support by playing one faction against another and in so doing he made his political situation worse. In 1982 there had been rioting in Khartoum over elimination of gasoline and sugar subsidies. This led Niameiry to close the University and the secondary schools. He then dissolved the Central Committee and Politburo of the ruling Sudan Socialist Union and replaced them with a forty-one member popular committee. He also shifted those who held major party offices. However successful these moves might have been, the next major domestic policy decisions were disastrous.

There had been relative order in the southern Sudan after the 1972 accord which had given the southerners a large measure of independence within the Sudan. Then in October 1981 Niameiry dissolved the southern legislature and created a transitional government more responsible to Khartoum. This action was preliminary to his announcement the following year of a reorganization of the south. He planned to divide the large area into three regions, Bahr al Ghazal, Equatoria, and Upper Nile, and bring southern autonomy to an end. Niameiry obviously was reacting to pressures from the conservative Muslims of the north. In pursuing the reorganization of the government, he detained twenty southern leaders who had formed a Council for the Unity of Sudan. The reaction in the south was immediate. There was a revival of the old opposition group, the Anya Nya II, which began to attack northerners residing in the south. Ultimately the most important group was formed by defectors from the Sudanese army. Niameiry planned to transfer southern soldiers north out of the troubled zone but his plan was discovered. Large numbers of officers and men simply deserted, taking with them their arms and equipment. These soldiers became the nucleus of the Sudanese Peoples Liberation Army (SPLA) commanded by Colonel John Garang.

In September 1983 Niameiry made another error. Attempting to moderate opposition from fundamentalist Muslims, he announced the application of the *sharia*, the Muslim law, in all cases and in all areas including the primarily Christian south. The prisons were emptied because the inmates had not been convicted by Muslim judges applying the *sharia*. A strict code of morality was enforced by floggings and public amputations of those convicted of robbery. These became commonplace. Police action to root out wrongdoers did not exempt foreigners and Niameiry's already oppressive regime became even worse. The southern sections of the country responded by giving more assistance to Colonel Garang's SPLA which was emboldened to kidnap expatriate workers and to attack Chevron Oil installations. The SPLA gained international attention and caused the Chevron Oil executives to close down their operations until the crisis had ended. The resultant loss of a projected $130 million in revenue exacerbated the government's economic problems. By the end of the year the external debt had grown to over $7 billion, a sum equal to the state's Gross National Product. The United States continued to pump aid to the Sudan, a total of $235 million in 1984, more than to any other African state. Nevertheless by the end of the year Niameiry's regime was under siege. There had been strikes by doctors, government clerks, and university personnel and students, all a clear indication that Sudan's middle class was preparing to desert Niameiry. The government's response was to declare a state of emergency, to impose a curfew, and to forbid public meetings. Much of the vast south, despite the strengthening of urban garrisons, was by this time controlled by the SPLA.

In this deteriorating situation the army acted. On April 6, 1985, after a new round of anti-Niameiry demonstrations in Khartoum by students, professionals, and workers, the Minister of Defense, Major General Suwar el Dahab, assumed control of the government. Niameiry fled to Egypt which granted him sanctuary, an act which further strained Egyptian-Sudanese relations. El Dahab immediately promised that the military regime would be short-lived and that the government would turn control back to civilians within a year. In October a temporary constitution was adopted which allowed political parties to operate and provided for the election of a parliament which was to develop the form of the permanent constitution. Despite the best intentions, el Dahab's tenure was not marked with signal success in areas other than planning for the future government. There was political infighting among members of the Transitional Military Council and the economy worsened. In early 1986 the IMF and the World Bank halted all aid programs.

By far the most difficult situation for the government was the spread of the revolt in the south. Colonel Garang repeatedly rejected peace overtures. He demanded immediate transfer of power to a civilian regime and autonomy for the south. Supplied in the main from Ethiopia, the SPLA took the offensive and by the end of 1985 controlled most of the southern provinces with the exception of the major towns and these were under siege. Garang's guerrilla force, well supplied with advanced equipment, much of it taken from the regular Sudanese army, had by then grown to over 20,000 men. The government's attempt to split the secessionist movement by supporting the rival Anya Nya II did not prove successful. The Sudanese army, generally confined to the larger towns, took heavy casualties. In September 1985 there was a mutiny of some northern troops in Khartoum who had been informed that they were to be sent south. Correlate with the escalation of the civil war were the problems of the refugees. There had been, prior to 1980, a significant refugee problem caused in part by the drought of the mid-1970s and partially because of the disturbances in Chad, Uganda, Zaire, and Ethiopia which forced untold thousands to flee to the Sudan. The return of the drought to southern Sudan in 1983 resulting in mass crop failures caused hundreds of thousands to crowd into the towns and the camps established by international relief agencies. In 1981 the production of sorghum, the major food crop, had reached 3.4 million tons. By 1985 the harvest resulted in only 1 million ton. The continuation of fighting in the south only worsened conditions. By 1985 an estimated 5 million persons were affected. The decision by the SPLA to prevent aid supplies not approved by their officials from being brought into the towns made the food situation desperate for hundreds of thousands. The destruction in the fall of 1986 of a Sudan Airways plane by the SPLA carrying relief supplies to Wau killing sixty-three persons brought international attention and general condemnation of the act but did not shake the SPLAs decision to control movement of supplies in the contested areas.

In the midst of all these difficulties elections were held in April 1986 for a new civilian responsible government. There was to be no president but a five man Council to act with the prime minister as a collective head of state. There were thirty-eight political parties involved. The two strongest were the Umma Party headed by former Prime Minister Sidiq al Mahdi and the National Islamic Front. The Umma Party won forty-eight percent of the seats and el Mahdi once again became prime minister having reached an agreement with the leader of the Democratic Unionist Party for a coalition. The problems faced by the new civilian government were the same as those which had bedeviled the previous regimes. All attempts including a face to face meeting between el Mahdi and Garang failed to end the war in the south. Al Mahdi, although moderating the enforcement of the *sharia*, did not believe he could immediately return to the previous type of civil code because of pressure from Muslim extremists. Al Mahdi did not announce the repeal of the *sharia* decree until late 1987.

Taking cognizance of the large numbers of Libyan sympathizers and attempting to end the potential threat of invasion, al Mahdi continued the rapprochement with Qaddafi. By the end of 1986 there were over 1,000 Libyans in Khartoum and al Mahdi was also utilizing many Palestinian and Syrian advisors. This more pliant attitude toward extremists Arab groups brought an immediate reaction from the United States which cut off all aid with the exception of emergency relief. On April 15, 1986, the day after an air strike by the United States against Libya, over 10,000 students and professionals demonstrated in Khartoum and attempted to storm the embassy. The following day an American envoy was assassinated. All non-essential embassy staff were subsequently evacuated. The worsening relations with the United States combined with the action of the IMF in February 1986 declaring Sudan ineligible for further loans meant that al Mahdi's government, faced with the civil war and millions on the verge of starvation, was in a potentially more grave condition than the government of Niameiry.

TEN
Epilogue

By concentrating on the political aspect of recent events, one can draw a pessimistic view of the future for sub-Saharan Africa. Certainly the growing influence of the military in the majority of states should cause a reexamination of the future of participatory democracy in most African states. Civil wars which have claimed hundreds of thousands of lives have made a mockery of the propaganda the nationalists used in the 1950s in their drive toward independence. The ideal of Pan-Africanism has also been battered by the outbreak of major wars between states and the practice of one polity allowing armed guerrillas sanctuary while they prepare to attack a neighbor. In the past decade some of these conflicts have escalated to the point where non-African states intervened directly. The power struggles attendant upon the cold war have thus been brought to Zaire, Angola, Rhodesia, Somalia, and Ethiopia and complicate already difficult problems.

Notwithstanding all such evidence of a general breakdown throughout the continent, perhaps a totally pessimistic view would, at this juncture, be as wrong as those projected by observers two decades ago who envisioned a swift onward and upward movement toward economic well-being and political democracy for the newly independent African states.

A few African polities have been relatively untouched by internal political turmoil. Zambia, Botswana, Malawi, Senegal, the Ivory Coast, Kenya, and Tanzania have each in its own way displayed considerable maturity and stability. Even some states whose names were once symbolic of violence—Nigeria, Zaire, and Guinea-Bissau—appear to have evolved, at least temporarily, government forms which are able to match their performance to a limited extent to the aspirations of the people.

Many other signs of growing maturity and responsibility are apparent. Julius Nyerere's program aimed at placing Tanzanians in responsible posts throughout the nation is a reflection of the success of that government's education policies. This is duplicated by most African states whose pool of educated and trained personnel is far larger than when independence was granted. Another portent of maturity is that despite the many conflicts, there is a greater degree of cooperation among some states. This cooperation is much more practical than the idealistic proposals for united action espoused by political leaders a few years ago. The Economic Community of West African States (ECOWAS) and the various regional associations all recognize the primacy of nationalism but strive to further economic cooperation where states can benefit mutually from concerted action. Even in the realm of politics there appears to be a more realistic appreciation of what can be achieved through political cooperation. The OAU has proved to be an imperfect structure but its very existence, as with the United Nations, represents a tremendous advance over what existed before its creation.

The crisis area for most African states is economic. Lack of natural resources combined with growing expectations has led to general overspending and subsequent huge debts to foreign investors or governments. Interest payments on what is owed is beyond the capacity of many African states. The ordinary expenditures to keep some governments functioning have to be met by additional loans or outright grants from European governments. Only a few countries in Africa have not relegated agricultural development to a secondary position, preferring instead eye catching development projects such as dams, freeways, airlines, or expensive public buildings. This attitude combined with doctrinaire socialistic practices and an oftentimes inefficient and corrupt bureaucracy has meant that food production once sufficient no longer meets the needs of a burgeoning population. Thus a large portion of foreign purchases is for food. Even the healthiest African states are in precarious condition. Those whose agriculture at best could barely support the population were extremely vulnerable to even minor climatic changes. The droughts of the 1970s and early 1980s proved disastrous to some. Mali, Niger, Chad, the Sudan, Mozambique, Somalia, and Ethiopia were devastated. Despite heroic international aid efforts, millions of persons died. The effects of the drought and the inefficient government responses to it linger and states such as Ethiopia may not recover for a generation.

Despite the evidence of maladministration in the economics of most African states, there are signs of a general awakening of many governments to the need for major changes. Although still maintaining Marxist rhetoric, the leaders of those states who have sought a socialistic revolution have been disengaging from their illusions since the state farms and state sponsored businesses have proven to be unsuccessful. In Tanzania, Guinea, Somalia, Mali, and Mozambique the governments have freed the economy allowing more individual enterprise while at the same time attempting to improve relations with the capitalistic West, so often villified during the decade after independence. The countries with valuable natural resources such as Nigeria, Liberia, Zimbabwe, and Zaire, often as a result of the prodding by the IMF, have altered their priorities, attempted to curb corruption, and developed balanced economic programs. Although the economic outlook for most African states grew even more grim in the 1980s, it remains possible for a reversal of the downward spiral if honest, efficient, practical leaders can be found to bring an end to the endemic civil strife and give stability to the governments. The interplay between government policy and the economic realities of African states will determine to a large degree whether this huge continent will achieve its full potential or be continually hampered by the internicine strife so typical of the period since 1965.

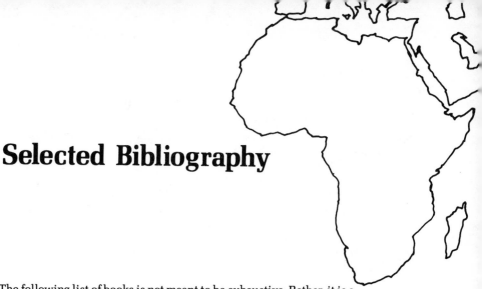

Selected Bibliography

The following list of books is not meant to be exhaustive. Rather, it is a selection of books and articles which the author found most useful for reference for specific subdivisions of the book. Many of these can also be utilized by students who wish to do reading corollary with the text. Those which might prove most useful have been marked with an asterisk (*). Books available in paperback editions have been noted with a plus sign (+). A number of books, particularly general histories, have application to several topic areas covered in this textbook, although each work is cited only once under the most appropriate chapter heading.

Chapter One

POSTWAR POLITICAL DEVELOPMENTS—FRENCH AFRICA

Adamolekum, Ladipo. "The Road to Independence in French Tropical Africa," *Tarikh*, II, No. 4, 1969.

Alexander, A. S. "The Ivory Coast Constitution," *Journal of Modern African Studies*, I, No. 3, 1963.

Berg, Elliott J. "The Economic Basis of Political Choice in French West Africa," *The American Political Science Review*, LIV, 1960.

Carter, Gwendolen. *African One Party States*. Ithaca, N.Y.: Cornell University Press, 1962.

LeVine, Victor T. *The Cameroons from Mandate to Independence*. Berkeley: University of California Press, 1964.

Morgenthau, Ruth Schacter. *Political Parties in French Speaking West Africa*. London: Oxford University Press, 1964.

Morgenthau, Ruth Schacter. "Single-Party Systems in West Africa," *The American Political Science Review*, LV, 1961.

Munger, Edwin S. "The Ivory Coast," *African Field Reports, 1952–1961*. Cape Town: C. Struik, 1961.

Senghor, Léopold Sédar. "West Africa in Evolution," *Foreign Affairs*, XXXIX, 1960–1961.

Skurnik, Walter A. E. "France and Fragmentation in West Africa: 1945–1960," *Journal of African History*, VIII, No. 2, 1967.

Skurnik, Walter A. E. "Senghor and African Socialism," *Journal of Modern African Studies*, III, No. 3, 1965.

*Thompson, Virginia and Richard Adloff. *The Emerging States of French Equatorial Africa.* Stanford: Stanford University Press, 1960.

Thompson, Virginia and Richard Adloff. *French West Africa.* Stanford: Stanford University Press, 1958.

Wallerstein, Immanuel. "Elites in French-Speaking West Africa," *Journal of Modern African Studies*, III, No. 1, May 1965.

Zolberg, Aristide. *One Party Government in the Ivory Coast.* Princeton, N.J.: Princeton University Press, 1964.

Chapter Two

POSTWAR POLITICAL DEVELOPMENTS—BRITISH AFRICA

WEST AFRICA

Austin, Dennis. "The Working Committee of the United Gold Coast Convention," *Journal of African History*, II, No. 2, 1961.

Munger, Edwin S. "Ghana's Finance Minister: Komla Agbeli Gbedemah," *African Field Reports, 1952–1961.* Cape Town: C. Struik, 1961.

Robson, Peter. "The Problem of Senegambia," *Journal of Modern African Studies*, III, No. 3, 1965.

Rothschild, Donald S. "Safeguarding Nigeria's Minorities," Duquesne University Institute of African Affairs, *African Reprint No. 17*, 1964.

Smythe, H. H., and M. M. Smythe. "Subgroups of the New Nigerian Elite," Duquesne University Institute of African Affairs, *African Reprint No. 5*, 1960.

CENTRAL AFRICA

*Clegg, Edward. *Race and Politics, Partnership in the Federation of Rhodesia and Nyasaland.* London: Oxford University Press, 1960.

Clutton-Brock, Guy. *Dawn in Nyasaland.* London: Hodder & Stoughton, 1960.

Cohen, Andrew. *British Policy in Changing Africa.* London: Routledge & Kegan Paul, 1959.

Franck, Thomas M. *Race and Nationalism: The Struggle for Power in Rhodesia and Nyasaland.* New York: Fordham University Press, 1960.

*Franklin, Harry. *Unholy Wedlock: The Failure of the Central African Federation.* London: G. Allen & Unwin, 1963.

Hanna, A. J. *The Story of the Rhodesias and Nyasaland.* London: Faber & Faber, 1960.

Kaunda, Kenneth. *A Humanist in Africa.* London: Longmans, Green & Co., 1966.

Leys, Colin, and R. Cranford Pratt (eds.). *A New Deal in Central Africa.* London: Heinemann, 1960.

*Mason, Philip. *Year of Decision.* London: Oxford University Press, 1960.

+Powdermaker, Hortense. *Copper Town: Changing Africa.* New York: Harper & Row, 1965.

THE HIGH COMMISSION TERRITORIES

Ashton, Edmund H. *The Basuto.* London: Oxford University Press, 1962.

Benson, Mary. *Tshekedi Khama.* London: Faber & Faber, 1961.

*Hailey, William M. (Baronet). *The Republic of South Africa and the High Commission Territories.* London: Oxford University Press, 1963.

Halpern, Jack. *South Africa's Hostages.* Baltimore, Md.: Penguin, 1965.

+Kuper, Hilda. *The Swazi: A South African Kingdom.* New York: Holt, Rinehart and Winston, 1963.

Munger, Edwin S. *Swaziland, the Tribe and Country.* New York: American Field Services, 1962.

Rosenthal, Eric. *African Switzerland: Basutoland of Today.* London: Hutchinson, 1948.

Sillery, A. *The Bechuanaland Protectorate.* London: Oxford University Press, 1952.

*Stevens, R. P. *Lesotho, Botswana and Swaziland.* New York: Praeger, 1967.

Stevens, R. P. "Swaziland Political Development," *Journal of Modern African Studies,* I, No. 3, 1963.

BRITISH EAST AFRICA

Chamberlain, John. "Kenyatta's Kenya," *American-African Affairs Association Paper,* April 1968.

Glickman, Harvey. "Some Observations on the Army and Political Unrest in Tanganyika," Duquesne University Institute of African Affairs, *African Reprint No. 16,* 1964.

*Ingham, Kenneth. *The Making of Modern Uganda.* London: Allen & Unwin, 1958.

Lansdale, J. M. "Some Origins of Natonalism in East Africa," *Journal of African History,* IX, No. 1, 1968.

Low, D. A., and R. C. Pratt. *Buganda and British Overrule, 1900–1955.* London: Oxford University Press, 1960.

Mboya, Tom. *Freedom and After.* London: Andre Deutsch, 1963.

*Rosberg, Carl G., and J. Nottingham. *The Myth of Mau Mau: Nationalism in Kenya.* New York: Praeger, 1966.

Tordoff, William. "Regional Administration in Tanzania," *Journal of Modern African Studies,* III, No. 1, May 1965.

Chapter Three

POSTWAR POLITICAL DEVELOPMENTS—BELGIAN AFRICA

Hennessy, Maurice N. *The Congo.* New York: Praeger, 1961.
*Hoskyns, Catherine. *The Congo since Independence.* London: Oxford University Press, 1965.
Lefever, E. W. *Crisis in the Congo.* Washington: Brookings, 1965.
+*Legum, Colin. *Congo Disaster.* Baltimore, Md.: Penguin, 1961.
Munger, E. S. "Conflict in the Congo," *African Field Reports, 1952–61.* Cape Town: C. Struik, 1961.
+*O'Brien, Conor Cruise. *To Katanga and Back.* New York: Simon and Schuster, 1962.
Young, Crawford. *Politics in the Congo.* Princeton, N.J.: Princeton University Press, 1965.

Chapter Four

THE PORTUGUESE SPEAKING TERRITORIES

+*Davidson, Basil. *In the Eye of the Storm: Angola's People.* Garden City, N.Y.: Doubleday, 1973.
+*Davidson, Basil. *The Liberation of Guiné.* Baltimore: Penguin, 1969.
*Ehnmark, Anders and Per Wastberg. *Angola and Mozambique.* New York: Roy Publishers, 1963.
*Henriksen, Thomas. *Mozambique: A History.* London: Rex Collings, 1978.
*Marcum, John. *The Angolan Revolution,* Vol. II. Cambridge, Mass.: M.I.T. Press, 1978.
Mason, Philip, et al. *Angola: Views of A Revolt.* London: Oxford University Press, 1962.
Munger, Edwin S. "Mozambique: Uneasy Today, Uncertain Tomorrow," *African Field Reports, 1952-61.* Cape Town: C. Struik, 1961.
Saul, John. *The State and Revolution in Eastern Africa.* New York: Monthly Review Press, 1979.
Segal, Ronald. *Political Africa.* London: Stevens, 1961.
Stockwell, John. *In Search of Enemies.* New York: W.W. Norton and Co., 1978.

Chapter Five

SUPRANATIONAL ORGANIZATIONS

+*Adam, Thomas R. *Government and Politics in Africa.* New York: Random House, 1965.
+Burke, Fred G. *Africa's Quest for Order.* Englewood Cliffs, N.J.: Prentice Hall, 1964.
+Dia, Mamadou. *The African Nations and World Solidarity.* New York: Praeger, 1962.
Haile Selassie I. "Toward African Unity," *Journal of Modern African Studies,* I, No. 3, 1963.

Hovet, Thomas. *Africa in the United Nations.* Evanston, Ill.: Northwestern University Press, 1963.

*Nkrumah, Kwame. *Africa Must Unite.* London: Heineman, 1961.

Nye, Joseph S., Jr. "East African Economic Integration," *Journal of Modern African Studies,* I, No. 4, 1963.

+Rivkin, Arnold. *Africa and the West.* New York: Praeger, 1962.

Segal, Aaron. "Africa Newly Divided," *Journal of Modern African Studies,* II, No. 1, 1964.

Chapter Six

THE SPECIAL CASE: THE REPUBLIC OF SOUTH AFRICA, 1910–1965

Carter, Gwendolen, and Patrick O'Meara. *Southern Africa: The Continuing Crisis.* Bloomington: Indiana University Press, 1979.

+*Davis, John A., and James Baker (eds.). *Southern Africa in Transition.* New York: Praeger, 1966.

De Beer, Z.J. *Multi-Racial South Africa.* London: Oxford University Press, 1961.

+De Kiewiet, C.W. *A History of South Africa: Social and Economic.* London: Oxford University Press, 1966.

+Drury, Allen. *A Very Strange Society.* New York: Pocket Books, 1968.

*Duignan, Peter, and L.H. Gann, *South West Africa—Namibia.* New York: American African Affairs Association, 1978.

*Feit, Edward. *African Opposition in South Africa.* Stanford: Hoover Institution, 1967.

+*Feit, Edward. *South Africa: The Dynamics of the African National Congress.* London: Oxford University Press, 1962.

+*First, Ruth. *South West Africa.* Baltimore, Md.: Penguin, 1963.

Gerhart, Gail M. *Black Power in South Africa.* Berkeley, University of California Press, 1978.

Hammond-Toke, W.D. "The Transkeian Council System 1895-1955," *Journal of African History,* IX, No. 3, 1968.

+*Hepple, Alexander. *Verwoerd.* Baltimore, Md.: Pelican Books, 1967.

Hill, C.R. *Bantustans.* London: Oxford University Press, 1964.

Legum, Colin. *The Western Crisis Over Southern Africa.* New York: Africana Publishing Company, 1979.

+Louw, Eric H. *The Case for South Africa.* New York: MacFadden Books, 1963.

Luthuli, Albert. *Let My People Go.* New York: McGraw-Hill, 1962.

+Marquard, Leo. *The Peoples and Policies of South Africa.* London: Oxford University Press, 1962.

+Mbeki, Govan. South Africa: *The Peasants' Revolt.* Baltimore, Md.: Penguin Books, 1964.

+Roux, Edward. *Time Longer than Rope.* Madison, Wis.: University of Wisconsin Press, 1966.

+Segal, Ronald. *Sanctions against South Africa.* Baltimore, Md.: Penguin Books, 1964.

Shepherd, George W. *Anti-Apartheid.* Westport, Conn.: Greenwood Press, 1977.

South African Bureau of Racial Affairs. "Apartheid—A Slogan or a Solution," *Fact Paper No. 30*, March, 1957.

South African Bureau of Racial Affairs. "Bantu Education Policy," *Fact Paper No. 39*, August 1957.

South African Bureau of Racial Affairs. "Bantu Labour in Industry," *Fact Paper No. 12*, June 1956.

South African Bureau of Racial Affairs. "Implications of the Separate Development Policy," *Fact Paper No. 17*, August 1956.

South African Bureau of Racial Affairs. "Is Separation the Answer to South Africa's Race Problem?" *Fact Paper No. 16*, August 1956.

South African Bureau of Racial Affairs. "The Origins and Essence of the Race Pattern in South Africa," *Fact Paper No. 61*, July 1958.

Thomas, Elizabeth M. *The Harmless People.* New York: Alfred Knopf, 1959.

+*Thompson, Leonard. *Politics in the Republic of South Africa.* Boston: Little, Brown, 1966.

Tötemeyer, Gerhard. *Namibia Old and New.* New York: St. Martin's Press, 1978.

+Vatcher, William H. *White Laager: The Rise of Afrikaner Nationalism.* New York: Praeger, 1965.

+*Woods, Donald. *Biko.* New York: Vintage Press, 1979.

Chapter Seven

TROUBLED INDEPENDENCE: WEST AFRICA

Afrifa, A. A. *The Ghana Coup.* London: Frank Cass, 1966.

Ayres, Robert L. *Banking on the Poor: The World Bank and World Poverty.* Cambridge, Mass.: MIT Press, 1983.

Bienen, Henry. *Armies and Parties in Africa.* New York: Africana Publishing Co., 1978.

Bauer, P. T. *Equality, the Third World, and Economic Delusion.* Cambridge, Mass.: Harvard University Press, 1981.

Clapham, Christopher, Ian Campbell, and George Philips, eds. *The Political Dilemmas of Military Regimes.* Totowa, N.J.: Barner & Noble Books, 1985.

+*Davidson, Basil, Joe Slovo, and A. R. Wilkinson. *The New Politics of Revolution.* Baltimore, Md.: Penguin, 1976.

+*Decalo, Samuel. *Coups and Army Rule in Africa.* New Haven: Yale University Press, 1976.

*First, Ruth. *Power in Africa.* New York: Random House, 1970.

Franke, Richard W., and Barbara J. Chasin. *Seeds of Famine: Ecological Destruction and the Development Dilemma in the West African Sahel.* Montclair, N.J.: Allanheld, Osmun, 1980.

*Gutteridge, W. F. *Military Regimes in Africa.* London: Metheun and Co., 1975.

Iliffe, John. *The Emergence of African Capitalism.* London: Macmillan, 1983.

Kennedy, Paul T. *Ghanaian Businessmen: From Artisan to Capitalist Entrepreneur in a Dependent Economy.* Munich: Weltform Verlang, 1980.

*Kirk-Greene, A.H.M., *Crisis and Conflict in Nigeria,* 2 vols. London: Oxford University Press, 1971.

*Levine, Victor. *Political Corruption: The Ghana Case.* Stanford: Hoover Institution Press, 1975.

Nafzinger, E. Wayne. *The Economics of Political Instability: The Nigerian Biafran War.* Boulder, Colo.: Westview Press, 1983.

Nkrumah, Kwame. *Neo-Colonialism: The Last Stage of Imperialism.* London: Thomas Nelson, 1965.

Nnoli, Okwudiba, ed. *Path to Nigerian Development.* Dakar, Senegal: Codesria, 1981.

Nolutshungu, Sam C. *Changing South Africa: Political Considerations.* New York: Africana Publishing Co., 1982.

Odetola, Theophilius Olatunde. *Military Politics in Nigeria: Economic Development and Political Stability.* New Brunswick, N.J.: Transaction Books, 1978.

+Ojukwu, C. Odemegwu. *Random Thoughts of C. Odemegwu Ojukwu,* 2 vols. New York: Harper & Row, 1969.

Rimmer, Douglas. *The Economics of West Africa.* New York: St. Martin's Press, 1984.

Robertson, Claire C. *Sharing the Same Bowl: A Socioeconomic History of Women and Class in Accra, Ghana.* Bloomington: Indiana University Press, 1984.

Touval, Saada. *The Boundary Policies of Independent Africa.* Cambridge, Mass.: Harvard University Press, 1972.

Uchendu, Victor C., ed. *Dependency and Underdevelopment in West Africa.* Netherlands: E. J. Brill, 1980.

Watts, Michael. *Silent Violence: Food, Famine and Peasantry in Northern Nigeria.* Berkeley: University of California Press, 1983.

Zartman, I. William, ed. *The Political Economy of Nigeria.* New York: Praeger, 1983.

_____. *Ripe for Revolution, Conflict and Intervention in Africa.* New York: Oxford University Press, 1985.

Chapter Eight

TROUBLED INDEPENDENCE: CENTRAL AND SOUTHERN AFRICA

Callaghy, Thomas M. *The State-Society Struggle: Zaire in Comparative Perspective.* New York: Columbia University Press, 1984.

Colin, Murray. *Families Divided: The Impact of Migrant Labour in Lesotho.* Johannesburg: Raven Press, 1981.

Copperbelt in Zambian Development. New York: Cambridge University Press, 1979.

Gibson, Richard. *African Liberation Movements.* New York: Oxford University Press, 1972.

Gould, David J. *Bureaucratic Corruption and Underdevelopment in the Third World: The Case of Zaire.* New York:

Kaunda, Kenneth. *Independence and Beyond.* London: Thomas Nelson, 1966.

Lan, David. *Guns and Rain: Guerrillas and Spirit Mediums in Zimbabwe.* London: James Curry Ltd., and Berkeley: University of California Press, 1985.

Muzorewa, Abel. *Rise Up and Walk.* Nashville, Tenn.: Abingdon, 1978.

Nyangoni, Christopher, and Gideon Nyandoro. *Zimbabwe Independence Movements.* New York: Barnes and Noble, 1979.

Seidman, Ann. *The Roots of Crisis in Southern Africa.* Trenton, N.J.: Africa World Press, 1985.

+Sithole, N. *African Nationalism.* London: Oxford University Press, 1969.

Young, Crawford, and Thomas Turner. *The Rise and Decline of the Zairian State.* Madison: University of Wisconsin Press, 1985.

Chapter Nine

TROUBLED INDEPENDENCE: EAST AND NORTHEASTERN AFRICA

Bager, Torben. *Marketing Cooperatives and Peasants in Kenya.* New York: Africana Publishing Co., 1980.

Barkan, Joel D., ed. *Politics and Public Policy in Kenya and Tanzania.* New York: Praeger, 1979, 2nd rev. ed., 1984.

Clarke, W. Edmund. *Socialist Development and Public Investment in Tanzania 1964–73.* Toronto: University of Toronto Press, 1978.

Firebrace, James, with Stuart Holland. *Never Kneel Down: Drought, Development and Liberation in Eritrea.* Trenton, N.J.: The Red Sea Press, 1985.

Kenyatta, Jomo. *Suffering without Bitterness.* Nairobi: East African Publishing House, 1968.

Kitching, Gavin. *Class and Economic Change in Kenya: The Making of an African Petite Bourgeoisie 1905–1970.* New Haven: Yale University Press, 1980.

McHenry, Dean E., Jr. *Tanzania's Ujaama Villages: The Implementation of a Rural Development Strategy.* Berkeley: Institute of International Studies, 1979.

Markakis, John, and Nega Ayele. *Class and Revolution in Ethiopia.* Nottingham: Spokesman Press, 1978.

Miller, Norman H. *Kenya: The Quest for Prosperity.* Boulder, Colo.: Westview Press, 1984.

Mittelman, James H. *Underdevelopment and the Transition to Socialism: Mozambique and Tanzania.* New York: Academic Press, 1981.

Nyerere, Julius. *Freedom and Unity.* Dar es Salaam: Oxford University Press, 1966.

*Ottoway, Marina, and David Ottoway. *Ethiopia, Empire in Revolution.* New York: Africana Publishers, 1978.

Odinga, Oginga. *Not Yet Uhuru.* London: Heinemann, 1967.

Peace, Adrian J. *Choice, Class and Conflict: A Study of Southern Nigerian Factory Workers.* Atlantic Highlands, N.J.: Humanities Press, 1979.

Selassie, Bereket Habte. *Conflict and Intervention in the Horn of Africa.* New York: Monthly Review Press, 1980.

Wai, Dunstan M. *The African-Arab Conflict in the Sudan.* New York: Africana Publishing Co., 1981.

For the most recent developments in Africa consult *West Africa, Africa Report, Facts on File, Time, Newsweek,* and comprehensive newspapers such as *The Times* of London, *The Observer, New York Times,* and the *Los Angeles Times.*

Index

Aba, 196
ABAKO-Cartel, 101
Abdul Muhammad (Babu), 88, 93, 95
Aberdare Mountains, 81
Abidjan, 216 221, 228
Abomey, 223
Aburi Agreement, 196
Accra, 193
Accra Conference (1959), 100, 125, 144, 150
Acheampong, General Ignatius, 190, 191
Acheikh Ibn Omar, 234
Acholi, 269, 270, 272
Action Democratique et Social de la Cote d' Ivorie, 14
Action Front for National Priorities, 174
Action Group, 49, 50, 52, 53
Acyl Ahmat, 229
Adamfio, Tawia, 46, 47
Addis Ababa, 197, 262, 278, 284, 286
Addis Ababa Conference, 36
Adegenbenro, Alhaji, 51, 53, 55
Adelazziz, Mohamad, 208
Adeji, Ako, 46, 47
Adoula, Cyrille, 104–105, 106, 107
Adowa, 284
Afars, 284, 285
Afars and Issas, 280, 285
African Development Bank, 147
African National Congress (ANC), 61, 131, 132, 163, 164, 168, 169, 175, 176, 179, 180, 185, 244, 249, 256, 257, 258, 259
African Peoples Party (APP), 83
Afrifa, Maj. General A. A., 48, 190, 191
Afrikaanse Nasionale Studentebond (ANS), 156
Afrikaners (see also Boers), 154, 155, 156, 157, 162
Afrikaner Party, 155, 167
Afrique Equatorial Francais (AEF), 1, 2, 3, 22–29, 176
Afrique Occidentale Francais (AOF), 1, 2, 3, 5–22, 25, 180, 205
Afro-Shirazi party (ASP), 94, 95, 262
Agacher region, 211
Agriculture, 125, 127, 129, 130, 132, 137, 138, 181, 193, 198, 208, 216, 220, 223,
230, 234, 239, 240, 243, 247, 248, 255, 257, 263, 264, 266, 269, 270, 283, 289, 290, 294
Aguiyi Ironsi, Maj. General John, 56, 195
Ahidjo, Ahmadou, 218–219
Ahmadu Bello University, 201
Ahomadegbe, Justin, 7, 9, 10, 223
Air France hijacking, 269
Akintola, Samuel L., 51, 52, 53, 55
Akouta district, 216
Akuffo, Maj. General Sam, 190, 191
al Dahab, Maj. General Suwar, 289
Algeria, 69, 134, 146, 207, 237
Alliance Démocratique Dahoméene, 10
All Peoples Congress (APC) (Sierra Leone), 58, 59, 194, 195
al Mahdi, Imam al Hadi, 286
al Mahdi, Sidik, 285, 286, 287, 290–291
al Myini, Hassan, 264, 265
al Niameiry, Col. Jaafar Muhammad, 233, 286, 287, 288, 289, 291
Amery, Leopold, 85
Amin, Idi, 199, 229, 262, 265, 268, 269, 270, 272
Amnesty International, 211–212
Ana Nya, 286, 289, 290
Andom, Lt. General Aman, 278
Anglo American, 182
Angola, 117, 118–127, 128, 133, 137, 148, 171, 173, 184–186, 237, 238–239, 249, 293
Ankole, 268, 272
Ankrah, Lt. General Joseph, 48, 189–190
Annobon, 229
Ansar, 285
Aouzau, 235
Apartheid, 164, 174
Aptido, Hassan Gouled, 285
Apithy, Serou, 7, 9, 10
arap Moi, Daniel, 264, 267, 268, 273
Arlit mines, 214
Armed Forces Revolutionary Council, 191
Army Congolaise Nationale (ANC), 104, 105, 106, 107
Arusha Declaration, 261
Asians, 265, 268, 271
Asmara, 278, 282

Assale, Charles, 30
assassination attempts, 34, 46, 54–
55, 103, 217–218, 222–223, 227,
230, 265, 268, 274, 291
Assemblées de Union Francoise, 2
Assimilado policy, 116, 119, 121, 124,
128, 133
*Association des Bakongo pour le
mantien l'Unité et l'Expansion et
la Defénse de Langue Kikongo*
(ABAKO), 99, 100, 101, 102, 105,
106, 109
*Association pour la promotion des
Masses* (APROSOMA), 111–112
Aubame, Jean, 29, 30
Aupias, Father, 216–218
Awolowo, Chief Obafemi, 38, 49, 51,
194, 195, 199

Babana, Horma Ould, 17, 18
Babangida, Maj. General Ibrahim,
201
Badouin I (King of Belgium), 102
Bafulero Pygmies, 106
Bagaza, Lt. Colonel Jean-Baptiste,
243
Bahr al Ghazal, 288
Bahutu, 110, 111, 112, 113, 114, 115,
241, 242, 243
Bakary, Djibo, 19, 215
Bakongo, 124
Balalis, 28
Balewa, Abubakr Tafewa, 49, 51, 54,
55, 139
Ballinger, Margaret, 166
Baluba, 102, 103
BALUBAKAT Party, 102, 104, 105,
106
Bamako, 15, 217
Bambara, 15
Bamenda, 220
Banda, Hastings, 40, 65–66, 246
Bangui, 226, 228
Bangura, Brig. General John, 194
Banjul, 198
Bankole-Bright, H., 56
Bantu, 157, 159, 160, 163–164, 166–

167, 173, 249, 250
Bantustans, 58, 169, 172, 180, 182–
183, 184
Banza, Colonel Alexandre, 226
Barclays Bank, 182
Bariba Tribe, 9
Basuto Congress Party (BCP), 70, 71,
72, 73, 256
Basuto National Council, 71
Basuto National Party (BNP), 71, 72,
73, 256, 257
Basutoland (see also Lesotho), 69–
73, 157, 172
Basutoland Council, 70
Bechuanaland (see also Botswana),
73–75, 169
Bechuanaland Democratic Party
(BDP), 75
Bechuanaland Liberal Party (BLP),
75
Bechuanaland Peoples Party (BPP),
75
Beira, 125, 128, 250
Belgium, 97–102, 108, 110, 111, 112,
114, 237, 240
Bello, Sardauna Ahmadu, 49, 53, 55
Benguela, 123, 124, 244
Benin, 205, 223–224
Benti, Brig. General Teferi, 278, 280
Bhekimpi, 257
Biafran War, 196–197
Bie, 124
Biha, Leopold, 114, 115
Biko, Steven, 173
Binaisa, Godfrey, 262, 270
Bioko, 229
Bissau, 133, 136
Biyogo, Macias Nguema, 229
Bloc Africain, 20
Bloc Africain de Guinée (BAG), 10
Bloc Démocratique Comerounais
(BDC), 30
Bloc Démocratic Eburneene, 32
Bloc Démocratic Gabonais (BDG),
29
Bloc Démocratic Senegalais (BDS),
20

Bloc Nigérien d' Action (BNA), 19
Bloc Progressiste Sénégalais (BPS), 20
Bloch, Dora, 269
Bobo Dioulasso, 216
Boers (see also Afrikaners), 153, 157
Boer War, 149, 153, 156, 157, 162
Boesak, Dr. Allan, 175, 176, 178
Boisson, Pierre, 1
Bokassa, Colonel Jean Bedel, 25–26, 226–227, 228, 230
Bolikango, Jean, 103, 104
Bondelswarts Hottentots, 154, 169
Bongo, Albert, 137, 225, 226
Boni, Nazi, 22
Bonny, 196
Bophuthatswana, 172, 183, 255
Border problems, 262, 265, 266, 269, 270, 271, 273, 274, 276, 277, 282
Botha, Pieter W. 125, 126, 131, 174, 175, 178, 179, 180, 181, 183, 184, 186
Botha, R.F., 182, 258
Botswana, 182, 253, 255, 258, 259, 293
Botswana Democratic Party (BDP), 259
Botswana Independence Party (BIP), 259
Botwsana Peoples Party (BPP), 259
Boucief, Colonel Ould, 206
Brazil, 193
Brazzaville, 27, 28, 29
Brazzaville Conference, 2, 26
British Commonwealth, 154, 164, 254
British Somaliland, 285
Broederbond, 174
Buganda, 90, 91, 92, 93, 268
Buhari, Maj. General Mohammad, 200–201
Bujumbura, 244
Bukavu, 237
Bull, Benjamin Pinto, 23, 133
Bunyoro, 89, 91, 92, 93, 268
Burkina Faso (see also Upper Volta),

193, 205, 211, 215–219
Burns Constitution, 43
Burundi (Urundi), 108, 110, 111, 112, 113–115, 240, 242
Busia, Dr. Kofi A., 45, 46, 190, 191, 193
Busoga, 92
Buthelezi, Chief Mangosuthu Gatsha, 178, 179, 181, 185
Buyoya, Major Pierre, 244

Cabinda, 120, 122, 124, 126, 127, 186
Cabora Bassa Dam, 130, 132
Cabral, Amilcar, 133, 134, 135
Cabral, Luis de Almeida, 135, 136
Caetano, Marcello, 118, 120, 130, 135
Cairo, 107, 142, 149
Calabar, 196
Cameroon, 30, 31, 218, 220, 221, 233
Cameroons National Federation (CNF), 31
Cameroons Peoples National Convention (CPNC), 32
Cape Colony, 143, 161, 162
Cape Colored, 154, 159, 161, 162, 167–168
Cape Town, 177
Cape Verde, 126, 135–137
Carrington, Lord, 251
Carter, Jimmy, 254
Casablanca Conference, 139, 141
Casablanca Group, 147, 151, 168, 188
Casamance, 209
Castro, Fidel, 282
Catholic Church, 241–242, 243–244
Central African Customs and Economic Union, 25
Central African Federation, 40, 59–61, 244
Central African Republic (Empire), 23–26, 226–228
Chad, 26, 27, 205, 231–235, 240, 289, 294
Chadian Liberation Front (FRON-ILAT), 232, 234
Chama cha Mapinduzi, 258, 260
Chef de Territoire, 5

Chevron Oil, 126, 290, 291
China, Peoples Republic of, 26, 29, 47, 84, 88, 89
Chipembere, Henry, 66
Chirwa, Orton, 247
Chissano, Joquim, 132, 184
Chiume, Kanyama, 62
Cholera, 229
Ciskei, 183, 255
Citoyens de Statut Civil, 3, 17
Citoyens de Statut Personnel, 3
Clark Amendment, 126
Cofie-Crabbie, H., 46, 47
Colonato, 129
Comité Démocratique Africain, 106
Comité du Liberation National (CLN), 105, 106, 107
Comité de l'Unité Togolaise (CUT), 33
Commercial Workers Union, 61
Committee on Youth Organization, 44
Communanté Economique de l'Afrique de l'Ouest (CEAO), 211
Communism, 12, 13, 29, 71, 164, 166
Compaoré, Captain Blaise, 218
Conakry, 211, 246
Concagou, Tairou, 10
Confedération des Associations du Katanga (CONAKAT), 102, 105, 106
Conferencia de Organizacoes Nacionalistas das Colonias Portuguesas (CONCP), 120, 122, 124, 128
Conféderation Générale des Travailleurs (CGT), 10, 11
Conféderation Générale de Travail Africaine (CGTA), 11
Congo, Republic of (Brazzaville), 27–29, 101, 230, 231
Congo, Republic of (Kinshasa) (see also Zaire), 100–110, 115, 121, 141, 149, 151, 152
Congolese Front for the Restoration of Democracy, 240
Congress Popular de Angola (CPA),

122
Congress for the Second Republic, 247
Congress of South African Trade Unions (COSTAU), 178
Conseil d'Administration, 17
Conseil Général, 3
Conseil de gouvernements, 4, 5
Conseil d'la Entente, 9, 13–14, 19, 22, 23, 213
Conseil de la République, 2–3
Conservative Alliance of Zimbabwe (CAZ), 255
Conservative Party (South Africa), 175, 186
Conté, Lansana, 212, 213
Convention Africaine, 20
Convention Nationale Congolaise (CONACO), 109
Convention Nationale Dahoméene, 10
Convention Peoples Party (CPP), 38, 44, 45–57, 187–188
Correia, Brig. General Paulo, 136
Cotonou, 18, 19, 214
Coulibaly, Ouezzin, 22
Council for the Unity of Sudan, 288
Coussey Commission, 44
Creoles, 56, 194
Crocker, Charles, 126–127
Cuba, 124, 125, 126, 134, 238, 282, 283
Cuenene River, 123, 173
Currency devaluation, 192, 200, 204, 212, 213, 237, 239, 245, 246, 254, 264, 266

Dacko, David, 25, 227, 228
da Costa, Manuel Pinto, 137, 138
Dahomey (see Benin), 6–10, 13, 19, 33, 140, 141
Dakar, 133, 176, 180, 211
Danquah, Dr. Joseph, 44, 45
Dar es Salaam, 87, 89, 244, 247, 263
da Silva, Jão, 136
de Andrade, Mario Pinto, 120
DeBeers Corp., 240

Decree 88A (Liberia), 204
Defferre, Gaston, 4
DeGaulle, Charles, 1, 2, 6, 11, 15, 20, 22, 23, 28, 142
Delamere, Lord, 80, 85
de la Rey, General J. H., 153
Democratic Front for the Salvation of Somalia, 277
Democratic Party (Gambia), 42
Democratic Party (Uganda), 91, 270, 271, 272
Democratic Salvation Front, 282
Democratic Unionist Party, 290
Dergue (Ethiopian Provisional Military Council), 278, 280, 282
d'Estaing, Giscard, 227
deWet, General Christian, 153
Dia, Momadou, 15, 16, 20–21
Diawadou, Barry, 10, 12
Dicko, Hamadori, 15, 16
Diop, Cheikh Anta, 21
Diori, Hamani, 19, 168, 189, 214, 215
Diouf, Abdou, 202, 208–209
Djibouti, 277, 280, 284
Doe, Sergeant Samuel, 203, 204
Dominion Party, 62
dos Santos, Eduardo, 124, 125, 127, 185
dos Santos, Maralino, 129
Douglas-Home, Sir Alex, 249
Drought, 135, 137, 181, 184, 189, 193, 197, 202, 205, 207, 208, 210, 212, 214, 216, 234, 239, 254, 259, 263, 276, 278, 283, 289, 294
Doula, 220
DuBois, W.E.B., 44
Durban, 152, 178, 184

East Germany, 125
Eboué, Felix, 130
Economic Community of West African States (ECOWAS), 203, 213, 294
Egal, Ibrahim, 274
Egba Omu Oduduwa, 49
Egypt, 233, 286, 287, 288, 289
El Ayoum, 207

Elizabethville, 103, 104
el Mokhtar, Sidi, 17
Endeley, Dr. Emmanuel, 31
Entebbe raid, 279
Enugu, 196
Equatoria Province, 285, 286, 288
Equatorial Guinea, 228–230
Eritrea, 274, 278, 280, 281, 282, 284
Eritrean Liberation Front (ELF), 277, 278, 281, 282, 283
Ethiopia, 127, 274, 276, 277–284, 285, 294
Ethiopian Civil War, 280, 281, 282, 284
Ethiopian resettlement, 283
Ethiopian-Somali War, 285
European Economic Community (EEC), 277, 285
Ewe, 32, 33
Eyadéma, Lt. Colonel Gnassingbé, 193, 218, 222

Falasha, 277, 283
Faya-Largeau, 234
Faye, Rev. J. C., 42
Federal Elections Committee (FEDECO) (Nigeria), 198, 199
Fernando Po, 169
Field, Winston, 62, 63, 64
Fizi, 108
Fon, 7
Foncha, John, 31, 32
Fonds de Solidarité, 140
Food and Agriculture Organization (FAO), 189, 283
Force Publique, 102, 103
Forces Armees du Nord (FAN), 233
Foreign debts, 124, 132, 137, 138, 193, 195, 200, 202, 205, 208, 213, 215, 222, 224, 230–231, 237, 238, 239, 243, 245, 264–265, 266, 289
Fort Hare University, 177
Fort Lamy, 263
France, 1–5, 10, 14, 21, 22, 25, 27, 181, 182–183, 196, 205, 211, 212, 215, 218, 219, 220, 224, 231–232, 233, 234, 241, 280, 284, 285

Franco-Burundi Committee on Economic Cooperation, 243
Free French, 1–2, 26
Freetown, 195
French Community, 6, 12, 14, 15, 17, 18, 22
French Equatorial African Federation (AEF), 1, 2, 3, 23–30
French Union, 2, 3, 33
French West African Federation (AOF), 1, 2, 3, 6–23
Frente da Libertaçao de Mocambique (FRELIMO), 128, 129, 130, 165, 258
Frente da Libertaçao Nacional de Angola (FNLA), 120, 122, 123, 124, 237
Frente da Libertaçao para Independencia Nacional de Guinea (FLING), 133
Frente Revolucionaria Africana para Independencia Nacional (FRAIN), 120
Front National Sénégalais, 21
Fula, 18

Gabon, 28, 29–30, 137, 189, 196, 225–226
Gaborone, 259
Gambia, 41–43, 134, 189, 201–202, 209
Gambia Congress party, 43
Gandhi, Mohandas K., 44
Garang, Colonel John, 284, 285, 286
Garba-Jahumpa, I. M., 42, 43
Garvey, Marcus, 44
Gbedemah, Komea, 186
Gbenye, Christopher, 105, 107, 109
Geneva Conference, 250
Germany, 274, 277
Ghana, 19, 23, 32, 34, 35, 43–48, 66, 109, 134, 141, 145, 146, 150, 187, 189–194, 200, 223
Gitega, 242
Goumba, Dr. Abel, 228
Gowon, Maj. General, 195, 196, 197
Grand Conseil, 4, 5

Great Britain, 36, 37, 38, 40, 41–42, 43, 49, 56, 60, 61, 63, 66, 68, 69, 75, 86–87, 88, 89, 92, 144–147, 149, 156, 248, 252, 253, 257, 265, 268, 269, 279
Great Nigerian Peoples Party (GNPP), 198
Grigg, Sir Edward, 85
Griqualand, 172, 173
Grunitsky, Nicolas, 33, 34–36, 222, 223
guerrilla actions, 120–121, 122, 123, 124, 125, 129–132, 134, 170, 171, 176, 184, 185, 207, 219, 237–238, 245, 248, 249, 265, 271, 277, 280, 282, 289, 290
Guéye, Lamine, 2, 20, 21
Guinea, 10–12, 13, 35, 48, 134, 188, 194, 203, 211–214
Guinea-Bissau, 130, 133–135, 136, 293
Gulf oil, 124
Gwambe, Adelino, 128

Habré, Hissene, 232, 233, 234, 235, 240
Habyarimana, Maj. General Juyenal, 241
Haidala, Lt. Colonel Khouna, 206
Haile Mariam, Mengistu, 274, 277, 278–280, 281, 282, 284
Haile Selassie, 189, 274, 277
Haiti, 196
Hancock, Sir Keith, 90
Hanga, Kassim, 88, 95, 261
Harare, 253, 254
Hassan II, 206, 207, 208, 234, 237
Hausa, 18, 53, 197
Haut Conseil de l'Union Francoise, 2
Heath, Edward, 249
Hendrikse, Rev. H. J., 175
Herstigte Nasionale Party (HNP), 175
Hertzog, James Barry, 148
High Commission Territories, 69–77, 255, 258

Hills, Denis, 269
Hilton-Young Commission, 85
Holy Spirit Movement, 273
Homadi, Sheikh Shamite, 94
Homoine Massacre, 132
Momolisa, General Bantu, 183
Hottentots, 154, 161
Houphouët-Boigny, Felix, 6, 7, 11, 12–14, 15, 29, 141, 146, 147, 150, 151, 211, 217, 218, 220, 221, 227, 228
Huambo Province, 124
Human rights violations, 227, 229, 269, 270, 283
Hume, Sir Alec Douglas, 64

Ibadan, 55
Ibo, 196
Ibrahim, Alhaji, 198
Ife, 199
Ijebu Ode, 199
Ijebu Province, 55
Ikhia, Zodi, 19
Ileo, Joseph, 103, 106
Imbokodova, 257
Imru, Michael, 278
Indegenas, 128
Indigénat system, 1
Indirect Rule, 38, 74
Indo China, 134
Infant mortality, 132–133
Inga Dam, 239
Institute of Commonwealth Studies, 90
International Court of Justice, 217
International Monetary Fund (IMF), 131, 192, 193, 195, 200, 204, 209, 213, 230, 238, 239, 245, 246, 254, 263, 264, 271, 288, 291
Issa, 284, 285
Italy, 284
Italian Somaliland, 285
Ivory Coast, 10, 12–14, 140, 141, 145, 147, 188, 189, 193, 196, 205, 209, 211, 220–222, 227, 293

Jabavu, John Tengo, 163

Jarden, Aggrey, 286
Jawara, Sir Dauda, 42, 43, 191, 202
Jehovah's Witnesses, 242
Jijiga, 282, 283
Johannesburg, 178
Johnston, Sir Harry, 89
Jonathan, Chief Lebua, 71, 72, 73, 256, 257
Jonglei Canal, 258
Jumbe, Aboud, 264
Juxton-Smith, Lt. Colonel Andrew, 194

Kaduna, 199
Kalenjen tribe, 266
Kalonji, Albert, 101, 103, 104, 105, 107
Kambona, Oscar, 88, 261
Kamerun United National Congress (KUNC), 31, 50
Kamougue, Lt. Colonel Wadal Abdelkader, 232, 233, 234
Kampala, 197, 262, 269, 270, 281, 282
Kano, 199
Kano, Mallam Aminu, 49, 198, 199
Karamojong, 271, 272
Kariba Dam, 69
Kariuki affair, 265
Karl-I-Bond, Nguza, 240
Karume, Abeid Aman, 88, 94, 95, 261–262
Kasai Province, 102, 103, 104
Kasavubu, Joseph, 235, 237
Katanga Province (see also Shaba), 102, 103, 104, 105, 106, 109, 233, 237
Kaunda, Kenneth, 40, 67, 68, 69, 244, 245, 246, 248, 249, 250
Kavirondo Association, 81
Kawawa, Rashidi, 87
Kayibanda, Gregoiré, 241
Keita, Modibo, 7, 15–16, 20, 209, 210, 213
Kenema, 191
Kenya, 79–84, 89, 92, 95, 148, 149, 188, 262, 263, 265–268, 269, 273,

277, 293
Kenya African Democratic Union (KADU), 82, 83, 84
Kenya African National Union (KANU), 82, 83, 84, 257, 265
Kenya Federation of Labor, 83
Kenyatta, Jomo, 81, 82, 83, 84, 89, 107, 265, 266
Kérékou, Mathieu, 223–224
Khartoum, 286, 287, 288, 290, 291
Kigale, 112, 241, 242
Kigene, 113
Kigere V (Mwami of Rwanda), 111, 112, 241
Kikuyu, 80, 81, 82, 83, 265, 266, 267
Kikuyu Central Association (KCA), 80
Kikuyu Independent Schools Association, 80
Kimba, Evareste, 109, 110
Kisangani University, 240
Kissinger, Henry, 250
Kivu Province, 102, 103, 106
Kiwanuka, Benedicto, 91, 268
Kolwezi, 237, 238
Konaté, Momadou, 15
Kongo, Colonel Koffi, 222
Kosah, Sir Arku, 47
Kotoka, Colonel E. K., 48
Koulmallah, Ahmed, 27
Kounteche, Colonel Seyni, 214, 215
Kumasi, 46, 48
Kundia Mine, 213
Kwa-Natal option, 180
Kwa-Nedebele, 183–184
Kwa-Ngwane, 258
Kwa-Zulu, 180, 182
Kwilu Province, 106, 109

Labery, Enrique, 133
Labor unrest, 198, 216, 240
Lagos, 49, 196
Lagos Youth Movement, 49
Lakwena, Alice, 273
Lamizana, Lt. Colonel Sangoule, 23, 216
Lancaster House Conference, 245

Lango, 269, 272
Lansana, Brig. General David, 194
League of Nations Mandates, 30, 84, 85, 86, 110, 169, 170
Lekhanya, Maj. General Justin, 257
L'Entente Mauritanienne, 17
Léopoldville (see Kinshasa), 97, 99, 101, 102, 103, 109, 118
Lesotho, 172, 182, 255–257
Lesotho Liberation Army (LLA), 256
Libandhla, 76
Liberia, 202–205, 294
Libreville, 226
Libya, 222–225, 232, 233, 234, 235, 268, 269, 286, 287, 288, 290, 291
Lightfoot-Boston, Sir Henry, 194
Limann, Dr. Hilla, 191, 192, 193
Limpopo River, 129, 183
Liqoqo, 257
Lisette, Gabriel, 26
Lissouba, Pascal, 29
Loi Cadre, 5, 6, 7, 11, 13, 15, 22, 26, 33
Loi fondamentale, 101, 103
Loi Lamine Gueye (1st Law), 4
Loi Lamine Gueye (2nd Law), 2
Lome, 193, 212, 222
London, 197
Lourenço Marques (see also Maputo), 129, 130
Luanda, 124, 125, 127
Lubaya, Andre, 105, 107
Lukiko, 90, 91
Lule, Yussuf, 258, 266
Luly, Lt. Colonel Mohammad Ould, 202
Lumumba, Patrice, 101, 102, 103, 104
Lunda, 102, 237
Luo, 81, 82, 84, 265, 266
Lusaka, 124–126, 247
Lyttelton, Oliver, 81

Macalle, 283
Macaulay, Herbert, 49
Machado, Ilidio Alves, 120
Machel, Samora, 129, 130, 131, 132,

184
MacKenzie, Professor W. J. M., 86
MacPherson Constitution, 49, 50
Maga, Hubert, 19, 223
Mahgoub, Muhammad, 285, 286
Mahjub, Abdul, 286
Mahlangu, Majozi, 183
Makalahari people, 73
Makonnen, Endalkachew, 278
Makotoko, Seth, 71, 72, 73
Malagasy Republic, 140, 146
Malan, Daniel, 153, 154, 155, 161,
    162, 164–165
Malange, 120
Malawi (see also Nyasaland), 40,
    65–67, 129, 132, 246–248, 293
Malawi Congress Party, 66, 247
Malawi Freedom Movement (MA-
    FREMO), 247
Malebo, 229
Mali Federation, 7, 13, 15–16, 20, 22,
    23, 140, 142
Mali, Republic of, 21, 26, 142, 144,
    145, 146, 188, 189, 205, 209–211,
    217, 218, 294
Malinke, 212, 213
Malloum, General Felix, 232
Malopo, C. D., 72, 73
Mandela, Nelson, 164, 169, 179
Mangalme district, 27
Mangope, Lucas, 172, 173
Mantizima, George, 183
Mantizima, Kaiser, 170, 171, 172, 173
Maputo (Lourenço Marques), 132,
    184
Marais, Jaap, 175
Marehen tribe, 276
Marematlou Freedom Party, 71, 72,
    73
Margai, Albert, 194
Margai, Sir Milton, 56–57, 58, 59,
    194
Marxism, 124, 126, 127, 130, 132,
    137, 184, 185, 208, 223, 252, 283,
    284
Maseru, 256
Masindi, 272

Masire, Quett K. J., 279
Massacres, 130, 132, 241, 242, 258,
    269, 271, 272
Massawa, 282
Massemba-Debat, Alphonse, 226
Matabeleland, 253, 254
Matan as Sarra, 235
Matthews, Baccus, 203
Mauritania, 16–18, 145, 146, 189,
    206–207
Mauroy, Pierre, 226
M'Ba, Leon, 29, 30
Mbabane, 258
Mbadiwe, Dr. Kingsley, 51
Mbasogo, Colonel Teodora Obiang
    Nguema, 229
Mbeki, Govan, 179
Mbida, Andre, 30
M'Bochis, 28
Mboya, Tom, 265, 267
Méatche, Idrisson, 224
Mende, 194
Mendy, Francisco, 133
Mensot, John Henry, 193
Mercenary troops, 108, 113, 237
Micembero, Michael, 115, 242
Mid-Western   Democratic   Front
    (MDF), 52
Military: Angola, 134, 185, 186; Bel-
    gium, 237, 238; Cameroon, 219;
    Chad, 232–233, 234–235; Cuba,
    124, 125, 185, 238, 274, 283, 284;
    Djibouti, 285; Egypt, 288; Ethio-
    pia, 274, 276, 277, 278, 282;
    France, 227, 231, 234, 237, 238,
    285; Ghana, 188; Guinea, 203;
    Guinea-Bissau, 134; Lesotho, 257;
    Libya, 234, 235, 270; Mali, 188,
    206, 210, 211; Morocco, 201, 237,
    238; Mozambique, 128–130, 131;
    Nigeria, 196–197, 199; Portugal,
    129–130, 133–134; Rhodesia, 245,
    248, 249, 252; Senegal, 202, 209,
    238; Sierra Leone, 188; Somalia,
    274; South Africa, 125, 126, 132,
    173, 176, 177–178, 184, 185–186,
    256, 259; Sudan, 286, 287, 290;

SWAPO, 125; Tanzania, 262, 270, 271; Uganda, 252, 269, 270, 271, 272, 273; UNITA, 124–125, 126, 127; Zaire, 237; Zimbabwe, 132, 252
Military Committee for National Rectification, 204
Mineral resources, 213, 215, 255, 257, 258
Mining, 222, 225, 226, 237, 238, 239, 244, 245, 257
Mitterand, Francois, 212, 218
Mobutu Sese Seko, 235, 237, 238, 239, 240
Mogadishu, 276, 282
Mokhehle, Ntsu, 71
Mokwa, Joseph, 226, 227
Mombasa, 266
Momoh, Maj. General Joseph, 195
Monckton Commission, 61, 62
Mondlane, Dr. Eduardo, 124
Mondu, Eugenio Abeso, 229
Monetary Union of West Africa (UMOA), 210
Monrovia, 202, 203, 204
Monrovia Conference, 139, 140
Morocco, 18, 134, 145, 146, 151, 206, 207, 209, 234, 237, 240
Moshoeshoe II, 71, 72, 256
Moundou, 232
Mouride Brotherhood, 209
Mouvement Démocratique Dahoméenne (MDD), 7
Mouvement Démocratique du Peuple Camerounais (MDPC), 219
Mouvement Démocratique Voltaique (MDV), 22
Mouvement de la Jeunesse Togolaise (JUVENTO), 34, 35
Mouvement de l'Evolution Democratique de l'Afrique Central (MEDAC), 25
Mouvement de Libération Nationale (MLN), 21
Mouvement National Congolaise (MNC), 101, 102, 104, 106, 109
Mouvement pour l'Evolution So-

ciale de l'Afrique Noire (MESAN), 25, 226
Mouvement Mixte Gabonaise, 29
Mouvement para de Libertaçao de São Tome e Principe (MLSTP), 137
Mouvement Populaire de l'Evolution Africaine, 258
Mouvement Popular de Libertaçao de Angola (MPLA), 120, 122, 123, 124, 240
Mouvement Populare de la Revolution (MPR), 238
Mouvement des Population Togolaises (MPT), 35
Mouvement Socialiste Africaine (MSA), 20, 27, 28
Mozambique, 117, 118, 124, 127–133, 148, 169, 176, 182, 184, 246, 248, 249, 252, 255, 256, 259
Mozambique Company, 127
Mozambique National Resistance Movement (see also RENAMO), 131–132, 184
Mpatanishi, 267
Mphephu, Chief Patrick, 172, 183
Msheshwe (Basuto ruler), 69, 70
Mswati II, 257
Mueda, 129
Mugabe, Robert, 132, 249, 250, 251, 252, 253, 254, 255
Muhammad, Maj. General Murtala, 197, 201
Muhirwa, Andre, 114
Muhsen, Sheikh Ali, 93
Mulamba, Colonel Leonard, 110
Mulder, Connie, 174
Mulele, Pierre, 106, 237
Munongo, Godefroid, 107, 109
Musa, Balarbe, 199
Musaveni, Yoweri, 272, 273
Muslim Brotherhood, 287
Muslim Congress Party (Gambia), 42
Musokotwane, 246
Mutesa II (Buganda ruler), 90–91, 268
Muwenga, Paulo, 270, 272

Muzorewa, Bishop Abel, 241, 245, 246, 249, 251

Mwakenya movement, 267, 268

Mwambutsa IV (Burundi ruler), 113, 114, 115

Nadiope, Sir William (Bunyoro ruler), 92

Nahfa, 283

Nairobi, 39, 80, 265, 266, 267, 273

Nairobi District African National Congress, 81

Namibia, 124, 125, 126–127, 170, 171, 174, 184–185

Namibian National Assembly, 170

Nasser, Gamal, 143

Natal, 172, 180, 182

National Alliance of Liberals (Ghana), 190

National Convention Party (NCP), 202

National Council of Nigeria and the Cameroons (later National Council of Nigerian Citizens) (NCNC), 50, 51, 52, 53

National Council of Sierra Leone, 56

National Democratic Party (Rhodesia), 62

National Democratic Party of Liberia (NDLP), 204

National Independence Party (NIP), 50

National Liberation Front of the Congo (FNLC), 237–238

National Liberation Movement (NLM), 46

National Party (South Africa), 153, 154, 155, 164, 173–174, 175, 177, 184, 186

National Peoples Party (South Africa), 175

National Reformation Council (Sierra Leone), 194

National Resistance Movement (NRM), 271, 272

National Revolution Movement, 29

National Revolutionary Movement for Development (MRND) (Rwanda), 241, 242

Native Recruiting Corporation (South Africa), 157

Ndebele, 252, 253

Ndjamena, 232, 233, 234, 235

Neto, Agostino, 120, 124, 171, 172

Ngala, Roland, 82, 83, 84

Ngei, Paul, 84

Ngorongoro, 263

Ngouabi, Marien, 230

Niamey, 197

Niger, 7, 13, 18, 19, 189, 205, 214–215, 294

Nigeria, 6, 31, 48–56, 144, 147, 188, 189, 195–201, 233, 234, 293, 294

Nigerian National Alliance (NNA), 54, 55

Nigerian National Democratic Party (NNDP), 49, 54, 55

Nigerian Peoples Party (NPP), 198, 199

Nigerian Reconstruction Group, 49

Nigerian Youth Movement (NYM), 49

N'Jie, Pierre Saar, 42

Njonjo, Charles, 267

Nkomati Agreement, 132, 184

Nkomo, Joshua, 61, 62, 63, 64, 244, 249, 250, 251, 252, 253, 254, 255

Nkrumah, Kwame, 38, 44–48, 142, 145, 147, 149, 150, 152, 187

Nkumbula, Harry, 62, 67, 68, 154, 156, 164, 244

Nobel Peace Prize, 176

North Vietnam, 274

Northern Elements Progressive Union (NEPU), 49

Northern Province United Association (NPUA), 83

Northern Rhodesia (see also Zambia), 61, 62, 67–69

Northern Rhodesia African National Congress, 67, 68

Nouakchott, 18, 206

Nqutu, J. J., 76

Nswam, 189

Ntare V (ruler of Burundi), 238
Ntombi (Queen Regent Swaziland), 253
Nujoma, Sam, 167, 185
Nyaragba prison, 223
Nyasaland (see also Malawi), 61, 62, 65–67
Nyerere, Julius, 86, 87, 88, 146, 262, 263, 264, 271, 293
Nyobe, Ruben Um, 30, 32
Nzeogwu, Major Chukwuma, 55

Obasanjo, Maj. General Olusegun, 197, 198, 199
Obock, 284
Obote, Milton, 91, 92, 93, 252, 268, 270, 271, 272, 273
Obrou, Fidel, 227
Ocran, Colonel H. R., 48
Odinga, Oginga, 81, 84, 265
Ogaden, 274, 280, 283
Ojukwu, Colonel Odemegwu, 196
Okello, Brig. General Basilo, 272
Okello, "Field Marshall" John, 95
Okigwi, 196
Okotie-Eboh, Festus, 55
Olympic Games, 249
Olympio, Sylvanus, 33–35, 36, 222
Omo-Osagie, Chief, 55
Ondo Province, 55
Onitsha, 196
Opangault, Jacques, 27, 28
Opango, Brig. General Joachim, 230
Organization of African Unity (OAU), 48, 65, 107, 108, 109, 122, 123, 128, 129, 140, 206, 207, 208, 219, 225
Organization Common Africane et Malagache de Cooperation Economique, 143
Organization Common Afrique et Malagache (OCAM), 144–145
Organization of Petroleum Exporting Countries (OPEC), 135
Oriental Province, 102, 103
Ormsby-Gore Commission, 85
Osadebay, Chief Dennis, 52, 56

Otegbeye, Dr. Tunji, 53
Ouagandougou, 23, 216, 217, 218
Ouddei, Goukouni, 228, 229, 230
Ouedraogo, Jean-Baptiste, 217
Ould Dadah, Mokhtar, 17–18, 31
Ounianga Kebir, 235
Ovimbundu, 172
Owerri, 196, 199
Owusu, Victor, 191

Pakistan, 277
Palma, 125
Pan African Congress (Manchester), 44
Pan African Freedom Movement, 75
Pan African Freedom Movement of East & Central Africa (PAFMECA), 94
Pan Africanism, 293
Paris Club, 131, 132, 204, 213, 288
Parti Africana Independencia para Guinea e Cabo Verd (PAIGC), 133, 134, 135
Parti Congolaise du Travail (PCT), 231
Parti Dahoméen de l'Unité (PDU), 241
Parti Démocratique de la Côte d'Ivorie (PDCI), 12, 14, 220, 221
Parti Démocratique Chritienne (PDC), 113
Parti Démocratique de Guinea (PDG), 10–11, 211, 212
Parti Démocratique Socialiste de Guinée, 12
Parti d'Emancipation de Hutus (PARMEHUTU), 241
Parti de la Fédération Africaine (PFA), 15
Parti de l'Unité et du Progres National du Burundi (UPRONA), 113, 115
Parti de l'Unité Nationale (PUNA), 104
Parti Lumumbiste Unité, (PALU), 109
Parti National du Patrice Lumumba,

104
Parti National Voltaique (PNV), 22
Parti Progressiste, 14
Parti Progressiste Nigérien, 18–19
Parti Progressiste Tchaden, 26
Parti du Régroupment Africain (PRA), 20–21
Parti du Régroupement Mauritanien (PRM), 14
Parti Régroupement Soudanaise (PRS), 15
Parti Républicaine Dahoméen (PRD), 7
Parti Républicaine de la Liberté (PRL), 22
Parti Social d'Education des Masses Africaines (SEMA), 22
Parti Socialiste (PS), 208
Parti Solidaire Africaine (PSA), 101, 102, 105, 106, 109
Parti Soudanais du Progrès (PSP), 15
Parti Togolais du Progrès (PTP), 33
Parti de l'Unité Nationale de Guinée (PUNG), 12
Patasse, Ange, 228
Paton, Alan, 165
Peace Corps, 269
Pearce Commission, 279
Pemba, 93
Peoples Caretaker Councils, 63
Peoples Congress Party (Uganda), 270
Peoples Defense Committees, 192
Peoples National Party (PNP) (Ghana), 191
Peoples National Party (PNP) (Sierra Leone), 58
Peoples Progressive Party (PPP) (Gambia), 42, 43, 201, 202
Peoples Redemption Council (PRD) (Liberia), 203, 204
Peoples Redemption Party (PRP), 198, 199
Peoples Revolutionary Courts, 191
Petroleum, 124, 136, 186, 197, 198, 199, 218, 219, 224, 225, 226, 230,
262, 263, 287, 288
Pereira, Aristides, 135, 137
Pirow, Oswald, 156
Plantations, 229
Pointe Noire, 230
Pokot tribe, 272
Polisaro, 206
Popular Front Party (PFP) (Ghana), 191
Population density, 240
Port Elizabeth, 184
Port Harcourt, 196
Port Sudan, 288
Porto Novo, 223
Portugal, 128–130, 249
Portugal and the Future, 134
Portuguese Guinea (see also Guinea Bissau), 128
Prazeros, 127
Press censorship, 192, 199, 200, 204
Pretoria, 184, 185
Principe, 137
Progress Party (Ghana), 190
Progressive Federal Party (PFP) (South Africa), 174, 186
Progressive Party (South Africa), 165
Provisional National Defense Council (PNDC), 192, 194

Qaddafi, Muammar, 227, 233, 234, 270, 287, 288, 290
Quiwonkpa, Brig. General Thomas, 204–205

Rajibansi, Amihand, 175
Rand strike, 154, 158
Raoul, Major Alfred, 226
Rassemblement Démocratique Africain (RDA), 7, 10, 12–13, 19, 22, 26, 27, 28
Rassemblement Démocratique Congolaise (RADECO), 106
Rassemblement du Peuple Camerounais (RPC), 33, 222
Rawlings, Flight Lieutenant, 190–191, 192–194, 218, 223

Red Sea, 284, 285
refugees, 241, 242, 254, 284, 289, 290, 292
relief activities, 282, 283, 289, 290, 292
RENAMO, 131–132, 184, 254
Renison, Sir Patrick, 83
Responsible Government Association, 61
Reunion, 127
Revolutionary Democratic Council (CDR), 234
Rhodes, Cecil John, 73
Rhodesia (see also Zimbabwe), 39, 40, 61–65, 129, 130, 244, 246, 248–250, 262, 293
Rhodesian Front Party (RF), 63, 64, 249
Rhodesian Native Association, 61
Richards Constitution, 37, 49
Rio Muni, 228
Roberto, Holden, 119, 123, 124, 128, 237
Rodriques, Alexandre, 126, 127
Rubasana, Rev. Walter, 163
Rudahigwa, Charles (Rwanda ruler), 111
Ruzzi River, 113
Rwanda (Ruanda), 84, 111–113, 144, 150
Rwangasore, Louis, 114

Sadat, Anwar, 233, 286, 287
Saharawi Arab Democratic Republic (SADR), 206, 207, 208
Sahel, 189, 212
Said Barre, Maj. General Said, 274, 276–277, 282, 283
St. Louis du Senegal, 18
Salazar, Antonio de Olivera, 117, 118, 120, 121, 122, 128
Saleh, Colonel Ibrahim, 219
Salek, Mustapha Ould, 206
Salim, Ahmed Salim, 264
Samatur, Lt. General Muhammad Ali, 277
Sandwe, Jason, 102, 104

Sandys, Duncan, 72
Sankara, Captain Thomas, 214–218
Santa Isabel, 229
Santa Maria, 120
Santos, Jos Eduardo dos, 124
São Thomé, 127, 137–138
Sara tribe, 232
Sassandra River, 220
Saudi Arabia, 276
Savimbi, Jonas, 123, 124, 125, 126, 127, 173, 186, 240
Sawaba Party, 19
Sawyer, Dr. Amos, 204
Schultz, George, 176
Sebe, Lennox, 183
Seibou, Colonel Ali, 215
Sekgoma (Bamangwato ruler), 74
Senegal, 4, 20–21, 42, 43, 141, 144, 189, 190, 202, 205, 208–209, 211, 238, 293
Senegambia Confederation, 202, 209
Senghor, Léopold Sédar, 4, 5, 15, 20, 21, 22, 34, 145, 148, 208
Serengeti Plain, 263
Seretse Khama, 74, 75
Seyyid Abdullah (Zanzibar ruler), 94
Seyyid Jamshid (Zanzibar ruler), 94
Seyyid, Sir Khalifa bin Harub (Zanzibar ruler), 94
Shaba Province, 237, 238, 239
Sharia, 289, 290
Shariff, Othman, 261
Shermarke, Abiderashid Ali, 274
Shona, 253
Sick, Dr. Abba, 232
Sierra Leone, 41, 56, 59, 194–195
Sierra Leone Peoples Party (SLPP), 56–59, 194
Sigcau, Stella, 183
Sissoko, Fely Dabo, 14–15, 16
Sithole, Ndabaningi, 64, 250
Smith, Ian Douglas, 64, 65, 69, 152, 170, 245, 248, 249, 250, 253, 254
Smuts, Jan Christian, 150, 155, 156, 163, 164, 165, 166

Soames, Lord, 251
Sobhuza II (Swazi ruler), 257
Socialism, 134–136, 138, 211–214, 230, 254, 261, 263, 264, 280, 282
Socialist League of Malawi (LESOMA), 247
Soglo, Colonel Christophe, 9–10
Somalia, 148, 149, 265, 273–277, 280, 282, 283, 285
Somali-Ethiopian War, 274–276, 280–281
Soudan, 13, 14–15, 20
South Africa: 65, 72, 124, 125–127, 131, 246, 247, 249, 250, 253, 254, 255, 256, 257; abolition of Influx Control Act, 180; agriculture, 181; Alien Act, 180; Asians, 175; censorship, 179; Chamber of Mines, 180; Coloreds, 174, 175; Constitutional reforms, 174, 175–176, 177; divestment, 181–182; economic sanctions, 179, 180–181, 183, 185, 186; elections, 174, 175, 184; foreign workers, 182; Homelands policy, 183; Immorality Act, 184; labor strikes, 177–178, 189; Mixed Marriages Act, 174; National Union of Mine Workers, 179; Restoration of Citizenship Act, 180, military, 173, 176, 185–186; state of emergency, 178–179; student riots, 173, 177, 178; unemployment, 182; urban violence, 173, 176, 177–179, 186; Verkrampte group, 174, 176
South African Act, 70, 161, 162, 168, 172
South African Bureau of Racial Affairs (SABRA), 155, 165
South African Native National Congress, 163
South African Party, 154, 156
Southern Front Party, 255
Southern Rhodesia (see also Zimbabwe), 39, 40, 61–65, 69, 85, 124, 148, 151, 152, 169
Southern Sudan, 285, 287, 288

Southwest Africa (see also Namibia) 153, 165, 169–171
Southwest Africa Peoples Organization (SWAPO), 124, 125, 126, 171–172, 184, 185
Soweto, 173
Spanish Empire, 228–229
Spears of the Nation, 176
Spinola, General Antonio de, 130, 134–135
Standard Oil, 288
Stanleyville, 103, 107, 108, 145
Stevens, Siaka, 58, 194, 195, 246
Steyn, M. T. 171
Strijdom, Johannes, 155, 167–168, 182
student protests, 192, 195, 199, 201, 205, 217, 224, 240, 267, 277–278, 280, 287, 288, 289
Sudan, 89, 108, 127, 231, 233, 234, 271, 277, 285–291, 294
Sudanese Civil War, 286, 288, 289, 290, 291
Sudanese Communist Party, 286, 287
Sudanese Peoples Liberation Army (SPLA), 289, 290
Sudanese Socialist Union (SSU), 287
Suez Canal, 284, 286
Sun City, 183
Susu, 213
Swahili, 261
Swaziland, 75–77, 172, 255, 257–258, 259
Swaziland Democratic Party (SDP), 76
Swaziland Progressive Party (SPP), 77
Syndicate Agricole Africain (SSA), 12
Syria, 286, 290

Tambo, Oliver, 176, 178, 179
Tanganyika (see Tanzania), 84–89, 94, 95, 110
Tanganyika African National Union

(TANU), 86, 87, 89, 261, 262
Tanganyika Elected Members Organization (TEMO), 87
Tanganyika Peoples Defense Force, 88
Tanganyika Rifles, 87
Tanzam railway, 244, 245, 262
Tanzania, 84–89, 124, 128, 129, 130, 150, 189, 196, 247, 249, 258, 261–265, 268, 270, 273, 293
Taya, Colonel Mouauia Sidi Mohamed, 207
Temne, 194
Tete, 130
Texaco, 126
Thatcher, Margaret, 251
Tibesti, 231
Tigre, 280, 282, 283, 284
Timbuktu, 210
Todd, Garfield, 62, 65, 249
Togo, 6, 32–36, 45, 46, 144, 146, 150, 193, 205, 222–223
Tolbert, William, 202, 203, 204
Tombalbaye, Francois, 26, 27, 231, 232
Toro, 91, 92, 93, 268
Toubou, 232
Touré, Sekou, 10, 11, 12, 13, 48, 142, 147, 207, 211, 212
Trade Union Congress (Gambia), 192
Transgabonaise railroad, 225
Transitional Government of National Unity (GUNT), 234, 235
Transkei, 159, 169, 171, 172, 183, 255
Transvaal, 73, 154, 157, 162
Traoré, Diarra, 212, 213
Traoré, Lt. Moussa, 210–211
Trarza, 17, 18
Truernicht, A. P., 174, 175
Tshakwe Association of Congo & the Rhodesias (AKTAT), 106
Tshekedi Khama, 74
Tshombe, Moise, 102, 103, 104–105, 107–108, 109, 110, 149, 235, 237
Tuaregs, 18, 210, 215
Tubman, W.V.S., 204
Tunisia, 151

Tutu, Bishop Desmond, 174, 178, 179
Twelfth of December Movement, 268

Ubangi-Shari, 22
Uganda, 89–93, 241, 262, 265, 268–273, 286, 287, 289
Uganda National Liberation Front, 270
Uganda National Movement, 91
Uganda Peoples Congress (UPC), 91, 92
Uganda State Research Bureau, 271
Ujamaa concept, 262, 263, 264
Uli, 197
Umkhonto we sezuie, 176
Umma Party (Sudan), 290
Umma Party (Zanzibar), 95
Uniao Nacional de Guinea Portuguesas (UNGP), 133
Uniao para a Independencia Total de Angola (UNITA), 123, 124, 185, 186, 238, 240
Union Africaine et Malagache (UAM), 144, 145
Union des Chefs et des Populations du Nord, 33
Union Démocratique Dahoméenne (UDD), 7
Union Démocratica Nacional de Mocambique (UDENAMO), 128, 129
Union Démocratique Nigerienne, 19
Union Démocratique de Population Malian (UDPM), 210
Union Démocratique des Populations Togalaises (UDPT), 33
Union Démocratique Voltaique (UDV), 22, 23
Union Féderation Générale des Travailleurs du Kongo (FGTK), 104
Union General des Travailleurs d'Afrique Noire (UGTAN), 11
Union National Dahoméenne (UND), 10
Union des Populations du Cameroun (UPC), 30, 219

Union Progressiste Sénégalaise (UPS), 20, 21
Union pour la Communanté Franco Africaine (UCFA), 19
Union pour le Progres du Tchad (UPT), 27
Union Sociale Gabonaise (USG), 29
Union Soudanaise, 16
Union of South Africa (see South Africa)
Union of Soviet Socialist Republics (USSR), 48, 72, 122, 124, 125, 136, 137, 196, 234, 268, 274, 282, 283, 284, 286
United Arab Republic (UAR), 94, 145, 146
United Democratic Front (South Africa), 175
United Democratic Party (UDP) (Sierra Leone), 194
United Federal Party (UFP), 59, 61, 64
United Gold Coast Convention (UGCC), 44, 45
United Middle Belt Congress (UMBC), 53
United National African Council (UNAC), 251
United National Independence Party (UNIP), 67, 68, 244, 246
United Nations, 31–32, 33, 43, 65, 71, 104, 105, 106, 108, 111, 112, 113, 114, 122, 125, 127, 130, 145, 147, 169, 172, 175, 176, 185, 216, 219, 271, 282, 283, 294
United Party (Gambia), 42, 43
United Party (Ghana), 46
United Party (Rhodesia), 61, 62
United Party (South Africa), 154, 162, 164, 165, 173–174, 202
United Party of Nigeria (UPN), 198, 199
United Peoples Party (UPP) (Liberia), 204
United Peoples Party (UPP) (Nigeria), 57
United Peoples Party (UPP) (Sierra Leone), 51
United Rhodesian Party, 62
United States: 83, 89, 107, 108, 122, 124, 126–127, 131, 142, 149, 162, 171, 173, 176, 177, 180–182, 185, 189, 196, 203, 204, 205, 207, 212, 233, 234, 235, 237, 250, 251, 253, 254, 266, 269, 274, 276, 283, 288, 290
United Swaziland Association, 76, 77
University of Nairobi, 267
Upper Nile Province, 288
Upper Volta, 13, 22–23, 189
Urundi (see Burundi), 84, 113–115
Usumbura (Bujumbuia), 105, 110, 114

Van Hemelrijck, Maurice, 99
Van Zyl Slabbart, Frederick, 184
Vatsa, Maj. General Maman, 201
Venda, 172, 183
Verwoerd, Dr. Hendrik, 75, 182
Vieira, Major João, 134
Viljoen, Gerrit, 174
Volta River Dam, 47
Vorster, Balthazar Johannes, 173, 174, 175, 250

Walls, General Peter, 252
Watutsi, 240, 241, 242, 243
Welensky, Sir Roy, 40, 59, 61, 62, 67
West Rand mining, 177
West Somali Liberation Front, 280
Western Sahara, 124, 205, 206
Whitehead, Sir Edgar, 62, 63, 64
Wilham Commission, 174
Wilson, Harold, 64, 65, 69, 151, 248
Workers Party of Ethiopia, 284
World Bank, 131, 137, 193, 204, 209, 213, 244, 263, 265

Xosa, 163, 172, 178

Yace, Philippe, 221
Yameogo, Maurice, 22–23, 130, 216
Yamoussoukro, 221
Yaoundé, 220

Yondo, 232
Youlou, Abbé Fulbert, 27, 28

Zaire (see also Republic of the Congo), 100–110, 124, 208, 234, 235–240, 271, 289, 293, 294
Zambesi River, 127
Zambia (see also Northern Rhodesia), 40, 64, 67–69, 124, 151, 169, 176, 182, 184, 196, 238, 244–246, 247, 248, 249, 250, 264, 293
Zambia African National Congress, 67
Zanzibar, 87–88, 93–94, 261, 264
Zanzibar National Party (ZNP), 93, 94, 95
Zanzibar Peoples Courts, 262

Zanzibar Peoples Party of Pemba (ZPPP), 44, 95
Zanzibar Revolutionary Council, 264
Zanzibar Township Council, 93
Zerbo, Colonel Saye, 216
Ziganchour, 209
Zimbabwe (see also Rhodesia), 132, 182, 184, 245, 248–255
Zimbabwe African National Union (ZANU), 64, 252, 254, 255
Zimbabwe African Peoples Union (ZAPU), 63, 252, 253, 254, 255
Zimbabwe National Party (ZNP), 63
Zinsou, Emile, 223
Zulu, 180